Dietrich Bonhoeffer
and the Resistance

Dietrich Bonhoeffer and the Resistance

SABINE DRAMM

Translated by Margaret Kohl

Fortress Press
Minneapolis

DIETRICH BONHOEFFER AND THE RESISTANCE

Cover image: © Gütersloher Verlagshaus, Gütersloh, in der Verlagsgruppe Random House GmbH, München
Cover design: Christy J. P. Barker
Book design: PerfecType, Nashville, Tenn.

Library of Congress Cataloging-in-Publication Data
Dramm, Sabine, 1943-
  [V-Mann Gottes und der Abwehr? English]
  Dietrich Bonhoeffer and the resistance / Sabine Dramm ; translated by Margaret Kohl.
    p. cm.
  Includes bibliographical references (p.   ) and index.
  ISBN 978-0-8006-6322-3 (alk. paper)
  1. Bonhoeffer, Dietrich, 1906-1945. 2. Theologians—Germany—Biography. 3. Anti-Nazi movement—Germany—Biography. I. Title.
  BX4827.B57D7413 2009
  230'.044092—dc22
  [B]
                              2009000228

13 12 11 10 09 1 2 3 4 5 6 7 8 9 10

Contents

one

Courier—In Whose Service?

The bearer of this card, Mr. Bonhoeffer, is traveling to Stockholm on May 30, 1942, with official documents and baggage of the Foreign Ministry. It is requested that the above-named person be granted whatever he needs to facilitate his trip and that protection and assistance be extended to him when necessary. Berlin, May 30, 1942.[1]

THIS IS THE INFORMATION on the Courier Identification Card No. 474 issued by the German Ministry for Foreign Affairs. It was in possession of these unexceptionable papers, issued on the morning of the same day, that on a Saturday in the middle of the war Dietrich Bonhoeffer, a thirty-six year-old Protestant theologian, set off on his journey. He left Berlin, the capital of the German Reich, on his way to Stockholm, the capital of a neutral state, traveling in the name of the Military Intelligence Foreign Office, which came under the army high command—to be more precise, in agreement with the officers in charge there, Hans von Dohnanyi and Hans Oster.

> A weekend flight to Stockholm, terrible storm. Magnificent city, very friendly but at the same time reserved, at least initially. . . . Strong anti-Bolshevist sentiment everywhere; that provides a certain shared foundation. . . . Theologically German influence seems in recent times to have unfortunately diminished sharply in favour of the Anglo-Saxon.[2]

So much for the entry in Bonhoeffer's diary. In his notes he also mentions someone he refers to as "B" who wants to become bishop of Stockholm (he means the Swedish theologian Manfred Björkquist) as well as the archbishop of Uppsala, Erling Eidem, with whom, however, he had only been able to make written contact because the time available was so brief—he had already flown back on Tuesday.

But these diary entries, allegedly of June 1942, were fictitious, actually only written nine months later, in February–March 1943, and had been deliberately backdated. They were intended to camouflage what belonged to the normal everyday business of an undercover agent in the service of the Military Intelligence when he was "in the field"—to test the atmosphere, note developing trends, and cultivate contacts. Bonhoeffer may indeed actually have corresponded with Eidem, even though there is no longer any evidence of it, either real or fabricated. He really was "very warmly received" by Björkquist, as he writes—but not only by him, but above all by his English guest, George Bell, and not only in Stockholm but also in the small Swedish town of Sigtuna, on Lake Mäler, between Stockholm and Uppsala. But neither Bell nor Sigtuna are mentioned in the diary entries, nor is a Hans Schönfeld, together with whom he flew back to Berlin on June 2, 1942. And there is quite definitely not the least indication of the real purpose of this extended weekend.

How can we unravel these tangled threads? How are the inconsistencies to be explained? After all, Bonhoeffer was not just *any* Protestant pastor, and certainly not a loyal supporter of the Nazi Party.

The struggle between church and state was fought out on many fronts and in many guises, the Confessing Church to which Bonhoeffer belonged being one of them. Like the Protestant churches as a whole, the Confessing Church was caught up in a struggle that was both external and internal. It was involved in an external struggle inasmuch as it resisted—as far as it was able and willing to do so—direct interference by the power machinery of a totalitarian state and the creeping erosion of the church's own autonomy. The struggle was an internal one inasmuch as it aimed to resist infiltration by the pro-Nazi German Christians and the "Germanization" of the Christian message that they propagated and practiced. This internal struggle also involved rejection of the official line taken by church authorities, which steered a course between conforming and actually currying favor with the National Socialist political system; it was a course that from time to time some of the regional Protestant churches willingly and even eagerly maintained.

In this Confessing Church to which he belonged, Bonhoeffer was not an unknown figure. He had belonged to it from the beginning and was one of the founding members of the Pastors' Emergency League (the *Pfarrernotbund*), the group of pastors who formed its nucleus. And in the years that followed, he proved to be a highly active member of its most resolute wing—not to say a radical in the service of the church. As such he was, then, by no means an unknown quantity for the officials of the National Socialist state either. There were a number of not inconsiderable complications to do with police requirements for registration in connection with conscription, and for a time he was forbidden to reside permanently in Berlin. But apart from that, he had headed one of the Confessing Church's preachers' seminaries in Finkenwalde until this was closed by the Gestapo in 1937. The last center of his work in the training and care of upcoming young theologians of the Confessing Church had been in Sigurdshof, like Finkenwalde situated in Pomerania. Like the latter, Sigurdshof too had been closed, in this case in 1940. Ever since 1940 Bonhoeffer had been forbidden to speak in public, and since 1941 he had been forbidden to publish.

So here was a Protestant theologian who was notoriously anything but conformist, and who avowedly belonged to the 'confessional front' (as the Confessing Church was also known in National Socialist jargon). What had a man like this to do with the military secret service? And what was he doing in Sweden? Theodor Heckel, who had been elevated to be head of the Church External Affairs Office, and who was a leading "state-supporting" churchman in Berlin, had termed Bonhoeffer a "pacifist and enemy of the state";[3] and he was not far wrong. It seems like a little irony of history that he should have described him in these terms six years before, in March 1936, when Bonhoeffer and members of his seminary had visited Sweden—and incidentally Sigtuna as well.

It is true that at the time of the brief Scandinavian journey in 1942 the Confessing Church had become tamer and somewhat less of a thorn in the flesh of the state authorities than it had been earlier. Moreover, Bonhoeffer was less popular within the ranks of the Confessing Church itself and necessarily occupied fewer prominent positions there, in part because of the exigencies of war. In spite of his not infrequent criticism of them, the leaders of the Confessing Church had generously left him his supra-congregational status and entrusted him with scholarly work; but he was and remained their pastor, a "shepherd of souls." But how could this pastor now travel abroad in the framework and name of the Military Intelligence? Had this "critical mind," this Protestant troublemaker, at long last discovered his duty to his country in a time of war?

The confusion is all the greater because this "independent" member of the clergy—this doctor of theology (a title he admittedly almost never used on everyday occasions)—this pastor (the title he himself always preferred)—had been granted reserved status at the instance of the Military Intelligence Foreign Office. That is to say, he was declared to be unavailable for military service on the grounds of a position important for the war. He was therefore excused from military service, at least for a certain time. Surely this was an unexpected privilege for a unreliable pastor. Or was it a decision necessary for the strategic employment of an indispensable patriot? The confusion is confounded, paradoxically enough, not by what we do not know but by what we have since come to know, knowledge acquired through hindsight, and which has thus—in the nature of things—often now become fixed. This dilemma in our perception of the past is, as we know, a fundamental problem in the writing of history: we cannot avoid describing the past through hindsight—*ex post*—yet this very perspective often enough distorts our view.

Attention is drawn here to this historiographical dilemma under a particular aspect. Of course we "know" that Bonhoeffer's function as undercover agent for the Intelligence was only camouflage, and that he was really pursuing other ends. We know that he was really acting against National Socialism—to put it briefly, as someone in the resistance. But what do we really know about this? How clear are our ideas about it, and how cloudy? What were his position and his role in the complicated warp and weft of what we are accustomed to call "the resistance movement"? What, for example, do the phrases "undercover agent" and "Military Intelligence" mean in more precise terms? What were Bonhoeffer's real goals? How did he try to fulfill them? What, for instance, was his intention on his whirlwind journey to Stockholm, officially described as courier in the service of the German Reich but really a courier of the conspiracy? And what did his everyday, practical life look like in this divided situation? What were the (underlying) reasons behind the varying facets of his existence, as a member of the Confessing Church, as an undercover agent for the Military Intelligence, as a member of the resistance? How do these things fit together—a pastor suspected of pacifism and yet a conspirator? But first of all, how did it come about?

Retrospectively, we have got used to talking about Bonhoeffer's activity in the resistance. In that same June of 1942, a few weeks after Sigtuna, he described himself more soberly in a letter to his friend Eberhard Bethge as being "in the worldly sector."[4] Bonhoeffer "joined the resistance movement"—so we sometimes say today, quite lightly, as if it were a matter of joining a club or a party, or a society open to all, or even a closed one, something he joined just as if it had been a common, casual diversion. Or we say it with a solemn undertone, as if it had been a once-for-all, solitary resolve. But the beginning of Bonhoeffer's conspiratorial activities cannot be pinned down to one simple "date of entry," a fixed point in his curriculum vitae. His decision to become actively involved in the preparations for an overthrow was not made at a particular hour on a particular day. That decision has to be seen as a component in the complex inner and outer development process of his life as a whole. It came about as part of the total fabric of circumstances and experiences, conditions and attitudes. When his sister-in-law, Emmi Bonhoeffer, was asked many years later why her husband, Klaus Bonhoeffer, joined the resistance, she replied, "One can only answer by saying that people do what they are compelled to do out of some inner necessity. . . . Many people think that resistance is a matter of the will, but often one has no choice."[5] And her answer is true for Dietrich Bonhoeffer too.

Yet for all that, there is something in his life that, though not indeed a conclusive answer, may count as a crystallization point for the question about the "Why?" and the "When?" It is a brief episode that took place in the key year 1939, which also makes that a key year in his career as well: his stay in New York during the summer of 1939. He had already been in New York once, in 1930–31, as a young student, on a scholarship to Union Theological Seminary. It was a breathing space between his doctorate, his years as curate, and his postdoctoral thesis, the *Habilitation*, which qualified him for a professorship at a German university. When he returned to Berlin, he took up a teaching post at the university. This time, in 1939, there was again a return to Berlin, although this return would not have been necessary.

At the end of the 1930s, after Bonhoeffer's professional situation in Germany had become increasingly difficult, American theologian friends invited him to come to the United States in order to sound out openings for living and working there. After the Community House in Finkenwalde was closed in 1937, an ominous cloud hung over Bonhoeffer's work. In addition he had a huge personal problem. It was only a question of time before he was called up. Constant maneuvering was required if the more or less still functioning "collective pastorates" in Pomerania were to continue; and the permanent incalculability of working on the edge of legality was wearing. He nevertheless clung to the work, as is evident from a card written to "My successor," which he wrote before he left for the United States, addressing it to a deputy as yet unnamed; he would find, first and foremost, "one of the finest spheres of work in the Confessing Church." The personal hints and working suggestions that follow end with the request: "Incidentally, go for walks with the brethren as often as possible, or be with them in other ways as much as you can."[6] In spite of all the difficult circumstances, this work in training and accompanying rising theologians in the northeasternmost part of Germany was one of the "finest spheres of work" not only in the Confessing Church but in Bonhoeffer's life too.

It was this precarious professional situation that was behind Bonhoeffer as he embarked on his second stay in America. Inwardly, for him it turned into a disaster. The political situation in Europe was worsening. When would the preliminaries to war turn into war itself? Uncertainty and anxiety paralyzed Bonhoeffer. His days were dominated by his waiting for news from home—from his parents, his friends, "the brethren." He felt completely out of place in New York. The attempts of his hosts to cheer him failed to reach him; their persistence had no effect. It was a time overshadowed by homesickness. His travel journal is in many respects a thought-provoking human document. It is the reflection of someone who sees himself at the mercy of a paralyzing self-blockage in a tormenting situation in which a decision was required of him. On the one hand, he felt helpless and powerless, and was plagued by self-doubt to the point of despair. On the other, he was possessed by a liberating certainty. The anxieties evoked by isolation and feelings of alienation were counteracted by experiences of warmheartedness and a sense of being valued. The loneliness of exile contrasted with experiences of loyalty and understanding. He interpreted the decision, once it was made, as having been shown him by God; and it seemed to him like an act of self-liberation: "It is strange that I am never quite clear about the motives that underlie my decisions. . . . The reason one gives to oneself and others are certainly inadequate. . . . In the last resort we are acting from a plane that is hidden from us." So he writes in his diary on June 20, 1939. And a day later: "I am at my wits' end, but he [God] knows what he is about." A week later the entry runs, "I cannot think that it is God's will that, if war comes, I am to stay here with no special task. I must go on the earliest possible date."[7]

Bonhoeffer broke off his stay in the United Sates so that—since the outbreak of war was undoubtedly impending—he could be in and remain in Germany, although he knew very well that for him personally he was renouncing the chance of emigration. After a good three weeks, on July 8, 1939, he set out from New York on his journey back to Germany, to the disappointment of his American friends, who had begun with no small expenditure of energy, time, and money to smooth his path to a professional future. As so often in the 1930s, he stopped over in London, where his twin sister, Sabine Leibholz, his brother-in-law, and his friend Franz Hildebrandt were living in exile. Bonhoeffer's sister and her family had flown to England via Switzerland in 1938 because of the "non-Aryan" origins of Sabine's husband, Gerhard Leibholz, who had until then been professor for constitutional law in Göttingen. Bonhoeffer was attached to his brother-in-law not only because of the relationship between them but because Leibholz had made him familiar with fundamental questions of constitutional law—and more: "with . . . the world of liberal constitutional politics,"[8] its claims, the dangers to which it was exposed, and its opponents. Consequently Leibholz took on a double significance in Bonhoeffer's life. He sharpened his political awareness and brought him directly face-to-face with stigma and threat.

The theologian Franz Hildebrandt, Bonhoeffer's friend and "spiritual brother," had fled to London in 1937, also because of his "non-Aryan" origins. Hildebrandt was a Christian with an intensive faith, and after 1933 he tried as long as he could to resist inwardly the traumatizing experience of being defined and discriminated against, in church as well as state, as a "Jewish Christian." After several weeks' imprisonment, he finally chose the path of emigration. With Hildebrandt, Bonhoeffer had tried in 1933 to protest against the appalling general assent to what went under the heading of the "Aryan paragraph" and the promptly beginning exclusion of Jewish Christians from a church that failed so miserably in this question. Through his ties with Hildebrandt, Bonhoeffer became highly sensitive early on to what was played down as "the Jewish question."

From 1933 to 1935, when he was pastor of the German church in London, Bonhoeffer had been confronted with the first waves of refugees from Germany. And at that time he formed a friendship in London with another "spiritual brother," even if in this case (and not only because of the difference in age) it might be more appropriate to talk about a "spiritual father," or father in God—George Bell, the bishop of Chichester.

Between Bell and Bonhoeffer's brother-in-law, again, a friendship then grew up during the war years that was both personal and politically motivated. The Leibholz family kept Bell up to date about Bonhoeffer's situation as far as was possible and, conversely, Bell did the same for the Leibholz family, according to circumstances and the possibilities open to him, which were in any case limited. But above all there was a lively exchange between Leibholz and Bell on the political level.

During Bonhoeffer's interim stay in London in the summer of 1939, to his great regret he was unable to meet George Bell. Bell was to see him again only three years later, in Sigtuna and Stockholm, during his mission as alleged courier for the Military Intelligence Foreign Office. For the moment Bonhoeffer could only tell him about his immediate situation by letter. He made it clear to Bell that it was with his eyes open that he had rejected the American offer of political and financial security, because—as he put it in his diary—he wanted "to return home so as to be again in the community of the brethren."[9] Among other things, he wrote to Bell that he had turned down a position as pastor for refugees in New York because there were many non-Aryan brethren who had a much greater right to such a position.[10] In another letter to a different theologian, Reinhold Niebuhr, Bonhoeffer wrote to England from New York at the end of June:

> Sitting here in Dr. Coffin's garden, I have had time to think prayerfully about my situation and the situation of my nation, and to arrive at clarity about God's will for me. I am convinced that I have made a mistake in coming to America. I must live through this difficult period of our national history with the Christian people of Germany. I will have no right to participate in the reconstruction of Christian life in Germany after the war if I do not share the trials of this time with my people. My brethren in the Confessing synods wanted me to go. Perhaps they were right to urge me, but it was wrong of me to leave. Everyone has to make a decision of this kind for himself. Christians in Germany will face the terrible alternative of either willing the defeat of their nation in order that Christian civilization may survive, or willing the victory of their nation and thereby destroying our civilization. I know which of these alternatives I must choose; but I cannot make that choice in security.[11]

In another letter to Niebuhr (then in Edinburgh), also written at the end of June, Paul Lehmann, one of Bonhoeffer's American friends, gives an account of things from his viewpoint. He tells of the failure of American friends to win over Bonhoeffer, writing with great sympathy, but not without spicing his account with some dry personal remarks about the political situation:

> Perhaps you have meanwhile heard all about Bonhoeffer. . . . My own conversation with him convinced me that he did the only thing he could. You must remember that his original concern was to avoid military service. He would have found the oath of allegiance to Hitler that would have gone with it unendurable. At the same

time, he didn't welcome the idea of going to prison earlier than was absolutely necessary because of that. . . .
During the short time that he was here he discovered
that he could not hope to make any contribution to the
German future—always provided it was given to him to
survive—unless he suffered through this present time.
This had not been so clear to him before his journey.
But in the seclusion of Coffin's summer house he looked
out over the sea and arrived at the conviction that vol-
untary exile would be a path into permanent inactivity.
. . . And of course the third factor in his decision was
the growing feeling that to remain here would amount
to a violation of the gospel's express instruction: he who
loses his life shall find it. On this point he could not
silence his conscience, and in view of the next critical
weeks he had simply to return. . . . As far as the expenditure is concerned, please let my small contribution be
added to the decencies which are still left in the world.
It wasn't very much. I can take it on, and do so gladly.
In case you want to rid yourself of the money that you
would have spent, give it to the Society for Drowning
the Present Prime Minister, always supposing that the
British are still men enough to organize it.[12]

two

A Change
of Course

BONHOEFFER'S RETURN FROM THE United States in the summer of 1939 was followed by a long-drawn-out change of course, as his bystander stance changed gradually into an independent role in the conspiracy. What from the summer of 1939 had been a passive position, gradually took on active form—not all at once, but successively. Bonhoeffer's own utterances in connection with his decision to leave America point in this direction. After the exile he rejected in 1939, the "silent partner" who in 1938 probably knew about first plans for a coup d'etat, now began to assume an active role.[1]

In the spring of 1938 there were for the first time signs of conspiratorial attempts—"to talk about plans for an overthrow would seem questionable"[2]—in leading military circles, the aim being to counteract the powerful position held by the SS and the Gestapo, as well as to counter Hitler's undisguised drive toward war. The instigator of these attempts was the so-called Blomberg-Fritsch group, and its purpose was not (as yet) to eliminate Hitler but to restrict the power of the Nazi leaders.

The overtly warlike policy had evoked the criticism and reservations of both Werner von Fritsch, the supreme commander of the army, and the minister for war, Werner von Blomberg, as a consequence of which Hitler dismissed them, making himself supreme commander and doing away with the War Ministry altogether. Internal Nazi intrigues and scandals resulted in the formation of a supreme military command that was loyal to Hitler and was put under Wilhelm Keitel (later field marshal), who was nicknamed "Lakeitel" ("lackey Keitel"); while after an infamous and slanderous campaign against Fritsch, amateurishly staged, the Ministry of Justice was entrusted with an investigation of the matter.

With this, "the Fritsch case" landed on the desk of the lawyer Hans von Dohnanyi, who at that time was still personal secretary to the minister of justice, Franz Gürtner, and was at the same time an out and out opponent of National Socialism. While working on the Fritsch case, Dohnanyi—Bonhoeffer's brother-in-law—came to know a man "belonging to Military Intelligence" (that is, the military secret service), with whom in the years that followed he came to be extremely closely associated in three ways: officially, as a collaborator in opposition to the regime, and as a friend. His name was Hans Oster. In agreement with his chief, Admiral Wilhelm Canaris, and with the assent of the then chief of staff, Ludwig Beck, during the spring of 1938 Oster attempted to persuade military leaders to end the supremacy of the SS and to bring about an end to Nazi rule.

These attempts came to an abrupt end in March 1938 through the event which at that time made the news and later the history books under the heading: "Hitler's Troops Enter Vienna." The frenetic enthusiasm on every side over this *Anschluss* seemed to make all attempts at a plot obsolete. At least for the moment. But from that time onward a conspiratorial group grew up, the center of whose organization was at the heart of the Military Intelligence, and which therefore had at its disposal special modes of operating.[3]

During the summer of 1938 there were renewed initiatives aimed at eliminating the Nazi regime, this time in connection with the Sudeten crisis, which arose from Hitler's undisguised strivings

for expansion in the direction of Sudetenland or the rest of Czechoslovakia. These initiatives have been a matter of controversy among
researchers into the resistance movement.[4] Nevertheless, a wide
range of secret activities and journeys abroad was set on foot from
the side of some Berlin "war preventers" in leading military positions. The occupation of the whole of Czechoslovakia (Hitler's next
annexation goal) seemed to be only a question of time, and a number of emissaries of what was later called the September plot tried
by means of a lively journeying diplomacy to get London to intervene. As a protest against the policy of conquest, Beck resigned from
his post as chief of staff—something new in the annals of German
generalship! Once again Hans Oster was one of the driving forces.
He was supported by Canaris and by Beck as the "head"[5] of the
group and was in constant contact with Hans von Dohnanyi, who
at the time in question was sometimes in Leipzig and sometimes
in Berlin. It had been decided with Canaris (the head of Military
Intelligence) that if war broke out Dohnanyi should immediately be
taken on by the Intelligence.[6]

In September 1938 England unexpectedly gave in to Hitler and
put an end to such plans, since at the instigation of Mussolini, Hitler
for his part—and equally surprisingly—gave way and purported to
be prepared for agreement rather than war. It seemed as if his urge
for war was at an end. The Sudetenland had to be ceded to the German Reich by Czechoslovakia, and in return Hitler declared that he
would renounce any further moves toward annexation. When the
representatives of England, France, Italy, and Germany (Chamberlain, Daladier, Mussolini, and Hitler) signed the Munich agreement,
the apparently peace-loving dictator was again met with only rejoicing on the part of the German people and was accounted a successful statesman. Was there to be a putsch just at this historic moment?
Was this a time for the prince of peace to be deposed? And by the
army, of all things? The chances for an overthrow seemed to have
slipped away.

It seems probable that in the spring of 1938 Bonhoeffer had
been told by Dohnanyi about these first beginnings of a military

plot against Hitler, and in the autumn of 1938 had been informed by him about initial ideas for an overthrow in prominent military circles. There was a constant exchange of ideas and information between them from the beginning of the 1930s onward. Dohnanyi was the husband of Bonhoeffer's sister Christine. But he was not just his brother-in-law; he was his friend, his discussion partner—occasionally his opponent—in short, an intimate confidant. The same was true for Dohnanyi: "You know me well; I think we are more that 'just' brothers-in-law."[7] Bethge offers a reminiscence from the mid-1930s that reflects the everyday situation and the everyday caution required, although it was not as yet a question of revolutionary plans but more probably had to do with practical help for threatened people exposed to the caprice of the state. It would have been a matter of warnings, of happenings in the Confessing Church, breaches of the law, attacks by the police, and the church's attempts to defend itself. This was the first time that Bethge accompanied Bonhoeffer to the Dohnanyis' house, and Bonhoeffer had warned his friend in advance that he might perhaps be excluded from certain discussions between Dohnanyi and himself:

> Things turned out just as he had thought they would: the two brothers-in-law retired to the study, and [Dohnanyi's] wife was left with the task of entertaining her brother's companion in the sitting room. I have forgotten the subjects with which we bridged the time. But I remember very well that the conversation was somewhat halting, and that I was secretly tormented by the knowledge that the mistress of the house (who shared completely in her husband's life and consultations as well as those in which her brother Dietrich was involved) would undoubtedly much rather have been sitting in the study instead of here with this visitor from the province, with his comparatively remote world of experience.[8]

In the years that followed, Bethge was no longer excluded from discussions of this kind. As far as the autumn of 1938 is concerned, he remembered that Bonhoeffer by no means greeted the Munich agreement with rejoicing. "His hope of a revolution had again come to nothing."[9] At that time his personal circumstances seemed to be in a limbo, but a permanent one. After the preachers' seminary in Finkenwalde had been closed by the Gestapo in the previous autumn, the era of the "Collective Pastorates" had begun; and from that time on Bonhoeffer led a nomadic existence. From December 1937 he had been registered with the police as permanently resident in the little town of Schlawe in Lower Pomerania, where—a not unimportant formality—he was registered in November 1938 in the *Wehrstammblatt*. The meetings and study courses of the students who were training for ministry in the Confessing Church initially took place in nearby Köslin and Gross-Schlönwitz, and then in Sigurdshof, until Sigurdshof too was closed by the Gestapo in March 1940.

Practically speaking, Bonhoeffer was "without any fixed residence." He had no home of his own in the usual sense, and the immediately succeeding years were given up entirely to travel. He had certainly a center for his life, inwardly and outwardly, in his parents' house in Berlin, and a prohibition against residence in Berlin was modified, though only through the successful influence of his father. After a meeting of Confessing Church pastors in the Dahlem church hall had been broken up by the Gestapo, Bonhoeffer was expelled from Berlin and Brandenburg in January of 1938. From that time on, only visits to his parents were exempt from the prohibition. Consequently, when he was in Berlin he could, or must, always live in his parents' house, Marienburger Allee 43. So much for his external situation in the second half of the 1930s.

When did Bonhoeffer make the transition from knowledge of conspiratorial plans to active participation? From what point in time—or more properly, from what period of time—can we at the earliest talk about Bonhoeffer's participation in the resistance movement? And how is the term "resistance" to be interpreted in general in this connection? What does "resistance" against National Socialism in Germany really mean?[10]

It would be fatal to overtax the German resistance and to equate it with the Résistance in France (which was a definite organization) or even with the partisan movements in other occupied counties. These were fundamentally different, being directed against an occupying power. They were fighting against the power of a hostile foreign state, not against their own government. It would also be fatal to dilute the term *resistance* to the point of elevating mere non-acceptance of National Socialism into resistance against it. A "conceptional inflation"[11] would then water down what resistance meant. Preliminary forms—silent or outspoken protest or disobedience— must be differentiated from resistance in the narrower sense. But the frontiers "between partial criticism, open opposition and active resistance were . . . inevitably fluid,"[12] and it cannot be too much stressed that there were different forms, degrees, and stages of resistance.[13] It can also hardly be sufficiently stressed that practical intervention on behalf of people who had been deprived of their rights and persecuted—e.g., by hiding Jews or helping them to escape— meant that in individual cases such intervention was a counteraction to state terror: resistance through action.

It is also worth remembering that the word 'resistance' was hardly used at all in resistance circles themselves.[14] And the fact that we find this surprising today is again an indication of the way we have retrospectively internalized things. The relationship between the term *resistance* and the thing it stands for is illustrated by an incident that demonstrates the complicated relations between words and realities, the past as it was experienced and the way it appears to subsequent, present-day awareness. Emmi Bonhoeffer, Klaus Bonhoeffer's widow, once reported:

> I heard the phrase "resistance movement" for the first time in 1947 in Switzerland. . . . My brother-in-law in Zurich said to me, "I hope that things will now be somewhat easier for you than it is for other people, since your husband lost his life in the resistance." "In what?" I asked. "In the resistance. That is what it is called here."

> I swallowed and said, "Well yes, one might call it that."
> Why didn't I know the word? It didn't exist among us.[15]

Nor was it in most cases a firmly datable resolve that led to *the* step into the resistance. Other reports by survivors of the 1944 assassination attempt, "the women of July 20," reflect this:

> "Today people generally imagine that resistance was something quite out of the ordinary, something heroic. We ourselves never used the word resistance at all; we felt that we were opponents of the Nazi regime. But we didn't call ourselves anything. We just did something." So Feya von Moltke said, looking back. Barbara von Haeften recapitulated, "One grew into it and couldn't say at any particular point, 'Now the resistance is beginning.' For at that time resistance didn't exist at all. One was in opposition from the beginning." For Marion Yorck von Wartenburg the resistance gradually coalesced and took concrete form, until the point of no return was reached and everything pointed inevitably toward the assassination.[16]

In the multitude of studies on the resistance in general and on the problem of defining the term in particular, I came across a sentence that gave me essential help: "The system depended on the permanence of fear."[17] It is fear that provides the key. Resistance is inconceivable without an understanding of the fear emanating from "the system." It is inconceivable without the surmounting of personal fear, inconceivable without the courage to endanger oneself and to endure the fear in the self-endangering—the goal being to bring about the end of the system of fear, in this case the Nazi system. If one central dimension of resistance is the resolve to destroy the power of fear and deliberately to put one's life at risk, another is the will to put an end to the system of government that is generating and perpetuating fear. Accordingly, part of resistance is the ability and readiness to risk personal consequences, to stand up to the system of fear and to wish to end it. In that context I understand by

resistance in the Third Reich an active, personally dangerous intervention with the goal of weakening or ending the regime, and putting an end to the National Socialist state.

Dietrich Bonhoeffer is an example that shows above all that
resistance was a process—and that the risk of death was an element
that had to be taken into account. I mentioned at the beginning of
this chapter that Bonhoeffer's return from the United States—from
the exile he would not accept—marks the beginning of a transition
from the informed Bonhoeffer to Bonhoeffer the active participant,
from passive to active resistance. Once before, during his "lesser"
exile in London in the middle of the 1930s, he had talked about a
transition "to a totally different opposition," without knowing how
true the reality he described would in fact prove to be. In April
1934 he wrote from London to Erwin Sutz, a theologian friend in
Switzerland:

> About what is going on in the church in Germany you
> probably know as much as I do. National Socialism has
> brought about the end of the church in Germany and
> has consistently implemented it. . . . And although I am
> working with all my might in the church's opposition,
> it is nevertheless fully clear to me that *this* opposition
> is only a quite temporary, intermediate stage leading
> to a totally different opposition, and that only the least
> number of the men involved in this first preliminary
> skirmish will be the men of that second struggle. And I
> believe that the whole of Christendom has therefore to
> pray with us that this "resistance unto blood" will come,
> and that people will be found who can endure it.[18]

His time in London from autumn 1933 until spring 1935 can
really be viewed as a probationary exile for Bonhoeffer, one not so
much in response to a real necessity as one chosen freely. It was
motivated, at least in part, by disappointment over the Confessing Church as it was coming to be. For him it was too hesitant, too
equivocal, too meek in its attitude to the state, too inconsistent, too

fearful—in a word, too "un–Protestant" in what it said and did. For
him it displayed too little opposition to the church politics of what
had become a National Socialist state. There was too little opposition to the anti-Semitism that the state required and was all too readily practiced—too little resistance to the fatal obsequious obedience
with which the Protestant churches hastened to comply with the
Aryan paragraph, and the increased stripping of the rights of "non-
Aryans." And not only that: there was too little opposition to the
threatened surrender of the Christian message to an ideology that
had a Christian gloss but an ingrained National Socialist coloring,
and sanctioned the unjust system instead of confuting it in Christ's
name and acting against it.

This being so, at the end of the 1930s Bonhoeffer finally changed
course, moving over to a "totally different opposition" in a double
sense. On the one hand, it was a change from opposition in the
church to political opposition, and, on the other hand (although the
two went together), it was a shift from passive to active participation
in attempts to bring down the regime. Perhaps the change of course
can be most concisely characterized as a transition from protest in
and by the church to political conspiracy, as a transition from contradiction to resistance.[19] As regards the precise date of this change, we
have only two hints, both dating from the time before his renounced
North American exile in the summer of 1939. These cannot suffice
as evidence but are nevertheless of interest. The first is as follows.
Hans Oster met Bonhoeffer in 1938 in Marienburger Allee 42, the
house adjoining that of Bonhoeffer's parents, where his sister Ursula
and her husband, Rüdiger Schleicher, were living with their family.[20]
But even if Bonhoeffer already knew from Dohnanyi about Oster's
conspirational activities, to assume that there were more specific
contacts between Oster and Bonhoeffer at that time is to enter the
realm of speculation. The second hint is this: in Bonhoeffer's diary
of 1938 the pages for February 10 to 20, 1938, the period covering
the Blomberg-Fritsch crisis, have been torn out; and so too have the
pages in his dairy of 1939 recording the periods when he was staying in Berlin, pages for January and April–May, as well as pages for

August and September 1939, the months following his return from New York. His biographer offers a convincing explanation:

> These pages contained Berlin addresses and telephone numbers that were not in Bonhoeffer's diaries of previous years, and initials and numbers of the Zehlendorf and Grunewald district, but especially of the Tirpitzufer, where the counter-espionage department had its headquarters. The Gestapo was not to be able to question him about such entries if his notebooks should fall into their hands in any search instigated into church affairs.[21]

Now, in a dictatorship especially, missing notebooks, addresses, notes, etc. would undoubtedly seem to suggest certain conclusions. But it would be a shaky argument to see the *nonexistence* of evidence as a definitive indication that in the months in question Bonhoeffer was already involved in the conspiracy, and Bethge too rightly terms this merely circumstantial evidence. Consequently, the question is still: When after his return from New York did Bonhoeffer change course and pass from passive to active resistance? The fact that this took place after New York can be established and is not in dispute. The question is exactly when?

three

When Did the Commitment Begin?

EVER SINCE BETHGE'S DETAILED biography, it has been assumed that Bonhoeffer's involvement in the resistance circle that had formed around Hans Oster in the Military Intelligence Foreign Office after 1938 dated from the second half of 1940. But there are indications that this assumption has to be corrected.

Dates can sometimes prove difficult to determine, especially when they have to do with the Military Intelligence, and even more with the resistance. An apt example is the question about the beginning of Bonhoeffer's work for the Military Intelligence or *Abwehr*, work that may count as his first practical step in the direction of resistance activities. On the basis of Bethge's biography, it has always been presupposed that August–September 1940 was the earliest period of his "final commitment to the *Abwehr*."[1] But new clues emerged afterward, at the latest with the publication in 1996 of volume 16 of the collected works (DBW), which in the English translation is titled *Conspiracy and*

Imprisonment 1940–1945. Here documents are published that, to put it cautiously, permit us to conclude that Bonhoeffer's activity for the Military Intelligence—or in reality for the resistance—clearly began earlier. What is the reason for this assumption?

The German preface to volume 16[2] stresses that the indictment against Bonhoeffer (which had then only recently been discovered in an archive in Prague) deserves particular attention. And this indictment of September 21, 1943, drawn up by the senior reich military prosecutor, contains extracts from Bonhoeffer's letters to the relevant district military recruiting station in Schlawe, Pomerania, which certainly make one prick up one's ears. In order to understand these letters, we must remember that at the beginning of 1938 Bonhoeffer had been forbidden to reside in Berlin (except for visits to his parents).[3] The background of the prohibition was his impending medical examination and call up, and they are evidence that relations between Bonhoeffer and Oster must already have been on record at least from October 1939—that is, three months after his return from the United States.

From these letters, the indictment quotes, first, a passage written on October 12, 1939: "In the meantime I have been given an assignment by the Armed Forces High Command that I must carry out in Berlin. Colonel Oster (Armed Forces High Command, Tirpitzufer 80) today authorized me to let you know that he is prepared to explain in case of further inquiry. For this reason I will be living for the time being in Berlin with my father." The indictment notes that the requirement to report to the appropriate military recruiting station in Berlin was not complied with. And a quotation from a further communication of Bonhoeffer's to the military recruiting station in Schlawe follows: "As always, when I am in Berlin on business, I live in my father's home. This time I was required to remain available in Berlin longer than was originally planned." The final passage, dated May 27, 1940, is as follows: "Since I will presumably need to remain a few days in Berlin, I am requesting, following consultation with my military department here, that my service record be sent to the chief of staff for the Foreign Office of Military Intelligence in the OKW. Address: Colonel Oster, Foreign Office of Military Intelligence, OKW, Berlin W 35, Tirpitzufer 80. Schlawe should remain my official military recruiting station."[4]

The indictment attaches special importance to this last-mentioned document, since when it was written its writer must already have received the summons to his medical examination on July 5, 1940. In the indictment against the prisoner Bonhoeffer, who is accused of evading his call up and subverting military authority, these quotations tend in a particular direction. They serve to prove that more than a year before he is named for the first time in the papers of the Military Intelligence Foreign Office—which can be shown to be only on December 11, 1940—the accused already appealed to that department. Consequently, he appealed to it inadmissibly—that is to say, before he had actually been appointed by the Military Intelligence—and the Intelligence from its side evidently and illegally covered up for him. In short, this was a dubious case in a dubious department. Incidentally, it would seem that the date December 11 given in the indictment is a typing error. What was meant was probably Bonhoeffer's letter to Dohnanyi of November 11, 1940—apparently written as a smokescreen—which was supposed to serve as an "application" from Bonhoeffer and was to have been deposited on purpose in the files.[5]

With regard to the question as to when Bonhoeffer can be proved to have had his first definite, documented contacts with Hans Oster of the Military Intelligence, these extracts from Bonhoeffer's incriminating letters to Schlawe provide a surprising answer under another aspect. They are unequivocal evidence that contacts evidently existed earlier than was long supposed—in any event (according to what we know at present), from October 1939 onward, and not just from the second half of 1940. Whether, however, this finding permits the conclusion that we now know about "some events that were previously unknown," such as Bonhoeffer's journeys to Bethel in the Rhineland and to Saxony on the instructions of Oster or the Military Intelligence Foreign Office[6] is a question that may be left open. The indictment certainly states in a different passage:

As the rationale for his letter of May 24, 1940, to the Schlawe District Military Recruiting Station, the defendant asserts that it is possible that he took trips at that time for himself to Bethel, to the Rhineland, and to Saxony, which "in accordance with the OKW agreement" he also used for his official concerns.[7]

We must nevertheless be clear about the fact that in later interrogations Bonhoeffer may have deliberately introduced a mention of journeys of this kind in order to lend verisimilitude to his—fictitious—work for the Military Intelligence, but that at the same time may have kept them vague—"it is possible"—so that what he said should not contradict anything said by others accused at that time, especially Dohnanyi. In any case, there is no other evidence for journeys of this kind; "it is possible" that they took place.[8] And it is possible, in spite of all the laborious reconstructions of Bonhoeffer's life, that there are still gaps that we know nothing about. The fact remains that he was clearly in contact with the Military Intelligence Foreign Office earlier than was long assumed.[9] What is questionable, however, is a statement made in another connection to the effect that Bonhoeffer already possessed a service passport from the Military Intelligence in 1939. Here, too, we can, in my view, establish only that this "was possible" as early as 1939.

This theory about the service passport—which at first glance is of no more than marginal importance—is discussed in more detail below, not so much for its own sake but rather as an example of the problematic nature of the documentary situation—or, to be more precise, the sources—where the resistance is concerned. This is even truer when we are considering the resistance that grew up within the Military Intelligence itself, an institution that as we know served as a military secret service.

My attention was drawn to this "service passport" theory in an extremely careful legal study of "the Dohnanyi case," which starts from the assumption that Bonhoeffer already possessed a service passport issued by the Military Intelligence in 1939.[10] In stating this, the author refers to Jørgen Glenthøj, one of the editors of DBW 16, which had not, however, yet appeared when her study was written. Glenthøj, undoubtedly an excellent authority on Bonhoeffer, had come across a paper from the Military Intelligence office in Munich to which Bonhoeffer was later assigned, from which he concluded that Bonhoeffer was in possession of a service passport as early as 1939. This finding was published in DBW 16 and was cautiously commented on there at another point and in another connection.[11] The document in question was a reply to a letter dated September 10, 1942, from the Military Intelligence office in Munich, addressed to Police Headquarters, Munich, in which Dietrich Bonhoeffer's passport was included,[12] and which contained an application for a visa for other official journeys abroad.[13] "Visa . . . issued for repeated journeys. Exempt from fees. (Service Passport no. II 1939–42 from Berlin Police Headquarters, valid from May 27, 1942, to August 26, 1945, issued for domestic and foreign travel." This appears among other things in the brief reply sent by Department II/1 of Police Headquarters Munich.[14] According to this, a service passport of Bonhoeffer's had been sent in, valid from May 27, 1942. With this service passport Bonhoeffer then flew to Sweden three days later, on May 30, 1942. Glenthøj's conclusion must have been that this was a service passport of 1939, which was renewed in 1942— "1939–42"—or that it was a succeeding passport (No. II), and that accordingly there must have been a passport No. I from 1939.

This is a tempting theory. In its favor is the fact that the renewal again follows in a three-year rhythm: 1939–1942–1945. But what speaks against it is that "No. II" may refer to the relevant department at the Munich police headquarters, which, it may be, was also responsible for passports, and that the occurrence of the numbers 1939–42 is merely a chance coincidence with the corresponding years. Without knowing the practices usual at the time in the issue of service passports, it is impossible to clarify this question. The end of research into the date of Bonhoeffer's entry into service with the Military Intelligence is still that, on the basis of the letters of 1939–40 quoted in the indictment, it may count as certain that in the autumn of 1939 he already officially claimed contact with

Hans Oster and the Military Intelligence Foreign Office, and that therefore consultations with Oster, of whatever nature, took place at least from October 12, 1939 onward. At that time he may even have already possessed a service passport from the Military Intelligence. However, substantial information about his activity for the Military Intelligence or the resistance is still available to us only from the second half of 1940.

In looking back, we must take into account several interlocking factors in the Bonhoeffer case. In the first place, in an institution such as the military secret service, a transparent chronology of events that could be precisely checked by an outsider definitely did not exist. No "account" true to reality was committed to paper about facts, people, operations, successes and failures, journeys and special missions. Camouflaged material and deceptive maneuvers for the purpose of misleading potential or actual opponents were part of the agenda. "A large part of the Intelligence work, and its most important part above all, is not recorded in the files."[15] Second, how much more will this have been true for a man who was only for form's sake active on behalf of the Military Intelligence. All the official events recorded in the files are no more than the scenery that provides the backdrop against which Bonhoeffer could, and was intended to, carry out his "real" assignments—assignments for the group around Oster who resisted their own government and were involved in resistance activities against it. Third, it is one of the main problems of historians of the resistance that in many cases there is no written evidence, neither personal statements nor documents. Nor could there be anything of the kind, because "conspiracy permits no detailed papers that could be discovered and could be a betrayal."[16]

Written notes about oppositional, let alone conspirational ideas and activities, carried a high risk—not only for those who compiled them but also for those with whom the authors were in contact. We shall therefore seek in vain for written personal statements, for example from Bonhoeffer, in which facts, reasons, and circumstances, perhaps about his first contacts with conspirational circles, are recorded.

It is obvious that there will be no written evidence regarding the date when, where, how, and why he talked to Dohnanyi and Oster about the beginning of his ostensible work for the Military Intelligence. In periods of dictatorship and the resistance to it, written testimonies about that resistance, of whatever kind, are unavoidably sparse. Letters and diaries, reflections and summaries, notes and lists of names, memoranda and the draft of plans—every text contained dangerous potential. And it is a fortunate chance for historians that there should be written material at all, and that of what there was, something should have remained, in spite of war and state terror.

In the first years of historical investigation into the resistance—and today the work of the early years itself already possesses historical status—there was a justifiable lament that there were hardly any records, hardly any documents.[17] Meanwhile, through research in the years that followed, the situation has improved considerably. We have now at our disposal many contemporary testimonies of considerable value, in spite of the requirement of silence necessarily imposed on the conspiracy, and in spite of the deliberate destruction to which many documents of the resistance fell victim. We have the diaries, for example, of Helmuth Groscurth, Ulrich von Hassell, and Helmuth James von Moltke; we have memoranda from Carl Goerdeler, Adam von Trott, and others; we have, for instance, numerous letters from, again, the Moltkes, from Hans von Dohnanyi's family, and from Dietrich Bonhoeffer. And in the case of Dohnanyi and Bonhoeffer, the documentary situation that provides the starting point is unusually good—in Dohnanyi's case because of the numerous posthumous papers that were preserved and have now been examined, in the case of Bonhoeffer because of the quantity of material: correspondence, manuscripts, and everyday documents.[18]

In Bonhoeffer's case, an additional point of decisive importance is the survival of the friend who for long periods of time was himself so close to events. Without the later work of the chronicler Eberhard Bethge, Dietrich Bonhoeffer would certainly not be the person he is today for those who have come after him. That this Bonhoeffer is seen very much through the eyes of his chronicler is in the nature of things. It is to Bethge's honor that he himself withdrew into the background and, wholly devoid of vanity, never took the stage himself, either in the biography or in his numerous other works on Bonhoeffer.

The Dohnanyi and the Bonhoeffer cases belong together. That at least was clearly seen at the time in the indictment. We may guess that without Hans von Dohnanyi, Bonhoeffer never would have come into contact with the conspiratorial circle in the Military Intelligence Foreign Office, which consolidated after Dohnanyi was appointed to his position there on August 25, 1939. On September 1 war broke out, as we are accustomed to put it, as if this had been some natural catastrophe. A few weeks later, on October 12, 1939—at least according to the later indictment—Bonhoeffer, in applying to his military recruiting station, referred for the first time to an assignment from the army high command and said (see above) that in case of doubt, "Colonel Oster" would be prepared to provide information.

four

A Monkey Wrench in the Machinery of the Intelligence

"ANYONE WHO SAW HIM in his study, talking with four discussion partners over the four secret telephones on his table, could take fright at the juggling involved in this game, especially if he knew that the man was working for two different camps."[1] The subject of the comment is Hans Oster, colonel and later major general, Berlin, Tirpitzufer. He was the head of Department Z, the central department of the Military Intelligence Foreign Office in the army high command—that is, the army's secret service, which was set up in 1938. His duties included the oversight and recruitment of personnel, the investigation and registration of everyone working for the Military Intelligence, and the administration of finances. The central department was first and foremost an administrative department; the real tasks of a military secret service—the often intersecting sectors of espionage, counterintelligence, counterespionage, and sabotage—were functions of other departments in the Military Intelligence Foreign Office. So the central department was not entitled to control its own agents, for example.[2]

Hans Oster was the son of a Reformed (that is, Calvinist) pastor, and according to his biographer, as a young man he was "unusually interested in theological questions."[3] He seems to have had a firm, matter-of-course faith that remained unshaken by the events through which he lived. In any case he was a man with joie de vivre, an optimist, someone who did not give up easily. He was practical, active, down to earth, but someone out of the way. An early report characterized him as "fresh, cheerful, very attractive. A correct attitude to his job. Good manners. Excellent conduct."[4] Oster was born in 1887. He was an officer by conviction in the First World War, was a monarchist through and through, and held a seemingly paradoxical Prussian-pacifist view of an officer's existence: "The professional officer should be the most convinced pacifist, because he knows what war is, and hence the responsibility."[5]

At the beginning, because of his basically monarchist views, Oster, like many of his like-minded contemporaries, viewed the new regime with a mixture of sympathy and contempt. But unlike most of the others, when he became aware of its injustice, he drew the appropriate personal conclusions. After the burning of the books and what is known as the Röhm putsch of 1934, Oster, fully aware of the risk, moved decisively away from the Nazi system and became its opponent. From that time on he was filled with an enduring fury, above all with the SS.[6] At latest from 1938 onward, after the dismissal and disgrace of the army's commander in chief, Werner von Fritsch, Oster made no attempt to hide his critical attitude to the regime. Moreover, he said later that he made Fritsch's cause his own.[7] As long as Ludwig Beck was still general chief of staff, Oster was permitted to occupy Beck's office for hours at a time. Beck had the highest opinion of this active man from the inner circle of the Military Intelligence who thought and acted so purposefully. And the respect was mutual.

Oster was at the center of the first conspirational plans in the years from 1938 to 1940, and in succeeding years, too, he did not allow himself to be turned aside, even though during this time the chances for an overthrow seemed to some of the combatants of those first years to have been lost for ever. He forced on plans for a coup d'etat whenever they promised the least breath of success and made continually fresh attempts to persuade the topmost generals to act. For this purpose he employed all the means and privileges his position offered, sometimes to the point of rashness; not even shrinking back— and so far we must anticipate—from what was clearly treason.

Fellow combatants of the most varied origin, and historians of the most varied provenance, have stressed Oster's supreme importance for the resistance.[8] It is all the more regrettable that, in the literature on the German resistance, extensive though it is, only few individual studies are devoted to him.[9] Oster had enjoyed the confidence of the head of the Military Intelligence, Admiral Wilhelm Canaris, ever since he had taken up his position in 1935. The two were friends, or became so. Canaris did not merely cover up Oster's subversive views and activities during 1938–39; he shared them, even took them further, until—from the summer of 1940 onward—he himself renounced active participation in plans for a coup d'etat, having become resigned to failure, in view of the continual refusal of the generals to act. Nevertheless, he continued to protect Oster and shielded him and other members of his staff whom he knew very well were actively involved in a conspiracy—above all Hans von Dohnanyi, but not Dohnanyi alone.

Immediately after the war and in the period that followed, Canaris's life and personality, his role in the Abwehr, or Military Intelligence, and the part he played in the resistance gave rise to a voluminous literature and a highly controversial and sometimes not very objective discussion. A profusion of biographies appeared.[10] He tended to be seen and described as a "mystery man," and the dictum that "the Intelligence was Canaris and Canaris the Intelligence" became almost a cliché.[11] The judgment of contemporaries and historians ranges widely.[12] Decades later the name Canaris still evokes stereotype descriptions. He is said to have been an ambiguous and contradictory character but highly intelligent. He is called the wily little Canaris, is described as enigmatic and inscrutable, impressively astute, and much more. In the mind of the public, Canaris was especially exposed to the cliché thinking customary where the Third Reich was concerned.

The same may be said of the Military Intelligence as a whole. For a long time, one of the commonest misunderstandings about it, for example, was that it was as a whole a shelter for the resistance. But "if one wishes to express it in terms of brutal statistics: at the peak of its activities the *Abwehr* (Military Intelligence) comprised 13,000 officers, officials and employees, of whom at most 50 can count as supporters of the resistance," that is, barely 0.4 percent.[13] This hard core was to be found in Department Z. In this central department Hans Oster had built up one of "the most important opposition groups in the army."[14] It viewed itself as bridgehead to other opposition groups in and outside the army, and in so far counted as "central department" in a special sense. It worked with the knowledge, approval, and (to a varying degree) active support of its head, Admiral Wilhelm Canaris. As far as Bonhoeffer's participation in the resistance and his formal integration in the Intelligence is concerned, Canaris himself rather played a marginal role. It was different in the case of Hans von Dohnanyi, to whom we must now turn in more detail.

Dohnanyi took up his post in Z Department on August 25, 1939. After the previous year's plans for an overthrow, Canaris and Oster had agreed with him that if war could no longer be prevented, he should be drafted into the Military Intelligence. From the outset the declared purpose of his recruitment—of course for each other and not officially—was that from this so to speak secure position Dohnanyi should continue to act in the interests of the conspiracy against the Nazi regime.[15]

Dohnanyi was a lawyer, a civilian by conviction, and he could offer neither any military service worth mentioning nor any military rank; so in 1940 he was given a special position as head of a group in a newly established group called "Reporting in the Central Department." This position carried with it the equivalent of a major's rank and entitled Dohnanyi to wear a uniform. The group centered on Oster consisted of members of staff critical of the regime. They were not as a whole regular officers and even less died-in-the-wool members of the Intelligence.[16] As well as Dohnanyi, the group soon included above all Justus Delbrück, a friend of Dohnanyi's since boyhood, and Karl Ludwig von Guttenberg, the editor of the conservative Catholic periodical *Weisse Blätter*. A photo dating from this period that shows this "Oster trio" is incidentally supposed to have been taken specially for the purpose of giving pleasure to Oster, the confirmed army officer.[17]

Dohnanyi's official function was to analyze all news, information, and reports with a view to their military and foreign policy significance. He had to keep Oster and Canaris up to date in this respect and to cultivate contacts with the Foreign Office. Canaris very soon also came to value him as personal adviser. With Oster, Dohnanyi was on friendly terms from the beginning, and there was cordial agreement between them, both in their official relations as well as on the level of Dohnanyi's "private practice," as his subversive activity in the Military Intelligence Foreign Office was called, in a phrase coined by his wife. In the first weeks, Oster even shared his office with him. Afterward he was given a room that could only be entered through Oster's and that was in direct proximity to that of Canaris.[18] When Dohnanyi entered the Military Intelligence, he already had behind him a busy professional life. He had brilliant qualifications, and a no less brilliant career seemed to lie ahead, if only he had not sometimes expressed his anti-Nazi views with positively insolent frankness. An official assessment from the Ministry of Justice, where he worked from 1933, includes the following comment:

> "Dohnanyi is a man of exceedingly keen intellect, with admirable grasp, great industry, polished manners, and a dextrous presentation, both orally and in writing." But later the report goes on, "He in no way agrees with the racial laws of the Third Reich, and is inwardly opposed to them. Thus he has expressed the view that the National Socialist racial attitude is impossible, because it contradicts the Christian standpoint of the Protestant church."[19]

Franz Gürtner, who was already minister of justice before Hitler came to power, let his personal secretary go after five years, unwillingly, but seeing that it was in the interests of Dohnanyi's future for him to be withdrawn from direct contact with the government if he were not to be professionally isolated or eliminated altogether. "If I were not completely confident that National Socialism will be got rid of, my whole life would seem to me no longer worth living," Dohnanyi once said to a friend in 1939.[20] It seems no exaggeration to sum up by saying that, from the beginning, he saw the meaning of his personal life in the struggle against this system, characterized as it was by injustice and violence, contempt for human beings, and their annihilation. And from the beginning, too, it was an existence in resistance. Nor does it seem an exaggeration to sum up by saying that he belongs at the center of the German resistance.[21]

During his work as the right hand of the minister of justice, Gürtner, Dohnanyi had been able to observe closely from 1933 onward the procedure of the National Socialist Party, government, and system. Not only that; he also had the chance to get to know personally its leaders, Hitler, Goebels, Göring, and Himmler. He knew the extent of their power and their greed for power. He experienced the way the law was perverted and broken. He noted the first acts of terror—and began to put them on record. He drew up dossiers in which, on the basis of specific cases, he was able to produce evidence of the way people were deprived of their rights and degraded. He described meticulously individual examples of attacks and lynch justice and collected all the information available to him about coercive measures and arbitrary acts. He was obliged to keep an official journal for the minister of justice, and out of that there grew a further chronicle of the dictatorship, which he continued on his own responsibility, a documentation of oppression and persecution.

Hans Oster drew up a secret collection of material on his own account (within the official secret information service) and outlined an overthrow scenario that he described as a "Study"; and for him Dohnanyi's collection of documents, which was termed his "portfolio of curiosities" or his "scandal chronicle," provided a welcome complement to his own, which he also went on to complete in the years that followed. In a similar way, after the devastating conquest of Poland, Canaris had begun to record measures that amounted to war crimes, his aim being to stir up the generals. In August 1938 Ludwig Beck had resigned his office under protest and, though now "in retirement," he counted as head of the resistance group gathered round Oster and as potential head of state after a putative revolution. For him these documents provided an invaluable and indispensable legitimating basis for a putsch. If a coup d'etat was to be able to count on the support of the people as a whole, overwhelming evidence was needed with which to demonstrate its necessity and legality. Consequently, after the outbreak of war particularly, Dohnanyi went ahead with his work of documenting National Socialist crimes. At the end of the war, his wife, Christine von Dohnanyi—who in my view was a partner in the resistance from the beginning—wrote about this chronicle:

> At that time almost all the internal party scandals, or scandals affecting the party organization, came before the minister of justice personally—generally with Hitler's instruction that the case be dismissed—and he passed these on without exception to my husband. Under the name of a "chronicle," my husband had put together a complete list of all these cases, and that meant recording the criminal acts of the powerful men in the party with all the details. . . . Over the years he had supplemented and completed this material. There were Hitler's speeches, accounts of the treatment of prisoners of war, films of crimes committed in Poland, reports about the reasons for the Bromberg "Bloody Sunday," Goebbels's instructions about the Jewish pogroms, and more material of like kind. My husband was convinced that these reports could be supplemented at will by experiences from other departments, and so he told me that these documents must be enough to open the eyes of anyone who was willing to see what Hitler and his regime were.[22]

It was not only this written word that was a potential monkey wrench in the machinery of the Intelligence but a number of acts as

well. Just as he had already done while he was in the ministry of justice in many individual cases that came before him either officially
or privately, Dohnanyi tried to intervene, stop, or help, whether by
himself or with the help of his chief Oster, but always shielded by
Canaris.[23] Even though they had been unable to prevent the outbreak of war, they hoped to undermine whatever would permit
its escalation into a world war. In order to be heard as the voice
of a German opposition to Hitler, they tried to make use of secret
contacts with countries abroad—the Vatican, Switzerland, Holland, Scandinavia. The previous year's scenario, which had been
designed to bring down the Hitler regime, was to be employed again
in the autumn of 1939. In thinking through this renewed attempt to
bring about the end of the system of violence, the assassination of
Hitler was now no longer completely excluded. But the plans for a
coup d'etat, which had been mainly planned by the group around
Canaris, Oster, Dohnanyi, and Beck, and was designed to prevent
the spread of the war into the west, and hence a World War, came to
nothing. The "November plot" again failed because of the renewed
hesitation of the generals. And there were other factors in addition.

On November 8, 1939, after three weeks' preparation, Georg
Elser made a single-handed attempt at an assassination in the Munich
Bürgerbräukeller. This abortive attempt, which must command
our admiration, resulted in security measures to protect Hitler that
seemed to banish to the realm of impossibility either the planned
arrest of the Führer (followed by legal proceedings against him) or
assassination through explosives. A day later "the Venlo incident"
followed, additionally bringing the German conspirators to a halt,
and discrediting their secret attempts to find foreign discussion partners.[24] Walter Schellenberg of the Security Section of the SS had set
up this incident with the help of the Gestapo, laying a false scent for
the English secret service. Near the Dutch town of Venlo, Gestapo
agents succeeded in kidnapping and bringing over the German frontier two British secret service officers, who were supposed to investigate these supposed peace contacts of German conspirators.[25]
Understandably enough, suspicion now fell on the men who under

the protection of the Intelligence or another official authority—perhaps the Foreign Office—really had sought contacts with England. Abroad, no one now put much trust any longer in alleged anti-Nazis in the service of the German Reich.

In the autumn of 1939, the Catholic lawyer Josef Müller was recruited as officer by the Military Intelligence office in Munich, on the instructions of the group around Hans Oster; and in the period that followed, he was several times sent to the Vatican as emissary of the Hitler opponents within the Intelligence and outside it. Because of his longstanding relations with the Vatican, Müller, apparently by way of Father Leiber, the pope's secretary, evidently managed to convince Pius XII that a German opposition existed, and that, via Müller, contact should be made with the English government. London was supposed to have signalized a possible readiness for negotiations with a new, non-Nazi government provided that the Hitler government fell.[26] On the basis of Müller's reports, at the end of January 1940 Hans von Dohnanyi drew up what was later called the X Report (X stood for Müller), which Christine von Dohnanyi in a tour de force typed overnight.[27] The hope that this report would galvanize the generals to act proved to be without foundation. So it was simply put aside with other secret material of the Oster group. When up to the spring of 1940 the secret opposition in Germany (of whose existence Müller had so vehemently assured the Vatican and England) had still failed to act, it was bound to look in London as if this opposition did not exist.

It seemed a little later as if the Oster group in the Military Intelligence Foreign Office, "the general staff of the German Resistance and of the chief link with the outside world,"[28] had given up, after Hitler's successful offensive in the West in the early summer of 1940. Canaris at least really did give up. With the capitulation of France, the diverse attempts of various opposition circles to move the generals as a whole to rebellion against the murderous war of a murderous system had failed. The conspiracy against the war[29] had come to an end. The escalation of the war into a world war was only a question of time. And the attack on Poland of September 1, 1939, turned into an annihilating war of indescribable proportions.

five

Fit for Active
Service

IN THE MONTHS FROM the autumn of 1939 until the spring of
1940, Hans Oster, fully aware of the possible consequences of what
he was doing, committed what is generally known as treason.[1] He
informed his friend Gijsbertus Jacobus Sas, the Dutch military atta-
ché in Berlin, about the date of the attacks planned in the west and
finally about those in the north too. At that time Oster told this
friend, "One can only say that I am a traitor, but I am not really one;
I believe that I am a better German than all the people who run after
Hitler. It is my plan and my duty to free Germany and the world
from this plague."[2] Since the dates he had named for the impending German attacks were continually postponed for various reasons,
his reports soon fell on deaf ears in the countries immediately concerned, and in England. The invasion did in fact finally take place
on April 9, 1940, in the north and on May 10, 1940, in the west,
and the troops of the "pan-German Reich" began to occupy first

Denmark and Norway, then Holland, Belgium, Luxembourg, and France. Oster had "betrayed" these dates too, but in vain.

The categories *treason* and *high treason* were formally distinguished, but in fact during the war the borderline was fluid. A classic case of this kind, the betrayal of military plans to the enemy, counted unequivocally as treason, and it was traditionally considered the worse crime of the two. High treason comprised attacks on the country's inner security, and consequently attempts at an overthrow belonged to this category.[3] Oster not only accepted the risk of incurring the stigma of high treason; he consciously risked the still worse condemnation of betraying his country to the enemy. He knew the reports about the Poland campaign, which made a mockery of the methods of all "normal" military campaigns, and his attempt was intended to prevent the war from spreading. He also made that attempt in the hope that the armed forces would use the chance to bring down their own government. In that context, Oster's behavior at this time was a precise example of the fact that under the conditions of the Second World War, German resistance "was in tendency always simultaneously both high treason and treason."[4] Both were as a rule subject to the death penalty or were punishable by yearlong imprisonment or by imprisonment for life.[5]

Hans von Dohnanyi knew about Oster's ventures, which, though undoubtedly well considered, were at the same time a counsel of despair. In countless contacts they discussed the possibilities and impossibilities of what they did. These discussions took place not only in their offices on the Tirpitzufer (today Reichpietschufer) but more intensively in the evenings in Oster's private apartment, which was at that time an important meeting place, particularly also for army officers who were not (or were no longer) on the active list, such as Ludwig Beck, the former chief of the general staff, who had retired in 1938.[6] Dohnanyi had taken his wife into his confidence about Oster's step (as was a matter of course in their marriage), and she "completely supported" his decision, as she later stressed.[7] From 1939 until 1941 the couple lived in Berlin in the house of Bonhoeffer's parents, which intensified the closeness to Dietrich

Bonhoeffer, who during his visits to Berlin had in any case to stay at Marienburger Allee 43, his parents' address, because he was forbidden otherwise to reside in the capital (a "Conditional Restriction of Residence" as it was called in civil service jargon).[8]

Bethge remembered that "one of the people whom Bonhoeffer met during these weeks [that is, immediately before April 1940] was Hans Oster."[9] On March 24—Easter Sunday in 1940; hence the precise dating—Hans Oster held a confidential discussion for the first time with Bonhoeffer in his parents' house.[10] But it can be deduced from another source that they had already met, at least, at the Schleichers' home.[11] And Bonhoeffer's letter of October 12, 1939, to his military recruiting station in Schlawe shows that there must already have been contacts, however fleeting, in the autumn of 1939.[12] So although the point when Oster and Bonhoeffer had gotten to know each other well cannot be clarified in detail, it can be established that they knew each other from 1938–39; and apparently the contact between them was intensified in the spring of 1940. That is also suggested by Bonhoeffer's later letter to Schlawe of May 1940. This would merely confirm the meeting "during these weeks," which I have already mentioned, and about which Bethge later reported.

It would seem that it was because of the burden on his conscience of repeated treasonable acts that Hans Oster wanted to talk to Bonhoeffer again—Bonhoeffer the theologian, the pastor, the spiritual counselor, and "the man of God." For an officer of Prussian origins, treason—apart from all its formal and legal aspects—was simply unthinkable, not open to discussion, always reprehensible. Of course, Oster always took a somewhat unusual view of his profession: "The professional soldier should be the most convinced pacifist, because he knows what war is and hence also the responsibility,"[13] and his opposition to the SS state did not permit him to shrink back even from treason, and had not done so for months. And yet he doubted the legitimacy of what he did. He tried to find the justification of which he could apparently not assure himself. Bethge describes Bonhoeffer's attitude in this borderland of treason:

Bonhoeffer regarded Oster's action on the eve of the Western offensive as a step taken on his own final responsibility. It seemed to him appropriate in a situation into which a presumptuous German had maneuvered his country, and in which all those who were capable of action were suffering from paralysis of the conscience. So the patriot had to perform what in normal times is the action of a scoundrel. "Treason" had become true patriotism, and what was normally "patriotism" had become treason. An officer saw the diabolical reversal of all values, and acted alone so as not in any circumstance, after his experience in Poland, to pave the way for new outrages in other countries—and the pastor approved of what he did.[14]

It was not a cheap acquittal that Bonhoeffer gave Oster. It accorded with his own thinking: while he did not fundamentally agree with treason, he saw it exclusively under the specific conditions of the specific situation. It was the answer of an individual in what had become an abnormal time, a time when to cling to the usual standards—people, country, defense—became a betrayal of these very standards themselves. From our perspective today, we can perhaps hardly understand why Hans Oster felt it necessary to draw on spiritual advice, and why he evidently found it difficult to come to terms with what at the time counted as treason—and was so in actual fact. It was clearly not fear of discovery that took him to Bonhoeffer. He evidently turned to him out of a burdened conscience, to use a concept that is nowadays somewhat out of fashion. But that would have had to do with the pastoral dimension of this conversation, and about that we know nothing, for good reason. Bethge reports that at that time there were often similar discussions between Dohnanyi and Bonhoeffer:

> In those crucial years, no one was nearer to him than his brother-in-law Hans von Dohnanyi. Bonhoeffer received from him information, counsel, and, later,

commissions, while Dohnanyi sought from him ethical certainty and enlightening conversation. . . . It was also he who one evening asked Bonhoeffer what he thought about the New Testament passage "all who take the sword will perish by the sword" (Matt. 26:52). Bonhoeffer's reply was that the word was valid for their circle too—we have to accept that we are subject to that judgment, but that there is now need of such men as will accept its validity for themselves.[15]

Bonhoeffer himself was at that time forced in the most highly personal sense to find an answer to this question about the sword. The question had to be asked on two levels: Can I perform military service; can I engage in war? May I, whether directly or indirectly, take part in the conspiracy, plans that do not merely imply the killing of human beings but have that as their goal? Looking back, it seems as if these were two fundamental questions, theoretically cleanly divided from each other yet in tense relationship. Or they are interpreted as if the questions are completely and wholly antagonistic. Or as questions that are in any case easy enough to answer, since today, after all, we know what was the right thing to do, and what was—or would have been—wrong. In the practical question Bonhoeffer had to solve, this question about the sword presents itself differently—in the context of his existence, so to speak. It was in very truth a question on two levels, and in answering the first, he found an answer to the second. Here it is necessary to go back a few years, to 1934.

At an ecumenical conference on the Danish island of Fanö in August of that year, Bonhoeffer gave a lecture with the title "The Universal Church and the World of the Nations." Its central statement was, "There should be peace because Christ is in the world."[16] Here, with the serpent's question, "Did God say?" he laid bare the lack of desire among human beings for peace, and the eternal justification of war. He described the peace dependent solely on the pillars of security politics as resting on a fragile foundation; and he set over against it the alternative—the will for peace that rests on a Christian foundation:

> There is no way to peace along the path of security.
> For peace has to be dared. It is a great and daring risk,
> and can never, ever be secured. Peace is the opposite of
> security. To demand securities means wanting to protect
> oneself. Peace means surrendering entirely to the com-
> mandment of God.

If the churches were to take such a resolute Christian will for peace
seriously, the bad word *pacifism* would become a term of honor. In
Christ's name the will for peace could wrest the weapons from Christendom and proclaim the peace of Christ over "the raging world." It
would counter Realpolitik's illusory idolatry of security through "a
radical call for peace."

> The hour presses—the world is bristling with weapons.
> . . . What are we waiting for? Are we willing to share in
> the guilt ourselves as never before.[17]

Ideas of this kind about war and peace, the church and peace, were
not usual, at least at that time.[18]

Another retrospect takes us back to the preachers' seminary in
Zingst in May 1935. Conscription had been introduced in the spring
of 1935, and the seminary members were discussing with almost
childish enthusiasm when the time would come for them too to be
called up. Bonhoeffer's biographer recalls that "a casual question
thrown out by Bonhoeffer . . . suddenly brought home to the unsus-
pecting students that his views on the subject might be quite different from their own." Elsewhere Bethge writes more precisely:

> That was for me the first time that I now heard from a
> Protestant theologian, a Lutheran, a competent mem-
> ber of the Confessing church, the question: is there
> then for a Christian not at least the option of simply
> trying to obey the Sermon on the Mount? Quite qui-
> etly, quite unfanatically, in a low voice, not as if he had
> now to convince us of something but simply personally,
> he reported that one day he had decided that when it

came to the point he really would become a conscientious objector.[19]

In most of the Christian churches—the Confessing Church not excepted—the justification of war, and consequently military service, was seldom called in question, and it was so much a matter of course for the students that Bonhoeffer's plea that conscientious objection should also be seen as a Christian option was for them an irritation. His purpose was not to proclaim pacifism in principle. He only wanted to open their eyes to the absurdity that human beings should destroy each other in the name of God, or at least with God's approval. He wanted them to face up to the fact that war is the will of men, not the will of God, and to perceive that a no to war is possible for faith's sake. He wanted to do no more than that—but also no less.

A third retrospect takes us back to London in March 1939. The danger of war could not be overlooked. Bonhoeffer visited his twin sister and her family in their English exile. He had to expect that he would be called up in the near future, and not only if war broke out. He was clear that he was neither willing nor able to swear an oath of loyalty to Hitler or to take up arms in the war Hitler had deliberately brought about. But if he were to declare himself a conscientious objector, he would have to reckon with immediate imprisonment and—at least after the outbreak of war—with the death penalty. He may already have heard about the arrest of Hermann Stöhr at the beginning of March.[20] Sabine Leibholz-Bonhoeffer wrote later:

> In those weeks in London we all discussed with Dietrich what he should do for the best in case he was called to the German forces. The Confessing Church had not defined its attitude toward conscription, and Dietrich's thoughts hovered between leaving the country, serving in the mission, or entering the Army Medical Service. To take up weapons in Hitler's war was for him simply

out of the question. He was not prepared to take part in
any other way than in joining the medical service. I can
still see him writing to the Bishop of Chichester in order
to ask his advice.[21]

In this letter of March 25, 1939, Bonhoeffer put before his friend
George Bell, the bishop of Chichester, the outward and inner difficulties from which he was suffering with regard to the war question. He told Bell that he was planning to leave Germany for a time.
His age group was due to be called up that year, and it seemed to
him "impossible in conscience to take part in a war under present
circumstances."[22] But if as a member of the Confessing Church he
were to come forward as a conscientious objector, he would only
damage the church, since its hostile attitude to the regime would
then be once more proved. He was uncertain and undecided, in
spite of much reflection and reading. But as things now were, to take
up arms would be to do violence to his Christian convictions. He
afterward had a long discussion with Bell in Chichester, and before
he left Germany Bonhoeffer thanked him warmly for the great help
this conversation meant for him. "I do not know what will be the
outcome of it all."[23]

The solution would have been America. No call-up—neither
conscientious objection nor war service, with perhaps deadly consequences in either case. Instead of that: security, professional advance-
ment, future. Nevertheless, Bonhoeffer returned to Germany in July
1939, leaving behind him a comfortable way out, and with unsolved
problems ahead. He took up his work again in the Collective Pastorates in Lower Pomerania as if nothing had happened, but because
of the imminent outbreak of war in that precarious border region,
he dismissed the summer course earlier than usual and arrived in
Berlin on August 26, 1939, one day after Hans von Dohnanyi had
taken up his post in the Military Intelligence Foreign Office.

On September 1, 1939, war broke out. Poland was subdued in
a few weeks, and on September 3 England and France declared war
on Germany. It was a radiant late summer. In Berlin there was business as usual. Bonhoeffer applied for a position as army and hospital

chaplain, but after months had passed the application was turned down. In October, contrary to expectations, a new course after all began in Sigurdshof. The second half of the semester, from the end of January until the middle of March, sounded the final chord in Bonhoeffer's training work for the Confessing Church. On March 17, 1940, Sigurdshof, the last phase of his preachers' seminary, was closed by the Gestapo.

During the first winter of the war, Bonhoeffer had stayed in Berlin as often as possible and would surely at that time have known about the plans of the regime's opponents in Oster's circle, even if he was not actively involved in them.[24] "Bonhoeffer [took] only a small part. [He] had not, as yet, any special commission to carry out, or any field of action for which he was responsible within the group. But he became more and more involved in it, and was sometimes present when tactics and principles were discussed."[25] His particular concern was the Confessing Church.

The existence of the Confessing Church was more than ever under threat, and its future was more than ever in jeopardy because so many of its pastors had been called up. For the group around Hans Oster, it was important to receive information about the reprisals to which the Confessing Church was exposed and to support and protect it as far as was at all possible. In the later trial documents of Oster and Dohnanyi, occasional reports of Bonhoeffer's are mentioned. These were at that time passed on via Oster to Canaris himself and to Colonel Helmuth Groscurth.[26] The statements about this are ambiguous. On the one hand, these reports deal with the church struggle, which was becoming more intensive, and, on the other hand, they were concerned solely with military policies. The fact that Groscurth "took an interest in Bonhoeffer's reports"[27] is stressed in Dohnanyi's defense brief; but their actual nature must remain an open question.[28]

Like Oster, Groscurth was a pastor's son, and until the spring of 1940 he was employed as liaison officer between the Military Intelligence Foreign Office and the army high command. In actual fact he was a liaison officer in a double sense. His diaries, discovered in the

1960s, document impressively that he was one of the most emphatic supporters of the conspiracy against the war-obsessed government, and as such he was decisively involved in the link between the Oster group and the generals who were perhaps prepared for an overthrow. Under the heading January 27, 1940, Groscurth noted among other things: "Again a new draft! In the afternoon an hour and a half's discussion with pastors belonging to the Confessing Church. Dreadful! But admirable men, resolved to fight. People like that make one feel ashamed."[29] He was referring to a conversation with representatives of the Council of Brethren of the Confessing Church, Kurt Scharf and Wilhelm Niesel, who were both imprisoned several times during the Third Reich. The main subject of that discussion was whether, or how, the large-scale call-up of pastors, which had an appalling effect on the Confessing Church and its congregations, could be checked. Bethge's biography makes it clear that this conversation came about through Bonhoeffer's mediation.[30]

After the end of the Sigurdshof semester in the middle of March 1940, Bonhoeffer again traveled to Berlin, where a few days later he learned that Sigurdshof had been closed. On March 24—and that brings us back to the beginning of this chapter—the conversation with Hans Oster on the question of treason took place in his parents' house. The fact that this conversation took place "at home" has in my view a symbolic significance. As if in a burning glass, it sheds light on the importance of his parents' home and his family for Bonhoeffer and illuminates especially the role they played during his progress into the resistance and in the resistance itself.

In this family, ever since Hitler had taken over the government, there was uncontested agreement about the no to National Socialism. "When governmental power passed into the hands of National Socialism, the Bonhoeffers' judgment was unanimous: Hitler means *war*."[31] The motives for this No may at the beginning have varied in their coloring among the individual members of the family, but about the matter itself there was no doubt. This No became vehemently intensified because the family was directly affected by the discrimination the state had authorized, and by the systematically increasing oppression and persecution of non-Aryans—we must remember the ultimate emigration of the Leibholz family. They also knew at firsthand from Dietrich Bonhoeffer about the effects of the repressive Nazi policy toward the church, and knew from Hans von Dohnanyi about the breaches of law and acts of terror committed against people of different political views.

As well as Dietrich Bonhoeffer, his brother Klaus and his sister Ursula's husband Rüdiger Schleicher were on the fringe of the resistance, so that when the "Kaltenbrunn Reports" noted "the opposing attitude of the whole clan,"[32] they were, according to their own lights, completely accurate. Bonhoeffer's parents and the Schleichers were neighbors, which made communication much easier. Consequently, their homes, and especially the home of the parents, Karl and Paula Bonhoeffer, were often the meeting point where those concerned could think and talk openly without mistrust or any misgivings. The conversation between Hans Oster and Dietrich Bonhoeffer at the end of March 1940 is an example.

In April and May, Bonhoeffer was forced to remain in Berlin; now that Sigurdshof, the last refuge of the Confessing Church for training its future pastors, had been closed, his further employment in the church was in question. But not only that. The Military Recruiting Station in Schlawe made a move. We know this from the letter Bonhoeffer addressed to it in May 1940, which is quoted in the indictment. The medical examination for military service was to take place in Schlawe on June 5, 1940. For this the indictment is, as far as I know, the only evidence, but it can hardly be called in question. Bonhoeffer was now classified as KV (*kriegsverwendungsfähig*),[33] which meant "fit for military service."

six

Interim

IN THE EARLY SUMMER of 1940 the war took on a new quality. The pan-German empire subjugated its neighbors in the north and the west. After it had occupied Denmark and Norway, Holland and Belgium and had forced a cease-fire on France, in Germany "the fruits of victory" were celebrated. The conditions of the cease-fire were dictated to France in the woods of Campiègne, in the same railway carriage in which at the end of the First World War the Germans had signed the Treaty of Versailles with the victorious powers—the treaty that was felt to be a dictate of shame. And now the German population rejoiced. Any attitude critical of the government and the war seemed to have been finally exposed as "defeatist." Open rebellion against National Socialist rule was made more difficult, not only from above because of the continually closer, continually more barefaced dictatorship, but also by the fatal, sometimes frenetic assent from below. The opposition in the army, which worked undercover, grasped that the time to act had slipped away. An overthrow seemed to have less prospect of success than ever.

Accommodation, deceit, and camouflage belonged to the permanent tactics of survival, if further plans to bring down the Nazi regime were to be in any way realistic. Life in resistance could often only be a life *between* accommodation and resistance. A scene that at first sight seems marginal illustrates the camouflage that belonged to the beginning of the double life Bonhoeffer began to lead from the summer of 1940 onward. On June 17, in the garden of a café in Memel, the loudspeakers boomed out the announcement of France's capitulation, which was greeted by the people present with enthusiastic rejoicing. Bethge describes how Bonhoeffer also sprang to his feet, raising his arm in the prescribed Hitler salute, while he himself stood beside him, dazed. " 'Raise your arm. Are you crazy?' he whispered to me, and later, 'We shall have to run risks for very different things now, but not for that salute!' "[1]

At that time they were on the first of what were known in the church as visitations. Bonhoeffer's professional situation had become precarious, and the Council of the Brethren, to whom he was responsible, came up with an assignment for journeys of this kind, on which, as "visitor" from the Old Prussian Council of Brethren, he acted as what we would now call a supervisor in questions relating to the buildup of the congregations. Bonhoeffer traveled through Lower Pomerania and East Prussia so as to lend support theologically and pastorally to the congregations there, and in order to strengthen and advise them. In the areas round Tilsit and Memel, conditions in the congregations of the Confessing Church, which were often without pastors, were often very depressing, but there were also signs of a lively Christian life that was not prepared to give up.

In July 1940, during the second visitation, there was a minor incident that nevertheless had far-reaching consequences. In Bloestau, near Königsberg, the Gestapo closed a Confessing Church retreat for theological students led by Bonhoeffer, with a vague reference to the law. Personal details were taken down, and there were interrogations. However, there were no arrests. Nevertheless, Bonhoeffer was worried, and the retreat did in fact have consequences about which he could at the time know nothing. "The Gestapo did not approve of speakers from other parts of the country, still less of speakers with his record."[2] Soviet soldiers had been conspicuously stationed on the other side of the frontier in what was earlier, and is now, Lithuania, in the wake of the "incorporation" of the Baltic states in the Soviet Union at that time; and there was accordingly unrest on both sides of the frontier. Bonhoeffer consequently broke off his journey abruptly and returned to Berlin sooner than expected. In any event, a discussion with Dohnanyi is already noted for July 29, 1940.[3]

At the beginning of August 1940, Dohnanyi and Bonhoeffer traveled to Potsdam together, a noteworthy journey, about which Dohnanyi wrote to his wife:

> The third man was Dr. Schönfeld, for whose sake the whole expedition took place. But I think it was worth it. There is considerable interest in Schönfeld in the office, and I think contact will be made with him in the next few days. For Schönfeld this is also extremely useful, and I think he is very grateful.[4]

This meeting is worth noting because it throws light especially on the relationship at that time between Dohnanyi's companions, Schönfeld and Bonhoeffer. They knew each other from the 1930s, when they were both in Geneva, working on behalf of ecumenical relations between the Protestant churches. The difference between them was that Bonhoeffer consistently followed the line of the Confessing Church, while Schönfeld, at least at that time, still adhered mainly to the external policy of the German Evangelical Church under Bishop Heckel, which was faithful to the regime. Schönfeld who— perhaps since the outbreak of war—had been in contact with opposition forces, was now to be drawn in, in some way or other, to the work of the Military Intelligence in order, on the one hand, to make use of his experience abroad and, on the other, to protect him from being called up. And it was in this connection that Dohnanyi wanted to meet him on August 5, 1940.[5] Dohnanyi's arrangement suggests a certain change in the relationship between Bonhoeffer and Schönfeld, which was originally very strained and seemed gradually to become more relaxed in the circumstances of their further existence in the resistance.

What also took place in August 1940 was a discussion in Berlin, in the house of Bonhoeffer's parents, which was followed by what was for Bonhoeffer a decisive determination of his course. He now came much closer to the circle of regime opponents. Dohnanyi and Oster were present as well as Bethge and Bonhoeffer, and also the lawyer Hans-Bernd Gisevius, at that time an officer in the Military Intelligence and a friend of Oster's.[6]

Gisevius was soon to move to Switzerland, where his official function as vice-consul in the German Consulate General in Zurich was intended to camouflage his real purpose. Although not intimate with Admiral Canaris, he was to act as "resident" of the Military Intelligence in Zurich, and as such to serve at the same time as middleman for the resistance circle in the Intelligence or, to be more precise, for the resistance group around Oster.[7] After the Nazis came to power, Gisevius had worked in a number of their administrative offices, including the Ministry for Home Affairs—at first with undoubted enthusiasm. But after the Röhm putsch in 1934, he became critical toward the regime, was friendly with Hans Oster (also from 1934 onward), and from 1939 acted as "special officer" in the Military Intelligence Foreign Office[8]—an obvious parallel to Dohnanyi; and, as in Dohnanyi's case, his appointment to the Intelligence served as camouflage for conspiracy against the regime. But whereas the relationship between Gisevius and Oster was extremely friendly—at least on Gisevius's side—Gisevius's relations with Dohnanyi were less so, to put it mildly; and in the postwar period this still had disastrous consequences.[9] Incidentally, Gisevius's dislike of Dohnanyi was at least partly mutual, and the relationship between Bonhoeffer and Gisevius does not seem to have been precisely unclouded either, as Dohnanyi's later notes show.[10]

But to return to the summer of 1940: What was the subject of the negotiations at this August meeting in the house of Bonhoeffer's parents? For they clearly laid down Bonhoeffer's further path, and have usually been (and often still are) taken to mark the beginning of Bonhoeffer's relations with the resistance. Dohnanyi and Oster wanted to draw him in the long term into their conspiracy work, and Bonhoeffer, the "complete civilian" and peace veteran, the pastor of the Confessing Church, finally took on himself an ambivalent role as protégé of the Military Intelligence. Outwardly he continued to act on Intelligence authority, just as he indicated to the recruiting station in Schlawe in his first comments of this kind in October 1939 and May 1940. The observations of such an innocent observer as a pastor, and a pastor of the Confessing Church at that, could on the face of it very well be of use to the Military Intelligence—especially in East Prussia, which was of particular interest as a potential area for the buildup of troops on both sides of the German-Russian border. So if Bonhoeffer were again to travel there, and if he were to be under observation by the Gestapo, for example, he could appeal to the assignments given him by the Military Intelligence; and from now on, observation of the concentration of Red Army troops, which was highly relevant for military policy, was one of his tasks. Perhaps in this way a call-up could initially still be avoided too. So Bonhoeffer, the church's "visitor," would travel with a double assignment: for the Confessing Church and for the Military Intelligence. But in the long run, with the help of the alleged Intelligence assignments, Bonhoeffer intended and meant to carry out assignments of a very different kind. His part in the work of the resistance now took on its own contours.

Bonhoeffer began his third visitation journey to East Prussia on August 25, 1940. He reported to the appropriate Military Intelligence office in Königsberg, in case some special occurrence should make an official screen necessary.[11] However, the planned meeting with the head of the Intelligence there came to nothing, but neither did the special occurrences that had been feared, apart from a sudden recall to Schlawe, where Bonhoeffer was still registered with the police under the address of the church superintendent. But the police for their part had been in touch with the Schlawe authorities; the Reich Central Security Office in Berlin, to which among others the Gestapo and the security service of the SS were subject, had issued an edict forbidding Bonhoeffer all public speaking anywhere in the country.

The background to this edict emerges from a letter, found five years later, from the head office of the Security Service in Königsberg, enclosing a detailed report to the Reich Security Office in Berlin. This discovery made it clear how denunciations functioned, and confirms that Bonhoeffer's uncomfortable feeling after the closure of the July retreat in Bloestau near Königsberg was not in fact unfounded.[12] One of the participants in the retreat, a student smuggled in as an informer by the Security Service, had evidently during the retreat itself alarmed his head office in Königsberg. According to his report,[13] "Pastor Bonnhöffer [*sic*] had among other things talked critically about the treatment of prisoners of war and of women and children belonging to the opposite side. He had said that the state viewpoint that these people were enemies was wrong from both a political and a Christian perspective," and the spy[14] sent by the Königsberg office of the Security Service also thought it worthwhile to mention Bonhoeffer's view that "the conception of death as heroic greatness is false." His report, incidentally, includes numerous other details, e.g., that the collections were intended for the support of imprisoned brethren and to finance the Confessing Church's circular letters. It had been one of Bonhoeffer's special pastoral activities since the beginning of the war—and remained so at irregular intervals until November 1942—to write circular letters to the "brethren," that is, to all former participants in his courses in the preachers' seminaries. Most of them were at the front, and more than half of the 150 or so men who had been in Finkenwalde were soon among those who had been killed, and were numbered among the millions of dead of this war.

What was disastrous in Bloestau in July 1940 was probably some personal remarks of Bonhoeffer's—that he was only in Pomerania in order "to foster the impression" that he had actually established his residence there, but that in fact he was constantly traveling on behalf of the Confessing Church "throughout the entire country"[15] in order to hold meetings. This was passed on by the zealous reporter. It was precisely these remarks that were probably decisive for the recommendation of the SS official who signed it and sent it on to Berlin, that "it would be appropriate to impose on Bonhoffer [*sic*] a ban on public speaking in the entire country."[16] The Reich Central Security Office then reacted promptly and accordingly. The "ban on public speaking within the entire German Reich" "because of his activity subverting the people" is dated August 22, 1940.[17] It meant an end to church services, devotions, lectures, retreats, every public occasion. To be forbidden to preach hurt him most. He made a written protest without success. A further measure about which he was informed at the same time in Schlawe was admittedly of greater importance, that "from that time on he was to report his movements regularly to the police at his place of residence."[18]

Bonhoeffer found himself in a highly critical situation. His professional perspectives were shrinking more and more; his personal situation was completely obscure. It was a vicious circle. A permanent domicile in Berlin was in any case forbidden. It was true that he could live outside Berlin and Brandenburg, but he could now no longer engage in any public activity. In Schlawe he must at least be present more than hitherto. That again would make all work for the conspiracy impossible. How could he be of use to the resistance in the long term if he were forced to live under continual state control? If he had to notify Schlawe before he undertook any journey? His position in the church was also affected by the dilemma. He was appointed as pastor without a particular congregation, but what could be done with a pastor who was no longer permitted to preach? And one who could not travel at will either? In the long term, where was he to live? And what should he do if he was called up? There seemed to be no way out.

But Oster and Dohnanyi saw a way. During the early autumn of 1940 they constructed for Bonhoeffer a new variant of his double existence that would stand up better to examination, and that would serve as a sustainable basis for future conspiracy work. In the meantime he had to lie low, so to speak. He was still least open to suspicion if he stayed not far from his official residence in Schlawe, until the final formalities had been settled. To clarify the terms of his further position in the church was a matter for Bonhoeffer himself. It would seem that among members of the Confessing Church in Berlin he took only Friedrich Justus Perels into his confidence.[19] Perels pleaded with the Old Prussian Council of Brethren that since Bonhoeffer was working on his book on ethics he should be given "a position that left him free for academic work";[20] in other respects, he suggested, Bonhoeffer would be immediately available for military assignments from Berlin. This, in time of war, was not unusual. More detailed information was not necessary—and it hardly would have been possible for Bonhoeffer to give it. He had no wish to incriminate his church by offering information about his future role. To take part in political resistance by working for the conspiracy against Hitler was something that in his view could only be interpreted "strictly personally." It was a special case for the Confessing Church and not an example for others. He knew traditional Lutheran-Prussian thinking all too well and the traditions in which it was still imprisoned, even though it was opposed to National Socialism. The former holy (or unholy) alliance between throne and altar still produced long-term side effects. Protest against the throne from the side of the altar had, indeed, meanwhile become permissible, if not even required in the name of God; but actual resistance was still hardly conceivable. Even Luther, let alone Calvin, had conceded to the church a right of resistance against the authority of the state; but for the Confessing Church this position was marginal. It was unable to decide in favour of direct resistance to the power of the state. The fact that in the course of the twelve-year history of the self-proclaimed Thousand-Year Reich, the Confessing Church became practically speaking "from time to time a 'resistance movement against its will' over against the National Socialist state"[21] remains a later trenchant characterization made by the theologian Ernst Wolf, one of the Confessing Church's most outstanding members.

In November 1940 the Council of Brethren approved "the Bonhoeffer project," so his professional situation seemed to be initially secure. He still held a position as one of the leaders of a training institution (nonexistent at the time); and as such he was entrusted with scholarly work—specifically, with a book on ethics. Otherwise he was to keep himself free. During the same period, between the end of August and the end of October 1940, the terms of this "Bonhoeffer project" were established on another level. In September and October Bonhoeffer chose Klein-Krössin as "waiting room" until he was finally given what were officially described as military assignments.

In Klein-Krössin in Lower Pomerania, between Stettin and Köslin and not far from Sigurdshof or Schlawe, was the country estate belonging to Ruth von Kleist-Retzow. Here he could concentrate on his new work. At the same time he was easily available if the police or the recruiting station in Schlawe were to require him. Here he had no need to set up a smoke screen as far as the owner was concerned. He had neither to play a part nor to conceal anything. He had no need to tell anything he didn't want to tell. Of her loyalty he could be certain. Bonhoeffer had met the elderly lady five years before. In fact, it was the other way around; it was she who decided to meet him, the new pastor of the Confessing Church, in the new preachers' seminary in Finkenwalde. At that time she was living in Stettin, looking after five of her grandchildren who were attending the high school there. On the last Sunday in September 1935 she came to Finkenwalde by train, her grandchildren in tow, to attend public worship in the preachers' seminary. Ruth von Kleist-Retzow was a highly interested and committed woman, both theologically and in the church—"even when she was very old, she read every new book written by Karl Barth"[22]—and she was a critical listener to sermons. One of her granddaughters told her biographer her reactions:

> The pastor's sermon fascinated Grandmother completely. Astonishingly enough it seemed to have the same effect on the ten-year-old Maria von Wedemeyer. Later it would emerge that the child had counted how often the pastor had used the word "God"—68 times, if the sermon and the prayers were added together.[23]

From that Sunday on, a firm friendship grew up between the coura-
geous matriarch and Bonhoeffer, a friendship that was warm, full of
trust and respect, and yet able to put up with the differences between
them.[24] Their joint birthdays on February 4 led in the years that followed to an occasional crisscross correspondence, and between Bonhoeffer and "RKR" there came to be a steady exchange of letters.
He was a frequent guest in the homes of the Klein-Krössin family, in
Klein-Krössin itself or in neighboring Kieckow, and he enjoyed his visits. In the second half of the 1930s, through Ruth von Kleist-Retzow,
Bonhoeffer got to know other families belonging to the Pomeranian
landed gentry. For him it was a new world, which seemed positively
progressive compared with the bourgeois, cultivated, upper-middle-
class milieu he was used to in Berlin. In this other world he also
learned from his own experience what it meant to be conservative—
in the extreme sense, but in the better sense of the word too.

Among the people he met during his occasional stays on the
Kleist family's estates was one of the protagonists of this conservatism, Ewald von Kleist-Schmenzin, a relative of Ruth von Kleist-
Retzow, who lived near Klein-Krössin and Kieckow. He was a
lawyer, a considerable landowner, a lone wolf, an unconditional
hater (not merely an opponent) of Hitler from the very beginning,
a "turncoat" and a "traitor," a Christian by both origin and conviction. They quickly got on well, relates Bethge, although it was
an understanding in spite of theological differences.[25] There may
have been a number of philosophical differences between Bonhoeffer and Schmenzin, but in faith, if not in theology, they were at one
in their ultimate solidarity with the Confessing Church and in their
unconditional rejection of National Socialist rule.

Ewald von Kleist-Schmenzin was an awkward character but a
straightforward one, who after 1933 had several times been harassed
and arrested by the Nazis. In 1938, at the time of the first putsch
plans in Berlin, he went to England on the instructions of Canaris,
Oster, and Beck, and managed to see, if not the prime minister,
Neville Chamberlain, at least Lord Vansittart of the Foreign Office,
as well as Winston Churchill, the subsequent prime minister who

was then still in the parliamentary opposition. The purpose was to inform them of Hitler's fixed ideas about conquest, and the plans of the anti-Hitler coalition, the hope being that if Hitler were to annex the Sudetenland, England might be moved to declare war.[26] Disappointed by his mission's lack of success, Ewald von Kleist-Schmenzin withdrew from further steady participation in the conspiracy but said that he would be available in case of need. It is hard to reconstruct what exactly Bonhoeffer knew about Schmenzin in this respect. It may count as certain, for example, that in Sigtuna, during his Swedish mission of 1942, he also had recourse to information provided by him.[27] The relationship of mind and spirit between these two men was perhaps closer than has generally been assumed.

In the autumn months of 1940, in the seclusion of the Pomeranian province, Bonhoeffer took up work on his new book, which he had begun to write in the summer, uncertain how and when exactly the other side of his work would begin. What initially seemed like a moratorium proved to be a chance for him to take stock personally. Work on his *Ethics* was to be the backdrop to the phase of his life that ran parallel to his work for the resistance.[28] It had been a lifelong wish of Bonhoeffer's to write a book on ethics, and with the assignment from the Council of Brethren at his back, he felt that this project was his particular contribution to the future of the church in the postwar era after the dictatorship. Now he had the chance to concentrate on scholarly theology once more. Ten years previously he had written his postdoctoral thesis, his "Habilitation," *Act and Being: Transcendental Philosophy and Ontology in Systematic Theology.* This followed his doctoral thesis, *Sanctorum Communio: A Theological Study of the Sociology of the Church.* These very titles and subjects betray a clear scholarly claim, whereas the books written during the second half of the 1930s, *Discipleship* and *Life Together*, have to do with faith as it is lived.[29]

The withdrawal of his permission to teach at the university in 1936 had put a rapid end to the start of Bonhoeffer's academic career. At the beginning of the 1930s, he had been a nonstipendiary lecturer at the university of Berlin, and originally there seemed to be no reason why he should not continue to go on working in this academic field later too—had it not been for the rise of National Socialism and, at its side, the authorities in church and university who were its faithful henchmen. Now, in the autumn of 1940, in Klein-Krössin, Bonhoeffer was suddenly for the first time once more in a position in which he was able to pursue theological work undisturbed. It was a curiously absurd situation, fragile and ambiguous, for while working intensively on the *Ethics,* he was simultaneously waiting for news from the Central Department in Berlin. On the one hand, he had to come to terms with the question of how life and action in accordance with Christ is possible; and at the same time he lived in uncertainty as to what his own life and action were going to look like in practical terms in the immediate future.

As far as the circumstances of the war permitted, Bonhoeffer had gotten together all the books on the subject of ethics he could find. But how was he to begin? A wealth of ideas, convictions, and approaches were before him, yet at the same time he was forced to write in cryptic terms. In the given circumstances, he had to reckon with interrogations and arrest, with house searches and confiscations by the Gestapo. So here, too, there had to be camouflage, a hidden existence, and ambiguity. The texts *must* be authentic and meaningful, but they *had* to be written in such a way that they would not endanger him, nor his friends and family, nor those who shared his faith and thinking.

Consequently, it is often the subtext of the *Ethics* that is the essential key to its understanding. In parts it can be read like a palimpsest: behind the visible text there is another that is harder to decipher. It contains theologically unambiguous and forceful statements beside others whose intention is hedged around by enigmatic ciphers and codelike words that can hardly be elucidated at first sight. It is true of the *Ethics* more than of any other of Bonhoeffer's books that "Any analysis and interpretation of these manuscripts must take into account their contemporary nexus of references."[30] There is another special point about this book. Bonhoeffer did not write it at a single stroke, continuously, so to speak, from beginning to end. He conceived of the individual parts separately and, in many fresh beginnings, redrafted them, rejected them, and varied them. What we know today as Bonhoeffer's *Ethics* is the posthumous amalgamation of the individual parts of the manuscript in the often unfinished state in which they then were.

On October 9, out of a period of intensive work and in the detachment of the apparently idyllic Klein-Krössin, Bonhoeffer wrote a few thought-provoking words to his friend Eberhard Bethge, who was apparently completely absorbed by his new job in the house of the Gossner Mission in Berlin-Friedenau, one of the last bastions of the "confessional front":

> You are presently leading a much more eventful and more productive life for the general cause than I am: only you must not let yourself be consumed and must reserve your own integrity as much as possible. I believe that a great deal of the exhaustion and sterility in our ranks is rooted in the lack of "selfless self-love." Since this topic has no place in the official Protestant ethic, we arrogantly disregard it and become work obsessed, to the detriment of the individual and of the whole. It belongs, however, to that humanum for which we are redeemed. Thus may this be a timely word for you as well. . . . Well-organized days make work and prayer as well as my interactions with people easy for me and spare me the spiritual, physical, and mental hardships resulting from disorder. Recently, however, a rough autumn storm left me quite depressed, and it was not at all easy to regain my equilibrium. My work progresses. I am writing the outline of the whole thing; for me this is always one of the greatest joys and trials. I will probably spend the rest of the week on it.[31]

Ten days later he had to interrupt his work on the *Ethics*. On October 20, 1940, he was once more in Berlin, and ten days later he traveled to Munich to report to the Military Intelligence department there.

seven

Ecumenism
Rewritten

IN MUNICH BONHOEFFER WAS to be incorporated, according to all
the rules of the Intelligence, as an agent in the ambiguous camouflage system of the conspiracy group, which had its own center in
Department Z, the central department of the Military Intelligence
Foreign Office in Berlin, and pursued its own purposes from the
basis of the military secret service. But why in Munich? Why not
in Berlin?

Dohnanyi and Oster had arrived at the notion of assigning
Bonhoeffer to the Military Intelligence office in Munich for several
reasons.[1] This was, after all, the not very easy proceeding of intro-
ducing him into the Military Intelligence (the Abwehr) and of push-
ing through, not too obviously, the required "*uk*" position that was
required (that is, the official confirmation that for reasons important
for the war he was not available for military service and could not
be called up). The requirement that he register with the police had
also to be canceled, for that would have made his future activity as

emissary—the future planned for him—impossible. It was therefore absolutely necessary for Bonhoeffer to be withdrawn from Gestapo observation and its extended arm, the special requirement to report to the police in Schlawe. But too great closeness to Canaris's "office" had to be avoided, for several reasons. Berlin itself did not come into question, if only because Bonhoeffer was forbidden to reside there, and unnecessary complications in connection with the necessary bureaucratic procedures were to be avoided. But there was something else in addition.

The official missions that were planned for Bonhoeffer belonged to the tricky no-man's-land on both sides of the line dividing the ground that had been negotiated in 1936 (and laid down in the so-called "Ten Commandments") between the Security Service and the Military Intelligence or, more specifically, between Reinhard Heydrich, as head of the security police and the Security Service, and Admiral Wilhelm Canaris, as head of the Military Intelligence.[2] The rivalry between the Gestapo and the Security Service on the one hand and the Military Intelligence on the other was common knowledge. The Military Intelligence Foreign Office under Canaris came under the army high command. The Reich Central Security Office (RSHA) was formed in 1939 and came under Heinrich Himmler and the SS, of which Himmler was the head. It united almost all the police and secret service agencies, and was a Nazi terror organization par excellence. It was also an expansive organization for which the—still—largely independent Military Intelligence was a troublesome outsider. Everything that seemed to encroach to the slightest degree on its claim to complete power had to reckon with intensified Gestapo or Security Service surveillance. This might even be true of a churchman, especially a churchman belonging to the Confessing Church, who was acting as agent for the Military Intelligence; for the battlefield of church politics was not one that belonged to the latter's sphere of competence. And it was in the capital that the omnipresence of the surveillance organizations of Himmler and Heydrich (which soon after the outbreak of war had been amalgamated in the RSHA) was felt most acutely.

Another factor against Berlin as the "location" for Bonhoeffer was that the central department of the Military Intelligence in Berlin was an administrative and personnel department that did not normally have agents of its own.[3] So Bonhoeffer could not be placed directly under it. Other departments in the Berlin head office would have been too risky, since this was in any case a matter of a bogus agent. From the beginning, Bonhoeffer's existence as agent—as representative—of the Military Intelligence served exclusively the purposes of the conspiracy; and about this special confidential position the department that controlled him must be at least partially informed.[4] The important thing was therefore to find such a department. And a construction would have to be found that would allow Bonhoeffer to be "stationed" far away from Schlawe, in order to make any possible investigation at least difficult. The choice fell on Munich.

Far removed as people then were from today's communication technology, with the possibilities it offers for passing on information and with the easy accessibility of data, it was by no means rare at that time, in spite of the totalitarian structures, for one authority to be ignorant about what the others were doing. That partly explains why the restrictions already imposed on Bonhoeffer by the state police—the at least partial prohibition of residence in Berlin, and the ban on public speaking—remained in force independently of his new status. Evidently because of these past restrictions to which this new agent was still subject, and as a precautionary measure, the Military Intelligence office in Munich contacted the Gestapo office there.[5] So from the viewpoint of the Intelligence itself, these restrictions were no bar to his employment.

The practices of the secret services were not very familiar to the newcomer Bonhoeffer. Even if in his case his existence as agent was only supposed to camouflage a different function, he had to learn to think in secret service categories. And according to the logic of military espionage, there was also no objection to applying for a "non-availability" declaration for a pastor belonging to the Confessing Church who was subject to Gestapo restrictions. The fact that an oppositional pastor, who moreover belonged to the radical wing of the Confessing Church, and who was exposed to state reprisals, should put himself at the disposal of the Military Intelligence was not particularly remarkable; nor was the Intelligence's interest in him. As far as his own doubts about his usefulness and plausibility as agent were concerned, he had first to come to terms inwardly with secret service ways of arguing. After all—and this was what was held out to him—the Military Intelligence worked together with everyone, including Communists and Jews, "so why not with people belonging to the Confessing Church too?"[6]

Ever since the putsch plans of 1939, Oster and Dohnanyi had had a special contact with Munich at their disposal. This was Josef Müller, to whom as courier of the conspiracy they had given the assignment of "negotiating with the Vatican."[7] Müller was employed as an officer of the Munich Intelligence office, and because of this relationship, it seemed to make sense for the new agent to be assigned to the Munich office too. During Bonhoeffer's first stay in Munich at the end of October, Hans von Dohnanyi was there as well for two days, in order to make the necessary practical arrangements.[8]

Now that Bonhoeffer had an official Munich domicile at the address of his aunt Christine von Kalckreuth, in Munich-Schwabing, he was registered there with the police, and the Intelligence office could apply to the recruiting station there for a non-availability (*uk*) certificate for Bonhoeffer as soon as the Schlawe recruiting station had confirmed his departure or move. As was to be expected, this took several weeks. In December 1940 Dohnanyi passed on the appropriate instructions to the relevant offices.[9] Would the bureaucracy function smoothly? Finally, on February 7, 1941, all the hurdles had been cleared. Bonhoeffer was classified as *uk*, at least "until further notice,"[10] and was consequently freed from the permanent obligation to register with the police as long as he was at the service of the Military Intelligence.

For Bonhoeffer, a new chapter in his life had begun on October 30, 1940, with his departure for Munich. He had finally put himself at the service of a state institution, which was "the positive embodiment of a grey zone."[11] He now definitely counted internally as informer for the Military Intelligence Foreign Office, which came under the army high command—in short, he was a "confidential agent" for the Intelligence.[12] The German word for this position is "V-Mann," a strange word for a strange thing, an ambiguous word for which there is no generally accepted definition—suitably enough, perhaps, for secret service vocabulary; but usually, then as now, and in Bonhoeffer's case too, it is taken to be short for *Vertrauensmann*—a confidential person.[13] By this is meant someone who at the instruction of a particular power—a state or an institution—working under cover and without revealing his real purpose, gathers information about a supposed or actual opponent, whether it be a country, an institution, a political party, or a person. As a rule these people are different from agents—and in the Military Intelligence a distinction was evidently made between a "V-Mann" and an agent.[14] The former was not actively concerned in practical measures, such as espionage, counterespionage, or acts of sabotage. Unlike informants who worked undercover, these "confidential agents" instead served largely as occasional purveyors of information without really belonging to the institutions from which they took their assignments.

Bonhoeffer was formally transferred to the Military Intelligence in Munich as "a sub-agent"[15] and was assigned, also formally, to an agent who was himself controlled by Department I of the Military Intelligence in Berlin, but who at that time worked from Munich and—once again formally—was supposed to act as Bonhoeffer's mentor.[16] His name was Wilhelm Schmidhuber. Schmidhuber held the position of "Portuguese honorary consul and major shareholder in Bavarian breweries"[17] in Munich. Like his friend Heinrich Wilhelm Ickrath, who was both his assistant and his secretary in the Portuguese consulate, he was a captain in the reserve. The biographies of Oster and Canaris do not give a very pleasant impression of Schmidhuber.[18] The central office in Berlin had contacts with him, both officially and in conspiracy matters. But at the same time they had mixed feelings about him. Dohnanyi was friendly with him, whereas Oster viewed the Bavarian businessman as a "wheeler-dealer" and an officer only by the way, and had considerable reservations about him. Together with Josef Müller, Schmidhuber, and Ickrath, Dohnanyi had put in the official claim to Bonhoeffer through the Military Intelligence office in Munich, and from then on it was Schmidhuber to whom Bonhoeffer was to apply should difficulties arise.

The official reason given for Bonhoeffer's employment was utilization of the excellent relations with prominent members of the ecumenical movement that derived from his earlier work. The ostensible purpose was to acquire information. The real reason was almost identical with this official one, except for the word *acquire*; for the actual purpose was to *pass on* information, of course information of a particular kind. Bonhoeffer, camouflaged as an agent of the Military Intelligence but really a guarantor and contact sent by opponents of Hitler, was supposed to establish links with countries abroad.

He was "a confidential agent" in several respects. His official role would permit him to travel unhindered abroad, while in fact he acted as agent for the resistance. Abroad, as a pastor of the Confessing Church, he would perhaps be trusted rather than other couriers of the conspiracy. Josef Müller had acted in a similar capacity in 1939–40, when as guarantor and contact of the conspiracy, he had been able to forge secret links with the British government in or via the Vatican, since he counted for the Roman Catholic Church as surety for the existence of a German resistance. Now an analogous role was planned for Bonhoeffer toward Protestant churches all over the world. As mouthpiece for the conspiracy against Hitler, he was meant to overcome the barriers of thought and speech erected by the Nazi dictatorship and to smooth the way to a shared world "afterward," that is, once the war had ended. In both cases the purpose was to activate relations with the major churches, with the aim of drawing them into the orbit of the political resistance.[19]

In the autumn of 1940 Bonhoeffer took the concrete and unequivocal step of—ostensibly—putting himself at the disposal of the Military Intelligence, letting himself be classified in the Munich office as—alleged—agent, and thus finally and actively joining the resistance group in the Military Intelligence Foreign Office. With this Bonhoeffer's path within the hidden existence of the conspiracy took on irreversible form. It was not indeed a straightforward path, decided on in advance. It seems rather that there was never one big heroic resolve, but that he was gradually drawn into a political existence that he took on himself (or rather, assumed) unpretentiously yet consistently, above all not looking for anything sensational, let alone seeking suffering. The practical official reasons and background of this "takeover" by the Intelligence can be seen from a letter that would appear to have been written in November 1940.

When in the spring of 1943 the fear of being exposed and arrested grew, Bonhoeffer, in agreement with Dohnanyi, composed this faked letter, backdated to the beginning of November 1940.[20] Dohnanyi knew that he was under observation by the Gestapo and was exposed to the increasingly covetous arm of the Reich Central Security Service, the RSHA; and he had good reasons for making Bonhoeffer's trustworthiness as agent of the Military Intelligence particularly watertight, as well as the *uk* (non-availability) position that went with it. What was needed was evidence that there had been contact between Bonhoeffer and the Military Intelligence in the autumn of 1940; and this was to be put on record as the beginning of Bonhoeffer's alleged activity as agent. The letter was supposed to show why a pastor belonging to the Confessing Church, under suspicion in state and party quarters, should have offered himself to the Military Intelligence.

It was a false trail, deliberately laid for the purpose of camouflaging the real date when his employment began. This letter of Bonhoeffer's was backed up by two other documents, backdated to November 29, 1940, which were supposed to lend additional support to his joining the Intelligence. The one contains information from Dohnanyi to Schmidhuber, to the effect that he was now sending him a copy of the letter of which he had already been notified by telephone. The other was a letter from Oster to the Military Intelligence office in Munich: "I hereby request the writer of the enclosed letter, whose name can be learned from Consul Schmidhuber,

Munich, Am Kosttor 1, from there to be declared *uk* for the purposes of the Abwehr."[21]

So in the spring of 1943 Bonhoeffer wrote a special kind of application, backdated, in which he explained to his brother-in law why he wanted to offer his special "services" to the Military Intelligence. (It was only with difficulty that the kind of writing paper usually sold in 1940, which Bonhoeffer had normally used, could be procured.)

> Dear Hans,
>
> In our recent conversation about ecumenical questions you asked me whether I would not be prepared, if need be, to make available my experience abroad and relationships to people in public life in Europe and overseas, in order to participate in acquiring reliable information about other countries. I have been thinking this over.
>
> Within the scope of the problems that interest you, the unique feature of ecumenical work lies in the fact that leading political figures of various countries are interested in this movement, in which all the major churches of the world (apart from the church of Rome) are united. This means that in fact it ought not to be difficult to ascertain the viewpoints and judgments of such figures through ecumenical relationships. Furthermore, I believe it to be altogether within the realm of possibility to enter even into new relationships in this way, which could perhaps be of significance for answering specialized questions.
>
> It is impossible within the scope of this letter to give you even a remote overview of the diverse connections that exist between the ecumenical movement and leading men of politics, economics, education, and science."[22]

But he is nevertheless quite prepared in the course of the letter to give an outline of his own "diverse (ecumenical) connections."

After he has described his own ecumenical career, with the emphases usual in an application, a list of several pages follows, with the names of prominent people in the ecumenical movement—that is, on the international stage—whom Bonhoeffer, as he stresses "knows personally—some of them very well—and with whom I can resume contact at any time." He names among others men who have been already mentioned here: Coffin and Niebuhr, Eidem and Björkquist, and naturally, the "lord bishop of Chichester," George Bell.[23] These passages seem like a roll call of the ecumenical movement as it was at that time. It includes prominent names from the United States, Scandinavia, Hungary, Romania, and Bulgaria, from the Balkan countries, Italy, Spain and France, England and—going far beyond the Protestant ecumenical movement—from India, since Bonhoeffer mentions the invitation that Gandhi and Tagore had passed on to him in the middle of the 1930s.[24] Of course he also had contacts with Catholic clergy.

At the end, he stresses that "the connection to such men ought to be particularly valuable," for example, in successfully combating "the anti-German propaganda, which took advantage of the German Church struggle and has sown a great deal of suspicion precisely in the church-oriented countries." He writes that he was now for the time being in Munich and "could—if this were desired—make myself available to the office there."[25] In this letter Bonhoeffer also incidentally mentions his knowledge of foreign languages, excluding his command of the three ancient languages, Hebrew, Greek, and Latin, which were not of interest in this context. In the (still existing) draft, he adds, "I am fluent especially in English but also in Spanish; I would be able to polish my French and Italian quickly."[26] It is not least this knowledge of languages, he says, that recommends him as emissary in the service of the Intelligence, and there is no question but that he would therefore prove especially useful for future missions (and for the missions of the conspiracy, which were what was really envisaged).

Read with the hindsight of a later time, the faked letter at the same time reflects Bonhoeffer's real intention. He wished, and was intended, to reactivate in the service of the resistance his earlier intensive links with the Protestant ecumenical movement. And what he had to offer was considerable: diverse experiences abroad and reliable personal contacts with prominent clergy in foreign countries that were now at war with Germany or were at best neutral. Above all, he had a considerable reputation as a man faithful to the Confessing Church, and was an incontrovertibly reputable emissary of an anti-Hitler *fronde* or faction[27] that was struggling to win credibility and trust.

Bonhoeffer and ecumenism is a chapter of its own. In 1931 Bonhoeffer's enthusiasm for the movement had been kindled, and it "took such a hold on him that it became an integral part of his being,"[28] or at least a task of considerable importance, personally and theologically, as well as for the policies of the church. In 1937 his involvement had come to a halt because of a number of disappointing experiences, the changed political situation in the church, and particular circumstances in Geneva and Berlin.[29] But it now came back into his life under completely different terms of reference.

In the context of that time, ecumenism meant the attempts of the (non–Roman Catholic) churches throughout the world to come closer to one another and to transform the unions between individual denominations that already existed into a binding community of worldwide Christendom with a firm institutional base. One of these transcending elements in Protestant ecumenism was expressed in one of Bonhoeffer's *Ethics* manuscripts, written in 1940, and echoes the affirmation of faith in the church's ancient creed, belief in the "holy catholic church": "The form of Christ is one and the same at all times and in all places. The church of Christ is also One, throughout all generations."[30]

Bonhoeffer hoped for an ecumenical community that the Roman Catholic Church too would not reject. In the winter of 1940–41 he himself experienced something of such an ecumenical community, which also functioned with unwritten laws. For this winter, the monastery in Ettal became the refuge for the courier-in-waiting.

At that time Bonhoeffer certainly did not live with his aunt Christine von Kalckreuth, but from the middle of November 1940 until the end of February 1941 was a guest in this Benedictine Abbey of Ettal, not far from Garmisch in Bavaria. At one point this incidentally led to a rather unpleasant situation, since the formalities of "the Bonhoeffer file" had not yet been completed:

> The Countess Kalckreuth had to conduct an exciting telephone conversation for the absent Bonhoeffer. "This is the secret state police. There is a Herr Bonhoeffer living at your house. He is to come here at once." With some trouble and anxiety she got her nephew out of Ettal monastery, and learnt that there was good news waiting for him, namely that his duty to report regularly was cancelled for the time being.[31]

The stay in Ettal had been brought about through the agency of Josef Müller, who was very closely connected with Oster and Dohnanyi through the already mentioned Vatican negotiations of 1939–40. Incidentally, as a result of these negotiations, and following Oster's betrayal of the impending Western offensive, in 1940 the Gestapo vainly searched for a time (under the code name *Schwarze Kapelle*, "Black Chapel") for a clique of traitors that it suspected was acting with the help of the church.[32] Müller and Oster seem to have got on well together from the time of their first meeting, Canaris having "ordered" the Munich lawyer to come to the Tirpitzufer in Berlin after the outbreak of war. Later Josef Müller recalled Oster's directness:

> "You have refused to join the Nazi Party or one of its organizations, giving as reason that you are a practicing Catholic. I myself am a convinced Protestant Christian, the son of a pastor. So we have the same firm basic attitude in the defence of Christianity." . . . During our conversation a young man came into the room, greeting me with a nod. Oster introduced him as *Reichsgerichtsrat* von Dohnanyi. "You two," he said "will talk to each other

and I hope work together too." Dohnanyi's brother-in-law, he said, was the Protestant pastor Dietrich Bonhoeffer. "We would welcome it if you would soon meet him too. There are undoubtedly interesting subjects of conversation, for example the struggle of Christianity against the dictatorship." "Of course we believe in the power of prayer," Oster went on, "but we mustn't just rely on God. We must contribute something ourselves so that God can help human beings."[33]

Müller was on particularly good terms with the clergy of the Catholic world and with the monastic orders, and in Munich he took up Bonhoeffer—in his autobiography he describes him retrospectively as his friend—and arranged for his possible temporary stay in the monastery at Ettal.[34] Bonhoeffer was lodged in the Hotel Ludwig der Bayer, which was owned by the monastery, and ate and worked in the monastery itself so he could concentrate on his further work on *Ethics* and could make contact with oppositional Catholic priests. Otherwise he had to wait. The monks were just reading his book *Life Together*, which reflects the almost monastic life and form of faith of the House of Brethren at Finkenwalde, and at the monastery's Christmas celebration there were readings from his book *Discipleship*. In Ettal he was evidently warmly and hospitably received. And yet it would seem as if the whole time there was some muted background music—that he continually called himself and the life he was leading at this moment in question. His letters to his friend Bethge show how much be strove for composure. On November 4 he writes:

> "At the moment I am attempting to gain a foothold, so to speak, in the circles that interest me; and I think this will be easier in this other confession than among our own people; we'll see." And on 18 November, "I have been here since yesterday, and was received most warmly. I eat in the refectory, sleep in the hotel, can use the library, have my own key to the cloister, and yesterday had a

long and good conversation with the abbot. In short, I have everything that one could desire." His letter of 23 November, however, betrays that inwardly he was not so contented: "Truly, how incomparably easy and pleasant our way has been through even these past years, in comparison with all that has weighed on the others for years! What right would I have to quibble with my own circumstances, which for others would be the very foretaste of paradise! So please do not imagine that I am giving myself over to resignation without restraint; I know clearly all that I have to be thankful for and repeat it to myself mornings and evenings." On 29 November he writes: "I find the mountain landscape difficult to tolerate physically. The insurmountable quality sometimes lies like a burden on my work as well. Does 'mountains' [*Gebirge*] actually have anything to do with 'to hide' [*bergen*]? At times I think this and also even experience it that way, though less frequently."[35]

But Ettal also meant an enrichment in his life, to which his affinity for monastic forms of living may have contributed. Even during his time as congregational pastor in London, he had interested himself in Anglican monasteries, and the "House of Brethren experiment" in Finkenwalde was something like a "temporary monasticism," a Christian community with a strict daily rhythm, with oral confession, meditation, fixed times for prayer and for silence, and with—though certainly only temporary—celibacy. On November 21, 1940, he wrote to his parents:

> This form of life is naturally not foreign to me, and I experience its regularity and silence as extremely beneficial for my work. It would certainly be a loss (and was indeed a loss at the Reformation!) if this form of communal life preserved for fifteen hundred years were destroyed, something that those here consider entirely possible.[36]

In Ettal Bonhoeffer discovered an unexpected closeness in political as well as in theological and pastoral thinking. His most important discussion partners in the monastery were the abbot, Angelus Kupfer, and Father Johannes Albrecht, who acted as "the monastery's foreign minister, so to speak."[37] The two of them were only a little older than himself. Through the medium of Josef Müller he met the Munich prelate Johannes Neuhäusler, who, however, was arrested in February 1941.[38] Through Müller Bonhoeffer also met Corbinian Hofmeister, the also oppositional abbot of the Metten monastery, in the Bavarian Forest. In spite of these diverse contacts and discussions, or perhaps just because of them, during this winter in Ettal two large manuscript sections of his *Ethics* were completed, the ones that are titled "the Last and the Penultimate Things" and "Natural Life."

Shortly before Christmas, Bonhoeffer had visitors from Berlin. Dohnanyi had "official" and personal reasons (his children were staying in Ettal), Bethge purely private ones. Bethge recalled: "At Christmas 1940 they sat up for half the night together: the abbots of Metten and Ettal, Fathers Leiber, Zeiger, and Schönhöfer from the Vatican, Consul Schmidhuber and Captain Ickradt, Josef Müller, Dohnanyi, and Bonhoeffer."[39] Later Bethge was also warmly remembered. It was not only Bonhoeffer who missed him; and on February 14 he wrote to him:

Today we are enjoying beautiful weather. Frost, sun, but no snow. Perhaps I shall go out for a bit. I miss having a partner! You see, you simply must come back. Johannes and Müller check in almost daily. "What is that Bättge up to?" They always want me to greet you from them; it seems as if they think something of you—strange![40]

eight

The Swiss Connection

BONHOEFFER SET OUT FROM Munich on his first "business trip," an ostensibly regular mission on behalf of the Military Intelligence, on February 24, 1941. His destination was Switzerland, which at that time was "one of the most important diplomatic listening posts."[1] The stages of his journey were Zurich, Basel, and Geneva. The journey was supposed to last a month. In Ettal he kept himself continually at the disposal of the "central office" in Berlin. The Munich Military Intelligence office, as the executive organ, was really in any case only interposed as the authority to which Bonhoeffer was responsible for pragmatic reasons of security, as cleverer camouflage. The vocabulary to be used by discussion partners in Germany was that these were "journeys for military purposes."[2] In Switzerland, however, he was to give purely scholarly interests as the reason for his journey. Unlooked-for difficulties had arisen about the visa, which Schmidhuber, the German consul, ironed out through his special relations with the Swiss. Consequently, Bonhoeffer was irritated when at the border the Swiss police suddenly demanded the name of a Swiss sponsor. He spontaneously named Karl Barth.

Bonhoeffer had known Barth personally for almost exactly ten years. In July 1931 he had traveled to Bonn specially, in order to experience at firsthand both personally and theologically the leading light and author of the *Church Dogmatics* before he himself took up his teaching position at the university of Berlin. Ever since then they had been in contact, even after Barth's departure from Germany in 1935. This contact was certainly not uninterrupted, but it was intensive and unreserved. Bonhoeffer was fascinated by Barth's personal directness and openness, by his political consistency and staunchness, and by the way in which from his Basel outpost he fulfilled his position as "guardian" of the Confessing Church. Barth, for his part, thought highly of the younger theologian, with his unorthodox stance both in the ecumenical movement and in the Confessing Church. He followed Bonhoeffer's career in the 1930s, even if from a geographical distance—not always with applause but occasionally skeptically, questioningly, and challengingly. Now, at the beginning of March 1941, Bonhoeffer visited him in Basel three times for what was evidently an exclusively theological exchange. On whose authority Bonhoeffer was really traveling does not in any event seem to have been mentioned in the spring of 1941.[3]

Bonhoeffer spent the first days after his arrival in Zurich. There he must certainly have met for the first time the representative of German Military Intelligence there, the vice-consul in the German consulate general, Hans Bernd Gisevius. Gisevius was also present during one of Bonhoeffer's visits to Barth in Basel. In any case, Barth's engagement calendar has a note to that effect.[4] It is admittedly not easy to imagine the meeting. What would they have talked about, especially since Bonhoeffer's real mission was probably not yet known to Barth at this point? What was the link between Gisevius and Barth, except for their shared opposition to the Nazis? And what were Gisevius's feelings when he met Bonhoeffer, the newcomer?

Gisevius does not seem to have been particularly delighted at Bonhoeffer's employment in his own sphere of authority. Hans von

Dohnanyi later once referred to a certain "competitor's jealousy"[5] on the part of the resident Military Intelligence representative where Bonhoeffer was concerned. "Gisevius was a particular enemy of Dietrich's because he didn't want anyone in Switzerland beside himself, and took it in bad part when Hans continually sent Dietrich to him," wrote Christine von Dohnanyi in a letter to her sister Sabine Leibholz in London in June 1946.[6]

Immediately after his arrival in Zurich, Bonhoeffer took the invaluable opportunity to send letters to England from this neutral ground: a long letter to the family of his twin sister, a shorter one to his friend George Bell: "When will we meet again? God knows, and we have to wait. But I cannot help hoping and praying that it will not last too long."[7] He visited his friend Erwin Sutz (who gladly put himself at Bonhoeffer's service as messenger from and to England) and also Friedrich Siegmund-Schultze, with whom he had worked during the heyday of his ecumenical work.

Siegmund-Schultze, a theologian and sociologist, had been dismissed from his job as professor in Berlin as early as 1933 and had emigrated to Switzerland. "In the early days of the war particularly, his Zurich apartment served as meeting point for exiles and emissaries of the resistance."[8] Bonhoeffer may not have confined his discussions with him to theological questions, for Siegmund-Schultze, a confidant of Goerderler's,[9] had on the latter's instructions constructed his own "Swiss road,"[10] in this case to England. While Neville Chamberlain was still prime minister, Siegmund-Schultze was in contact with London, and he tried to keep these contacts alive under Churchill too, in the interest of peace feelers put out by Goerdeler. In the summer of 1941 he saw to it that a memorandum of Goerdeler's came into the hands of the British government.[11]

At the time of the meeting between Bonhoeffer and Siegmund-Schultze at the end of February or beginning of March 1941 in Zurich, neither Siegmund-Schultze nor Goerdeler, neither Bonhoeffer nor Oster, neither Dohnanyi nor Beck could know that on January 20, 1941, Winston Churchill had already issued an "unambiguous instruction"[12] to the effect that there should be absolute silence on the part of the English government and the Foreign Office in response to inquiries or proposals of whatever kind from the German side. It was a policy that in the future he was actually to intensify rather than modify: "Our attitude toward all such inquiries or suggestions should henceforward be absolute silence."[13]

What was Bonhoeffer supposed do for the resistance in the situation of that time? What could he achieve? What were the goals of his Swiss mission? Oster and Dohnanyi, the men on whose immediate instructions Bonhoeffer was traveling, hoped that by virtue of his personal relations and his steadfast will for peace, as well as his authenticity and integrity, he could resume, modify, and deepen the contacts that had been broken off with church bodies in Geneva. In this way, earlier loyalties could prove themselves in the drastically altered circumstances of the war. They were something that could be relied on, even in the future and in perhaps tricky situations.

Bonhoeffer was faced with a complex task. He was supposed to renew his ecumenical ties and discover how far they could prove strong enough for new ways forward—that is to say, for contacts with the Western governments, especially the British. He was supposed to indicate that continual attempts at resistance were still going on in Germany and to discover whether peace conditions for a post-Hitler government were conceivable, and if so, what these conditions would be.[14]

The main goal of his journey was accordingly Geneva, which he knew well from his earlier stay in Switzerland when he was working on ecumenical affairs. Geneva was the home of the central office of the World Council of Churches, which from 1938 had been in the process of formation. Its head, as general secretary, was the Dutch Reformed theologian Willem Visser't Hooft. In his autobiography, he described this first meeting with Bonhoeffer in London in March 1939, which took place at Paddington Station. Bonhoeffer was in London visiting his sister Sabine Leibholz and her family. He was uncertain whether he should stay in Germany or not, uncertain whether he should do military service and swear the oath of loyalty to Hitler, or whether he should refuse to do either.[15] He knew from Bishop Bell that Visser't Hooft was also in London, and he very much wanted to meet him personally. The opportunity finally arose—between trains, as it were—in the last week of March:

> Since I had to take the train to Aberdeen, we made an appointment to meet at Paddington Station. We talked together as we walked up and down the station platform. I had expected that he would want to discuss the relations between the Confessing Church and the World Council. So I was surprised that he began immediately to tell me about the grave choice concerning the future which he had to make. . . . I remember his urgent questions better than my answers. It was not simply the old issue of pacifism. The question was whether a Christian could participate in a war started by a ruthless regime which would bring untold misery to many nations. On the other hand, what would happen to the Confessing Church if he were to become a conscientious objector and others follow his example? The best help I could give was perhaps simply to show a real understanding for the awful dilemma which he was facing.[16]

Remembering this memorable railway station meeting, Visser't Hooft wrote immediately after the end of the war: "In the hazy world between 'Munich' and 'Warsaw,' in which hardly anyone dared to formulate the real problems clearly, this questioning voice had a liberating effect on me."[17] Two years later, in March 1941, Bonhoeffer and Visser't Hooft met once more, in Geneva. The trust on the one side and the understanding on the other that had marked their first meeting meant that they now felt as if they were old friends. Later Visser't Hooft remembered his impressions:

> During the two years since our first meeting he had become more deeply informed of the conspiratorial activities of the opposition to Hitler. But he did not give the impression of a man torn apart by the tensions of

his dangerous life. With his round, almost boyish face, his cheerful expression, his eager enjoyment of a good story or a good meal, he seemed to have a more affirmative attitude to life than many of us who lived in the comparative quiet of neutral Switzerland. This time we had an opportunity for long discussions. I was glad to find that with regard to theological as well as political issues we were on the same wavelength and could speak together with complete frankness.[18]

"Could speak together with complete frankness": the notes in Nils Ehrenström's diary give us exceptionally good information about Bonhoeffer's stay in Geneva. Ehrenström, a Swedish theologian, a close colleague of Visser't Hooft at the World Council of Churches (WCC) in Geneva and head of the church's institute in Sigtuna, seems to have been the "manager" during Bonhoeffer's first week in Geneva in his new role as emissary of the anti-Hitler group in the Intelligence. His diary entries for March 8–15, 1941, meticulously record times, meeting places, subjects of conversation, and participants.[19] For example, we see from them that on the morning of March 10, 1941, a Monday, Visser't Hooft, Freudenberg, and Ehrenström met Bonhoeffer and talked about "the work among Jewish refugees" and about ecumenical studies. In the afternoon, "the same, plus Guillon, re the situation in France."[20]

Adolf Freudenberg had an unusual career behind him. In 1933 he left the Foreign Office as legation counselor because he had a "non-Aryan" wife. After studying theology in Berlin, he was ordained by the Confessing Church in Berlin-Dahlem. First in London and then as émigré in Geneva, he took over leadership of the secretariat for refugees at the WCC. When he mentioned "work among Jewish refugees," he knew what he was talking about.

Charles François Guillon belonged to the Protestant minority in France and came from a no less remarkable situation. Guillon was a Reformed (Calvinist) pastor in Le-Chambon-sur-Lignon, a village in the central French *massif*, had an apartment in Geneva because of his ecumenical work, and was at the same time the mayor of his village. But Chambon-sur-Lignon was not just a village like any other; it later became part of the history of the French resistance and is an example of practical humanity worthy of reflection and imitation.[21] The village with its neighboring hamlets was a stronghold of French Protestantism. Many of its inhabitants were consistent members of the resistance, and together with other resistance groups they succeeded in organizing extensive help for the persecuted, and above all for Jews. In this way a cooperation between Christians and non-Christians developed in the French resistance that saved Jewish lives.

Under March 11, 1941, Ehrenström noted a similar group and similar subjects of conversation as on the previous day, but this time supplemented by an important heading: "peace aims." On the following day Ehrenström, Visser't Hooft, and Bonhoeffer worked mainly on a memorandum about Christian peace aims. The program for March 13 was particularly full. Bonhoeffer, Visser't Hooft, and Ehrenström discussed the memorandum to which Visser't Hooft had given a final polish, and Bonhoeffer and Ehrenström continued the discussion they had begun the previous day on "Roman Catholic–Protestant problems."[22] In the evening Visser't Hooft, Bonhoeffer, and three other ecumenists, among them Jacques Courvoisier, professor of church history in Geneva and chairman of the organization for prisoner-of-war aid in the WCC, met in Freudenberg's apartment. It was probably the discussion on this March evening in 1941 that Visser't Hooft later described:

> We also spent an evening with Swiss friends in the apartment of Adolf Freudenberg. One of us asked Bonhoeffer: "What do you pray for in the present situation?" He answered without hesitation: "Since you ask me, I must say that I pray for the defeat of my country, for I believe that this is the only way in which it can pay for the suffering which it has caused in the world." That crystal clear answer characterized the man. Truth was to be served without reservation whatever the cost. I knew him now well enough to realize that this hard saying

was not a denial, but rather an affirmation of his love for his country.[23]

The climax and end of this Geneva week seems to have been the afternoon of March 15, a Saturday. We have three reminiscences, which bring out Bonhoeffer's passion for theology. Ehrenström's diary records: "Lunch and afternoon, in Bellevue. A theological colloquium. . . ." In what follows the purpose of the colloquium is briefly indicated and the participants—"Bonhoeffer in the centre of them"—are listed.[24] According to Courvoisier's recollection, during the morning there was a discussion among three people, Visser't Hooft, Bonhoeffer, and Courvoisier, in the Avenue de Champel 41, which at that time was the home of the WCC. This discussion turned on "many things," church and politics, God and the world:

> It so happened that at the end of this conversation Bonhoeffer explained to us that everything we had discussed had been very interesting, but that he was very keen that we should talk about things which were still more important and fundamental. He asked whether we could not meet some theologians during the afternoon in order to "pursue serious theology." So it came about that during the afternoon we spent a few hours with a number of Geneva pastors on the bank of the lake.[25]

In Visser't Hooft's reminiscences, we also hear about what was evidently the last shared afternoon during this Swiss journey of Bonhoeffer's, which was spent at the See Restaurant Bellevue. At the same time we are given essential information about the starting point of departure for his *Ethics,* and its conclusion:

> Bonhoeffer was eager to meet other theologians so as to get their reactions to the line of thought he was developing. So we got a group of Genevese friends to join us for a long discussion in the garden of a restaurant on the shores of the lake. Bonhoeffer told us of the approach he was taking in his *Ethics.* He wanted to overcome the

dualism which had characterized Christian ethics for so long. The sacred and the secular, the church and the world, had been kept separate. But in Christ we receive the invitation to participate at the same time in the reality of God and in the reality of the world. Bonhoeffer quoted often the first chapter of the Epistle to the Colossians and especially verse 16, which says that the world is created "unto Christ." In this way Christians could get rid of that dangerous pietism or otherworldliness which really left the world to the forces of darkness. And they had a strong starting point for their task *in* the world.[26]

To meet old and new friends in the ecumenical community, people of the most varying nationality and that in wartime; to renew a personal theological exchange at long last; to catch up with ecumenical literature in the WCC library; to talk about help for refugees and prisoners, the situation of neighboring and now enemy countries, and the political situation of the church—all this was unquestionably important, both the meetings themselves and the subjects discussed. But what had Bonhoeffer been able to achieve for his real work for the resistance?

Bonhoeffer's biographer Bethge does not give the impression that he originally viewed the fruits of this first journey as very great. The earlier relationship of trust had been restored, the continued opposition had been indicated, and the hindrances that faced the people involved had been convincingly described. No more had as yet been arrived at.[27] Over against this, on the basis of sources discovered later, from the angle of church history this journey should not be underestimated. Bonhoeffer had immediately put his cards on the table and had put into words the central question of the German resistance: what would the peace conditions for Germany look like once the Nazi government had been eliminated? And with this, the ecumenical community, at least, was given essential stimuli for thinking about future peace goals, even if this was not true for political quarters abroad.[28]

The really new aspect, and the question that affected a German involved in the resistance movement, was one that Bonhoeffer brought to the notice of his discussion partners in Geneva. We discover this in Visser't Hooft's account of the week, written at the time or soon afterward. His letters and his accounts of Bonhoeffer's visit can be seen as a summing up and a record of the reactions to it; and they bring out what he wanted to pass on abroad at the instructions of the resistance group in the Military Intelligence, as well as what he himself felt about the future of Germany.

On March 12, 1941, Visser't Hooft wrote to two men who were both concerned with ecumenical relations. One was the English theologian William Temple (who in 1941 was still archbishop of York, later becoming archbishop of Canterbury). The other was John Foster Dulles, later United States secretary of state, who in 1941 was chairman of the Commission for a Just and Lasting Peace in the North American Council of Churches. This paper was entitled "Some Considerations concerning the Post-war Settlement,"[29] and in later research into the resistance it came to be known as the "Bonhoeffer Memorandum."[30] Visser't Hooft wrote that these thoughts about was to happen after the war were the outcome of a discussion in a small group of people belonging to different sides in the war. In later retrospect, he described the ideas of that time as follows:

> The main points of the document were that Europe was rapidly becoming a political vacuum, that after the war no regimes should be allowed to exist which were totalitarian in character, that several countries might have to be under authoritarian rule for a period, but that this should be phased out in due order, together with the introduction of free speech and the right of opposition, and that Europe should be organized as a Federation with a certain limitation of national sovereignty.[31]

The response from the United States was sibylline and led to nothing. John Foster Dulles wrote politely that the text was helpful for the formation of opinion in his commission; he had found it "particularly interesting," and it clearly reflected thinking that "while idealistic was also realistic."[32] The answer from the United Kingdom was more fruitful. Although it was not really more favorable, it was at least unambiguous. This may have been due to the fact that, in an accompanying letter to Archbishop Temple, Visser't Hooft had talked openly about the existence of a German resistance grouping and described the questions that were preoccupying them:

> I have to add a point of considerable importance. By friends who belong to a group which I need not mention by name since you can guess who they are, the question is often raised: What are the minimum-conditions on which peace would be possible? . . . Would their country have a chance of being offered acceptable terms if it would change its regime? Or would such a change of regime be used to crush their country altogether? This is a problem which is much discussed, and it is clear that a clear answer on this point may be of considerable importance for the decisions which this group may take. At present their fear is that it is too late for an action of this kind. If, however, they could be convinced that this is not the case, they might get busy again. This whole matter is, of course, very confidential.[33]

This passage describes precisely the questions asked in Germany by people belonging to the civilian opposition, and especially also those who belonged to the group around Beck, Oster, and Dohnanyi. It puts into plain words the inquiry of their emissary. Both question and answer seem fundamentally to touch on a dilemma that was to crop up again and again in the future, and for which there was hardly a solution—and which in fact was never solved: the German resistance would and could act if the foreign enemy—in this case England—would promise in advance, first, not to make use of a possibly obscure situation during the coup d'etat, but would call a halt to military operations; and second, if a Germany after Hitler could reckon with fair peace conditions.

From the viewpoint of Germany's opponents, however, in this case England, German resistance would only be convincing if it were to act first—that is, if it were first to get rid of the Nazi regime and furthermore was prepared from the outset for far-reaching peace conditions. In short, the resistance would act if the enemy would keep quiet; the enemy would perhaps keep quiet once the resistance had acted. England wanted to see proofs and deeds, and the secret opposition wanted a promise *before* it acted. The answer from the English side, given at the end of April 1941, also contains in nucleus all later reactions to inquiries on the part of the German resistance, inasmuch as such reactions were forthcoming at all, in view of Churchill's command for silence. Visser't Hooft recapitulated:

> On 29 April the Archbishop replied:
> "I was immensely interested in your letter. . . . It is very hard to say what would be the minimum conditions of peace put forward in this country, but I think that the main body of opinion would support the start of negotiations if the following conditions were fulfilled: 1. the disappearance of the Nazi regime; 2. the evacuation of all the occupied territory; 3. the cessation of that type of tyranny which is represented by the Gestapo."
> The Archbishop added that Czechoslovakia and Poland were of course included in the occupied countries. That was a relatively encouraging answer.[34]

It was at least a concrete answer that at once made the situation clearer. For the question remains: was it really a dilemma on the part of the German resistance? Was it not rather its fundamental miscalculation of the whole situation, in which it thought it could come forward as a potential negotiator? There is no doubt that in the resistance its own situation was interpreted as being dominated by this quandary, this dilemma. It is a viewpoint that to some extent still persists in later research, where there is repeated talk about the "vicious circle" of the resistance's "foreign policy," as if the members of the resistance had to be viewed as equal negotiating partners for the opposing side in the war.[35]

But this was by no means the case. The countries that were at war with Germany followed their war aims irrespective of developments within the German Reich—and according to their own logic they were bound to do so. This is perhaps hard to accept. But was it not understandable, legitimate, and perhaps even necessary, not only for the war but for the peace too, to pursue consistently "the cessation of that type of tyranny which is represented by the Gestapo," as the archbishop put it to Visser't Hooft—without respect of persons, so to speak? Was this not absolutely essential, even as early as the spring of 1941? Was it not essential, after the attack on Poland and the strategy of annihilation practiced by the general government? After the outrageous disregard of the neutrality of neighboring states? After the occupation of France and the destructive air attacks on England? After the beginning of the Africa campaign and immediately before the Balkan offensive?

Other letters of Visser't Hooft's, written in March 1941, show the traces left by Bonhoeffer's visit in Geneva. These are remarkable with regard to the personal impression he made, as well as for his information about the conspiracy, and for his own view of things. On March 1941 Visser't Hooft wrote a long letter to George Bell, the bishop of Chichester, who was his own friend as well as Bonhoeffer's:

> He was a week with us and spent most of his time extracting ecumenical information from persons and documents. It is touching to see how hungry people like him are for news about their brothers in other countries. . . . On the other hand we learned a lot from him. The picture which he gave is pretty black in respect to the exterior circumstances for the community which he represents. The pressure is greater than ever. But fortunately he could also tell us of many signs that their fundamental position has not changed at all. . . . Many

of them have really the same reaction to all that has
happened and is happening as you have or as I have.[36]

The new element that Bonhoeffer had introduced into the Swiss
meeting appears in the "Notes on the state of the church in Europe"
that Visser't Hooft sent to England at the end of March 1941. The
third section of these notes, which was devoted to Germany, was also
based, as Visser't Hooft said later, on his conversations with Bonhoeffer.[37] He wrote at that time from Geneva to England that in the
Confessing Church there was a group that clung to the "inner line"
and concentrated on the building up of the spiritual life. And there
was another group that gave preference to the church's prophetic
and ethical function for the world, and prepared for the time when
it would be able to resume this function. It was generally recognized
among believing Christians that a Nazi victory would have the most
disastrous consequences for the church in their own country as well
as elsewhere. On the other hand, Germany's defeat would probably
also mean its end as nation. Whatever the outcome, for Germany it
would be in either case "an evil thing." And then follows the statement that echoes Bonhoeffer's fundamental attitude: "One hears,
however, also voices which say that after all the suffering which their
country has brought upon others they almost hope for an opportunity to pay the price by suffering themselves.[38]

That was the tone in which on that already mentioned March
evening Bonhoeffer had answered Freudenberg's question when he
asked what Bonhoeffer prayed for in the present situation: "Since
you ask me, I must say that I pray for the defeat of my country, for
I believe that this is the only way in which it can pay for the suffering which it has caused in the world."[39] With this he expressed the
notion of defeat as atonement, and that at a time when all the omens
in Germany still pointed to victory, even in the resistance circles for
whom he was the emissary.

To accept the defeat of his own country as the price for the
endless suffering it had caused—to imagine such a thing, and even
more to hope for it as necessary for the future, meant daring to pursue a solitary path between all the fronts, at least in the spring of

1941. Just as he had seen his decision to place himself at the disposal of the active resistance as his own personal decision, so within this resistance it was his voice that now, still as the voice of an individual, took the personal responsibility of talking about atonement. It was the same tone in which in 1929, as a young curate in the German congregation in Barcelona, he had once said, in a lecture on "Fundamental Questions of a Christian Ethic": "The Christian stands on his own before God and the world, without any backing. . . . In ethical decisions we are led into the most profound loneliness, the loneliness in which a human being stands before the living God."[40]

nine

Networks

BONHOEFFER'S EVERYDAY LIFE DURING the 1940s was marked by a variety of contacts in a number of different circles. The way they overlapped is particularly evident in the last week of March 1941.[1] After a month's stay, he left Switzerland; stopped over briefly in Munich on March 24 to call on his official "office," where he met his mentor, Wilhelm Schmidhuber; and on March 29 was again in Berlin after an absence of five months in all. He had interrupted his further journey from Munich to Berlin (where he had to report to the "central office") for a stopover in Halle, his purpose being to talk to Ernst Wolf, one of the leading theologians in the Confessing Church, about the changed perspective of his work; for on March 19 a renewed restriction had been imposed on him: the prohibition to publish. This forbade "every activity as a writer"[2] and future publications of whatever kind. It finally put an end to the publication of his *Ethics*, which he had in any case hardly dared to hope for anymore. Nevertheless, he worked intensively on the book during the following months, now seeing it as "his life's work."[3]

Ernst Wolf had been transferred to Halle as a disciplinary measure. Like Eberhard Bethge, Wilhelm Niesel, Wilhelm Jannasch, and Wilhelm Rott,[4] he was one of the clergy whom Hans von Dohnanyi, with the support of Oster and the knowledge of Canaris, head of the Military Intelligence, had saved from military service by means of a temporary *uk* (non-availability) position. Bonhoeffer had forwarded a tentative but urgent request to Dohnanyi in this or a similar connection: "Forgive me for upending this vat of requests and needs over you, but by now you must be used to it. Many thanks for all your help."[5] The opposition group was to be strengthened whenever possible. "The main idea here was that in the period following the successful overthrow at least a few capable younger people should be available to shoulder the new responsibility."[6] In addition, Dohnanyi and Oster were concerned to keep the Confessing Church from being bled white, for their congregations were without pastoral care, the clergy having been "given the preference" in the call-up. This concern was shared by Ludwig Beck and Carl Goerdeler, although they acted rather in the background. So the Confessing Church received help from the side of the political resistance without perhaps being fully aware of its extent.[7]

It was Ludwig Beck especially who attached importance to contacts with officeholders in the church who were connected with the opposition to Hitler. It was his idea and at his wish ("which like all his wishes had for us absolute authority"[8]) that in 1939 Canaris and Oster had the lawyer Josef Müller transferred from Munich to the Tirpitzufer in Berlin, in order to win him over for resistance work, and to send him to the Vatican as negotiator with the British. From that time on he was in constant touch with critical members of the Catholic clergy on behalf of the Intelligence.[9] Later Josef Müller described Beck as a convinced and zealous Christian;[10] Eduard Spranger certified that he "was truly religious" and in 1947 wrote in typically emotional style, "I would not dare to define the religious certainty from which the General acted. What is certain is only that it *was* a religious sense and that alone, a combative one and that alone."[11]

Spranger's characterization may well be correct, but the question must, in my view, be left open.[12] Beck's "religious sense" and the fact that for him the decision to support an overthrow was also a question of his Christian existence is given credence by an anecdote. Helmut Gollwitzer, who at the end of the 1930s was pastor of the well-known Confessing Church congregation in Dahlem, Berlin, reported later that Beck came to him at that time and raised the question of an overthrow. Gollwitzer, spontaneously thinking specifically of the elimination of Hitler, said, " 'The fellow must be got rid of.' Whereupon Beck declared, 'I didn't really want to hear your opinion about people or politics. I came to you as a clergyman and pastor.' "[13]

Undisputed is Beck's central importance for the civil and military resistance, if this is what the loose association of different opposition groups within the spectrum of the resistance can be called, a complex that contained civilians as well as members of the armed forces.[14] For the Oster group in the Intelligence, Beck was eminently important from its beginnings in 1938, the year before the war. From the time of his resignation as general chief of staff, he was the link between leaders in the army high command who were at least critical of the government, and the resistance group in the Military Intelligence.

Irrespective of the hopes and disappointments of the civil and military resistance in those years, Beck served as the fixed point and stabilizing element. He was the guarantor of Prussian integrity, an officer in civilian dress and a protesting general in retirement, who in his own particular way had put himself at the service of his country. "The only man I am afraid of is Beck. That man would be in a position to take steps against me," Hitler is supposed to have said in the course of the intrigue against Werner von Fritsch, the commander in chief of the army.[15] But in January 1938 Beck had countered Lieutenant General Halder, who tried to get him to take part in the putsch during the Fritsch crisis by saying, "Mutiny, revolution—these words are not part of the vocabulary of a German officer."[16] Yet in July 1938, shortly before he resigned on the grounds of Hitler's warlike policy (which had emerged openly in the Sudeten crisis), he said in some notes for a lecture:

> Here what is at stake are final decisions about the state of the nation. At the bar of history these leaders [that is, the generals] will be seen to have blood on their hands if they fail to act according to their professional and political consciences. Their obedience as soldiers comes up against its limits when their knowledge, conscience and responsibility forbid them to carry out a command. . . . It shows a lack of greatness and a failure to realize the task he is called to when at such times a soldier in the highest position seeks his duty only in the limited framework of his military assignments, without being conscious of his supreme responsibility for the whole people. Exceptional times demand exceptional acts.[17]

On August 17, 1938, Beck acted accordingly and resigned as general chief of staff; and from that time he worked personally to end the Nazi regime because of his "supreme responsibility for the German people."[18] Through Beck, the resistance circle in the Intelligence had essential contacts with members of the military who were still active but critical of the government and potentially prepared for an overthrow. These included Franz Halder and Erich Hoepner, Friedrich Olbricht and Erwin von Witzleben.[19]

If Beck was the bridgehead to the forces of resistance in the army, the lawyer Carl Goerdeler exercised the same function toward groups of the civilian opposition—more: he himself counted as no less than their central figure.[20] Goerdeler was to be head of the government, Beck was to be head of state; after a successful coup d'etat, Gordeler was to take over the post of chancellor in a first, newly formed government in a post-Hitler Germany. About this the people involved in the conspiracy were at one, disparate in their thinking and disunited though they sometimes were, just as they were equally agreed that the office of German president must pass to Beck.

In 1937 Carl Friedrich Goerdeler had resigned in protest from his office as lord mayor of Leipzig. What finally led him to this step was the removal, without his agreement, of the statue of the composer Mendelssohn, which had stood in front of the Leipzig concert hall, the Gewandhaus. He himself, a conservative in his thinking, set himself consistently against Nazi rule, without fear or favor and with a confidence that apparently never failed. What is particularly striking is his sometimes high-flown, apparently almost irrationally wild and optimistic attitude, which was sustained by his unshakable hope, his courage, and his openness.[21] Especially striking, too, are his untiring readiness and ability to maintain contacts with the most varying groups in the resistance, and to make ever new attempts to keep in touch with countries abroad—later, the Nazi "people's court" described him as "a traveling salesman of defeatism."[22] He was also the author of a throng of memoranda and appeals.[23]

After he had resigned from his post in Leipzig, Goerdeler worked mainly for the Stuttgart firm of Robert Bosch, which enabled him to take numerous journeys abroad and also offered him material security that was not to be despised. Under the protection of this position, which he used to a considerable extent for his conspiratorial activities, Goerdler had at his disposal to a degree rare in wartime, time, money, and contacts—all privileges he used for the purposes of the resistance. Robert Bosch, incidentally, was one of the few industrialists who was a declared Nazi opponent and supported the Confessing Church. Among his special friends was the Württemberg bishop Theophil Wurm, who is known particularly for his vociferous opposition to the euthanasia murders.[24] Goerdeler's opinions were sometimes extremely conservative, but in the interests of a broader opposition basis, he nevertheless worked with leading trade-union orientated and Social Democratic groups in the resistance, for example with Jakob Kaiser, Wilhelm Leuschner, and Ernst von Harnack, who, again, had contacts with Klaus Bonhoeffer, one of Dietrich Bonhoeffer's brothers.

Before we consider Goerdeler's contacts with Dietrich Bonhoeffer, we must look briefly at the relationship—or perhaps non-relationship—between these two brothers. In spite of their family ties and their avowed opposition from the beginning to National Socialism, and in spite of the readiness of them both for risky conspiracy, they seem to have been somewhat reserved toward each other. In the biographical literature about Dietrich Bonhoeffer, when his family is under discussion, relatively little is said about the relationship between Klaus Bonhoeffer and his younger brother. Perhaps their ideological orientation, their political preferences, and their professional perspectives were too different.

Klaus Bonhoeffer held a doctorate in law and was employed as chief corporation counsel for Lufthansa. He was opposed to the Nazi regime from the outset. His special contribution to the resistance—especially together with his collaborators and friends, the brothers Hans and Otto John—was to make contacts and set up personal meetings between people with the most widely differing *Weltanschauung* and political background. Examples are the links between the Hohenzollern prince Louis Ferdinand, the trade unionist Jakob Kaiser, and the archconservatives Ewald von Kleist-Schmenzin and Ulrich von Hassell; or between the trade unionist Wilhelm Leuschner and Ludwig Beck. And in the framework of such contacts, the two Bonhoeffer brothers of course often had to do with each other. There was a meeting, for example, between them and the John brothers, as well as Klaus Bonhoeffer's brother-in-law Justus Delbrück (who worked in Department Z of the Military Intelligence Foreign Office) and Dietrich Bonhoeffer's friend Eberhard Bethge.[25]

But Klaus Bonhoeffer's profile is always only vaguely drawn. In my view, it would be a worthwhile task for research into the resistance to determine his specific importance and to free his memory from the overshadowing remembrance of his "little brother."

We know something about Carl Goerdeler's specific contacts with Dietrich Bonhoeffer from Bethge and through Christine von Dohnanyi. For one thing, in 1941 Goerdeler, Bonhoeffer, and Bethge met twice for talks in the Berlin Fürstenhof.[26] For another, via Dohnanyi, Bonhoeffer received financial help from Goerdeler to cover his living expenses and his conspiratorial activity. Dohnanyi again met Goerdeler on May 20, 1941, for example, a meeting, which, as his wife wrote, "again brought in something for Dietrich." As Christine von Dohnanyi explained later, the background to this was that from 1941 neither the Confessing Church nor the Intelligence paid her brother a salary; instead, via her husband, he received money from Goerdeler, who "got together about 500 RM every month by way of a collection. No one was supposed to know, so that Goerdeler did not get into difficulties. The fact that Dietrich received the money was so that it could reach the Confessing Church without its source having to be revealed. That was what Goerdeler preferred."[27]

This leads to the question, what did Bonhoeffer live on after the autumn of 1940, that is, from the time of his (fictitious) employment as agent for the Military Intelligence? For in this role—not to say, for this role—he unquestionably received no money, either from the Military Intelligence Foreign Office or from its office in Munich. His biographer maintains vehemently, "To avoid any misunderstanding, of course he never expected or received any remuneration for his activity in the Abwehr—as 'agent,' for instance."[28]

In this connection Dohnanyi's biographer stressed his efforts for "the financial security of his brother-in-law, who had been released officially for the purposes of the Intelligence, as cover for the opposition group."[29] She emphasizes that he had repeatedly discussed this question with Goerdeler (see above). And this again only confirms the fact that Bonhoeffer was not paid by the Military Intelligence.[30]

With regard to the payment of a salary by the church, Bethge mentions that Bonhoeffer wanted to relieve the Confessing Church of a burden, since it was in any case in difficulties, and from the turn of the year 1940–41 he had taken advantage of "regular allocations which, in spite of existing difficulties, his Leibholz relatives were able to make him from their German account."[31] Since a good deal of his time and energy was now devoted to nonchurch activity, about which his church knew nothing and was to know nothing, he thought it right to relieve it of salary payments, at least in part. In fact, he had meanwhile saved the Council of Brethren between a third and half of his salary.

In the correspondence between Bonhoeffer and Bethge, it occasionally sounds as if Bonhoeffer would also have liked to make his friend his treasurer, who would have had to deal with tax payments as well as with bills and similar troublesome matters.[32] Luckily for him, money seemed for Bonhoeffer to be relatively unimportant. Even in the House of Brethren in Finkenwalde he had dispensed with a salary as seminary director and had it paid into a common stock, together with his own books, furniture, etc. But this salary was a far from negligible matter for the committee of the Confessing Church that had to make the payments. With an affectionate, ironic undertone, Bethge writes, "His very inadequate talents for the essentials of book-keeping caused a great deal of difficulty to the financial experts of the Council of Brethren in their dealings with the tax authorities, and occasionally led to his having to answer further enquiries."[33] An embarrassing inquiry of this kind was once sent from Stettin by the Council of Brethren of the Evangelical Church of Pomerania to the Pastors' Emergency League in Berlin, saying that the finance department responsible had complained that taxes had been paid by or for Bonhoeffer, but no salary, and that the whole procedure in this matter "was in general exceedingly strange." The letter went on:

> This cannot be disputed. At the moment Brother Bonhoeffer receives his salary through private contributions. Sometimes they do not amount monthly to the equivalent amount of the salary, sometimes, again, they appear to exceed it. Occasionally Brother Bonhoeffer sends a larger round sum (e.g., the last time RM 1,000) which is supposed to represent the amount for tax payments. But this mode of procedure is of course not precisely the correct one.[34]

This should be enough to confirm what, as we have seen, Bethge calls Bonhoeffer's "very inadequate talents for the essentials of book-keeping." It was precisely his conscientious renunciation of a regular and "normal" salary from the church during his alleged work for the Military Intelligence—a renunciation demanded by his conscience—that sometimes made for confusion among those responsible for salary matters in the church. Ultimately speaking, however, this confusion, though unintended by Bonhoeffer, was completely in accord with Goerdeler's wishes. Christine von Dohnanyi writes that "Dietrich got the money so that it could reach the Confessing Church in this way, without its source having to be revealed."[35] Bonhoeffer was evidently someone for whom money was not important. A friend of his from the Finkenwalde era, Wolf-Dieter Zimmermann, recalled that for Bonhoeffer sharing was a matter of course:

> Bonhoeffer . . . was very generous with what he possessed. Once when we were talking about a certain book, he wanted to let me have it immediately—he wanted to give it to me. I was shocked, and refused, but he rebuked me, saying, "What kind of a notion do you have about property? Property doesn't mean private possession." As one of the "haves," it was for him a matter of course to take over the costs . . . if one of us was in personal difficulties. He once explained this by saying, "I should like always to have enough money not to have to think about it; anyone who thinks about money takes on the character of money as well."[36]

Bonhoeffer's generosity may have been connected with the optimism he radiated. His trust in God's "crooked paths" and patient endurance gave him a confidence that was sometimes startling in view of the real situation. The longer state terror and war lasted, the more Bonhoeffer seems to have developed hope and confidence in the future—unlike, for example, his brother-in-law and friend Dohnanyi. For example, on May 25, 1941, Dohnanyi wrote to his wife in deepest depression. It was a Sunday, and looking back over the past four weeks he had tried to render an account to himself of what these weeks had really brought: "Result: nothing." Even if

Sunday was included, he had made no progress, either in his work or his private life:

> But all that means nothing compared with the pain of my ever-increasing awareness that in this world I shall probably never again be permitted to lead a useful life in which I am my own master . . . it is nothing more than a laborious marking time in the face of an uncertain future . . . and with the sad certainty that the things that enrich human life are slowly withering away.[37]

It would seem as if for Dohnanyi this Berlin Sunday meant a bitter taking stock. His scepticism easily became resignation, and in such situations especially, Bonhoeffer was evidently his opposite number, refusing to surrender the future to hopelessness.[38] And yet Bonhoeffer himself had approaches to depression, and from time to time suffered severely from them.[39] Dohnanyi's biographer stresses the unquestioning and unbroken loyalty between Dohnanyi and Bonhoeffer, and—quoting Bethge, the friend of both of them—he writes that Dohnanyi valued Bonhoeffer's "sturdy realism," theologian though he was, as well as his ability to help others to reach decisions at a time when decisions were lacking.[40]

Following his return from the United States in the summer of 1939, after a period of extreme tension, marked by feelings of isolation and an inability to reach a decision, Bonhoeffer evidently achieved an inner stability that he passed on to others. He lived from the assurance that in spite of all appearances the world is in God's hand. And he was convinced that this assurance has a foundation and a name on which we can rely in the forsakenness of this world, and in that forsakenness above all. Sometime in the months after the first conspiratorial journey to Switzerland, Bonhoeffer composed a text designed for his *Ethics* called "Christ, Reality, and Good." There he wrote, "The world belongs to Christ, and only in Christ is the world what it is . . . Christ has died for the world, and Christ is Christ only in the midst of the world."[41] That was the basis of his indestructible hope for the present and future of the world, even and above all a world where this fact was not evident. Perhaps for the conspiracy especially, part of Bonhoeffer's special charisma—I use that great word with deliberation—was to give a sign of this hope for the world, to believe in its future and in the greater power of God, and again and again to put this faith in God and the future into words. Perhaps it was as "Pastor" Bonhoeffer, Bonhoeffer the shepherd, that he was particularly in demand. His optimism was literally "foundational." It had nothing to do with glossing over the facts, but very much to do with what can most aptly be described in the old-fashioned term "trust in God"; and this must occasionally have sufficed, even for Dohnanyi, and for him especially—vicariously, so to speak. But sometimes even that was not enough, as we see from the already quoted letter he wrote from Berlin on that Sunday in May in the war year 1941.

A month later, on June 22, 1941, the war was extended to the Soviet Union. "Attack," "invasion," "campaign," "conquest"—with whatever terms the systematic policy of annihilation was and is paraphrased, its consequences were appalling. What had begun brutally in Poland became a doctrine. The war in the east was pursued beyond the usual categories of war and was accompanied by the criminal practices of the deadly machinery of the SS. In the wake of these events, far-reaching cross-connections developed among resistance circles in the capital, groups that functioned more or less parallel to each other, and the contacts between military and civilian opponents of the regime became closer. In the face of the overtly inhumane and criminal conduct of the war, as well as the decreed disregard of all the laws of war that was part of the daily agenda, in the period between the early summer of 1941 and the end of that year there was a phase of closer rapprochement between Hans von Dohnanyi and Helmuth James Graf von Moltke,[42] probably the two most important regime-critical civilians in the Military Intelligence Foreign Office. Also in the second half of 1941, in the Central Army Group, led by the first officer of the general staff, Henning von Tresckow, one of the most important resistance groups in the army, coalesced more definitely than ever before.[43] One result was that that in the autumn of 1941 Tresckow tried via Fabian von Schlabrendorff to make contact in Berlin with the group in the Military Intelligence Foreign Office around Hans Oster and Hans von Dohnanyi.[44] As a consequence, out of horror at the criminal conduct of the war enjoined by their own side, links were forged between civilian and military attempts at resistance. These were to have far-reaching consequences, even though from today's standpoint the attempts were perhaps much too hesitant, too belated, and too inconsistent.[45] Moltke and Tresckow were exponents of two different resistance groups that crystallized within the civilian opposition. And in the much discussed interaction of civilian and military resistance,[46] the "little radical resistance group" gathered around Oster[47] played a decisive part.

These two resistance activities concentrated around Moltke and Tresckow are examples that make it clear that in Germany as a whole there was no unified resistance movement, but rather a loose cooperation and parallel activity. Nor can even the civilian resistance be seen as a unified movement. The multiplicity and diversity of the opposition strivings and activities in their various separate camps naturally led to deficits in planning, coordination, support, and effectiveness. But the decisive difficulty was that, in the nature of things, it was impossible in the conditions of the dictatorship for firm forms of organization and publicly declared agreement to develop. The very fact that such groups existed at all could not be made public. They were bound to close their ranks toward outside influences, and even less could they discuss loudly and distinctly their aims and ways forward, their ideas and methods.

Even within the individual circles there could be no organized links between the initiated. In order to reduce the danger for the individual members (which is really an inappropriate term) all those concerned had to walk the tightrope between trust and caution. Inevitably, often not even closest members of the family could be told about particular actions. As an example, the biographer of Friedrich Justus Perels, the Confessing Church's legal adviser and one of Bonhoeffer's confidants, reports that although his family was certainly informed about his connections with the conspiracy, on principle he did not inform them about the aim and purpose of some of his journeys, out of consideration for them. He also recounts that although Dohnanyi and Bonhoeffer were completely convinced of Perels's loyalty, specific contacts were to be confined to Bonhoeffer and Bethge, in order to avoid unnecessary risk. Too many meetings between representatives of the Confessing Church and representatives of the Military Intelligence Foreign Office would only arouse suspicion.[48]

Disparate though the different circles seem on the one hand to be, on the other there were many overlappings. The resistance group around Oster especially constituted an important interface between military and civilian circles, and between people in the church and in politics; Beck and Oster, Dohnanyi and Bonhoeffer are examples. In the attempt to see one's way through the kaleidoscope of the civilian resistance groups, one becomes aware of the ramifications both within the individual groups as well as between them. One discovers reliable teams, emotionally bound together, that grew up out of a close friendship, and there are others that rest on a common university, profession, or career. A wealth of relationships emerges—not merely ties of blood, but also truly lived ties between relatives, as well as others based on a similar class and background. But in addition there were evidently contacts that depended solely on sympathy and a shared wavelength, philosophically or humanly, ethically or politically. A basic mutual trust and reliance on secrecy belonged to the fundamental equipment of the people who tried to find a shared path of resistance.

One thing cannot be too highly estimated when we are considering the civilian groups of regime opponents. That is the importance of family background and youthful and undergraduate friendships, a feeling of being able to rely on relationships that had grown up over the years and on unquestionable support from relatives. "Among those belonging to the traditional elite, the extended family, which included even the most remote cousin, still existed as a unit of interaction and loyalty."[49] Attention has at various times been drawn to this fact—that a "close network of family, professional and friendly connections"[50] existed in the civilian resistance and especially in the orbit of the Bonhoeffer (extended) family. It has even been said that the "organizational chart" of some resistance groups, such as the one around Dietrich Bonhoeffer, reads like part of a family tree.[51] There is evidence enough that the relationships between relatives and friends formed a complex fabric. Here we may look at only a few examples of the ramifications both inside the resistance group in the Military Intelligence Foreign Office and in other civilian resistance groups with which it was connected.

Dietrich Bonhoeffer had met Hans Oster through Hans von Dohnanyi, who was married to Bonhoeffer's sister Christine, and whose own sister was married to Dietrich Bonhoeffer's brother Klaus Friedrich. The latter was a close friend of Adam von Trott, who was one of the regime opponents in the Foreign Office and belonged to what was later called the Kreisau circle (a resistance group centered on Helmuth James von Moltke). Hans Dohnanyi was also friendly with Adam von Trott. Trott's mother and Trott himself were friendly with Willem A. Visser't Hooft, the ecumenist who cooperated with West European resistance movements, and who himself was friendly with the English bishop George Bell, who again was a friend of Dietrich Bonhoeffer's. Adam von Trott's sister Vera had been at school with Sabine Bonhoeffer, Dietrich's twin sister. Adam von Trott was well known to Sabine and her husband, Gerhard Leibholz. One of Adam von Trott's closest friends was Hans Bernd von Haeften, a member of the Confessing Church and, like Trott, employed in the Foreign Office, like him active in the conspiracy, and again like him belonging to the Kreisau circle. Hans Berndt von Haeften and Dietrich Bonhoeffer had been vaguely friendly since the confirmation classes they had attended together. Haeften's brother, Werner von Haeften, was adjutant to Claus Schenk Graf von Stauffenberg, who was directly involved in the assassination attempt on Hitler of July 20, 1944. One of Stauffenberg's cousins was Peter Yorck von Wartenburg—apart from Moltke the most important of the Kreisau circle. Peter Yorck's wife, Marion, was in Dietrich Bonhoeffer's high school class in Berlin. Dietrich's sister Ursula was married to Rüdiger Schleicher, a friend, both personally and professionally, of Dietrich's brother Klaus. Klaus Bonhoeffer married Emmi Delbrück, the sister of one of his best friends, Justus Delbrück, who was later active in the conspiracy as a colleague of Hans von Dohnanyi and under the protection of Department Z of the Military Intelligence Foreign Office. Delbrück was also friendly with Rüdiger and Ursula Schleicher. Dietrich Bonhoeffer's friend Eberhard Bethge married the Schleichers' daughter Renate. The lawyer Rüdiger von der Goltz was a cousin of Ursula Schleicher and of Dietrich Bonhoeffer. He was later to be one of Dohnanyi's defending counsel. During the so-called Fritsch crisis, Goltz was Fritsch's counsel, Fritsch then being commander in chief of the army. It was through these events that Hans von Dohnanyi and Hans Oster met. In the years that followed, a relationship of particular trust grew up between Dohnanyi and Oster, professionally, privately, and in the framework of the conspiracy, just as there came to be a relationship of unconditional trust between Dohnanyi and Bonhoeffer.

Bonhoeffer's much older kindred spirit, Ruth von Kleist-Retzow, was the grandmother of his later and very much younger fiancé Maria von Wedemeyer. Another of Ruth von Kleist-Retzow's granddaughters had married Fabian von Schlabrendorff, who was therefore Maria von Wedemeyer's cousin by marriage. He knew Bonhoeffer from the time when he was staying in Lower Pomerania. Schlabrendorff was also a relation by marriage of Henning von Tresckow, one of Ruth von Kleist Retzow's nephews, and was one of his closest confidants in the military resistance group in the Central Army Group. On Henning von Tresckow's instructions, in 1941 Schlabrendorff made the first contact with the resistance group around Hans Oster in the Military Intelligence Foreign Office, having already met Oster in 1938 through his father-in-law, Herbert von Bismarck. Hans Oster, again, had as we know, met Dietrich Bonhoeffer through Hans von Dohnanyi.

It is impossible to say that in this way the circle closed, for it was open toward many sides—toward other military authorities, toward representatives of both Protestants and Catholics, toward left-wing members of the resistance, and yet, through Julius Leber, also toward such eminently conservative lone wolves as Ewald von Kleist-Schmenzin. Similar linked relationships can be shown for others, such as Adam von Trott or Helmuth James Graf von Moltke, both of whom, each in his own way, seems to have had to a particular degree a special gift for friendship. In Bonhoeffer's life too—and not just during these years—friendships played a central role and, as with so many of the resistance people round him, even apart from these personal friendships the number of reliable contacts seems to have been unusually great.

In not a few cases, it was also and especially the wives of the men concerned who did not merely offer unshakable support in the passive sense but who were actively involved, and often enough counterbalanced the inward and outward isolation of the participants. These partners and comrades of the resistance people—Christine von Dohnanyi, Freya von Moltke, Marion Yorck von Wartenburg, and Clarita von Trott, to mention only a few—belong to the history of the resistance no less than their later renowned husbands.[52]

And yet the impression of a supportive and protective community, living in solidarity, in which a conspirational existence could be confidently lived, is deceptive. It was an existence at one's own personal risk. There was no point of reference within a firm group, no background support, no safety net. In spite of the diverse experiences of reliable, matter-of-course solidarity, there was serious loneliness. That the two existed side by side reflects the contradictoriness and fragility of the human condition, in resistance especially. "Resistance was increasingly practiced from an exposed position. There was no appeal to organized support, let alone to support through any institution."[53]

Moreover, especially people who wanted to resist tyranny because of their faith, and came to political resistance for that reason (like Bonhoeffer, or the Jesuit Alfred Selp, who belonged to the Kreisau circle round Moltke), felt that they were "solitary Christians"[54] and were in fact seen by their orders or their churches to be on their own. This was also the Confessing Church's attitude to Bonhoeffer. "There is one thing left: the venture of action." This sentence comes from one of the rare passages that indirectly describes the way Bonhoeffer viewed his own involvement in the conspiracy against Hitler. There he talks about "the venture of responsibility"; about the refusal to obey in a specific historical situation "which can only be a venture of one's own responsibility."[55] Understandably enough, he seldom put these ideas into words, and if at all, then only in a roundabout way. But they can be found in a theological position paper entitled *State and Church*, which he probably wrote after April 1941. During these spring and summer months, in which he commuted between his parents' house in Berlin and the manor house of the Kleist-Retzows in Klein-Krössin, giving priority to his work on his *Ethics*, he held himself in readiness for new instructions from the opponents of the regime in the Military Intelligence.

ten

Signals for
the Future?

"AMAZING NEWS: THE OPPOSITION plans to get rid of Hitler and
the Nazi regime are getting increasingly crystallised." This note can
be found in the Geneva diary notes of Swedish WCC staff member
Nils Ehrenström for the evening of September 3, 1941.[1] Bonhoeffer had visited him at his home, and the most important subject of
their conversation had been "the whole German situation."[2] In that
year Bonhoeffer was in Switzerland for the second time, and for the
second time he tried to draw the attention of countries abroad to the
existence of a conspiracy in Germany prepared to intervene. Now
of all times?

North Africa, the Balkans, Russia—it seemed as if there were no
limits to the unstoppable advance of the German war machine, and
as if, with its victories, the critical voices at home and at the front—
which were few enough in any case—were falling completely silent.
Yet contrary to expectation there were also signs of renewed hopes
for an overthrow, admittedly sparse, but perhaps not unrealistic.

Would this expansion of the war not inevitably lead to an implosion of the Nazi imperium? Might not its end, for that very reason, be conceivably and palpably coming closer? In view of the manifest and enjoined cruelties in the conduct of the war, couldn't the indecisiveness of some high-ranking officers who were undoubtedly critical of the regime turn into a decisive no? So couldn't the different opposition forces join together and be made to act? Wouldn't countries abroad then call a halt in order to give the coup d'etat a chance? And couldn't the result then be a new solution for Europe?

By way of the channels open to the churches in Europe or, more specifically, by way of the excellent links existing between the World Council of Churches in Geneva (which was still in the process of formation) and the English churches, Bonhoeffer was supposed to pick up and deepen the contacts with countries abroad that had already been reactivated in the spring.

His function was to put out feelers about peace conditions, to provide information about the regime opponents, and to win support for them. Countries abroad were to know that there really were "officers against Hitler,"[3] and civilian opponents too, people who stood for "another Germany,"[4] hoped for an end of the Nazi dictatorship and were developing points of departure for a future Germany in a future Europe.

In the last week of August 1941, Bonhoeffer traveled to his official office in Munich, probably in order to receive instructions, papers, and currency. He visited "his" monastery in Ettal and met Josef Müller, who through Vatican channels cultivated "contacts with the wider world"[5] on behalf of the resistance group in the Military Intelligence.

His first stop in Switzerland was in Basel, where he paid a short visit on Sunday, August 30, 1941, to Alphons Koechlin, a Swiss churchman prominent in Basel and Bern. He then, of course, also saw Karl Barth. His next stop was Geneva. There he met ecumenists he already knew, among them Ehrenström, Visser't Hooft, and Courvoisier. At this new meeting at the beginning of September, Visser't Hooft was surprised at Bonhoeffer's interpretation of world events.

In those early weeks of the German invasion of Russia the general impression was still that the German army had met little effective resistance and that Hitler might succeed in the East as he had succeeded in the West. So I was taken aback when [Bonhoeffer] opened the conversation by saying: "So this is the beginning of the end." He saw my startled expression and added: "The old man will never get out of this." He felt sure that Hitler was making the same mistake which Napoleon had made.[6]

Visser't Hooft wrote to Bishop Bell about this Geneva visit of Bonhoeffer's, saying that he had come for a double purpose, on the one hand to keep alive ecumenical contacts and the exchange of ideas, and on the other to discover as far as possible on behalf of the resistance groups in Germany what peace conditions could be expected.[7]

Visser't Hooft, as general secretary of the WCC, was its representative par excellence, and Bonhoeffer and he wanted to point the way to the future for their friends in politics and the church in England and the United States, and to do so more distinctly than they had done in the spring. But they chose a very complicated method. In England a book had appeared in July published by the English theologian William Paton, who was also a member of the leading committee of the WCC. Its title was *The Church and the New Order in Europe*. At their meeting in Geneva, Bonhoeffer and Visser't Hooft decided to make this book the occasion for a rejoinder of their own, a memorandum on the question of a postwar order in Europe. This was to be sent to politicians, church leaders, and "peace aims" groups in England and the United States.

Bonhoeffer spent a few days preparing the memorandum at the Freudenbergs' holiday house on Lac Champex. His host remembered him as "a man sure of God's compassion," who in spite of everything was able quite consciously to enjoy the beauty of these days. "He had switched off completely from German worries and haunting thoughts, was relaxed and cheerful, and enjoyed without reserve the freshness and scents of the early autumn which is especially brilliant in the Valais Alps."[8] After another brief stop in Geneva, Bonhoeffer traveled to Zürich, staying there from September 15 to 24, 1941, as the guest (as the guest book attests) of Otto Salomon, his former editor at the Munich publishing house Christian Kaiser. Salomon had emigrated in 1938, and Bonhoeffer visited him each time he was in Switzerland. Salomon later reported:

> We learned nothing about his activity in the German resistance and his telegrams to the bishop of Chichester [George Bell]. He slept in our little guest room and worked at night until the early morning. But we spent a few hours together during the afternoons.[9]

With Karl Barth it was a different matter. Barth wanted to know how Bonhoeffer came to be so privileged that he could actually turn up in Switzerland for a second time in wartime. This had aroused suspicion in some Swiss circles. When he visited Barth in Basel again three weeks later, during this second stay, traveling from Zurich on September 19, Barth openly expressed a certain discomfort in view of various rumors that were circulating. "Since Bonhoeffer was under suspicion from various sides, Barth asked him directly, 'My dear Bonhoeffer, let me ask you quite frankly: why are you actually here in Switzerland?' In response Bonhoeffer talked openly about plans to remove Hitler."[10] Barth was certain of Bonhoeffer's integrity, but he wanted to eliminate every doubt:

> I was . . . always certain that B. was not a "Nationalist"— but when I was asked (understandably in view of the various double agents who were at large in Switzerland at the time) how he was able to spend three weeks in our country with a German passport (issued by the Security Service!) and with currency, I was unable to give an answer. Hence my question.[11]

Bonhoeffer had in fact received his passport not from the Security Service (which was under the SS and the Nazi Party) but from the military secret service; but that was a minor matter.[12] Not minor for Bonhoeffer however, was to be exposed to suspicion. It was a misunderstanding that weighed on him and had to be cleared up. At least for the time being, Barth was also astonished at Bonhoeffer's account of the way the secret opposition in Germany imagined (at least at that time) the possible beginning of peace negotiations: a government composed of generals was proposing, not to withdraw the German troops, but initially *to leave them where they were* (wherever the fronts might then be), and in the occupied territories as well, and to negotiate with the Allies on that basis.[13] Bonhoeffer, for his part, was equally amazed that Barth should consider it out of the question that the Allies would agree to this.

Would they consider the other messages that Bonhoeffer wanted to pass on to them as emissary of this opposition? The project had been discussed in detail with Visser't Hooft and had meanwhile been largely realized: in response to Paton's already-mentioned book, Bonhoeffer had submitted a draft in German in the first half of September, on the basis of which Visser't Hooft had composed an English version, which, as the latter later stressed, was intended to put forward their shared convictions, its wording having been agreed upon between them.[14] Bonhoeffer's text was entitled *Gedenken zu William Paton: The Church and the New Order* (Reflections on William Paton's "The Church and the New Order"), and it is only extant in incomplete form. It seems to be initially a theological review, but for all that it is not hard to detect its intention, which was to send out signals from German opponents of the regime.

Some of its comments are particularly striking because they are both politically and theologically challenging. He is critical of British radio propaganda policy, stressing—undoubtedly realistically—that "any worker revolt would lead to a bloody repression by the SS" and "in terms of sheer power, only the military is capable of removing the present regime." "One must take this into consideration when broadcasting these peace aims to Germany."[15] This last comment was certainly not very realistic. The theologically challenging character of the text emerges, for example, when he formulates the right to exclusive [Christian] representation; for although this is of course justifiable within the boundaries of the Christian faith, it is incomprehensible outside them:

> The foundation of a new world order can be sought in the will of God revealed in Jesus Christ. Because the world holds together only "in Christ" and "for Christ" (Colossians 1), any consideration of humanity "in itself" or the world and its order "in itself" is an abstraction. By the will of God, everything stands in relation to Christ, whether it realizes this or not.[16]

In what follows Bonhoeffer describes his hope, which is for "a legitimate earthly order according to God's will. . . . Until recently this order was threatened by liberal anarchy in all spheres of life." Today, he goes on, "it is threatened by the omnipotence of the state (it could next be threatened by economic omnipotence). This omnipotence of the state must be broken in the name of a legitimate order that submits to the command of God." And now Bonhoeffer comes down to brass tacks. Such a state order in Germany will become evident "in the total removal of the Nazi system, including and especially the Gestapo; in the restoration of the sovereignty of equal rights for all; in a press that serves the truth; in the restoration of the freedom of the church to proclaim the word of God in command and gospel to all the world." The entire question "is whether people in England and America will be prepared to negotiate with a government that is formed on this basis, even if it initially does not appear to be democratic in the Anglo-Saxon sense of the word. Such a government could establish itself at once. Much would depend on whether it could count on the immediate support of the Allies." The extant text ends, or breaks off, with the following assessment: "It is not pan-Germanism but rather pan-Slavism that is the coming danger. Since a new Germany completely of its own accord will have the desire to disarm—even for economic reasons—the continuing insistence on this as a primary demand is not very shrewd, especially at the present time."[17]

Visser't Hooft's existing English text, which is entitled *The Church and the New Order in Europe*, is very much more detailed. A proper comparison with the German draft is hardly possible, since the original version of the latter is no longer extant. Passages from the German draft have sometimes been taken over word for word, but are sometimes softened or formulated in more differentiated terms. It is the undertones that reveal a number of differences.[18]

Visser't Hooft prefaced the document with a comment of his own, pointing out that it represented the thinking of two Christians from two different nations who found themselves on opposite sides in the war. The leitmotif for the discussion about peace conditions and peace goals seemed for him to be the question whether or how a postwar and post-Hitler Germany would be accepted by the Allies as partners to a peace within the community of the nations. Christians on all sides had the right and the duty to participate in this discussion. But the particular situation in Germany had to be taken into account. The attitude of those groups—considerable in number—which were against the regime but were at the same time good patriots, would depend on the answer to the question, how will Germany be treated if it loses the war?[19]

Visser't Hooft took over into the English text Bonhoeffer's thesis that now something could be undertaken against the Hitler regime from the military side. But he added that it was improbable that the people concerned would act unless they had good reason to hope for an acceptable peace. He then put forward as a suggestion, for British radio propaganda especially, that statements about the future should give the opposition existing in Germany a certain basis for acting. In the passage touching on specific conditions and the results of a possible overthrow, Visser't Hooft raised the question as to whether a German government that broke completely with Hitler and everything he stood for could hope for a peace that would offer some chance of survival. As peace terms to be offered by such a government, he named the evacuation of all—explicitly

all—occupied territory, the dismissal of all Nazi leaders, and preparedness for disarmament.[20]

Bonhoeffer, in contrast, at least in the already mentioned conversation with Barth in that same September of 1941, seems not yet
to have assumed that there must be a complete withdrawal. Visser't
Hooft also found slight variations of emphasis in the question about
the form of state that would probably initially be set up under a
new government; Bonhoeffer had simply said that it would have
a pre-democratic character. Visser't Hooft now justified this assertion, explaining it and giving a reason. In large countries that had
been dictatorships or had been occupied for a long period, a strong
centralized authority would be necessary for a considerable time; in
Europe it was mainly only the smaller nations that had democratic
traditions. Under the heading "The Russian Problem," he finally
cautiously explained (though without taking over Bonhoeffer's wording) the thesis, which Bonhoeffer formulated in apodictic terms: that
it was pan-Slavism, not pan-Germanism that was the coming danger.[21] Probably it was Visser't Hooft's intention in this way to take
account of Anglo-Russian relations at that time. He did not want to
see his chances of being listened to at all in England reduced to a
minimum from the outset. He acted similarly when he struck out the
sentence in Bonhoeffer's draft that claimed that an anti-Nazi government could be formed immediately, but that this would depend
on whether they could count on the immediate support of the Allies.
Visser't Hooft, who later stressed that they had both also agreed to
cut out this sentence specifically, justified the omission by the dimin-
ishing credibility in England of German opposition groups because
of all too frequent secret announcements of a coup d'etat which
then came to nothing. In addition he pointed to a contradiction:
"You could not say at the same time: 'The attitude of the opposition
groups in Germany will depend on the answer which they will get
from the Allied governments' and 'The opposition is ready to act in
any case.'"[22]

Visser't Hooft sent this Geneva memorandum to carefully
selected addressees in England in the autumn of 1941 through

channels open to him. But it was not destined for success. True, Visser't Hoot received from Paton himself an acknowledgment that was at first sight enthusiastic, but he waited in vain for the "considerable reply" that Paton promised him.[23] True, an enthusiastic reply came from New York too, but that was not followed up either. An important American theologian and ecumenist wrote to Visser't Hooft at the end of November 1941 saying that the anonymous commentary on Paton's book was one of the most valuable documents on the peace question at the present time, and he had passed it on to Dulles among others.[24] But that was all. The response from church quarters was reserved. The people to whom it was actually addressed did not react. Thirty years later Visser't Hooft wrote:

> The commentary on Paton's book was in fact an SOS, an attempt to elicit sufficient help from the Allied nations to enable the rather small group of determined resistance men to convince the large group of the hesitant, including the generals who would not make up their minds.[25]

The fact that this call for help was not heard, or not answered, was in accordance with the line Churchill had laid down for the Foreign Office in London at the beginning of 1941 in a directive that was later repeated: absolute silence.[26] Absolute silence in response to all attempts of a secret German opposition to make contact with England belonged to the logic of the war and the logic of the Allies, especially after the British-Soviet Mutual Assistance pact of July, which excluded a separate peace and therefore also separate contacts with Germany. Consequently, it is not surprising that Visser't Hooft could record only a "meagre result," not, however, without adding, "It is all the more remarkable that Bonhoeffer did not give up."[27] It seems to have been one of Bonhoeffer's most persistent characteristics, one of his "immutable marks," so to speak, that he never became resigned in spite of all disheartenments, even when no noticeable response to signals from the resistance came from any side, neither from the church nor from political quarters. In England it was only Bishop Bell who was convinced of their authenticity and soundness.[28]

On his last day in Switzerland, September 25, 1941, Bonhoeffer again took the opportunity to write a letter to his English friend. At the end of this letter to George Bell, he admits that personally he is quite optimistic in his hope for better days and does not lose hope that they will meet again in the coming year: "What a strange day that will be!"[29]

At this point Bonhoeffer could not yet know that in Berlin there really was a reason for fresh hope. In the autumn of 1941 Fabian von Schlabrendorff turned up in Berlin for the first time, in order to signalize in the name of Henning von Tresckow that among the staff of the Central Army Group there was no longer any hesitation about participating in an overthrow of the government. Dohnanyi was even spinning further threads. Ulrich von Hassell was the foreign-policy expert among the civilian regime opponents, and his diary entry for October 4 records that a few days previously, through the mediation of Guttenberg (a member of Dohnanyi's staff), Schlabrendorff had come to see him, "having been commissioned to discover if at home there were useful crystallizing points, and who assured him that there 'one' was ready for anything."[30]

With this a solid link between the resistance circle in Berlin and military groups capable of action seemed at last to be in sight. The fact that at least some men belonging to what was then the most important contingent in the army were now really prepared to surrender their inward flight from the reality of their criminal methods of waging war in the east and were prepared to resist both these and their government gave the conspiracy a not inconsiderable new impetus.[31]

What offered less ground for hope, on the other hand, was another event in Germany soon after Bonhoeffer's return from Switzerland. In October 1941 the first deportations of Jews took place in Berlin.

eleven

"The Desperation Is Unprecedented . . ."

THE SYNAGOGUE IN LEVETZOWSTRASSE in the Moabit quarter of Berlin was to serve as the collecting and shipment point for people who were to be deported. In the night of October 16, 1941, they were fetched out of their homes and taken to the appropriate police station and then to the synagogue, which had been cleared for the purpose. On October 18, a Saturday, that is, a Sabbath, they were taken away in three stages—morning, midday, and evening—their destination being places in the east. So at least rumor said about the goals of the deportations. This first batch comprised about fifteen hundred people, and that was only the beginning. On October 24, October 29, and November 1, 1941, deportation transports were noted as leaving Berlin for the ghetto of Lodz, taking more than a thousand people each day.[1]

The deportations were preceded by precise bureaucratic measures. The families involved in the first wave of those arrested had received a letter during the week of October 5 to 12 saying that their apartment was to be evacuated and that a form was to be filled out with an inventory and a statement of any bank assets. Immediate attendance at the housing office was required, with a statement of all personal particulars, such as family status, origins, employment, etc. Then in the evening, or during the night, the Gestapo or the normal Berlin police arrived unannounced, allowed the family one to four hours to pack for what were called "normal requirements" (that is, fifty kilos of hand luggage), and then took them away. Information was passed on to other "non-Aryan" families precisely at the point when the first batch arrived at the synagogue, as a forced intermediate stop. "Since these newly affected families now already know what these communications mean, the desperation is unprecedented. Grave illnesses among those suffering heart disease, gallstones, etc., and the danger of suicide are the understandable results." So wrote Friedrich Justus Perels in a "Report on the N.A. Evacuation" (N.A. standing for non-Aryan).[2]

Perels was a friend and comrade-at-arms of Bonhoeffer's in the Confessing Church and, apart from Bethge, he was probably the only fellow member of the church to know about Bonhoeffer's conspiratorial connections. On October 17, immediately after the first "collective action," Bonhoeffer and he had already set on foot precise investigations and had immediately compiled an initial report about the mass deportations of Jews in order to document the deportation measures.[3] During the next few days, Perels wrote a second report, the one about "the N.A. Evacuation." Bonhoeffer had meanwhile taken ill with a severe and (as it turned out) prolonged pneumonia and could no longer contribute actively himself, but he saw to it that the reports were passed on to his brother-in-law, Hans Dohnanyi.

Perels must have been particularly shocked by the deportations, because his family was directly affected by the "non-Aryan" laws. One of his uncles, a professor of law, had been forbidden to teach as early as 1933 and since 1940 had been interned in the Gurs camp in the south of France. Another uncle, Perels's father, and Perels himself suffered under the regulations that discriminated against so-called non-Aryans and in most cases practically meant that they were forbidden to practice their profession. Perels joined the Confessing Church early on and acted as adviser to the leading committees and the Pastors' Emergency League in the many and difficult legal problems that faced them.

Perels, who came from the tradition of young people's Bible groups, was in the best sense of the word a committed Christian, an opponent of National Socialism, and resolutely resistant. "Because of his clear and consistent opposition, his friends jokingly called him 'the church's secret police.' "[4] In 1936 at the latest, Bonhoeffer had gotten to know him personally in connection with a tax matter that he had found very complicated, and that had to do with the illegally functioning preachers' seminary; this had been confronted by the financial authorities in Stettin with a requirement for a turnover tax declaration. Perels cleared away other bureaucratic hurdles too where necessary and, as Bethge—at that time Bonhoeffer's closest assistant—later recollected, "he delighted Bonhoeffer by his ability to cope with the official pedantry the latter found so distasteful."[5] The two complemented each other and got on excellently, their cooperation during these years, their joint involvement in the Confessing Church's theological training, and their shared uncompromising opposition to National Socialism all leading to a firm friendship. That explains why Perels was one of the people whom Bonhoeffer initiated into the background of his contacts with the military secret service.[6]

Perels's competent, circumspect, and fearless work was one of the pillars of the Confessing Church in Berlin and in its congregations in the wide hinterland of the Protestant church of the Old Prussian Union. Perels was able to work undisturbed as legal adviser for the Confessing Church at least until 1940, but then one of its active members, an attorney, offered him a post in his chambers. There were various reasons for this transfer. Above all, in his previous position he had been unable to advise imprisoned Confessing Church pastors and was himself continually exposed to the danger of arrest. From that time on Perels pursued well-considered and persevering work with those imprisoned, at considerable cost to himself. It was a special kind of pastoral care for the imprisoned; if the term existed, one might call it care for the legal rights of the imprisoned. Yet he still hesitated to join conspiratorial groups. Although his specific work in the service of the Confessing Church was often enough a subversive one, he had not hitherto wished to participate in explicit plans to get rid of the National Socialist regime. But now he took a further decisive step.

What Perels and Bonhoeffer meant to do in October 1941 was to provide objective evidence in objective words for the inhumane measures employed. By recording in writing the proceedings of the state authorities, they wanted to alarm Nazi opponents in military circles and strengthen their readiness to act. Dohnanyi was to see to the duplication of the reports and arrange for their distribution. In this way they would get into the hands of Oster and Beck, and from them be passed on to critics of the regime, above all in military circles, in order to galvanize them into intervention.

Apart from that, the reports were useful for the "chronicle" that Dohnanyi had kept for years. This was also important for Oster and Beck as a dossier of the terror and was continually kept up to date. It was intended to serve as a legitimating basis for a coup d'etat and as a body of evidence against the SS state.[7] Perels's and Bonhoeffer's reports about the deportations of Jews in Berlin also drew attention to other deportations planned and already implemented in other cities; and they are among the first of any such reports in opposition circles.[8]

They also presumably reached the headquarters of the WCC in Geneva, since a member of its staff, Hans Schönfield, happened to be in Berlin at this very time and was able to act as courier. Visser't Hooft, in any event, had himself given an account of the October deportations in his *Notes on the Situation of the Churches* of November 1941. Moreover, a copy of the reports, without a sender's address, was sent by normal post, evidently from Geneva, to William Paton, the English general secretary of the WCC, and was intercepted by the censor. It was thought that it had been sent by Visser't Hooft.

In any case, through these strange channels several copies arrived in diverse English ministries. So in a curious way information that rested on the secret cooperation between Berlin and Geneva nevertheless reached the highest quarters in London.[9]

Arrests, interrogations, collecting points, transports, the number and gravity of acts of violence committed against Jews in Germany—all these increased drastically, quite apart from the inconceivable mistreatment and the murders perpetrated in the conquered territories. From October 1941 at the latest, Jews in Germany had to expect deportation; and from September 1941 they had to wear the yellow star in public places.

One of the people affected was Charlotte Friedenthal. She was a committed and highly qualified member of the staff of the Confessing Church. At that time she was working as secretary, but practically speaking as managing director, of the illegal central office of the Confessing Church in Berlin, the provisional church authority. Her chief, Martin Albertz, its chairman, was also chairman of the examining committee of the Old Prussian Council of Brethren, and as such was responsible for theological training in the Confessing Church. But he had been in the Berlin-Moabit prison for the previous six months. After his arrest in May 1941—the leading administrators of the Confessing Church had been arrested on May 6—Charlotte Friedenthal, together with a small remaining team, had kept the work going. From the beginning, she had been personally and professionally committed to the Confessing Church and was especially active on behalf of "non-Aryan" Christians. Because of her own biography—her Jewish parents had had her baptized as a child—she brought sympathy and never-failing inventiveness to the task of finding practical ways in which the church could help at least those persecuted Jews who were church members and who waited despairingly and generally in vain for their "brothers and sisters in Christ" to intervene on their behalf.

In October 1941 at the latest, after the first wave of Berlin deportations, a way out had to be found for Charlotte Friedenthal herself. The ball was set rolling by her imprisoned chief who, by way of

Perels, instructed Wilhelm Rott, a member of his staff, that Charlotte Friedenthal "should immediately be provided with a chance to emigrate."[10] But where to? Since Charlotte had a cousin living in Lausanne, she hoped that Switzerland might be a possible place of exile, although the immigration policy there was already enforced highly restrictively. Rott turned to Bonhoeffer for help, the two having been on friendly terms since Finkenwalde, where Rott had worked as academic inspector. Could Bonhoeffer's many and varied contacts with influential people in the Swiss churches be of use? Bonhoeffer had meanwhile been reduced to a passive role by his severe pneumonia, but he was able to suggest to Rott a path he could pursue, and he was able to bring into play his contacts with Courvoisier, Freudenberg, Koechlin, and Barth, and not least with Schmidhuber, at the Military Intelligence office in Munich, who was able to deal with the complicated formalities in courier and frontier matters.

Bonhoeffer was also immediately able to put Rott in touch with Jacques Courvoisier, theology professor in Geneva, since in his function as chairman of the prisoners-of-war commission of the WCC, Courvoisier was at that time in Berlin, seeing how the land lay. Courvoisier did not hold out much hope to Rott (who had also asked for his help in two other cases) but promised to do what he could as soon as he was back in Switzerland. Having returned, he appealed immediately to Adolf Freudenberg, the head of the WCC's refugee relief, who again wrote a moving letter to Alphons Koechlin, the president of the Swiss Protestant Church Federation. Almost at the same time, he received "through a messenger," a similarly moving letter from Berlin written by Rott after detailed advice from Perels— Bonhoeffer was already ill—and which came via this unusual postal route through Bonhoeffer's special Munich "office." Rott took this detailed letter to Munich, where he gave it to Schmidhuber, who personally passed it on to Koechlin. Schmidhuber wrote:

> Since around the middle of October, authorities have begun to deport non-Aryans from Berlin and other cities to the East. The entire matter opens the Christian churches to questions and needs that we are almost

helpless to face. We know that your hands are also more or less bound. . . . Our question to you today is whether, by means of an urgent introduction and an official action by the Swiss churches, a door could not perhaps be opened for a very few people or at least for the one single case we especially endorse.[11]

For Charlotte Friedenthal "a door could be opened," but for her alone; and here no small part was played by Karl Barth in Basel. Schmidhuber was also supposed to involve Barth. Did he do so personally in Basel, or by post, or by way of a third person? The question has still never been completely cleared up, and ultimately speaking *how* he did it was not decisive; the important thing was that he did it. Nevertheless, special attention has been drawn to this relatively unimportant detail and to an afterward-discovered, much later letter that touches on the same matter, for they show how illuminating later findings are, however unimportant they may seem at first glance. It again shows how risky it was to document sabotaging and subversive steps against the system and once more sheds light on the dilemma that there could be no written evidence at that time for things of which today we should like to have proof. The letter in question, dated Zürich, October 29, 1941, was found in 1998. It begins, "Dear Baroness," and evidently accompanied a letter from Rott and Bonhoeffer to Barth or Koechlin, a letter that had earlier been presumed but was no longer extant. Up to now it has still not been established who the writer or signatory of this accompanying letter was; but I have good grounds for supposing that the writer was Gisevius.[12]

Barth immediately went into action, and by the beginning of November, by means of dogged and ingenious efforts and with a good deal of persuasion, had finally succeeded in getting the head of the alien branch of the Swiss police in Berlin and the police authorities in the canton of Basel to give Charlotte Friedenthal an entry and resident's visa. Nothing now stood in the way of her emigration to Switzerland. She now needed "only" the agreement of the German emigration authorities and hoped to be in Basel at the beginning of December. But meanwhile the door had been slammed shut from the other side. "The head of the SS and chief of the German police has ordered that the emigration of Jews has from now on to be prevented (the evacuation measures remain unaffected)."[13] This edict of October 23, 1941, had not at first been made public, and Charlotte Friedenthal waited for weeks in vain for her German papers. There was no longer any assent to emigration. There were only "evacuations."

A second attempt was then started to keep her from being deported. Since the beginning of the year she had had to live in a so-called Jewish house but spent most of the time at the house of a friend, in which, incidentally, at that time the Rotts were also living. But this was only seemingly a protection. The only uncertain point was not *if* she would be taken away, but when. "Since this hiding place could at most offer a little security against a surprise move by the Gestapo, Dietrich Bonhoeffer asked his brother-in-law Hans Dohnanyi to place Charlotte Friedenthal under the protection of the Military Intelligence."[14] With this protection it was possible for Charlotte Friedenthal to be several times struck off the deportation lists at the last moment. At the beginning of September 1942 preparations for bringing her into the safety of Swiss exile in another way had been completed via "Operation 7."

This is the name for an action that later became famous: "An action to save those threatened by the Holocaust [initiated] by the Military Intelligence Foreign Office in the Army High Command." That was the subtitle of the pioneer study on Operation 7, and its detailed research findings give an impressive picture of the background and motives, implementation, and consequences of this project.[15] In February 1942, under the impression of the escalating persecution and extermination measures, Dohnanyi resolved to try a daring rescue operation—first on behalf of two lawyers of Jewish origin and their families, who had long been known to him and with whom he had close ties. At the express wish of Canaris, the head of the Military Intelligence, the circle was extended to take in other families too.

Dohnanyi now drew Charlotte Friedenthal into this group as well—"undoubtedly at Bonhoeffer's suggestion."[16] The group was to be smuggled into Switzerland in order to escape the threatened deportations. Thus with the knowledge—more: with the resolute support—of the head of the Military Intelligence, an escape was prepared, first for seven, and in the end for fourteen Jewish men and women, in the form of an ostensibly legal, that is, officially approved, emigration from the German Reich. The trick was that they were to start their journey from Berlin disguised as Intelligence agents, that is, on the instructions of the military secret service, equipped with unexceptionable papers. What appeared to be a "normal" operation under the cloak of the Intelligence was nothing other than the attempt to save fourteen people from extermination.

It was a risky operation, and there were irritations on the personal level, unlooked-for difficulties, and exceptional formal hurdles. When Dohnanyi revealed the plan, one of the people who was to be rescued protested that the rescuees would never be prepared to serve the interests of this concern, that is, the Military Intelligence; but the misunderstanding could quickly be cleared up.[17] Ostensibly they were destined for special missions in South America and were to use Switzerland only as a transit country. This fiction was necessary, especially for SS, Gestapo, and security service spies, who had long cast a suspicious eye on the Military Intelligence, and who would in any case have liked best to divest it of power by means of a "hostile takeover." It was essential that passports and the exceptionally issued permission to leave the country were absolutely watertight; and in order for the "false" agents to travel with genuine papers, the relevant officials in the relevant departments had to be convinced or tricked. At the end of June 1942, during a dinner, Canaris personally got Heinrich Himmler (at that time the head of the Reich Central Security Office) to agree that Jews might be employed as agents, which meant that they had permission to leave the country.

It was not "only" the conditions hitherto usual for emigrants that had to be fulfilled. Additional requirements were a certificate

of good conduct issued by the police, certificates from the tax
authorities and the labor office, saying that there was no objection
from their side, a statement of financial circumstances, the payment of a tax on leaving the country, a baggage check, etc., etc.
All this was left to Dohnanyi's efforts, contacts, and inventiveness.
Complicated financial transactions were also necessary in order to
secure the future material existence of those concerned once they
had emigrated. On the other hand, it had to be ensured that the
people who had emigrated to Switzerland in this curious, apparently legal way were not suspected of being spies and promptly
arrested. This was to be avoided through contacts with church
groups, who were given a certain amount of background information. In these matters Bonhoeffer's excellent relations with Koechlin proved useful.

Numerous bureaucratic hindrances on the side of the Swiss
authorities had to be surmounted. For this purpose Dohnanyi had
to travel to Zürich at the end of August 1942 with a passport made
out under his code name, Dr. Donner, in order to discuss the situation with Hans Bernd Gisevius, the Military Intelligence representative there, and to sound out Swiss contacts.[18] He was equipped with
a written recommendation from Bonhoeffer, his brother-in-law, to
Alphons Koechlin. Koechlin was the chief representative of Swiss
Protestantism and had influence with the authorities in both church
and state. Bonhoeffer had gotten to know him in the 1930s. In his
letter of August 26, 1942, Bonhoeffer wrote:

> May I beg you for the great favor of receiving my
> brother-in-law, who is in Switzerland for a few days and
> will deliver this letter to you, and of assisting him with
> your advice and aid in a situation which lies very close
> to our hearts? I would be extraordinarily grateful to you
> for this.[19]

We do not know whether Dohnanyi presented this letter personally.[20]
But the important thing is that Koechlin did in fact exert his influence vigorously in the proper quarter, that is, with the head of the

alien branch of the police, to whom Barth had turned successfully on behalf of Charlotte Friedenthal at the beginning of November 1941. Her original entry visa had fortunately been extended several times so that she was able to travel even before the final formalities for the other ostensible agents had been completed. She was supposed to take the night train from Berlin to Basel on September 4, 1942. But did she have to wear the yellow star on her journey, or would it be better not to do so? Charlotte Friedental remembered later:

> The sun shone through the windows of my compartment, which I had to myself. A lady watched me from the corridor. Finally she came to me and asked how I was able to travel, since I wore the yellow star and travel was then forbidden. I told her soothingly that everything was in order. . . . The train was an hour late but about 12 o'clock we crossed the frontier. On the station . . . I followed the few travelers . . . I completely forgot or did not notice that I was on Swiss soil. Two officials drew my attention in a friendly way to the fact that I could take off the star. What a moment!! A Swiss official smiled at me and said, "You're in luck." That's a miracle.[21]

The other ostensible agents of the Military Intelligence arrived in Switzerland at the end of September 1942 (a latecomer in the middle of December) and were viewed as out-of-the-ordinary exotics, wearers of the yellow star who had nevertheless managed to escape from persecution. Only a very few knew the background. The rescue operation, "Operation 7," was at an end. For fourteen Jewish men and women there was now a future, and for Charlotte Friedenthal too.

Bonhoeffer unquestionably contributed a not unimportant part to the rescue of Charlotte Friedenthal. But a clear distinction must nevertheless be made between two phases of the action on her behalf. This distinction is frequently ignored because of the account in Bethge's definitive Bonhoeffer biography of 1967. "Rott's efforts for a Swiss entry visa, in which he was helped by Bonhoeffer and Perels . . . were not yet connected with 'Operation 7' set up by the Military Intelligence Foreign Office, as Bethge thought; they had to do only with the—ultimately unsuccessful—attempt to secure a legal emigration for Charlotte Friedenthal." That is an important objection made by a historian.[22] In the initial phase of the attempt to help Charlotte Friedenthal to flee, in the autumn of 1941, Bonhoeffer brought into play his many good relations with Swiss churches and with the Munich Military Intelligence, arranging first contacts, smoothing the way for further important links, and arranging specific courier trips. Steps of this kind were always risky at that time, even if from our secure vantage point, with its reproachful hindsight knowledge, the steps perhaps appear to be only small.

In the second phase of Charlotte Friedenthal's rescue, that is, from the spring of 1942, Bonhoeffer's contribution was to draw in Dohnanyi, so that Charlotte Friedenthal was put under the protection of the Military Intelligence and was "incorporated" into Operation 7. Indirectly, in the course of this rescue operation, his Swiss contacts came into play, and of these Dohnanyi also made use. But Bonhoeffer was not active in either the planning or the implementation of Operation 7, nor could he be. It was a project initiated by Dohnanyi, worked out and put through in the Berlin office under his leadership, evidently like one of the usual Intelligence projects. Apart from Canaris, Dohnanyi's immediate chief, Hans Oster, was initiated with two members of his staff in the central department, Delbrück and Guttenberg, as well as a colleague in the double sense, Helmuth James von Moltke, from another department of the Military Intelligence Foreign Office.[23]

To sum up, it may be said that there is no evidence for a direct link between Bonhoeffer and Operation 7 in the sense that he cooperated with it personally and was therefore able to save fourteen Jews from deportation. What is undisputed is that after the failure of Charlotte Friedenthal's first attempt to escape to Switzerland, he played a large part in having her included by Dohnanyi in Operation 7, and that she was saved as a result. "Under the protection of Bonhoeffer and Dohnanyi"[24] and in the framework of this unusual Military Intelligence project, she was actually able to escape on September 4, 1942, with the permission to enter Switzerland issued a month before, which remained in force for only one more day, with an authentic passport and visa, and with a valid permission to emigrate—and wearing a yellow star, which according to the regulations had to be clearly visible. Perhaps what Bonhoeffer did for her was not much. But for Charlotte Friedenthal it was a great deal.

The detailed description of the conditions under which her rescue took place has been given here not only out of purely historical interest. It was also in order to do justice to Bonhoeffer today. For in today's circumstances, only a reconstruction of the events of the time can help us to avoid from the outset the danger of a blind and excessive idealization of him. This is both dishonest and pointless, and ultimately speaking can only lead to absurd dis(illusion).[25] In addition, the detailed account of this specific historical case and of events in the autumn of 1941 is given because in the present framework that is more necessary than yet another discussion in fundamental terms about the question of "Bonhoeffer and the Jews"[26] or even "the German resistance and the Jews."[27]

From Bonhoeffer himself we learn something, even if only indirectly, about these questions in his *Ethics*. Probably during the spring and winter of 1941 he worked on a text that dealt with the perception of guilt and the admission of guilt, and which he called "Guilt, Justification, Renewal." In this he opposed both the building up of guilt and the minimizing of it; he pointed people to their own responsibility. Sometimes he wrote in the first person: "I cannot pacify myself by saying that my part in all this is slight and hardly noticeable,"[28] and he gave concrete form to the *mea* in the *mea culpa*, "my own most personal guilt": "I am guilty . . . of cowardly silence when I should have spoken; I am guilty of untruthfulness and hypocrisy in the face of threatening violence; I am guilty of disowning without mercy the poorest of my neighbors."[29] It may be that in "the hubris of hindsight"[30] Bonhoeffer did too little for the Jews. But even at that time he understood that it was the guilt of individual Christians and the guilt of Christendom not to have resisted the extermination of Jewish people.

twelve

Is There Such a Thing as Spring?

THE WINTER OF 1941–42 brought the deaths of countless men and women, and the escalation into a world war was irreversible. On December 7, 1941, Japan attacked the United States fleet in Pearl Harbor in Hawaii, and this finally made the global dimension of the war clear. On the following day the United States, Great Britain, and other countries declared war on Japan. Three days later, Germany and Italy declared war on the United States. At the same time the German attack on the Soviet Union came to a halt before Moscow, and the German troops were pushed back by a Russian counter-offensive. Hitler took the opportunity presented by this stall in the Russian campaign to dismiss the army's commander in chief, Field Marshal Walther von Brauchitsch, and to take over the post himself. On January 20, 1942, the Wannsee conference decided under Heydrich's leadership on what was called in Nazi language "the final solution of the Jewish question." And with that the systematic extermination of European Jewry was only a question of time.

The opponents of the regime and the war had to come to terms with their disappointment over the change in the high command. For Brauchitsch had shown himself to be at least no longer completely opposed to their plans for an overthrow. So a lever, at least in tendency, for a coup d'etat at the highest military level had now been removed. Under the impression of the unrestrainedly growing inhumanity of the Nazi system in every sector—the brutal conduct of the war and the undermining of international law, the systematic extermination of Jews especially, the cynical disregard of human dignity, and the permanent oppression within Germany itself—since the autumn of 1941, the hopes of the conspirators had grown, and the communication network between the different cells had become denser. So now Dohnanyi, the "special leader" in Department Z of the Military Intelligence Foreign Office, met more often with Helmuth James Graf von Moltke, who worked in the same building in the field of international law and who was the initiator of the resistance group that came to be known as the Kreisau circle.[1]

Dohnanyi also conferred more frequently with the former German ambassador in Rome, Ulrich von Hassell, who had been retired against his will and was now a member of the resistance. We learn about the numerous contacts developed during these months by these three negotiators on behalf of the resistance through Christine Dohnanyi's diary, through Moltke's letters to his wife, Freya, and through Hassell's journals. It would not be true to say that they are *the* "mirror of a plot,"[2] but they do reflect something of the everyday existence of the conspirators. Vague hints and encoded information, code words and ciphers, abbreviations and pseudonyms were all necessary for communication under a dictatorship. "Resistance made disguised language necessary,"[3] and inventive minds were needed to deal with codes and espionage channels.

For example, "Ulrich" was the pseudonym used by Hans and Christine Dohnanyi for Goerdeler, while for Hassell he was "Pfaff."

Hassell called Dohnanyi "Freda," probably after his secretary in the Intelligence, while Beck was "Geibel" and Oster "Hase." The "Josephs" were the generals. "Emil" came to be the name used for Hitler. In Bonhoeffer's correspondence, which contains a number of code names for people, actions, and events, a certain "Onkel Rudi" (Uncle Rudy) continually turns up. His name was used when the subject was the outbreak of the war or its progress. News about arrests was passed on in a roundabout way. For example, on February 8, 1941, Bonhoeffer wrote to his friend Bethge from Ettal monastery, telling him that the Munich prelate Neuhäusler had been arrested: "On Wednesday N. in M. suddenly became ill and went into hospital: The diagnosis is still uncertain (might he have brought home a disease from the mission field?) and it is possible he may need specialized treatment."[4] Specialized treatment is in fact just what he received—in concentration camps in Sachsenhausen and Dachau.

A necessarily "divided trust"[5] also played a not unimportant role in communicating even with people whom one knew well—for the protection of both parties. Oskar Hammelsbeck, one of Bonhoeffer's comrades-at-arms in the Confessing Church, reported later that Bonhoeffer had told him about his participation in the conspiracy but had kept strictly to the principle: no names![6] Important though relationships of trust were within the individual resistance groups, the links between them were important too, and as frequent an exchange of information as was possible. Yet in both cases certain unwritten laws were unavoidable; the groups had sometimes actually to cut themselves off from each other. Precautions of this kind were necessary for reasons of security in the "normal" everyday life of the conspirators. Above all, they were vitally necessary in case one of them should be arrested and tortured. "The most elementary precautions demanded that one knew only what was absolutely necessary, and above all that one knew as little as possible about the identity of the people involved."[7] Under the conditions of the contact system used by the conspirators, central figures might not even know each other personally at all, even though they knew a great deal about each other and did the groundwork for each other. Hans

Oster and Henning von Tresckow, for example, are supposed never to have never met personally.[8]

Caution was even required in one's own family circle, so as not to endanger the children or oneself unnecessarily. Emmi Bonhoeffer, Klaus Bonhoeffer's widow, recalled one small incident: one day her son's teacher called her and said that she ought to be a bit more careful about expressing her political views to her children. In an essay about the invasion of Czechoslovakia, her son had written, "Only a few Germans are living there, and they are at daggers drawn with the Czechs. I hope the Führer won't find himself in trouble there." Emmi Bonhoeffer's comment was that "he had probably picked up something at table and misunderstood it. It is true that we were a bit careless where the children were concerned."[9] Everyday life was a strain in general. During the day there was the usual work, at night secret meetings. "As far as the *daily* routine goes, I would rather talk about a *nightly* routine. For everything had to happen at night, and everything had to be only by word of mouth. One couldn't even telephone or write letters."[10] During the nightly meetings held in her house, she herself used to walk round the block, so as to see whether the house was under observation.[11]

The fact that for reasons of security direct contacts by word of mouth were given absolute priority became a matter of course. Telephone calls were risky, and letters and notes were always dangerous. As we know, that has led to the dilemma that today written records for the resistance are sparse.[12] Perels's widow told that her husband used the telephone only for conversations to which anyone could listen in. He telephoned a great deal, but always from public telephone booths. Whenever he made a written note, he considered carefully whether he should write it at all, and if so, how he should formulate it.[13] Hans von Dohnanyi decided in the winter of 1942 to destroy all notes of a personal nature and in the future to dispense with any more written records. Christine von Dohnanyi acted differently. From the beginning of 1942 she kept a diary, apparently harmless, a kind of journal—the notes of a housewife and mother, wife and hostess.[14] She records numerous visits by her brother Dietrich and his friend Bethge. Bethge, for his part, noted that Bonhoeffer now also met his brother Klaus more often. For example on January 23, 1942,[15] he met him at the "Venetia" café in Berlin, together with Moltke, Guttenberg, and Dohnanyi's assistant Delbrück.

Although the opposition had hoped that it was gaining ground and was moving closer to the goal of an overthrow and a new beginning, this optimism was once again considerably damped, particularly by the depressing situation both at home and in foreign relations. At the beginning of February 1942, Hassell felt constrained to say that "everyone feels somewhat intimidated."[16] Oster and Dohnanyi had been warned by what we should today call "well-informed sources" that the security service was trying to keep certain people and activities in the Military Intelligence Foreign Office under closer surveillance. However, for Oster and Dohnanyi, in spite of this writing on the wall, the motto was "business as usual."

From November 1941, because of his severe pneumonia, Bonhoeffer was at first only able to operate to a limited extent. He had spent December convalescing in his "refuge," the Kleist-Retzow estate at Kieckow, but was in Berlin during the first months of the new year. He could now go on working on his *Ethics* and could send his circular pastoral letters to his "brethren" or former students at the front. At the end of October 1941, Ruth von Kleist-Retzow had written to him in Berlin, asking him about these letters, "What has happened to your letter to the brothers?"[17] And she saw to the practical arrangements involved. While he was staying in his country retreat, she wrote from Stettin, saying, "I still have five hundred sheets of typing paper and two hundred sheets of office paper ready for you, as well as one hundred envelopes. . . . What should we do with them now? Should I send the package to Berlin? Or do you still need it in Kieckow?"[18]

By means of these circular letters, Bonhoeffer tried to keep up his connections and personal ties with former members of the Finkenwalde seminary. The most difficult thing he had to do was to tell them about the men who had meanwhile been killed in action. He did not try to put a fine patriotic gloss over the pain, the horror, and the absurdity of these deaths in war. His concern was to let the former members of his seminary feel, even in the border situation of the war that faced them every day, that they could be sustained by faith; but he did so without whitewashing the grief and despair. In unpretentious, matter-of-course words, he picked up the experience they shared—the knowledge that they were in safekeeping with God. This "nevertheless" of faith was not a rebellious, defensive nevertheless. It was a trusting one, in Job's sense. It was anchored in the assurance of God and was held fast in the language of hope. In the circular letter of the beginning of March 1942, he writes:

> Today, March 1, is the first day a warm spring sun has shone; the snow is dropping from the eaves, the air is clear, and the earth is beginning to appear again. Our thoughts are with you who in the past months have endured unimaginable things on the front and during the winter, wishing for you that the sun and warmth and earth will soon give you joy again. "He gives snow like wool; he scatters frost like ashes. . . . Who can stand before his cold? He sends out his word, and melts them; he makes his wind blow, and the waters flow" (Psalm 147). God will one day break even the winter and the night of evil and allow a spring of grace and joy to draw nigh.[19]

On this first day of March 1942 all seven Lutheran bishops in occupied Norway resigned in protest against the spirit and practice of the German occupying power and the policies of the prime minister, Vidkun Quisling, whom the Germans had appointed exactly a month previously and who was zealously subservient to the Germans. Within a month the conflict spread. Eivind Berggrav, the bishop of Oslo, was put under house arrest on April 2. On Easter Sunday (which fell on April 5 in 1942) this measure led to a confrontation between the church and the Norwegian resistance movement on the one side, and the pro-Nazi government and the occupying power on the other. Out of solidarity with the action of their bishops, and in protest against the jettisoning of Berggrav, the Norwegian clergy resigned from their pastorates in the state church. On April 8, Berggrav was arrested. Bonhoeffer was again visiting Lower Pomerania over Easter. But on the day when Berggrav was arrested, Dohnanyi recalled him by telephone to Berlin, and on April 9, in his brother-in-law's house, he was given more precise instructions for the journey on which he was to start on the following morning. His destination was to be Oslo. The official purpose was to minimize the damage done through the bishop's arrest. But the secret purpose was to encourage further resistance. Moltke was to accompany him.

Helmuth James Graf von Moltke was the great-great-grandson of the Prussian field marshal Helmuth Graf von Moltke. But he had not taken up a military career. He had studied jurisprudence and constitutional law in Berlin, was a doctor of law and the owner of the Kreisau estate in Silesia. From boyhood he had had a special affinity with the Anglo-Saxon world. He had spent a good deal of time in England, spoke perfect English, and had also completed a legal training there. He was opposed to the Nazi regime from the beginning and therefore found it impossible, even in 1933, to take up a post as judge. Instead, he decided to work as an attorney. The outbreak of war put an end to his plan to settle in England as a barrister. As war service, he was made responsible for questions of martial and international law in the foreign division of the military secret service under the army high command—in fact the Military Intelligence Foreign Office, where at the same time Hans von Dohnanyi took up his job as "special leader" and member of Oster's staff.

In numerous cases, by means of submissions, applications, and counsel's opinions, Moltke succeeded in quashing infringements of the most elemental principles of martial and international law, and in fact was able "to prevent worse things from happening."[20] What was specifically in question were methods of waging war, the treatment and mistreatment of prisoners of war, actions against partisans, and the taking of hostages, things that made a mockery of all war conventions. In 1943, by means of a risky personal intervention, he helped to have the Danish Jews warned in time about their threatened deportation, so that most of them got away to Sweden.

In the same way he warned Norway about raids against the Jews, so that rescuing transports to Sweden could be organized. In this way he unquestionably later achieved what he had once tried to do in the autumn of 1941, "to put at least an obstructive spoke in the wheel of the Jewish persecution."[21] Moltke's letters to his wife, Freya, show the degree to which he suffered under the burden of the information with which he was daily confronted through his work.

From 1940 onward, Moltke, "an advocate for the future,"[22] together with Peter Yorck von Wartenburg developed ideas and increasingly specific plans for "the time afterward"—for a democratic Germany that would have said no to the incessant infringement of human rights, and which would find a new place in "the family of man." Up to now, practical plans for an overthrow were still far from his mind. But through diverse contacts arising from his work, as well as through personal friendships, an oppositional group, at first loosely organized, gradually came together and met regularly in Berlin and at Moltke's Kreisau estate. In the context of the German resistance as a whole, this group was specially characterized by the fact that people of very different ways of thinking belonged to it. There were conservatives, liberals, Social Democrats, and socialists, Protestants from both the Confessing and the "official" Protestant church, as well as Catholic priests. What many of those close to the Kreisau circle had in common was that they lived from the Christian faith that provided their common foundation. This was especially true of their two "prophets," Moltke and Yorck von Wartenburg. Among those who belonged to the inner circle of the group, and whose paths crossed Bonhoeffer's during those years, we may mention as examples Hans Bernd von Haeften and Adam von Trott of the Foreign Ministry, the theologian Eugen Gerstenmaier, who belonged to the External Affairs Office of the official Protestant church (the DEK, or Deutsche Evangelische Kirche), and Karl Ludwig von Guttenberg, who was a member of Dohnanyi's staff. And another was Theodor Steltzer.

Bonhoeffer got to know Steltzer in Norway. He had a doctorate in economics and was transport officer on the staff of General von Falkenhorst, who was head of the German High Command in Norway. At the same time he developed excellent relations with the Norwegian church and the Norwegian resistance (the two in fact belonged together) and had had good contacts with the Swedish church in addition. He was a friend of Moltke's and was politically associated with him through their work in the Kreisau group. He was active in the liturgically interested Brotherhood of St. Michael and in the Confessing Church. Steltzer's straightforward sincerity was once laconically judged (in whichever sense one wishes to take the word) by saying that "his strong confessional ties largely determined everything he thought and did."[23] It only remains to add that he enjoyed a lasting friendship with Bishop Berggrav, who in occupied Norway counted as the symbol par excellence of the resistance; and this was even more so after the reprisals against the bishop and the Easter disturbances in Oslo in 1942.[24]

These Easter disturbances were now the background for Moltke's and Bonhoeffer's Norwegian mission. The tense atmosphere in the Norwegian population irritated the occupying power. On the German side, following the bishop's spectacular resignation at the beginning of March, and even more after the still more spectacular act of solidarity on the part of the clergy at the beginning of April, the authorities were nervous. As if that were not enough, the protest had been compounded for weeks by a boycott and strikes by teachers out of protest against the edict forcing all Norwegian young people to become members of an organization similar to the Hitler Youth. The Norwegian prime minister Quisling, leader of the Fascist *Nasjonal Samling*, was always ready to oblige the German commissar, Terboven, and was himself always true to the Nazi line; and he insisted on obedience to the occupying power of "Greater Germany." Among the Norwegian people, collaborating "quislings" on the one side were matched by members of the resistance movement "Milorg" on the other. The Norwegian church, at least to a large part, tried to resist the government (which existed by grace of the Germans) as well as the occupying power itself, and was prepared for strikes and sabotage to the point of direct resistance.

Steltzer, who tried to make contact with Norwegian resistance circles through the Norwegian church, regularly enjoyed the useful honor of dining with the highest army representative in Norway, Nikolaus von Falkenhorst. On these occasions he was the recipient, in passing, of the most recent information from the German Reich commissar and the prime minister, and he had no hesitation in passing this on to the appropriate quarter. Steltzer had discussed with Moltke particularly the unstable mood of the people in general and the massive reservations in the church toward the people in power. "Moltke and I had agreed on a special word which would be a sign that Berggrav had been arrested."[25] Under this code word, he informed the regime opponents in the Berlin Military Intelligence Foreign Office by telegram that the arrest of the Oslo bishop was immediately impending. In view of this, and because of the protests that followed among the Norwegian people, the Intelligence decided to intervene, sending two people with a double assignment: "After the receipt of this telegram Canaris and Oster decided to send two members of their staff to Oslo, to clarify the situation."[26] For this assignment Moltke and Bonhoeffer were chosen.

Entirely in line with their official status, Moltke was assigned to the army high command as the member of staff responsible for foreign affairs in the Military Intelligence Foreign Office, while Bonhoeffer was sent as an expert in church affairs. The two were intended to approach leading political quarters, to make sure that army interests in Norway were safeguarded. The motto was to be *pas de vagues*—"Just don't attract any attention!" In practical terms that meant no unnecessary unrest among the people, no conflicts with a rebellious church, no unnecessary provocations, such as the arrest of a prominent churchman, no attacks or sabotage to bring the army into difficulties. The conspiratorial side of the mission, on the other hand, was supposed to support the Norwegian church in its readiness to resist and to establish links with the Norwegian resistance.

The course of the Norwegian journey undertaken by Moltke and Bonhoeffer can be broadly reconstructed. For this we have Bonhoeffer's still extant handwritten diary entries for April 10 to 18,

1942,[27] and, in much more detail, the sometimes highly amusing letters Moltke wrote to his wife during these days.[28] On April 9, a Thursday, he gave her a broad outline of the plans for his journey and mentions at the end: "On Friday morning Dohnanyi and Bonhoeffer are coming to me at 8:15, and the train leaves at 10."[29] The train left at 10:35 from the Stettin station in Berlin in the direction of the island of Rügen; and the two travelers to the north were forced to make a long intermediate stop at the port of Sassnitz on the east coast of the island because the ferry that plied between there and Sweden had stuck fast in the ice.

Bonhoeffer notes that they spent the night in the Victoria Hotel, and from there Moltke wrote to his wife, not precisely with enthusiasm: "Now we're off to have dinner and are then going to the cinema. I let myself be talked into it because I didn't want to desert the good Bonhoeffer."[30] But the next morning things seemed to Moltke much more promising. He told his wife about a long walk they took together, and about their onward journey to Oslo:

> I was keen to take this walk because I wanted to clarify our game plan, and it seemed to me easier to do this during a walk than in the hotel room. We then walked from 9 until 1:30, I should think about 6 km, to the chalk cliffs of Stubbenkammer, and about the same distance back, the whole way through beech woods, high above the sea. . . . Apart from a woodcutter we didn't meet a soul. We were also able to reach some conclusions that have proved satisfactory, at least up to now.

In the afternoon they were actually able to continue their journey by ferry to Trelleborg—a sea voyage during which Moltke suffered greatly, both psychologically and physically.

> The ship was comfortable, the other passengers simply embarrassingly awful. I should really have liked only to talk English in order to dissociate myself from that band of thieves and louts. Apart from one or two people who

were bearable, the stewards, and a few German fore-
men, who were going third class, there was no one on
the ship except the scum of the German lower middle
classes.

They were hopelessly late in arriving, and that day only got as
far as Malmö. After a train journey lasting many hours, they finally
arrived at their destination, the Norwegian capital, at midnight on
the night from Sunday to Monday, April 13, 1942.

At 12 we were in Oslo, where Steltzer met us at the
station and took us to the hotel, where I am lodged in a
huge, princely suite, half drawing room, half bedroom,
with bathroom etc, on the belle étage; whereas my companion, as he is called here, has a room on the third
floor.[31]

According to Bonhoeffer's pocket diary, they stayed at the Grand
Hotel in Oslo for three days and carried out an intensive program of
discussions, one official and one unofficial, the first on the business
for which they had been officially sent, the other subversive. "Bonhoeffer and I always ate together in my room, because that gave us
the best opportunity to coordinate our plans for the day."[32] Moltke
held official discussions—apparently without Bonhoeffer—mainly
with high-ranking members of the army and the civil administration, for example, with the heads of the Military Intelligence office
in Oslo, with the immediate staff of the commander in chief in Norway, or with the commander in chief, General Nikolaus von Falkenhorst himself. He lunched with him, but only with some discomfort:
"On Wednesday evening I didn't eat at all because I felt rotten and
didn't want to give my body the additional labor of digestion," he
wrote to his wife. "The general is really a dreadful piece of work. He
is incapable of listening, holds forth in monologues, tells silly stories
and is really quite extraordinarily stupid."[33]

Moltke felt happier about the unofficial meetings, especially the
(outwardly completely legal) meeting with Theodor Steltzer. Moltke

felt rather unwell during the whole journey because of a feverish cold: "Perhaps that was the reason why his Norwegian hosts thought he looked like St. Sebastian."[34] He found the arrangements made for them on Monday evening (probably by Steltzer) "the high spot of our stay." "At 8:30 for the first time we visited three quite splendid Norwegians, who entertained Steltzer, Bonhoeffer, and myself to a positively princely meal, luckily with a lot of coffee, so that I got over my tiredness. The talk went on until 1:30, which was really a bit too long."[35]

It seems that the Norwegians who took part in this meeting on the evening of April 13 were two pastors who were actively involved in the struggle of the Norwegian churches, and the painter Henrik Sörensen, a friend of Bishop Berggrav; or it may have been the professor of sociology Arvid Brodersen, who was a friend of Steltzer's and belonged to the Norwegian resistance. The reports we have and specific recollections from people who might have been there leave us uncertain as to who was definitely present on that evening and what people involved in the discussion remembered in detail, especially about Bonhoeffer.[36] There seems to be no doubt, however, that discussion turned to the explosive atmosphere connected with the struggle of the Norwegian churches, the future of Bishop Berggrav, the internal links between the church opposition and the Norwegian resistance movement, and potential links with German opposition groups.[37]

Whereas Moltke was most concerned with the last of these complexes, Bonhoeffer saw his function as being to support the Norwegian church in its rejection of Nazi thinking and its system of oppression. Were these his past dreams about an unequivocal and consistent testimony in the church to the Christian life? He probably remembered his own vain hopes nine years previously, when he looked for resignations and a strike by the clergy. In any case, he tried to cheer the Norwegian Protestants, encouraged them not to weaken in their protest and not to surrender the difficult path they had chosen in exchange for one smoother and more compliant. A Lutheran church that said "Yes" and "Amen" to every authority would no longer be a church that could appeal to the name of the Reformer himself. The conversations begun on this evening were continued. In any event, as Moltke told his wife, there was again "a discussion from 3:30 until 8 with the three Norwegians of the previous evening, in order to settle details. B. had plans to meet another [Norwegian] discussion partner."[38]

Moltke and Bonhoeffer spent three days in Oslo. Bonhoeffer's diary and Moltke's letters to his wife show that they left the capital for Stockholm by train on April 16, a Thursday.[39] Writing to his wife about his Oslo visit, Moltke summed up: "Practically speaking, I have the impression that it was a success, both the ostensible and the concealed part. I was at one with all the soldiers involved— except for the general—about the content of my report to Admiral Canaris and its requests, and for me that was of course very important." He again mentions to her the account of the situation that was designed for Canaris, apparently quite suddenly at the end of April, in a letter from Berlin, after she had visited him there. They had evidently talked the matter over together: "This morning the opus has gone off to Bonhoeffer, and tomorrow morning he will bring it back. So I hope that tomorrow I can say goodbye to it in the course of the day."[40]

Moltke's and Bonhoeffer's double game was unquestionably extremely risky. Officially they had to play down the problem, soothe the people involved, get the exceedingly nervous occupation authorities to relax—all this ostensibly in the interests of the army. Yet in fact their aim was to strengthen the attempts at resistance in the Norwegian church and among the people. And there is also no doubt that the two were fully aware of the risk. For example, the day before he left, on April 9, 1942, Bonhoeffer wrote a short note to his friend Bethge with only the following message: "Just in case, you should know that it is my wish for you someday to receive my books, musical instruments, and pictures."[41] Their journey was without any doubt a conspirational one, and in what they were doing they were risking their lives. It was not just an honest attempt, it was more: it was an attempt worthy of the greatest respect.

An idealization of the kind that followed (even if unintentionally) at the end of the war and in the succeeding years is therefore
superfluous. But the Norwegian journey demonstrates in several
ways the small but important distortions of the picture of Bonhoeffer to which this idealization occasionally led. One example
touches on Bonhoeffer's effectiveness in Norway. In 1957, fifteen
years after the journey, Bishop Berggrav, in a letter to Theodor
Steltzer, recalled the impression that Bonhoeffer left behind him
among his Norwegian discussion partners during those days. He
wrote, "Bonhoeffer seems to have made a deep impression. First,
because he was the member of a commission, and second because
he said so little."[42] But both in Bethge's splendid biography and the
equally splendid volume 16 of Bonhoeffer's works, only the beginning of the reminiscence is quoted; Bonhoeffer seemed to have
made a deep impression.[43] In his biography Bethge quotes another
passage from Berggrav's letter to Steltzer: "Bonhoeffer insisted on
resistance *à outrance*—even as far as martyrdom." But Steltzer himself, in a letter written to Bethge a short time later, pointed out that
he was doubtful "whether Bonhoeffer really insisted on substantial
resistance to the point of martyrdom. To me he never said anything
of the kind."[44]

A second example touches on the importance of Moltke and
Bonhoeffer for the fate of the Norwegian bishop Berggrav. In recording the events in Norway during those days in April, an inescapable question is what really happened to the bishop of Oslo at that
time. As already mentioned, before Easter he had been put under
house arrest, and after Easter he was imprisoned, two days before
Bonhoeffer and Moltke left Norway. Influence was brought to bear
from the highest quarters in Berlin to damp down events in Norway. The German Reich commissar, Terboven, received a telegram
from Himmler himself, the head of the SS, asking him why Berggrav
(whom Himmler knew personally) was being kept in custody. On
April 13, the Monday that was the very first day of Moltke's and
Bonhoeffer's stay in Oslo, and that ended with the evening meeting that Moltke touched on so enthusiastically, people in Norway

expected that Berggrav would be brought before a "people's court" by the Quisling government and would be condemned. Contrary to this expectation, nothing of the kind happened. Instead, on Wednesday another telegram arrived in Oslo from Berlin, this time sent by Martin Bormann, the head of the Party Chancellery, instructing the authorities to release Berggrav immediately.

A day later, on April 16, Berggrav was in fact released from prison, although he was supposed to be immediately interned for three years in his "country house," the legendary Wildhütte in Asker, not far from Oslo.[45] During the internment that followed, the bishop—an exponent of the church's refusal to obey the occupying power and an informant for the Norwegian resistance—managed to keep up these subversive contacts in an astonishing way, incidentally with the help of his prison guards.

> The guards told the bishop that they were on his side and were ready to do everything they could for him. If he wanted to go into the town, he could put on the uniform of one of the policemen. A dummy was then placed in his bed, and when the guards changed they were told, "The bishop is asleep." One day I was very urgently asked by the bishop's brother to come for a talk. As we were sitting together, the door opened, a Norwegian policeman came up to me and showed me his badge. I was a bit surprised and not very happy about the situation. Then the policeman took off his little moustache and asked, "Don't you know me any more, Steltzer?" It was the bishop. I asked, astonished, "How did you managed to get here [to Oslo]?" and he replied, "With the suburban train."[46]

The fact that Moltke and Bonhoeffer were sent to Norway at the height of the disputes about the Oslo bishop and of the Norwegian church's struggle generally, and the circumstance that they left the country again on the very day when Berggrav was released from prison, at first sight suggests an inescapable causality. And in fact, the coincidence in time between the events surrounding Berggrav's arrest and Moltke's and Bonhoeffer's mission to Norway and their stay there—in a word, their Oslo mission—has in the past sometimes led to conclusions that would seem to be self-evident, but which are in fact hardly tenable. Their official task was to analyze the situation and—as far as possible—to calm things down. Formally, they came as emissaries from the Military Intelligence, although in fact as spies for the German opposition.

As the events were later reconstructed, it seemed obvious (though it was mistaken) to interpret the role they in fact played as belonging together with Berggrav's "amnesty."[47] Intentionally or unintentionally, the impression at least was given that Berggrav was released from prison through their intervention.[48] All that need be said here was already said more than twenty-five years ago by a competent source. The fact that Berggrav was again only put under house arrest instead of remaining in prison was probably at the insistance of Himmler (and Bormann). "It certainly had nothing to do with any ideas the two emissaries may have had."[49] In order to avoid misunderstanding, it should emphatically be pointed out here that neither Moltke nor Bonhoeffer require any interpretative idealization of this kind. The way they thought and acted during these years—and here specifically in connection with the journey to Norway—was an example of firm resistance toward the Nazi dictatorship, even if we are not obliged to ascribe to them a degree of influence and power that neither of them in actual fact possessed.

Moltke and Bonhoeffer returned to Germany via Stockholm, and here we are once again on firm historical ground. Moltke's official assignment was to confer with the German ambassador in the Swedish capital about business conflicts between Sweden and the German occupying power in Norway; and he took the opportunity of this neutral ground to send a long letter to his English friend Lionel Curtis, part of which runs as follows:

> We now have a realistic chance to persuade our people
> to at last get rid of this reign of terror, if only we can
> show them some prospect at the end of the frightful and

hopeless future that is imminent. A prospect that would make it worthwhile for the disappointed people to strive for, work for, and believe in, and for which it would be worth making a new beginning. For us, Europe after the war is not so much a matter of frontiers and soldiers, complicated organizations or great plans. Europe after the war is the question of how the image of the human being can be restored in the hearts of our people? . . . Can you imagine what it means to work as a group when one cannot use the telephone, when one can't mention the names of one's best friends to other friends, for fear one of them might be caught and that the names could be betrayed under pressure?[50]

Bonhoeffer also took the chance offered by this neutral ground to write to his twin sister Sabine Leibholz and her family in London. When he was talking about the political situation, he used the internal family codes, in which "Uncle Rudy" was the code name for Hitler's conduct of the war:

When I wrote to you last I thought Uncle Rudy would not live much longer, but in January and February he recovered a little though I am quite convinced only for a very short time. He is so weak that I and my people do not believe that he can live longer than a few months.[51]

On April 18 the two emissaries flew back to Berlin from Malmö via Copenhagen, and apparently went immediately to the central office. Bethge later recalled that he collected his friend from the Military Intelligence Foreign Office. Bonhoeffer was very much taken with the days he had spent with Moltke and found them "stimulating." But Bethge also remembered him saying, ". . . but we are not of the same opinion."[52]

At first glance there was more in common between Moltke and Bonhoeffer than what divided them. The facts of their lives were almost identical, and in the recollection of those that came after them they were leading figures and representatives of the resistance.

The parallels are obvious, but they cannot and should not disguise the differences, even the contrasts, between the two. They were both markedly Anglophile, and their close contacts with England were an intrinsic part of both their biographies. Their friendships bridged Great Britain and the Continent, and lasted over the years, surviving the enmity between their two countries. "I now have more friends in London than I have in Berlin," reported Moltke in 1937 from England; the important thing for him, as he already wrote in 1935 to Lionel Curtis, was to keep up "ties with the wider world."[53]

Both Bonhoeffer and Moltke were immune from National Socialist thinking and its ruling system from the beginning of the Nazi era, Moltke being a convinced republican, Bonhoeffer a Confessing Christian. Both were practicing Christians with Protestant backgrounds. Moltke grew up in the Lutheran tradition but early on came into contact with Christian Science.[54] He was originally somewhat reserved in questions of faith and only arrived at a fully developed, personal devotional life through the experiences of dictatorship and resistance. Bonhoeffer's churchmanship was originally Protestant-Lutheran in character and was later influenced by the dialectical theology of Karl Barth. It was largely his faith that fired his oppositional attitude to the Nazi dictatorship. Moltke and Bonhoeffer were at one in their uncompromising rejection of the "Thousand-Year Reich" and in the resolute character of their faith.[55]

We know very little about their relationship to each other. "The affinity between the thinking of Moltke and Bonhoeffer is inescapable. It is not that the two were in any way personally attuned to each other."[56] As far as their personal relationship is concerned, apart from Moltke's already quoted comments in his letters from Oslo and Stockholm during their time together there, we have no further comments from the two directly concerned. We know only what was said by the two people who, at least at that time, were closest to them: in Bonhoeffer's case, his friend Eberhard Bethge; in Moltke's, his wife, Freya von Moltke.

According to her reminiscences, the two discovered on their Norway journey "that they did not have much to say to each other.

Moltke, the squire, was not on the same wavelength as, and indeed was a bit bored by and impatient with the man of the Book,"[57] and this Norwegian journey was evidently also the last occasion in which the two encountered each other. In any case, it was and remained their only joint undertaking. "Moltke and Bonhoeffer probably never met again, although they were both Christians and both inexorable opponents of Hitler. But Moltke already had good connections with the Protestant church and did not want to expand the circle of his personal contacts unnecessarily."[58] Bethge's explanation of why the two had no further contact after their return from Norway is not dissimilar. But he explains the explicit disagreement between them— Bonhoeffer's "we were not of the same opinion"—by saying that Bonhoeffer, unlike Moltke, pleaded that the assassination of Hitler was necessary, unexpected though this opinion might seem for an ordained member of the church.[59] Moltke worked energetically for the end of the regime and was not prepared to exclude a coup d'etat outright; but he was nevertheless unable to accept plans to murder Hitler. At least at this point, he was still against an attempt to assassinate the dictator: "Moltke fought against this—unlike Bonhoeffer— for reasons of principle."[60] One of these principles was that wrong could not be combated by wrong, and that the machinery of murder could not be stopped by murder; and Moltke found it hard to call this principle in question.[61]

In any event, his companion on the Norwegian journey in April 1942 did not arrive at an easy answer. A remark he once made in the house of his sister Christine and his brother-in-law Hans von Dohnanyi was probably made during the last weeks of 1941. He was talking about the problem of whether a coup d'etat was conceivable and possible without the previous assassination of Hitler, and said, according to his biographer, that "if it fell to him to carry out the deed he was ready to do so, but that he must first resign, formally and officially, from his Church, as the Church could not shield him, and he had no wish to claim its protection." However, Bethge immediately qualified this statement by saying, "That was certainly a theoretical position, for Bonhoeffer knew nothing about how to handle guns or explosives."[62] Of course, what Bonhoeffer said was purely hypothetical, for at that time the notion that he might ever be given the chance to assassinate Hitler was hardly realistic And yet it throws light on the path Bonhoeffer pursued in the conspiracy. It was one that he was deliberately prepared to take without the backup of his church—and one that in the end he did in fact have to take.

In spite of the personal differences of which Moltke and Bonhoeffer were themselves evidently aware, and in spite of some differences in their philosophies and backgrounds, there was one especially striking affinity between them: their no to National Socialism did not merely embrace the risk to their own existence but was also deliberately prepared to pay the price of the defeat of their own nation. The two were not afraid to risk their own lives, not out of any yearning for martyrdom but out of the readiness for what Bonhoeffer termed in the manuscript for his *Ethics* (probably written in the summer of 1942) "willingness to become guilty."[63] Where they were divided, at least in 1942, was in the question about an assassination attempt on Hitler; at that time they disagreed about a yes to this murder, a political murder out of the most extreme necessity. They were at one in their awareness of their own share in the guilt. The closeness of their thinking is reflected—in its ambivalence too—in a passage in one of the letters Moltke wrote to his friend Curtis in the April of 1942 from the stopover he and Bonhoeffer made in Stockholm. He wrote:

> Perhaps you may remember that in our discussions before the war I said that I thought that belief in God was not essential in order to arrive at the point where we now are. Today I know that I was wrong—completely and utterly wrong. You know that from the very first day I have fought against the Nazis, but the degree of endangerment and the readiness for sacrifice which is required of us today, and will perhaps be required of us tomorrow, presupposes more than sound ethical principles, especially since we know that the success of our struggle will probably mean the total collapse of our national unity But we are willing to face that.[64]

thirteen

Under
Suspicion

ON MAY 11, 1942, Bonhoeffer set off on a journey to Switzerland for
the third time during the war. It was a journey not without irritations. We have no more than suppositions about its specific intentions, and these seem to come to an abrupt end. The progress of the
journey can be more or less precisely reconstructed from parts of
the still extant letters from both Bonhoeffer and Barth. But its place
in the conspiracy remains cloudy. The picture of this journey is like
a mosaic that cannot be properly fitted together. It is overshadowed
by disappointment, misunderstandings, and mistrust; but it is also
marked by elements of trust, joy, and friendship.

Bonhoeffer's first stop was Zurich, where he probably met Hans
Bernd Gisevius, the representative there of the Military Intelligence
Foreign Office. This meeting probably took place at the beginning
of his stay, but perhaps only toward its end. In any case, he passed
on Gisevius's Zurich address to Barth, in case Barth was able and
willing in the future to supply him in Germany with books.[1] He,

Bonhoeffer, would then willingly act as a "lending library" for other interested people, and Gisevius would willingly act as messenger; moreover, Gisevius himself was very anxious to meet Barth again.[2] In any event, on May 12–13 Bonhoeffer was again the guest in Zurich of some friends of Barth's, as he had already been once before. Afterward, also as before, he visited Otto Salomon, formerly his editor at Christian Kaiser Verlag. At the same time, incidentally, Barth wrote from Basel to Otto Salomon:

> I hear that Mr. Bonhoeffer is already in the country. I knew of his coming from the police here, who enquired of me regarding clearance for his entry. Would you quietly suggest to him that he be most circumspect when discussing politics with Swiss people? If I discern rightly, German public credibility has sunk considerably since he was last here.[3]

However, Salomon was unable "quietly" to pass on this piece of advice to Bonhoeffer, since the latter first intended to follow up his days in Zurich by withdrawing for a week or so to a guesthouse on Lake Geneva, "armed with the galley proofs of your new *Dogmatics* volume," as he wrote to Barth.[4] The volume in question with which Bonhoeffer now went on retreat for a few days was *Church Dogmatics* 2/2, *The Doctrine of God*; for Bonhoeffer's passion was theology, in spite of the events of the time, and just because of them. It was a passion for God *and* the world.

But of course the world did not leave him in peace even during these days. During his Swiss journey particularly, Bonhoeffer suffered from the cloud of suspicion, which—understandably enough—hung over his person, his mysterious privileges, and his obscure projects.

A frank, unreserved exchange of letters in May of 1941 with Karl Barth or his assistant, Charlotte von Kirschbaum, documents the ups and downs on both sides between mistrust and trust, skepticism and hope. About a week after his arrival, on May 17, he confided to Barth what dismayed him and left him feeling uncertain of what to do. During his self-chosen retreat on Lake Geneva, he had evidently not confined himself to reading Barth's *Church Dogmatics*, as he had said in his letter; he had already been in Geneva:

> When, last week in Zürich, I first heard someone say that you found my stay here "disturbingly mysterious in its objectives," I simply laughed; when shortly thereafter I ran up against this purported statement of yours a second time in Zürich, I thought it would be best simply not to respond. Now I have heard the same thing twice here in Geneva, and having pondered the matter for a few days, I simply wish to let you know of it. . . . In a time when so much simply has to rest on personal trust, *everything* is lost if mistrust arises. I can, of course, understand that this curse of suspicion gradually affects us all, but it is difficult to bear when for the first time it affects oneself personally.[5]

Bonhoeffer recalled and reminded Barth of their conversation during his last stay in Switzerland.[6] He had thought that this conversation had cleared everything up, but now, on his side, he felt somewhat uneasy about Basel too. Barth replied by return of post through Charlotte von Kirschbaum—"What a pickle to be in!"—and vehemently denied that he himself was distrustful. Admittedly, friends had from time to time expressed surprise at the liberty and freedom of movement that Bonhoeffer was able to enjoy abroad. But Barth had always defended him in response to awkward questions of this kind. What he in fact found worrying was something else: "For Karl Barth there is in fact something 'disturbing,' and that is all the attempts to rescue Germany by means of further 'national' endeavors from the immense predicament into which it has now been swept. This also includes the attempts that may be undertaken if necessary by the generals." She wrote that Barth hoped to be able to exchange ideas with Bonhoeffer about this and wanted him to know that "we shall be *overjoyed* at your coming." In response, on May 20, Bonhoeffer wrote back that he proposed to visit Barth on the following Monday, that is, Pentecost Monday, and that he was very happy about his reply.[7]

In these very days a stone was set rolling in Prague that was certainly seen to be dangerous in the Berlin Military Intelligence Foreign Office and in its Munich office, but that the far-reaching consequences of which could not at this point as yet be seen. Inquiries by a German customs official in Prague had led to investigations by the respective customs authorities into a mysterious currency affair, and these were to lead to other proceedings of a very different kind. Inquiries were started in Munich as to whether Schmidhuber and Ickrath were guilty of a currency offense, and if so, to what extent.[8] This raised alarm in the central Military Intelligence office in Berlin. Canaris and, above all, his colleagues Oster and Dohnanyi, as well as Josef Müller in Munich, were uneasy because they were afraid that this was a stone that might release an avalanche.

These investigations were so potentially dangerous because, for one thing, the "odd bird" Pastor Bonhoeffer was answerable, purely formally, to Schmidhuber, the consul and captain in the reserve. He was Bonhoeffer's "control" as agent, to use secret service jargon. This meant that the man who was Bonhoeffer's official contact with the Military Intelligence was suspected of smuggling, and the probability was that the investigators would be only too delighted to track down the internal secret service affairs of the Canaris office. In addition, it was all too possible that, in the course of intensified interrogations, Schmidhuber's complicity and involvement in conspiracy activities might be discovered, the more so since the customs investigation office came under the Gestapo. And the Gestapo's hankering to bring the Military Intelligence Foreign Office at long last into line, or to get rid of it altogether as an independent secret service under the command of the army, had long been no secret. This department, since it came under the army high command, was the only secret service in the SS state that was still independent of the Reich Central Security Office (the RSHA). Since 1939 the security police and the SS's own security service had been incorporated into the RSHA, to which since 1940 the Gestapo too was subordinated. And its long-term goal was to use whatever pretext was offered in order to compromise the Military Intelligence, so as finally to annex it.

In addition, what was not unimportant for the history of Canaris's office and concern was that on May 1, 1942, a truce had been made in Prague castle that was anything but favorable for the Military Intelligence. The two rivals, the head of the Military Intelligence Foreign Office, Admiral Canaris, and the head of the Reich Central Security Office, the SS's chief lieutenant Reinhard Heydrich (who was therefore, as we have seen, head of the other security services and of the Gestapo too), had newly regulated afresh the powers of the different security (that is, secret) services and had made an agreement that blurred the dividing lines between them. For all practical purposes, this whittled down the autonomy of the Military Intelligence.[9] Any diminution of Canaris's powers meant danger for the group around Oster and Dohnanyi, which till then had owed its relative safety to Canaris's loyalty. Another event in May 1942 was bound to diminish yet again the conspirators' hope of making successful contacts with countries abroad. On May 26, 1942, in London, the Soviet Foreign Minister Molotov signed a more specific and expanded treaty with the British ally that explicitly and finally excluded any separate peace. This was a further disappointment for those who were working toward a coup d'etat and hoped thereby to be able to count on the support of the Western Allies.

During these days Bonhoeffer had to swallow another, very specific disappointment, which was the absence of Visser't Hooft. His most important accomplice in the conspiracy in Switzerland had managed to get to England by way of southern France and Spain, his purpose being to put into the hands of political and church leaders a memorandum (drawn up under the oversight of Adam von Trott) about the attempts, goals, and hopes of the German opposition. He also wanted to take the opportunity to draw attention once again to the paper he and Bonhoeffer had worked on in the autumn of 1941.[10] His success was negligible. Trott's memorandum did indeed reach the people it was supposed to reach, and Churchill even judged it favorably as "very encouraging"; yet he believed that the existence of an opposition in Germany that was really resolved to act was a pious fiction: "But the point is that they must *do* something,

like Belgians and Dutch, Norwegians and French, before we are prepared to believe even in their existence." This is noted in the Foreign
Office papers and dated May 20, 1942.[11]

Visser't Hooft was personally and politically close to both Adam
von Trott and Dietrich Bonhoeffer, although his two confidants themselves only knew each other slightly. There had been opportunities
and common ground enough, and Trott had been a close friend of
Bonhoeffer's oldest brother, Karl-Friedrich, for years. But it was only
after 1939–40 that there were evidently occasional meetings between
the two, and in the years that followed, they were not often in direct
contact, either via Berlin, as was conceivable, or via Geneva.[12] In
Geneva in May 1942, Bonhoeffer was forced to discover that Visser't
Hooft was at that very time in London, trying to do his utmost for
the cause of the Hitler opponents in Germany; so this time he was
not available as a discussion partner.

The general secretary of the World Council of Churches "in
process of formation" (as the term was) had become unofficially one
of the couriers and coordinators of resistance groups in Europe.
He made use of the tried and tested "Swiss road" and built up and
developed a special "Swiss road"[13] both from the Geneva office of the
WCC in the Avenue de Champel No. 41 and from his private apartment. For example, three months previously he had set up a courier
service to Amsterdam via Brussels. "The Intelligence information
was transported on microfilm concealed in objects of everyday use,
such as fountain pens and pocket torches. Visser't Hooft then sent
the films on by the normal post, hidden inside book bindings, to
Portuguese or Swedish accommodation addresses. From there they
arrived by air in London."[14] It was in the nature of things that the
kind of double life that Visser't Hooft led was objectively speaking
no less dangerous than the life led by the conspirators against Hitler. But subjectively it must have been very much less nerve-racking
for him, since it lacked the permanent strain of a "divided existence" to which the conspirators were subjected.[15] When they were
abroad especially, Adam von Trott and Bonhoeffer were painfully
conscious of this dichotomy with which they were forced to live. So

Bonhoeffer no doubt found Visser't Hooft's absence in May 1942 especially depressing and must have felt Karl Barth's loyalty as all the more liberating.

Looking back on Bonhoeffer's third Swiss journey, and especially if we compare it with his journey to Norway, it is not very clear, on the one hand, what his ostensible mission for the Military Intelligence consisted of and, on the other hand, the nature of the real assignment given him by the resistance group in the Military Intelligence Foreign Office. We know many of the details, but a central thread linking them with a specific mission cannot be detected. We know, for example, that just before Pentecost 1942 he met other ecumenically interested people in Freudenberg's apartment in Geneva, Freudenberg being at that time responsible for the WCC's refugee aid.[16] And we know too that on Pentecost Monday, May 25, he traveled from Zurich, to Basel in order to spend the afternoon with Barth. Charlotte von Kirschbaum and Barth later recorded some impressions of this visit.[17] These bring out the openness and inner closeness between Barth and Bonhoeffer, even though, as had already emerged in the autumn of the previous year, they differed in some respects in their assessment of the political situation.[18] When Bonhoeffer was in Zurich, he probably also visited Alphons Koechlin, the president of the Swiss Federation of Protestant Churches, in order to talk to him in connection with Operation 7 about the power and the powerlessness of Swiss bureaucracy.[19]

Bonhoeffer's visa only ran out on May 28, the Thursday after Pentecost. But he seems to have already broken off his visit two days earlier[20] and to have started back to Berlin via Munich on May 26.

*George K. A. Bell (1883–
1958), Lord Bishop of
Chichester* © Gütersloher
Verlagshaus, Gütersloh, in der
Verlagsgruppe Random House
GmbH, München

*Major Hans Oster (General from 1943),
head of the Central Office of the Abwehr
(counterespionage)* © Gütersloher
Verlagshaus

*Dietrich Bonhoeffer and Eberhard Bethge setting off for Chamby, August 18,
1936* © Gütersloher Verlagshaus

Helmuth James von Moltke's passport © Gütersloher Verlagshaus

Courier document of identification of the Foreign Office for Dietrich Bonhoeffer. Photo: SBB. Staatsbibliothek zu Berlin, Stiftung Preussischer Kulturbesitz, Berlin, Germany © Bildarchiv Preussischer Kulturbesitz / Art Resource, NY

Storefronts of Jewish-owned businesses damaged during Kristallnacht: A Nationwide Pogrom on Leipziger Straße, Berlin, November 9-10, 1938. Photo: Abraham Pisarek © Bildarchiv Preussischer Kulturbesitz / Art Resource, NY

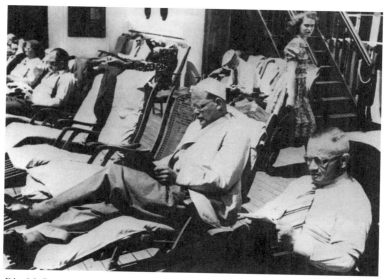

Dietrich Bonhoeffer on a ship traveling to America, Summer 1939. Photo: Rotraut Forberg © Bildarchiv Preussischer Kulturbesitz / Art Resource, NY.

Members of the Confessing Church and English clergymen at a conference in Oxford during World War II, 1940. Photo: Renate Forberg © Bildarchiv Preussischer Kulturbesitz / Art Resource, NY.

Dietrich Bonhoeffer sometime after his arrest © Gütersloher Verlagshaus

fourteen

Sigtuna

SHORTLY BEFORE THREE O'CLOCK on the morning of May 13, 1942, an aircraft with a Norwegian pilot and a single passenger on board landed at the Stockholm airport. The bishop of Chichester, George Bell, had come to Sweden on a mission from the British Ministry of Information. He was supposed to fly back to England on June 2. His envisaged purpose was to sound out cultural relations between England and Sweden, and especially to renew personal contacts between members of the Anglican and the Swedish churches. During his stay in Sweden there was a brief episode that may be summed up under the name of Sigtuna, for which we have detailed documentation and which has been much discussed.[1]

The English bishop's stay began at almost the same time as Bonhoeffer's third visit to Switzerland. This Swiss journey, which he undertook on behalf of the regime opponents, was surrounded by rumors and uncertainties, incompletions, and new departures. On May 1, Bell had already sent a telegram to Geneva telling Visser't Hooft, the general secretary of the WCC, that he was planning to go to Sweden. But at that time Visser't Hooft was already on the way to

London with the Trott memorandum. Whether—as is most probable—the central office of the WCC in Geneva had told Bonhoeffer
about the content of the telegram or whether he read in the Swiss
newspapers that the bishop was in Sweden is of secondary importance. It is also conceivable that he had heard this from the "central
office" in Berlin while he was still in Switzerland, or perhaps only
after he had arrived in Berlin himself. In any case, it was decided
at short notice that Bonhoeffer might still be able to meet Bell in
Sweden, at literally the last moment, shortly before Bell's planned
departure.

It was different in the case of another member of the clergy.
Hans Schönfeld, one of Visser't Hooft's colleagues and the head
of the research department of the WCC, had traveled north from
Geneva earlier and had been able to arrange for a personal meeting
with Bell in Sweden. On May 6, 1942, he had written from Geneva
via Madrid to his assistant, the Swede Nils Ehrenström, who was
then in his home country: "You will meanwhile have probably also
heard that you are going to have a visitor for three weeks from May
11 on. . . . I am sure you will understand that I would then like to
have a long talk with George Bell. . . ." And he telegraphed him
a week later, on May 13, via the "Ekumeninstitut Sigtuna": "Beg
immediately . . . instructions to Berlin for a ten-day visa. I leave here
Monday."[2]

Schönfeld used the stopover in Berlin to get the visa he had
requested from the Swedish embassy, as well as to receive final
instructions for the conversations with Bell from the Berlin representatives of the civilian resistance, with whom he was at that time
in contact. Schönfeld could hardly be said to belong to a particular
group of Nazi opponents—the groups overlapped in any case—but
at this period he was loosely connected with critics of the regime in
the Foreign Office and with people belonging to the Kreisau circle.
But he hardly had any contact with the group around Goerdeler,
Beck, Dohnanyi, and Oster.[3] We may assume that he was given his
instructions for the Swedish project primarily by Hans Berndt von
Haeften, who belonged to the Kreisau circle.[4] Schönfeld arrived in

Stockholm at Pentecost 1942, the time when Moltke's friends met for the first time at his estate in Kreisau and when Bonhoeffer visited Barth in Basel. On Pentecost Monday, May 26, Schönfeld met Bishop Bell for the first time during his stay in Sweden.

On Tuesday of the same week, Bonhoeffer (at least in all probability) broke off his Swiss journey prematurely. His sister Christine von Dohnanyi's notebook shows that he already spent Thursday evening with them at their home in Sakrow near Potsdam.[5] His old service passport had been renewed or extended the previous day, May 27, 1942.[6] He would have spent brief, hectic days in Berlin in order to prepare with Oster and Dohnanyi for his surprising visit to Stockholm—which at that time, incidentally, was "an espionage center of the first rank."[7] The official version of this undertaking—a special mission for the Military Intelligence—had to be constructed by Canaris's staff; the real mission had to be thoroughly thought through, and every detail on the technical side—papers and tickets— had to be organized.

The main purpose of the ostensible Military Intelligence mission was to make contact from the side of Canaris's office with a critic of the British government, one who was well-disposed toward the Germans—"a man of balance and understanding,"[8] which was what Bishop Bell seemed to be. The chief objective of this operation was allegedly to gain background information about war perspectives and the real relations between the United Kingdom and its American and Soviet Russian allies. In particular, the Military Intelligence contact was to investigate Swedish-Soviet relations and discover what was going on in the Swedish church. With regard to the nature and intention of Bonhoeffer's real commission, Oster and Dohnanyi had consulted with Ludwig Beck, the moving spirit of the conspiracy against Hitler. As emissary of the conspirators, Bonhoeffer was supposed to give Bell information about their existence, their goals, and their questions. How would the enemy side react to the coup d'etat and an assassination? Bonhoeffer was thoroughly briefed. After the war, Christine von Dohnanyi remembered exactly the real assignment given to her brother as courier:

He was supposed to put across the following message: if a putsch were to take place under the leadership of certain people—my husband gave my brother their names—this would under all circumstances be the guarantee of a peaceful intention, even if the men involved had at first had to conceal their intentions from the people, until the true explanation could be given. Bonhoeffer was consequently supposed to ask that the armed forces should not make use of this moment to strike, but should give the new government a period of grace in which to clear matters up internally.[9]

It has meanwhile emerged that it was not only the anti-Hitler conspirators around Beck, Oster, and Dohnanyi who prepared Bonhoeffer for Sweden during his brief stopover in Berlin as negotiator for the opposition. Later Barbara von Haeften recalled several times that her husband and Bonhoeffer had conferred both before and after the journey. At that time they took a long walk together through the streets of Berlin and in the Grunewald.[10] They had known each other for more than twenty years; on March 15, 1921, Dietrich Bonhoeffer and his sister Sabine had been confirmed in the Grunewald church at the same time as Hans Bernd von Haeften and his sister had been.

Haeften, meanwhile councillor in the Foreign Office, was from the beginning an active member of the Confessing Church and a convinced supporter of nonviolence. Almost all his life he was unable to reconcile the assassination of Hitler with his personal beliefs. He knew more theology than many a contemporary theologian, and his uncompromising faith increasingly made him, ideologically speaking, an outsider in an aspiring "Thousand-Year Reich" and in a largely conformist, unprotesting Protestant church. He was evidently strikingly characterized by great sensibility and a highly developed feeling for justice. Closely associated as he was with the ideas of the Kreisau circle, he devoted himself with dogged energy to work for a "new Germany."

There is much to suggest that Haeften prepared both Schönfeld and Bonhoeffer for their mission in Sigtuna and that this is probably the solution to what Bethge still called "the riddle of the two messengers."[11] What Schönfeld was for the Kreisau circle, Bonhoeffer was for the resistance group in the Military Intelligence: a mouthpiece for a fundamental German opposition to the Nazi system. And especially where contacts with Bishop Bell were concerned, a "double cast" would not be counterproductive—or not, at least, in the eyes of Hans Bernd von Haeften. Through Haeften, Bonhoeffer was probably informed about Schönfeld's mission, whereas Schönfeld could not have known anything about the second "messenger," or not at least before Bonhoeffer's arrival in Stockholm. It must be remembered that Bonhoeffer left Switzerland at earliest (and most probably) on May 2, whereas we know that Schönfeld already had a discussion with Bell in Stockholm on that day.

In any case, during these brief days in Berlin in May, Bonhoeffer was given not merely vague, generally formulated statements, but specific information about plans for a coup d'etat. In addition he had to be equipped with absolutely unexceptionable papers. Forged passports would have been amateurish and too risky. That was also the reason for the attempts at that time to provide collaborators and agents—and above all, those who like Bonhoeffer were traveling on a mission connected with the conspiracy—with authentic papers, service passports, visas, etc.

In this case, a courier visa issued by the Foreign Office was needed. It may have been issued by Adam von Trott by way of relations between another member of the Military Intelligence staff (that is, Moltke) and the Foreign Office, and it was handed over to Bonhoeffer himself only early in the morning of the day he left. In short, on Saturday, May 30, 1942, Bonhoeffer, a courier in the service of the German Reich, armed with a courier passport issued by the Foreign Office, serial number 474, flew from Berlin-Tempelhof to Stockholm. Incidentally, there is a later report about this departure written by the theologian Eugen Gerstenmeier; but this shows only how problematical such recollections can occasionally be.[12] In his fictitious dairy, written some months later, Bonhoeffer, courier to Scandinavia, noted down his first impressions, seemingly thereby toeing the party line. This entry, which was already quoted at the beginning of the present book, runs:

> A weekend flight to Stockholm, terrible storm. Magnificent city, very friendly, but at the same time reserved, at least initially. Great astonishment, then warming up. . . . Always very difficult without knowing the language. Waiters often act as if they understand no German and respond only when addressed in English. . . . Strong anti-Bolshevist sentiment everywhere; that provides a certain shared foundation.[13]

As things turned out, he was able to discover on his arrival in Stockholm that on Sunday there would be a chance to meet the bishop in Sigtuna, the small town on Lake Mälar, a little less than 50 km northwest of the center of Stockholm. This was the home of the Nordiska Ekumeniska Institutet. Bonhoeffer was probably familiar with the Nordic ecumenical institute from hearsay. It had been founded in 1940 by Manfred Björquist, later bishop of Stockholm, and was at the time of Bonhoeffer's visit headed by one of Björquist's colleagues, Harry Johansson, who later became the institute's director.

Sigtuna counted as the trademark both in Sweden and internationally for further education in the church and for adult education generally. In addition, it served officially to further contacts between the WCC in Geneva and the Scandinavian churches and—again beyond that, but needless to say unofficially—as the clearing house for information between the WCC, the Scandinavian churches, and resistance groups. Ecumenical couriers from Germany and the occupied countries, often at considerable risk, used this "Swedish line," which linked Geneva and Sigtuna, but not theses two centers alone. Among the couriers was, for example, Hans Schönfeld and also his Swedish colleague in the WCC's research department, Nils Ehrenström, who also belonged to the Sigtuna team.[14]

For the last Sunday in May 1942, a meeting was planned in Sigtuna between three Swedish theologians—Björkquist, Ehrenström, and Johansson—and the English bishop Bell; but this meeting led unexpectedly to another with two other participants, Dietrich Bonhoeffer and Hans Schönfeld from Germany. Johansson remembered later that during tea in Björkquist's private apartment in Sigtuna the telephone suddenly rang: two Germans were standing on the station in Märsta, on the railway line between Stockholm and Uppsala, and wanted to see Bell. It was arranged that the two Germans should take a taxi for the few kilometers to Sigtuna and should get out at the main entrance to the institute. Meanwhile the Swedes, with their English guest, would take "a path along the lake so as to reach the house unnoticed from the garden side, without being seen from the street by any possible observers."[15]

Whatever the details may have been—in Bell's various reminiscences there are small discrepancies, for example, as to the simultaneous arrival of Bonhoeffer and Schönfeld[16]—there was certainly a meeting of Bell, Schönfeld, and Bonhoeffer in Sigtuna on May 31, 1942; and its circumstances and consequences bring out particularly clearly the conspiratorial side of Bonhoeffer's life. "Sigtuna" stands as hardly any other event as a code word or symbol for the circumstances of Bonhoeffer's existence—allegedly as agent for the Military Intelligence, and really as the trusted go-between of the men in the Military Intelligence who were involved in the resistance. That double existence is exemplified particularly clearly by this lightning trip to Sweden, and it is therefore treated here in detail. Moreover, the reconstruction of the events in Sigtuna repeatedly raises questions about the reliability of specific recollections. It shows how insubstantial matter-of-course assumptions can be and calls in question the objective character of human perceptions. To look back at Sigtuna is to see Bonhoeffer in the limelight and Schönfeld in the shadow, Bonhoeffer at the center, Schönfeld on the sidelines.[17] Who was this Hans Schönfeld?

Schönfeld held a doctorate in economics and was an ordained theologian. From 1931 onward he headed the department for study and research in the WCC, then "in process of formation" in Geneva. Until about the beginning of the war, he largely supported the loyal party line followed by the Church External Affairs Office of the DEK (the official Protestant church in Germany) and by its chairman, Bishop Heckel, who allied himself with the National Socialist government. Formally, and from time to time financially, Schönfeld came under Heckel's department, which itself was linked with the Foreign Ministry. A secret instruction issued by the ministry made it possible, for example, for him and other representatives of the WCC, without any control from the side of the Nazi authorities, to acquire a visa for the other European countries, that is, for the occupied territories too; this enabled him to undertake an astonishingly extensive program as traveler and courier.[18]

Schönfeld's service to the ecumenical cause may count as undisputed, in spite of all criticism. In his own way and irrespective of his ambitions in the official church, he seems to have done excellent work.[19] During the 1930s he was undoubtedly well disposed toward the government, and in church politics clearly and often very readily obedient. But over against this we have to note risky and diverse efforts on behalf of victims and opponents of the Nazi regime during the 1940s. The later comments of his Geneva chief, Visser't Hooft, were admittedly still ambivalent. Schönfeld had certainly garnered a rich harvest of information and documents from the occupied countries, but he, Visser't Hooft, was never sure "as to whether he was carrying out the policy of the World Council or his own." At that time "we were, to put it mildly, not on the same wavelength. Our relations improved in the following years [that is, after 1939] when Schönfeld identified himself more clearly with the resistance against the Nazi regime."[20]

Schönfeld's relationship with Bonhoeffer was similar. When they met in Sweden at the end of May 1942, they had known each other for about ten years. In his early years in Geneva, Schönfeld represented the official German church in the ecumenical "family," while Bonhoeffer supported the Confessing Church, and its more radical Dahelm wing at that. So there were reasons enough for controversy in theology and in church politics. After Schönfeld had seen the text for Bonhoeffer's rousing and controversial 1934 Fanö lecture, "The Universal Church and the World of the Nations" (a text that in retrospect might be called Bonhoeffer's pacifist manifesto), he wrote to his colleague Ehrenström, "I must confess that I am a little dismayed by Herr Bonhoeffer's material and its narrow concern with the problem of war."[21] Or in 1936 he recommended his friend Gerstenmaier (from the church's External Affairs Office in Berlin) to at last appoint a new youth secretary for the WCC: "Personally, I have long thought it an impossible state of affairs that this part of the work should be determined by, or almost only by, a man like Bonhoeffer."[22]

Yet by the early summer of 1942 the relations between Bonhoeffer and Schönfeld had passed their nadir. After periods of considerable reserve and mutual alienation, in the first war years their relationship changed. Schönfeld's growing contacts with critics of the regime and a number of meetings in 1940—for example, with Dohnanyi in Potsdam[23]—may have contributed essentially to this change of attitude.

Schönfeld's commitment to the resistance has been very variously judged, as it is still, from the most diverse sides. Moltke is supposed to have known him well; he is said to have got on excellently with Adam von Trott; and the head of the American secret service in Switzerland, Allen W. Dulles, found his contacts with Schönfeld important and valued Schönfeld's extensive links with churches and resistance groups all over Europe.[24] His efforts on behalf of occupied Holland and Dutch resistance groups is much praised; of the services he rendered, it is said that he helped lay the foundation for an agreement between the German and the Dutch resistance.[25] His intensive courier journeys between the European churches involved a permanent risk that must not be underestimated. And one of his contacts was the English bishop Bell, whom he had known personally since the beginning of his time in Geneva.[26]

Bell spent the first two weeks of his stay traveling through Sweden in order to reactivate old friendships—he had known the Swedish church exceptionally well since the First World War—and in order to forge new links. The Swedes were visibly impressed by the trust, confidence, and cheerfulness he radiated. His goodwill tour was a complete success, as can be seen from the fact that on Pentecost Monday more than a thousand people attended a service in which they had to listen to a sermon in a foreign language. The following evening the young pastor Ehrenström, who was also, as has been said, assistant in the research department of the WCC in Geneva, took the bishop with him to the Student Movement House[27] in Stockholm, where to his surprise Hans Schönfeld appeared.

An extremely interesting discussion followed, noted Bell in his diary,[28] in which Schönfeld seemed to the bishop to be in a state of considerable tension; and the discussion soon turned on "his real concern," the situation of the hidden German opposition to Nazi rule.[29] The quintessence of what Schönfeld told Bell was that there was a strong resistance movement drawn from a broad spectrum of the population—civil servants, trade unionists, and army officers— and that this was supported by leading figures in both the Protestant and the Catholic churches. Their goal was "the complete destruction of the entire Hitler regime."[30] Schönfeld outlined the further political goals of this resistance movement, and also, somewhat more specifically, gave a broad outline of the planned coup. He said that the central question for the resistance movement was: Would the Allies behave cooperatively? Later, in the autumn of 1945, Bell wrote that Schönfeld wanted to find out on behalf of the resistance movement whether the British government would support a revolt of this kind against Hitler, and whether, if it was successful, they would be prepared to negotiate with a new German anti-National Socialist government. In his diary of 1942 he had noted, "Would government encourage such rebels to hope for negotiations when the arch-gangsters were eliminated?"[31]

Three days later, on the afternoon of May 29, 1942, Bell and Schönfeld had another conversation, which turned mainly on the reality and effectiveness of the church's resistance to the Hitler dictatorship. Bell, protagonist and chronicler in one, jotted down what was said in note form in his diary: "All the generals in opposition related to church"; or, "no longer capitalist ideas [or views] of property." In the account he wrote in 1957 he summed up by saying that this time their conversation lasted for about an hour. He asked Schönfeld to give him what they had said in writing, which he promised to do. But, he adds, the next day, Sunday, May 31, was decisive.[32]

It is not surprising that in his description of the dramatic events that began on May 26[33] Bell should have attached special importance to the day on which, after his meeting with Schönfeld, he also met Bonhoeffer as courier for the German resistance. For he was not just bound to Bonhoeffer through a solid working relationship, which endured through all the ups and downs of events. In addition they were firm personal friends. This is indicated by the fact that in Bell's diary notes of that time, Schönfeld is referred to as "S" but Bonhoeffer as "D."[34]

Bell and Bonhoeffer had been drawn to each other from the time of their first meeting, and this affinity was hardly affected by distance in time and space. In October 1933 Bonhoeffer had taken up his pastorate in London and, as a young theologian, was recommended from Geneva to the Bishop of Chichester as "one of the most promising young men in Germany."[35] Their first conversation took place at the beginning of November 1933. Bell had invited him to dinner at the Athenaeum in Pall Mall, one of the most famous London clubs. This occasion was followed by a lively correspondence and, at the end of the month, by a visit from Bonhoeffer to the bishop's house in Chichester. They soon became close friends, as Bell wrote in his reminiscences about their meeting in Sigtuna.[36] Even after he had left England, Bonhoeffer remained in constant contact with Bell. Letters, visits, and conversations in the years that followed show that they greatly esteemed each other and trusted one another unreservedly. "Their sympathy for each other expressed itself in mutual trust."[37] After war broke out, Bell wrote, "My dear Dietrich, you know how deeply I feel for you and yours in this melancholy time."[38]

Of course the structure of their relationship was influenced by the difference in age between them, separated as they were by almost a quarter of a century. Bonhoeffer's friend Franz Hildebrandt had emigrated to England because of his "non-Aryan" origins, and Bell had done his utmost for him professionally; and he is later said to have referred to Bonhoeffer and Hildebrandt as "my two boys."[39] Were they like sons for him? And was Bell for Bonhoeffer in some sense a father figure, who filled a gap that had been left vacant by church and theology? Their birthdays fell on the same day, February 4, and they exchanged good wishes on that occasion as long as the war and the times permitted it.

George Bell was a nonconformist character in both church and society, with a remarkable career. In the 1920s he was in the service of the archbishop of Canterbury and was already in some sense especially responsible for international relations. From 1929 on, as bishop of Chichester, he held leading positions in the Anglican church as well as in national and international bodies connected with what was later to become the World Council of Churches. From 1937 on he held the title of lord bishop, and as such had a seat in the House of Lords. Obstinate and unnervingly tenacious, during the war he was smiled at by the British public as a naïve idealist, was occasionally eyed mistrustfully as suspect, and was even severely abused. A bishop as an unpatriotic malcontent? Certainly, even in the leaden, hostile atmosphere of the war, it never occurred to him to break off his relations with people of whose integrity he was convinced. He refused to equate *all* the Germans with Nazi Germany. At the same time, he openly castigated the criminal character of the Nazi system. Without thinking twice, he helped people who were trying to escape the grasp of the persecuting machinery of "greater Germany." This irksome political bishop opposed the British bombing of German cities, protesting against it from the pulpit, in the House of Lords, and in letters to the *Times*. In the media this gave him the reputation of sympathizing with the Germans and called down on him a spate of polemical caricatures.

Bell was a bridge builder; that seems to have been his special charisma. His vision of a Christian brotherhood that would break down national barriers did not only make him a pioneer in ecumenical relations; in the eyes of the Confessing Church this vision made him the epitome of loyalty, and for the opponents of Hitler he was their hope. "Uncle George,"[40] as he was affectionately and respectfully called in Confessing Church circles because of his steadfast commitment, counted for the German resistance as a potential ally in a hostile country. In the early summer of 1942, it was he who came into question as perhaps the only person who could convince the British government that a revolt against the Nazi regime was really planned, and that the people concerned were urgently hoping for help from outside.[41]

Bell and Bonhoeffer had met exactly three years previously, on June 6, 1939, when Bonhoeffer stopped over in London on his way to the United States. Now, on May 31, 1942, they suddenly came face-to-face in Sigtuna. Irrespective of whether Schönfeld arrived in Sigtuna later than Bonhoeffer on that Sunday (as Bell remembered), or Schönfeld and Bonhoeffer arrived together (as in Johansson's precise reminiscence), in either event Bell and Bonhoeffer first had a long private talk,[42] and in the evening they came to talk about Bonhoeffer's political activity.[43]

With regard to the question of his military service—in the spring of 1939 Bonhoeffer had turned to Bell in all his uncertainty[44]— Bell notes in his diary of 1942 that Bonhoeffer had talked to a high-ranking officer in the War Ministry, a friend of the Confessing Church, who had told him that "he would try to keep him out of it" and subsequently managed to get him a position as courier.[45] Here it is clear that only Colonel Oster and the Military Intelligence Foreign Office in the army headquarters (formerly the War Ministry) could have been meant. In addition Bonhoeffer filled him in about the present attitude of leading churchmen in Germany, beginning with Wurm and ending with Heckel (Wurm "now very good," Heckel the same as always, though now critical of the government—"a regular seismograph").[46]

Bell told Bonhoeffer, at least in outline, about his conversations with Schönfeld and about the mistrust he, Bell, would certainly encounter from the side of his government. He therefore asked whether Bonhoeffer could give him, in complete confidence and in spite of all the danger, names of the men most concerned in the anti-Hitler movement. According to Bell in 1957, Bonhoeffer readily agreed, although Bell could see that the matter weighed very heavily on him.[47] Bonhoeffer then gave him the most important names known to him, not without adding a brief commentary in each case. The organization was supported by people in all the ministries and major cities, as well as by generals who were in command at the front and in the home forces. He mentioned that a coup had become more difficult; Hitler was barricading himself in the Führer's headquarters in East Prussia and had recently canceled a visit to the headquarters in Smolensk at short notice.

In his diary Bell jotted down a few key names: General Beck: trusted in the army, a Christian, conservative, in touch with trade union leaders. General von Hammerstein: a little more Prussian, a convinced Christian. Goerdeler: highly esteemed by civil service people, the leader on the civil front. Leuschner: president of the United Trade Union, before its dissolution. Kaiser: Catholic Trade Union leader. A few others were ambivalent, e.g., Schacht: a seismograph of contemporary events. If Beck and Goerdeler came up: "worth trying." Most of the field marshals were reliable: von Kluge (a Christian), von Bock, Küchler, Witzleben (not so likely to come to the fore). Bell stressed that an act of repentance was necessary ("We are sorry").[48]

At this point in Bell's diary the account of this confidential discussion breaks off. It begins again with notes about the talk that followed in a larger group. According to this, the private talk between the bishop and Bonhoeffer then passed over into a wider discussion, in which Schönfeld and the three Swedish theologians Björnkquist, Ehrenström, and Johansson now joined. Bell's notes and his reports concentrate on the contributions to the discussion made by Schönfeld and Bonhoeffer, as well as the remarks he himself threw in. The main theme of the conversation, according to his account, was the question about the existence of a military and civil opposition movement in Germany, and about the postwar future. Schönfeld stressed that it was impossible to assess the number of people supporting an anti-Hitler coalition but that opponents occupied key positions in radio, the police, industry, and energy supply (water, gas, etc.). But he appealed to the Allies to remember that the German army held "a thousand miles of Russian territory."[49] Perhaps it might be possible to defuse the German-Russian relationship and to arrive at an understanding. Would the Allies feel responsible for the suffering of the many oppressed people in the occupied territories, and would they therefore search for ways and means to prevent still greater crimes? Would they therefore soften toward Germany? What chances of understanding could be considered?

Bell had the impression that Bonhoeffer was worried by the thrust and intention of Schönfeld's remarks and therefore interrupted him. In his diary Bell noted Bonhoeffer's objections:

> Christian conscience not quite at ease with Schönfeld's ideas. There must be punishment by God. We should not be worthy of such a solution. We do not want to escape repentance. Our action to be such as will be understood as an act of repentance and spoken out [*sic*]. . . . Christians do not wish to escape repentance or chaos, if God wills to bring it on us. We must accept this judgment as Christians.[50]

Bell backed Bonhoeffer up in saying that an expression of repentance was important. There was evidently a greater measure of agreement in the rest of the discussion about the role of the Allied forces, and perhaps the neutral and conquered countries, if Germany were to be occupied. The fears and hopes of the Dutch and Norwegian people were mentioned. Would England incidentally favor a restoration of the monarchy in Germany? This would not be inconceivable. Prince Louis Ferdinand would perhaps be available as a representative of the imperial family.[51] In his 1942 diary Bell added here that Dietrich knew the prince, that he was a Christian and had "outspoken social interests."[52] In his later accounts he sums up in strong terms the purpose and goal of the Sigtuna conversations. He, Bell, was asked—more: commissioned—to inform the Allies about the existence of an opposition movement in Germany that was ready to strike. Its aim was to eliminate Hitler and set up a new government, devoid of National Socialist ideas, which would be prepared for negotiations, the withdrawal of troops, and indemnification. But—and this was no small "but"—in spite of their readiness for an overthrow, the Germans must be able to rely on the willingness of the Allies to cooperate. Bell said that it was put before him in the most emphatic terms that there was little point in the resistance movement taking on themselves all the dangers to which they were exposed in the pursuance of their goals if the Allied governments intended to treat a Germany that had been purified of Hitler and all his henchmen in exactly the same way as it would a Hitler Germany.[53]

The conversation ended with considerations of a practical kind. What channels could be used for further contacts between the regime opponents and Bell? How could an answer from the Foreign Office in London reach them? Perhaps by way of other possible representatives of the resistance who could contact Bell? Apart from Bonhoeffer? And apart from Schönfeld? According to Bell's diary, Adam von Trott was explicitly mentioned as a possibility; at least Bell noted him down.[54] In favor of the 'Trott–Visser't Hooft–Bell' line of approach, or the 'Trott–Sigtuna team–Bell' line, much was certainly to be said in favor of Trott's proven connections, with their many ramifications. He had good contacts with Geneva as well as with London and Stockholm, and through his work in the Foreign Ministry had excellent opportunities to travel. A carefully worked out scenario would be open to several variations, depending on the character of the answer from London. As contact places on the continent, Sigtuna or Geneva were considered, and as middlemen Johansson or Ehrenström. A code for fixing times and places for possible meetings was also arranged.

The guest book in Sigtuna is also in its own way a record of the discussion group of May 31, 1942. There is an entry with Bell's official signature as bishop—George Cicestr.—as well as the signatures

of Manfred Björkquist and Nils Ehrenström. Bonhoeffer signed
merely with his initials. Schönfeld—evidently more cautious—did
not sign at all, and neither did Johansson, since he was acting as
"host."[55] The next day there were a number of follow-ups in Stockholm. Björkquist asked Johansson to tell George Bell that the Sigtuna institute was after all not available as potential contact point
between the English bishop and the German regime opponents;
he gave Swedish neutrality as the reason for this reversal. Consequently, only Geneva now came into question as the exchange
point for information. It was also Johansson who arranged another
meeting between Bell, Schönfeld, and Bonhoeffer. They met "in
the room in the St. Clara church, Klara Östra Kyrgata 8, used by
the parish council, because it too had different entrances from two
different streets."[56]

We know nothing in detail about the content and character of
this discussion. Bell thought he could remember that Schönfeld gave
him a short written message from Moltke, simply signed "James,"
with the request that it be passed on to his friend Lionel Curtis.[57]
Bonhoeffer may also have taken this opportunity to send the personal messages to his brother-in-law Gerhard Leibholz in London,
to which Bell's notebook entries refer (the entries that provided the
basis for those in his diary). There is also a note about Bonhoeffer's other brother-in-law, Dohnanyi: "Hans in high command, and
very active in good sense"; and the question to his sister whether she
would want to return to Germany after the war; if so, he (Bonhoeffer) was "ready to do utmost for finding position" [sic].[58]

It was in fact after the war that Sabine Leibholz-Bonhoeffer
remembered a June day in Cambridge 1942 on which she met an
excited bishop who had just arrived from Stockholm:

> The Bishop had done his utmost to dissuade Dietrich
> from returning to Germany and had sought to take him
> straight to England with him. But Dietrich was quite
> resolute in refusing this, in view of all those who were
> in contact with him in Germany. He did not want to be

the means of bringing disaster on anyone. The Bishop
was very sad as he told us this.[59]

Also after the war, in the lecture he gave in Germany in May
1957, George Bell too recalled the end of that day in Stockholm,
June 1, 1942. He told that as it ended he was given two personal
letters, [60] one from Schönfeld and one from Bonhoeffer. Schönfeld
also gave him a longer text, for which Bell had asked him during the previous week: he had envisaged a brief documentation
describing the present situation in the resistance, with a quintessence of their aims. Schönfeld had meanwhile compiled this text,
heading it "Statement by a German Pastor at Stockholm 31st May
1942." In his letter to the bishop, he expressed to him his extreme
gratitude:

> I cannot express in words what this fellowship you
> have shown for us, for myself and my fellow-Christians
> who were with us to us means with their thoughts and
> prayers. [*sic*]

Bonhoeffer wrote similarly:

> I think these days will remain in my memory as some of
> the greatest of my life. This spirit of fellowship and of
> Christian brotherliness will carry me through the dark-
> est hours. . . . The impressions of these days were so
> overwhelming that I cannot express them in words. . . .
> Please pray for us. We need it.[61]

On the following day, a Tuesday, Schönfeld and Bonhoeffer flew
back together to Berlin. Schönfeld immediately went to a conference in the Hotel am Steinplatz with, among others, Hans Bernd
von Haeften and Adam von Trott. On his arrival, Bonhoeffer went
directly to Sakrow, to the Dohnanyis' house.[62] George Bell was
originally also supposed to end his Sweden visit on June 2, but bad
weather prevented him, and he was only able to fly back to England
a week later.

For Bell this was the beginning of a laborious undertaking. At that time, to interest the British government in statements by two German pastors about a resistance movement in Germany that allegedly existed and was actually in a position to act, was not exactly easy, to put it mildly. There had already been too many SOS's of this kind without any proof that an effective fundamental opposition even existed, let alone that concrete actions leading to a coup d'etat were on foot. How could the Allies get involved in something that might prove to be a pure myth? There were a number of reasons for the skepticism. Had emissaries of this kind not perhaps been sent by the secret service? And could it not be another secret-service trick, designed to sow confusion, for them to come forward—allegedly only ostensibly—as spies commissioned by the secret service? And apart from doubts about the part played by the secret service, how trustworthy were emissaries who came in the name of the very men who in the same breath determined what was going on in the war?

Messages about putsch plans hatched by the generals were not rated very highly in London. Ever since 1940, information about alleged plans for an overthrow conceived by high-ranking German officers had been ridiculed in the Foreign Office as "the good old story." Information coming from a military opposition in Germany was received in the Foreign Office with commentaries such as "The generals again," or "This is the old story about the German army generals who, we are told, want to overthrow Hitler." And Churchill's 1941 directive that there should be absolute silence in response to secret emissaries of an anti-Hitler and pro-peace pact remained unchanged.[63] Why should this wall of silence be broken through just because these men were guaranteed by the bishop of Chichester?

In order to lend emphasis in London to his mission, on June 18, 1942, Bell wrote a personal letter to Anthony Eden, the foreign secretary. He referred to very important and confidential information about "a big opposition movement in Germany"[64] and stressed the absolute reliability of his sources. These were two German pastors, both of whom he had known for years, and one of whom was a close friend. Bell did not give their names. He asked the foreign secretary for an appointment at which he would hand him the appropriate documents. The next day he composed a paper, which, together with Schönfeld's text, he handed to Eden on June 30, 1942, at the end of the conversation he had asked for. In his diary Bell wrote, "He was much interested."[65] The paper that the foreign minister was asked to read was conceived as an up-to-date dossier about the resistance in Germany. Here the authentic account written by one of his informants, Schönfeld's paper of May 31, 1942, appeared in two versions, one the original and another in the form in which Bell incorporated it in his paper. The bishop called the whole paper he gave to Eden: *Memorandum of Conversations and Statement by a German Pastor.*[66]

  This statement of Schönfeld's—his paper, and at the same time the sum of his information to Bell—was intended to describe the situation of resistance groups in Germany, and essentially speaking covered the following aspects: strong, active centers of opposition had now crystallized, their goal being the overthrow of the Nazi regime and a complete changeover of power. They were recruited from some of "the key men in the highest command of the army" and others from the central state administration, former trade unionists and "liaison men to large groups of workers," as well as church leaders "acting together . . . as centers of resistance and reconstruction. He mentioned Bishop Wurm by name. The whole leadership in government, party, Gestapo, SS, and SA would at the first opportunity be eliminated, and the change of power would be brought about not by a military clique but by a government whose aim would be "to bring about a complete change of the present system of lawlessness and social injustice." Its main aims were among other things a "reconstruction of the economic order according to truly socialistic lines" and "a European federation of free nations" orientated toward the Christian faith. Would the Allies be prepared for a peace settlement along these lines? If, on the other hand, the Allies insisted on "a fight to the finish," the German opposition for its part would be prepared with the German army to go on with the war "to the bitter end," in spite of its wish to end the Nazi regime.

In the case of agreement, the opposition government would, after a coup d'état, withdraw forces from all the occupied and invaded territories, would contribute to their reconstruction, would bring about the end of the war in the Far East, would rehabilitate Jewish people, "cooperate in finding a solution of the colonial problem," and much more. It would be extremely helpful if the opposition groups were "to be encouraged in any way to go on."[67]

Bell basically took up what Schönfeld had said in his own memorandum, adding in part his own emphases, and including information given him by Bonhoeffer—of course without naming his sources in detail. Here he kept roughly to his own diary notes. He lists the names Bonhoeffer had given him: "The following names were given as those of men who were deeply involved in the opposition movement" and, following his own notes, he stresses Beck and Goerdeler. Bonhoeffer had mentioned the dubious political attitude of Hjalmar Schacht, but here Bell only refers to his "less clear Christian character." He goes on, "Most of the Field Marshals are reliable, especially von Kluge, von Beck, Kuchler, and possibly Witzleben." The passage about a conceivable restoration of the monarchy is followed, in a slightly modified form, by the reference to the churches in Germany. "The leaders of the Protestant and Catholic Churches are also closely in touch with the whole opposition movement." Along with Bishop Wurm, he mentions Konrad von Preysing, the Catholic bishop of Berlin. He then adds in brackets what, as we know from later reports, had apparently especially impressed him about Bonhoeffer in Sigtuna: "At the same time it should be said that included in the opposition are many who are not only filled with deep penitence for the crimes committed in Germany's name, but even say, 'Christians do not wish to escape repentance, or chaos, if God wills to bring it upon us.'" Finally, Bell passed on two questions to the Allies. First, would the Allied governments be willing to deal with a new German government of this kind? The answer to this might be given privately to a representative of the opposition. Second, would they be prepared to declare publicly to the world that they were willing to negotiate with a government formed after the overthrow of the Hitler regime?[68]

The answer can be quickly given: they were not willing. There was no discussion of the substance of either the first or the second question, and consequently the possible means of communication offered by Bell could be ignored. Bell's dossier was read in the Foreign Office in London, commented upon, discussed, answered, and laid aside as closed. On July 30, 1942, a month after Bell had spoken to Eden, he made a similar approach to the American ambassador in London, at that time John Winant. Winant listened to him, accepted the same documents, and promised to inform Washington. Bell wrote in 1957, "But that was all, and I heard nothing more."[69]

Rather more trouble than that, however, was undoubtedly taken in London with regard to the bishop's information. The Foreign Office minutes reveal interesting details. In reference to the discussion with Eden that Bell had asked for, it was discreetly indicated in the understated English manner that the Foreign Minister might perhaps take the opportunity to impress on the lord bishop "the great importance of secrecy in matters of this kind." One of Eden's close colleagues, G. W. Harrison, described the document Bell had passed on as "the most elaborate and illuminating [document] we have so far received." But he added the reminder that "the list of names . . . does not inspire confidence." Goerdeler, Beck, and Hammerstein were "old friends who have cropped up often in the past and who have so far achieved nothing." He had instituted inquiries about Leuschner and Kaiser. His general impression was that these people were genuine, though hitherto unsuccessful anti-Nazis, and, he went on, "if the German secret service wanted to put up a plausible facade, these are just the names they would be likely to pull out of the hat."[70]

On July 17, 1942, the Foreign Office sent the bishop an unequivocal refusal: "These interesting documents have now been given the most careful examination, and without casting any reflection on the *bona fides* of your informants, I am satisfied that it would not be in the national interest for any reply whatsoever to be sent to them."[71] Following this refusal, on July 23 Bell telegraphed to Willem Wisser't Hooft, the general secretary of the WCC in Geneva, saying, "Interest undoubted, but deeply regret no reply possible."[72] However, Bell did not give up completely; but his attempts through further correspondence to change Eden's mind came to nothing. Eden commented on the bishop's persistence in a note in the margin of Bell's letter of July 8, 1942: "I see no reason whatsoever to encourage this pestilent priest."[73] The hopes of Sigtuna and Stockholm were in vain.

The fact that the attempts to make contact with the Allies from the side of the resistance generally and in particular after the Sweden mission of 1942 were not crowned with success has been sufficiently and zealously discussed by historians of the resistance—occasionally not without emotion, occasionally highly simplistically, occasionally without any comprehension of the situation and the arguments of the Allies at the time.[74] The emissaries of "the other Germany" and people on the Allied side, especially the British government, were the victims of a failure in communication of a special kind. And this endured. The German opposition expected, indeed demanded, a sign of cooperation. The other side was not prepared to give any kind of undertaking as long as nothing happened in Germany to prove the existence of that opposition. And even then—at least in 1942 and in what was after all the fourth year of the war—an isolated British initiative, based on a possible revolt by a marginal minority with uncertain credentials, was highly improbable; and in addition it would have been a breach of the agreement made with their own allies. From the standpoint of the British government, there was no alternative to what it did, but its justification was hardly understood by those involved in the German resistance. Insofar, this was a failure of communication between two unequal partners. Leaving aside other attempts, this also applies to the bid made from Sigtuna, which was also bound to come to nothing.

With regard to the special question about the part played by Bonhoeffer in Sigtuna, the following point should perhaps be remembered. There is no doubt that he underwent a great personal risk when he traveled to Sweden on a mission from the Oster group in order to meet the English bishop and to inform him about the situation in Germany and the members of the military opposition. The risk for Schönfeld was just as great. Yet the Bonhoeffer picture built up in the years after the war allowed Schönfeld's situation to pale into insignificance in comparison. Bonhoeffer versus Schönfeld? An appropriate Bonhoeffer reception has, in my view, no need to extol his merits at the expense of others, in this case at the expense of Schönfeld.

There are several understandable reasons why Schönfeld's role in Sweden as a whole has been set in a less positive light than Bonhoeffer's, and why his importance in Sigtuna as emissary of the resistance forces has been less highly estimated. In the first place, through his ties with Heckel and Heckel's Church External Affairs Office, Schönfeld was "tainted" in a way that Bonhoeffer most certainly was not. Second, the events in Sweden were from 1945 onward seen largely through the eyes of Bishop Bell and later also from the perspective of Bonhoeffer's biographer Bethge, both of whom (and to say this is no criticism) were very much closer to Bonhoeffer theologically, personally, and in church politics than they were to Schönfeld. Third, in retrospect, the fact that Schönfeld was one of the survivors while Bonhoeffer was not, has inevitably played a role that should not be underestimated.

It is incidentally to Bell's honor that although in his account of 1945 he drew attention warningly to the relationship between Heckel and Schönfeld (and in this respect clearly differentiated between Bonhoeffer's integrity and Schönfeld's), he at the same time mentioned Schönfeld's courage and his sympathy for the Confessing Church.[75] In 1957 Bell no longer drew attention to Schönfeld's earlier association with the Church External Affairs Office. He talked about his later ties with the Kreisau circle, and after he had spoken about Bonhoeffer's death, also mentioned, obviously moved, Schönfeld's too: "Hans Schönfeld's sufferings were different, but they were very severe."[76] It is also to the honor of Eberhard Bethge, Bonhoeffer's biographer and friend, that his account of Sigtuna is at the beginning markedly careful; cautious evaluations and presumptive formulations predominate at the beginning of this chapter of his Bonhoeffer biography.[77] But in the course of the account, he described the protagonists Schönfeld and Bonhoeffer with an emotional coloring that cannot go undisputed: "Schönfeld negotiates, Bonhoeffer informs; . . . Schönfeld threatens with German strength . . . Bonhoeffer asks. Schönfeld warns, Bonhoeffer talks of repentance. Schönfeld is tactical, Bonhoeffer fundamental."[78]

Bethge goes on that here Schönfeld was undoubtedly "the more politic," but that in his approach—he means his interpretation of the overthrow as an act of repentance—Bonhoeffer was "the better and more effective diplomat."[79] And here we must again agree with Bethge. And yet, looking back, it must be said that it was rather an inward-looking political stance. In the Foreign Office, at least, it was evidently not felt as diplomatic but as best as an interesting theological sleight of hand on the part of oppositional clergy in Germany, which might impress an Anglican bishop but was irrelevant for present-day *Realpolitik*. As an internal political stance, addressed to members of the German resistance, these ideas of Bonhoeffer's could become increasingly influential: to see and accept as an act of repentance one's own preparedness for an assassination and overthrow—and if necessary for complete defeat—this stance, carried to these lengths and at this point in time, was a novelty in the thinking of the resistance groups with which Bonhoeffer was associated.[80]

The very fact that in Sigtuna Bonhoeffer, seemingly quite inappropriately, introduced a theological category such as "repentance" into a political context, has received much attention. It is striking that in the discussion about Sigtuna, not only in the Bonhoeffer reception but in the literature about the resistance too, Bonhoeffer's preaching of "repentance" has moved into the center of attention.[81] But a careful exegesis of what Bonhoeffer then said soon comes up against its limits. In the first place, what we have is only by way of oral transmission. Second, even in the case of the "first witness," Bishop Bell, there are different strata of oral transmission in his different written testimonies of 1942, 1945, and 1957.[82] Third, we are faced with not inconsiderable semantic problems. The terms or concepts shift—repentance, act of expiation, punishment, judgment.

How are they to be understood in each case? And how should they be translated from German into English?[83] *The fact* that in Sigtuna Bonhoeffer interpreted—and demanded—the overthrow as an act of repentance seems to be clear. And yet what Bonhoeffer specifically said in Sigtuna about this, and what he meant, still remains open, although it was later moved so firmly into the center.

What he passed on to Bell were primarily names rather than new facts. Most of these names indicate the background, politically and in general outlook, of the circles for whom Bonhoeffer was speaking; this was the conservative wing of the resistance.[84] In the wider discussion group with the bishop, as we have seen, even the possible restoration of the monarchy was considered, coupled with a specific personal suggestion. And here Bonhoeffer's personal contacts with the Hohenzollern prince Louis Ferdinand were mentioned, however important these may or may not have really been.[85]

Bell noted that in their private conversation Bonhoeffer mentioned ten important people, the first of whom, Beck and Goerdeler, von Hammerstein, Leuchner, and Kaiser, were without any doubt (and not just seen from the perspective of later years) convinced opponents of the regime.[86] Bonhoeffer was explicitly cautious in his mention of Hjalmar Schacht.[87] The second group of names was problematical. Why did Bonhoeffer pass on the names of von Kluge, von Bock, and von Kühler, of all people? The fact that Bonhoeffer mentioned them as if they were guarantors of the overthrow in leading military circles is at least surprising, and is even disconcerting.[88] The only really convincing name here—and not only in retrospect—is that of Erwin von Witzleben; he was one of the few on whom the opponents of the regime could rely.[89]

In spite of the critical questions about the factual value and point of the information, and in spite of critical questions about an inappropriate buildup of Bonhoeffer's role and importance in Sigtuna, we may sum up by saying the following.

First, Sigtuna was until then Bonhoeffer's most resolute and certainly most spectacular attempt to inform countries abroad about the conspiracy against Hitler and to try to win their support, indeed, to plead for it. It was not his fault that this potentially most effective project in his political work met with no response from the side of those to whom it was addressed.

Second, great importance is ascribed to Sigtuna, not only in Bonhoeffer studies but in the historiography of the resistance too. According to the editors of the afterword to volume 16 of Bonhoeffer's *Works*, its "historical significance has long been acknowledged."[90] It is all the more important, for the sake of Bonhoeffer himself, to ensure that Sigtuna historiography does not, even if unintentionally, turn into a Sigtuna hagiography.

Third, Sigtuna especially exemplifies the questions about Bonhoeffer's role in and for the German resistance—questions about intentions and purposes, motives and means, rivalries and cooperation, extent and aims, success and error, good fortune and failure. "Sigtuna" contains in miniature all the elements of his existence as an agent of the conspiracy, and apart from its historical importance, it can be seen as the quintessence of Bonhoeffer's activity in the resistance.

fifteen

Home Affairs

ON JUNE 25, 1942, a week after Bishop Bell had written his first letter about Sigtuna to Anthony Eden, the British foreign secretary, Bonhoeffer was sitting in the train from Berlin to Munich writing a long letter to his friend Bethge. This gives us some slight impression of these summer weeks, about which we do not in general know very much:

> Greetings from this train once again. . . . I will be flying out tomorrow and shall return with Hans on the tenth (not the ninth!). . . . My recent activity, which has been largely in the worldly sector, gives me much to think about. I have not written to Maria. It is truly not time for that yet. If no further meetings are possible the pleasant thought of a few highly charged minutes will surely eventually dissolve into the realm of unfulfilled fantasies, a realm that in any case is already well populated. On the other side, I do not see how a meeting could be brought about that would be inconspicuous

and not painful for her. . . . I am in fact still not at all
clear and decided about this.[1]

A week after his return from Sweden, Bonhoeffer had withdrawn to his Pomeranian retreat on Ruth von Kleist-Retzow's estate
in Klein-Krössin in order to take up work on his *Ethics* manuscript
once more. During his stay he (again) met Maria von Wedemeyer, a
meeting that was evidently crucial for them both. Ruth von Kleist-
Retzow's granddaughter and Bonhoeffer had in fact already known
each other for some years. In autumn 1935 the eleven-year-old Maria
had passed the time during a church service by counting the time
Pastor Bonhoeffer used the word God.[2] At the beginning of June
1942 she had just passed her *Abitur*, the school leaving examination,
and was spending a few days holiday with her grandmother, with
whom she had an especially affectionate relationship. She recalled
later:

> I had been there a week when the celebrated Pastor
> Bonhoeffer came to stay. I was a bit put out at first, to
> be honest, but it very soon emerged that the three of us
> got on extremely well together. . . . We went for a stroll
> in the garden. He said he'd been to America, and we
> noted with surprise that I'd never before met anyone
> who had been there.[3]

Next day she had to leave. How long Bonhoeffer stayed we do
not exactly know. It is certain that from June 21–24 he was staying
with the Dohnanyis in Sakrow, and that during the month he was
twice at his "office" in the Bavarian capital. He wrote a letter to his
friend "in the train to Munich" on June 18, and another on June
25, the one in which he mentions Maria von Wedemeyer for the
first time. This letter contains another concrete clue to Bonhoeffer's
"present activity in the worldly sector," since it refers to the flight he
was about to take. He does not mention its destination, but it is clear
from his letter that Bethge was fully informed. This was one of Bonhoeffer's journeys about which we have very few details—his visit to
Italy in the summer of 1942.

The following can be deduced from the sparse and occasionally contradictory information we have. On June 26 Bonhoeffer evidently flew first to Venice from Munich. Hans von Dohnanyi followed only on July 3, arriving in Venice from Berlin via Vienna. They seem to have spent a few days in Venice together with Wilhelm Schmidhuber and, during the stay in Rome that followed, Josef Müller evidently joined them—either in addition to Schmidhuber or instead of him.[4] They hoped that they might receive a signal through Roman-British channels telling them whether the Foreign Office had reacted to Bishop Bell's Sigtuna information and, if so, how; but this hope proved illusory.[5]

The day before he left Rome, Bonhoeffer took the opportunity to write a few lines to his sister and her family in London. He wrote (in English) with his apparently unbroken confidence: "I am still optimistic enough to believe that it will not last long till we meet again."[6] On July 10 he and Dohnanyi flew back to Berlin. In the fragments from Bonhoeffer's faked travel diary, which were supposed to be the notes of the keen Military Intelligence agent, we read under the date July 16, 1942 (but in fact the notes were probably written in February or March 1943), a mixture of facts and hints, deliberately ambiguous formulations, and mild political slogans:

> Two weeks in Italy, Venice and Rome. It is good to see Italy again from time to time. . . . Exhaustive visit to the catacombs! Many problems. Above all, why does the symbol of the cross appear only so late? Questions about some of the paintings. Splendidly well-informed guides. But much too little time for real research. Later, after the war! . . . The great heat did not leave enough energy after the work of the day for areas of personal interest. The food was adequate. Unfortunately a question of money again. The poor appear to be getting by, while those with property can afford everything. Why can these plutocratic conditions not be eradicated, even with good will? The Italians' lack of talent for organization does seem to play a significant role, however.[7]

Apart from short breaks in Klein-Krössin and Munich, Bonhoeffer spent most of the summer and autumn of 1942 in Berlin. An examination of the documents, letters, and notes gives the impression that this was a time of waiting, like the beginning of his activity for the Oster group. It was an interim with an uncertain end. In the first half of August he seems to have been relatively often with his friend Eberhard Bethge, and among other things, on August 11 the two met Carl Goerdeler again (as once before in 1941)[8] in the Fürstenhof in Berlin. We have no details about the reason for the meeting. It is conceivable that it once more had to do with Goerdeler's financial contributions to Bonhoeffer's work and to the work of the Confessing Church in general. At the end of August, Dohnanyi had to travel to Switzerland for a few days in order to clarify final details about the departure of the families involved in Operation 7, which was immediately impending. He took with him two letters from his brother-in-law, one being a letter of recommendation to Alphons Koechlin, the president of the Swiss Protestant Church Federation, which contained a veiled appeal for help for Operation 7,[9] and another with some brief lines for Bishop Bell:

> Things are going as I expected them to go. But the length of time is, of course, sometimes a little enervating. Still I am hopeful that the day might not be too far when the bad dream will be over and we shall meet again.[10]

Again and again, Bonhoeffer's hopes for the future! He tried to radiate optimism and confidence in the face of all the waiting and all the uncertainty, and in spite of it—and in the face of reality, and in spite of it. Meanwhile preparations were afoot for his next journey. On September 10, 1942, the Military Intelligence office in Munich applied to police headquarters there for a travel visa for his passport, "for repeated travel to and return from Hungary, Bulgaria, Greece, Turkey, Croatia, Italy, for a period of three months."[11] It was immediately issued. His service passport, which I have already mentioned in an earlier connection,[12] was duly returned. He received the requested permission, to extend from September 10 to December 10, for all the countries named, and accordingly "for all the border crossing points . . . for repeated use. Exempt from fees."[13]

On October 3, 1942, Bonhoeffer traveled to Munich in order to set out from there on the first of these journeys. But on October 14 he returned to Berlin without having started. Further preparations for the journey had been broken off for the time being, apparently because of confidential warnings from a source that would otherwise be considered far from trustworthy: SS Major General Arthur Nebe, criminal director of the Reich Central Security Office.[14] It is still not clear even today what specific assignments went along with these journeys. We know neither the official ones, for Bonhoeffer the alleged Military Intelligence agent, nor those for Bonhoeffer the conspirators' courier. He "was to visit ecumenical friends in the Balkans and Switzerland," says the biography cautiously. According to a less guarded comment, "There is no way today to know the purposes and intentions of these travel plans."[15] The plans were scrapped several times, sometimes only at the last minute, because the journeys would have been too risky. The Schmidhuber inquiry made it seem advisable to Oster and Dohnanyi to be more circumspect. As far as possible no shadow or suspicion of insubordination in official matters was to be attached to department Z in the Military Intelligence Foreign Office, or to the Munich office.

Bonhoeffer had made a short detour to Freiburg, not so much as emissary of the Oster group, but rather as a theologian of the Confessing Church. He had convinced the Provisional Administration of the Confessing Church in Berlin that if, at the end of the war, there were to be a conference of the World Council of Churches, the Confessing Church should present its own memorandum on a viable future for postwar Germany.[16] On October 9, 1942, he arrived in the famous university city with two professors who had close ties with the Confessing Church, Constantin von Dietze, professor of economics, and Erik Wolf, professor of law. His practical suggestion to the Freiburg group, made in the name of the Church Provisional Administration, was that a memorandum should be prepared, its subject being the new form Germany should take and a future peaceful order on the foundation of the Christian faith. The memorandum was to be a programmatic document "in which as far as possible all the main branches of public life should be treated under the aspects of Christian social ethics."[17]

It was not just by chance that this suggestion was addressed to the Freiburg circle, for it maintained a regular working party that seemed to be positively made for the composition of just such a memorandum. Ever since the autumn of 1938, as a reaction to the crimes of the so-called Night of Broken Glass (the Jewish pogrom), Protestant professors at Freiburg university who were either members of the Confessing Church or were sympathetic toward it had regularly met with clergy of the local Confessing Church and sometimes with Catholic clergy too. As well as Dietze, the historian Gerhard Ritter and the economists Walter Eucken and Adolf Lampe constituted the core of this Freiburg group.[18] This group of Protestant scholars was politically largely conservative in its views. Its members combined a no to National Socialism with an active acknowledgment of their Christian faith.

Bonhoeffer's suggestion was immediately accepted. Erik Wolf notes in his diary on October 9 that there was a discussion between Dietze and Bonhoeffer that lasted from five o'clock until late in the evening.[19] Extant notes written by Bonhoeffer and Dietze on this October 9, with (for outsiders hardly comprehensible) abbreviations, terms, and headings, have been deciphered and elucidated.[20] They deal with preliminary plans for a bigger meeting, to take place November 17 to 19, 1942, in Freiburg, at which it was planned that Bonhoeffer should speak on "The church's proclamation to the world."

However, Bonhoeffer did not after all participate in this three-day conference in Freiburg, at which the previous suggestions for the memorandum were discussed. But we do know that Carl Goerdeler was present at this decisive meeting. Earlier, probably at the end of October or the beginning of November, there seems to have been another discussion in Berlin with Dietze, with Friedrich Justus Perels (the Confessing Church's lawyer and Bonhoeffer's confidant), as well as with Bonhoeffer and other members of the Confessing Church.[21] Finally, there were two further meetings with Dietze in a select group in Berlin, probably around December 20 and again on February 6–7, 1943.[22] After that, work on the memorandum ceased. Its main section, which was entitled "The Political Form of the Community," was written by Gerhard Ritter, who saw to it that during the war it was buried on a farm in the Black Forest. It was published immediately after the end of the war.

Of course, seen as a whole "much still remains obscure"[23] about the conflicts in philosophical viewpoint and practicality between Bonhoeffer and the Freiburg group, but there are meanwhile clear indications that it was Bonhoeffer, together with Perels, who ended the cooperation with the Freiburg group.[24] Afterward, but as early as December, the text that was already finished was "sharply criticized" by Bonhoeffer and Perels; and finally, "at the meeting in Berlin on February 6–7, 1943, Bonhoeffer's and Perels's annihilating criticism of Ritter's work . . . was the prologue to the end of the planned continuation."[25] So although Bonhoeffer initiated the work on the memorandum and was for that reason in Freiburg in October 1942, he dissociated himself from it after some working sessions in Berlin at the beginning of February 1943. The fact that forty years later this Freiburg circle that had worked on the memorandum was called "the Bonhoeffer circle" seems "artificial and somewhat misleading[26]— even actually inadmissible.[27]

At the same time, it is clear that the differences between Bonhoeffer and the Freiburg group were theological rather than political, and that the basically conservative approach of the memorandum did in fact conform to his political thinking at that time.[28] The no to the heresy of parliamentarianism in the memorandum is matched by a yes to aristocratic constitutional forms, an authoritarian order of society, a salutary "leveling down of all ranks of society,"[29] and the formation of a new elite—ideas that were not all too far removed from Bonhoeffer's political world view. We read in the memorandum: "It may be actually viewed as an ideal goal of creative politics in the future to distil out of the indistinguishable mass a new stratum of notables with political insight and moral reliability."[30] Bonhoeffer wrote something similar in a text meant personally for Oster and Dohnanyi, although it is certainly rather different in detail and tone: "We are witnessing the levelling down of all ranks of society, and at the same time the birth of a new sense of nobility, which is binding together a circle of men from all former social classes. . . . Quality is the greatest enemy of any kind of mass-levelling."[31] And in a theological position paper[32] on "State and Church," which as a whole reflects Bonhoeffer's affinity with a somewhat conservative understanding of the state, we can read in the final theses:

> The relatively best form of the state will be that in which it is most clear that government is from above, from God, and in which its divine origin shines through most brightly. A properly understood divine right of government in its glory and in its responsibility belongs to the essence of the relatively best form of the state.[33]

At the same time, in this text he also demands "the venture of responsibility," the possible duty of disobedience, and "the venture of action"—categories that play an important part in his *Ethics*.[34]

During the second half of 1942, Bonhoeffer had more time for writing. His travel plans for the resistance cell round "the Canaris office" had repeatedly to be postponed. Apart from work on his *Ethics*, he mainly devoted himself to theological position papers for the Confessing Church—"mainly shorter contributions he had been asked for and occasional papers"[35]—and in addition drew up two drafts that were meant for Day X. The first, which remained unfinished, was designed to be a message from the pulpit to be delivered after the overthrow. Its tone is pastoral but unequivocal. It begins with the promise of God and ends with hope for the future of the Confessing Church. The heart of the message is guilt and forgiveness:

> God has not forgotten his church. . . . In the midst of a Christendom enmeshed in guilt beyond all measure,

the word of forgiveness of all sins through Jesus Christ
and the call to a new life in obedience to God's holy
commands shall be allowed to go forth once again. . . .
We call to personal confession. For long years oppressive
guilt has made our hearts callous and numb. Christ has
given his church-community the power to forgive sins in
his name. . . . Only in repentance and conversion can
we be helped.[36]

The other draft deals with a new order in the church after the
coup. As so often, the idea goes back to Dohnanyi. His wife recalled
later that an expertise of this kind was to be passed on via Canaris
to Field Marshal Keitel, the chief of the army high command, and
via Goerdeler to General Alexander von Falkenhausen, who was
critical of the regime.[37] We may presume that Beck was also one of
the potential addressees.

This was a project Perels and Bonhoeffer had agreed on. Parallel to Bonhoeffer, Perels, the Confessing Church's company lawyer
in Berlin, had drawn up a skillful legal draft, closely organized and
with suggestions about the people who should be involved. Here
Bonhoeffer's name was also mentioned—incidentally in connection
with a committee for reorganization of the Church's External Affairs
Office, of all things, which was so hostile to the Confessing Church.
Its long-standing director and Bonhoeffer's arch enemy, the Hitler
sympathizer Bishop Theodor Heckel, was to be relieved of his post.
In spite of the different language, the substance of the two drafts
is similar. The main emphasis of Bonhoeffer's draft is that the sole
and indispensable premise for a new ordering of the relationship
between state and church, and for a new beginning inside the church
itself, had to be the ending of the internal church struggle and the
establishment of an administration "operating in accordance with
the confessions":

The special interests of the regional churches, still rooted
in certain traditional historical and confessional scru-
ples, would certainly be overcome in the near future

by means of a strong church leadership. As the new church is reorganized, the reactionary circles associated with the official church bureaucracy must not under any circumstances be given new leadership responsibilities. For state and church that would be a regressive solution to the church question. A solution that is intended to place the relationship of church and state on new ground must have recourse to the young generation of pastors and laypersons who were tested in the Church struggle.[38]

The same Bonhoeffer who in "State and Church" talked about the glory of the divine grace of authority, properly understood,[39] pleads here for brotherly ideas in a future church; and Perels developed a legally safeguarded set of rules, divided into sections. The idea informing the draft is the concept of a church liberated from state oppression, independent of state influence, a free and independent and at the same time publicly effective church, a church that confesses Christ in the world. It is evident here, for example, that in questions of church policy, Bonhoeffer was markedly more progressive than he was in general political questions. The reader of this "outline of a church" gets the impression that here—perhaps at last?—he is in his real element. A living theology and a living church is for him only a dream, but he clings to his dream. Direct and yet differentiated, realistic and yet with courage for the future: it seems that he had a rare power to cling to this basic trust and not to capitulate before the superior power of hard facts.

Because of the restrictions laid on him by the state, Bonhoeffer could only pursue his activity in the church to a rudimentary degree. His "activity in the worldly sector," as he had called it, had come to a halt because of the warnings that had reached the central department in Berlin. He led a literally homeless existence. He was continually on the move. The question of where he should live was still unsolved. There would have been little point in renting an apartment in Munich, and he was still not allowed to stay in Berlin. His relationship to Maria von Wedemeyer was still not clear either.

When Bonhoeffer returned to Berlin from Munich in the middle of October 1942 (we know that instead of a new foreign journey in the interests of the Oster group he only got as far as Freiburg), he met her next day at the family house of his sister, Ursula Schleicher, at a farewell party for his nephew, whose military service was beginning. The same evening Maria von Wedemeyer wrote in her diary:

> I had a very interesting conversation with Pastor Bonhoeffer. He said it was a tradition with us that young men should volunteer for military service and lay down their lives for a cause of which they mightn't approve at all. But there must also be people who are able to fight only from conviction. If they approved of the grounds for war, well and good. If not they could best serve the Fatherland by operating on the internal front, perhaps even by working against the regime. It would thus be their task to avoid serving in the armed forces for as long as possible—and even, under certain circumstances, if they couldn't reconcile it with their consciences, to be conscientious objectors.[40]

They met again several times during these autumn weeks. Both of them had come to wish for a common future, a shared life, but there was hardly any practical and specific hope that this future would soon be a reality. In the middle of November, for example, he wrote to her: "I hope my travels will be over by the beginning of December, unless the whole situation changes again."[41] But quite apart from the permanent uncertainty about his own immediate future, at the end of the month Maria's mother insisted that there should be no contact between her daughter and Bonhoeffer for a year. They were neither to meet, talk, nor write to each other.

"Unless the whole situation changes again"—the constant uncertainty overshadowed both everyday life and thoughts about longer-term vistas and projects. The risk of arrest had grown considerably. In the second half of the year some of these arrests were particularly alarming for the Oster group. On August 31, 1942, the first members of the resistance groups were taken into custody, having been picked up by the Gestapo in connection with the "Rote Kapelle" group. In October others were arrested. After long preliminary investigations, two members of the Military Intelligence office in Munich were arrested, Ickrath on October 13, 1942, Consul Schmidhuber, his "chief" and friend, on October 31. A little later they were taken to the Berlin Reich Central Security Service's Gestapo prison, and in their interrogation the names of Dohnanyi and Bonhoeffer played a not unimportant part. The point at issue was Schmidhuber's "currency affairs" and financial transactions in connection with Operation 7. These were interpreted as a move made by the Military Intelligence people in their own interests and for the benefit of the Jewish families who had just, that very autumn, been able to leave Germany unscathed as "agents." In addition here was perhaps the very chance to discredit even the higher echelons of the Reich Central Security Office's own competitors, the Military Intelligence: for as we know, the former had long wanted to get rid of the Military Intelligence Foreign Office altogether. So it did not look as if an accusation against Schmidhuber would be confined merely to currency offences. Bonhoeffer put off his journey.

During November 1942 there were two family meetings, one with Dietrich's brother Klaus and one with his brother-in-law Rüdiger Schleicher. These were anything but merely family gatherings. The guests outside the family were among those whose names had been mentioned in Sigtuna, Carl Goerdeler and the Hohenzollern prince Louis Ferdinand, as well as Jakob Kaiser, the former representative of the Christian trade union movement, and the Social Democrat and trade unionist Wilhelm Leuschner. No details are known about the content of these November discussions, but the list of guests reflects to some extent the changes that gradually took place in the course of 1942 in the circles of the civilian opposition. In retrospect, we can see that during this period three main trends crystallized: the most conservative, around Hassell and the Freiburg group; a later Goerdeler-Kaiser-Leuschner group; and the Kreisau circle.[42]

Of course there were contacts and interactions between these three groups, but also competition and conflicts. In the winter of 1942–43, Goerdeler, the potential chancellor in a potential post-Hitler era, developed the idea that once the army had deprived Hitler of power, the monarchy should be restored under the Hohenzollern prince. In the late autumn of 1942, he had initiated promising contacts between leading army people who were prepared to act— between Tresckow of the Central Army Group and Olbricht, the head of the general army office in Berlin; and together with other members of the civilian opposition, he awaited the actions of this newly coalescing opposition among the officers.[43]

Dietrich Bonhoeffer as a monarchist? The idea that the monarchy might be restored in Germany seems to those of us who came afterward as an anachronism, so it is not easy to imagine Bonhoeffer as supporter of a future monarchical constitution. But at the beginning of the 1940s this idea, in diverse variations and with diverse intensity, repeatedly played a role in groups hostile to the regime, and especially in the case of Goerdeler.[44] And there is no reason to assume that Bonhoeffer rejected in principle the idea of the establishment of a constitutional monarchy or that he supported it for merely pragmatic reasons.[45]

The fundamental conservatism of those around him at the time is clearly reflected in texts and theoretical approaches in his *Ethics*, and it also belonged to his own political thinking. This was undoubtedly "conservative" rather than "national-conservative," but it was certainly conservative in the original sense of "conserving."[46] It aimed at restoration—that is to say reinstatement, and a reinstatement of a "divinely bestowed authority," properly understood.[47] And its aim was not, as it might have been, to reinstate the Weimer Republic, the first German democracy and its first democratic constitution. At least there are no explicit comments in his writings to suggest that his ideas moved in the direction of a parliamentary constitution, a pluralistic party state, or democratic social structures. This is hardly surprising. We can only understand Bonhoeffer in the context of his time and the world in which he lived. He was rooted in a "restorative" political world view. This characterized the resistance group that he had joined and large sections of the civilian resistance movement as well.[48]

Bonhoeffer's rejection of National Socialism must be seen against the background of an upper-middle-class liberal view of the world. It was certainly not uncritical of totalitarian trends, but that did not necessarily imply a democratic understanding of the state. The possibility that Bonhoeffer also favored monarchical elements cannot be excluded. As far as his general political viewpoint is concerned, it is in any case hardly possible to define Bonhoeffer's specific political tendencies. Moreover, he made few definite statements about his personal political ideas, and when he did, they were somewhat tentative. He had thought only about the "relatively best form" of the state and the church.[49] "I hope there will [be] something like an authoritarian 'Rechtsstaat' as the Germans call it," he wrote to a friend in the United States in 1941.[50]

Events on the eastern front at the end of November 1942 rendered obsolete all thoughts about constitutional law, in whatever direction they tended. The reality of the war Hitler had wanted caught up with the "unstoppable rise" of what was supposed to be the "Thousand-Year Reich." The Soviet offensive against the German Sixth Army in and round Stalingrad had begun.

sixteen

The Dilemma of Guilt

TO LOOK BACK AT the people who at that time wanted to resist the National Socialist system is, from today's standpoint, to be struck by their hesitancy to use force against the representatives of a system that itself depended on force.[1] This undoubtedly seems surprising to some extent, because in our own day political murder, assassination, and suicide missions are part of the daily political agenda. We have evidently become used to them, and nowadays the murder of a tyrant would often seem to be even less of a problem. It is no longer a "questionable" act. But at that earlier time, there were a good many people among supporters of the resistance for whom assassination presented a grave ethical problem.

The hesitation of the army officers involved in the resistance is surprising for another reason too. In the profession to which they belonged, killing was not something completely alien. These men were not just "entangled" in acts of war. They were actively involved in them. But to kill the people who embodied higher authority per se, and people to whom, in addition, they had taken an oath of loyalty, was for them forbidden by what they felt to be their duty to the state to which they subordinated themselves, and by their soldierly and Christian consciences. To call in question the categories of command and obedience, above and below, duty, discipline, and loyalty was hardly conceivable. There was a highly effective inhibition threshold that made them hesitate to act in a situation where they were preeminently in a position to do so. At the end of 1942 Bonhoeffer described this particular scruple:

> No one who confines himself to the limits of duty ever goes so far as to venture, on his sole responsibility, to act in the only way that makes it possible to score a direct hit on evil and defeat it. . . . It was an unmistakable fact that the German still lacked something fundamental: he could not see the need for free and responsible action, even though that might mean opposition to his profession and his calling.[2]

It was probably the progress of the war that in the end contributed to the growing realization among exponents of the civilian and military resistance that an assassination was necessary. In most of the loosely associated military and civilian circles, the view gradually consolidated, although with varying nuances (and much less in the Kreisau circle, for example), that the killing of the dictator was the precondition for a coup d'etat, and that this coup d'etat, again, was the precondition for a new beginning.

To depend on a halt to the war and a consequent change of government was meanwhile bound to appear illusory. Only a change of regime brought about by force could now bring about the end of the war and the mass crimes. Without an assassination of the dictator himself, it would be futile to hope for an end to the regime. In historical studies of the resistance, there is an assumption that, at least after the beginning of the Soviet Stalingrad offensive against the German troops, this view increasingly came to prevail among the regime opponents. So Oster in particular could again begin to hope that plans for an overthrow would finally be put into practice. From the end of 1942 onward, "the threads of the military plans for a coup conceived by Oster, Olbricht, and Tresckow came together."[3]

According to the recollection of Bonhoeffer's biographer, Eberhard Bethge, Bonhoeffer probably already gave a first assent to plans for an assassination in the autumn of 1941, and in his account of the Norwegian journey of April 1942, Bethge points out that Bonhoeffer, unlike Moltke, pleaded that an assassination was necessary.[4] But if we disregard the question of the actual point after which Bonhoeffer definitely supported an assassination, there seems to be general agreement (apart from some differences in detail) that he did agree to it, at least from 1942 onward, and even paid the price of resulting differences between him and some of his political associates.[5] In spite of the change of mood among members of the civilian opposition, even at the end of 1942 and in the period that followed, there were still reservations and fundamental rejection, especially among the most resolute opponents of the Nazi system, although the intensity of the objections and the reasons for them varied. We know that this was true of Goerdeler, and also of Moltke, Peter Yorck von Wartenburg, Hans Bernd von Haeften, and Theodor Steltzer, all of whom were members of the Kreisau group.[6]

Bonhoeffer too did not find it easy to feel compelled to come to terms with "tyrant murder." Just as he did not move into the resistance movement in a single step, so there was not, in my view, a definite point at which he said yes to the assassination. It seems as if both decisions were arrived at though a process, perhaps a laborious one; and in the nature of things he did not commit himself in writing. Since we lack clear statements in his texts, we are dependent on oral traditions and on subtexts. In the writings of that period we find these, for example, just where we should least expect to find them, in "State and Church." In this theological position paper, Bonhoeffer puts forward in good Lutheran categories the duty of Christians to obey "the powers that be." But they are only bound by this duty "up to the point where the government forces them into direct violation of the divine commandments, thus until government overtly acts contrary to its divine task and thereby forfeits its divine claim." If it exceeds its task—and this too is good Lutheran doctrine—"then at this point it is indeed to be disobeyed for the sake of conscience." But this refusal to obey must not be the rule, only the exception. "Disobedience can only be a concrete decision in the individual case."[7]

We find clearer and more differentiated statements about the question of political murder in his *Ethics*. Here we find the theological substantiation for his specific affirmation of the assassination and his general commitment to resistance. He neither legitimates them nor does he generalize: "Bonhoeffer did not justify his participation in the resistance; he took the responsibility for it."[8] As he already said in "State and Church," it is a decision in the individual case, not a fundamental judgment. But in the *Ethics* the yes has a different emphasis. It is justified and made plausible, but at the same time it is of course expressed in veiled terms. In the situation of the time, it would be absurd to expect an open discussion about the right of resistance, let alone a justification of tyrant murder. In a letter dated the First Sunday in Advent 1942, Bonhoeffer wrote that he was afraid that his "forced silence about personal matters has . . . become second nature,"[9] and it will also have become second nature to mention political affairs in cryptic terms.[10] Nevertheless, he found a clear answer to a question he was not able to ask openly. This appears from a text in his *Ethics* headed "The structure of responsible life," which probably dates from the first half of 1942.

In this text Bonhoeffer developed his specific understanding of an ethic of responsibility along the lines of the sociologist (of religion) Max Weber, though without using the same terminology.[11] An approach to an ethic of responsibility, for example, emerges when in the face of a specific situation someone ventures, as a last resort, to break through an ethical principle, and takes responsibility for the consequences of what he does—out of ultimate necessity, that is, in order to avert some dire emergency that cannot be averted in any other way. This is the background to Bonhoeffer's reflections, as he develops an approach to an ethic of responsibility, and it tacitly includes his answer to the question about tyrant murder. The main statements in this passage from the *Ethics* make this clear:

> Extraordinary necessity appeals to the freedom of those who act responsibly. In this case there is no law behind which they could take cover. . . . Instead, in such a situation, one must completely let go of any law, knowing that here one must decide as a free venture. This must also include the open acknowledgment that here the law is being broken, violated. . . . The ultimate question remains open and must be kept open. For in either case one becomes guilty, and is able to live only by divine grace and forgiveness. . . . From the discussion thus far, it follows that the structure of responsible action involves both *willingness to become guilty* and *freedom*.[12]

Bonhoeffer certainly did not arrive at an easy answer to the question as to whether the murder of a tyrant is legitimate or even required, but his answer was unequivocal. It is a question that can only be asked in the face of a specific situation in which there is no way out. Everyone has to take responsibility for his decision, for himself and before God. A yes can be necessary, simply as a responsible act, but it nonetheless remains a violation of the commandment against killing. The yes in the broader situation must not turn into a principle about the use of force; it must not become a general maxim of behavior. In other words, and in the words of another, "The act of violence must preserve its unique character as a *breach*, as a crime. That is to say it is permissible only in conjunction with *personal* responsibility."[13]

The special point about Bonhoeffer's answer to the question about assassination is that it shows that Christian existence is always an existence tensed between responsibility and forgiveness, and that there is no such thing as an existence free of guilt. He maintains that responsibility and the admission of guilt belong together, that people become guilty both through doing nothing and through acting. There is no third possibility. "There was no way of remaining guilt-free."[14] As Bonhoeffer said at that time, the only possibility was deliberately to accept guilt—and hope for God's forgiveness. His yes to the assassination attempt on the dictator did not rest on an astute justification. He did not provide any slick legitimating basis, let alone a charter excusing murder, under the motto, perhaps, that the end justifies the means. His analysis was not suited for a neat distinction between just and unjust killing. It was a yes in awareness of the risk of misuse—and the risk of endangering his own existence.

It is not only "the structure of responsible life" in Bonhoeffer's *Ethics* that has a subtext; there are other passages in the *Ethics* especially that must be read—indeed must positively be deciphered—in the light of the question about his position regarding the assassination attempt on Hitler and, more generally, his involvement in the resistance. The elucidation is occasionally a laborious undertaking but of the greatest interest. There is another statement of Bonhoeffer's, on the other hand, that sounds somewhat simplistic. This is current in its English (and, later, German) version as an oral tradition. We find it in the early historical studies on the resistance and sometimes still come across it today. It is taken from George Bell's Sigtuna report, which was first published in October 1945 under the title, "The Background of the Hitler plot."[15] There Bell wrote that he knew of a meeting in the summer of 1940 between the men engaged in subversive activities "where it was proposed that further action should be postponed, so as to avoid giving Hitler the character of a martyr if he should be killed. Bonhoeffer's rejoinder was decisive: 'If we claim to be Christians, there is no room for expediency. Hitler is the Anti-Christ. Therefore we must go on with our work and eliminate him whether he be successful or not.'"[16]

Since this report of Bell's was published in a number of places, it is not surprising that Bonhoeffer's assessment of the situation quickly made the rounds, especially since in tone and content it was excellently suited to conjure up the picture of a "resistance fighter" who from the beginning, undoubtedly armed, was resolved to go to the limit. It was the picture of a lone voice crying in the wilderness of apathy, who defied the apocalyptic Antichrist, as the quintessence of evil, in order to eliminate him. Much speaks in favor of the presumption that these martial sentences were subsequently ascribed to Bonhoeffer by Bell; and incidentally Bethge, with the appropriate caution *and* decisiveness, already found an explanation for them in his Bonhoeffer biography.[17] They are not questionable only because of the alleged situation in which they were supposed to have been involved—a full-scale meeting of all the German resistance in the summer of 1940, with Bonhoeffer casting the decisive vote? They are also dubious because of their terminology. Nor is it easy to believe that Bonhoeffer set so high a valuation on his own importance in resistance circles. But above all, as Bethge especially stresses, to identify Hitler with the Antichrist is not typical for Bonhoeffer, and Bethge backs this up with another reminiscence. When he was once asked this question, Bonhoeffer answered, "No, he is not the Antichrist; Hitler is not big enough for that; the Antichrist uses him, but he is not as stupid as that man!"[18]

However, by the time Bethge put forward his objections, it was evidently already too late to correct the image of Bonhoeffer that these statements convey. They had meanwhile found an entry into Bell's own book and into his biography, so that in the long term this picture took firm root, above all in the English-speaking world.[19] The great importance ascribed to them in early studies on the German resistance did the rest (in the German-speaking world too), and even in recent work on the subject we still come across Bonhoeffer's disputed Antichrist formulation.[20] In the Bonhoeffer reception, however, it plays only a marginal role, and not just because of Bethge's objections. In any case, the manifold interpretations of Bonhoeffer's writings from the period in question, especially the *Ethics*, fail to support the impression that George Bell's description conveyed.[21]

How long do certain images, ascriptions, and quotations hold their ground in general works about the resistance, even when they have elsewhere long since been called in question? In Bonhoeffer reception in the German-speaking countries, this description has remained a peripheral one; this may be because of the immense

relevance Bethge's biography has always had for the German understanding of Bonhoeffer.

Another example of oral tradition that sheds light on Bonhoeffer's attitude to an assassination attempt on Hitler can be found
in the reminiscences of the theologian Wolf-Dieter Zimmermann.
Zimmermann had been friendly with Bonhoeffer from the time
when the latter was working on his doctorate in Berlin, and afterward from the period of the preachers' seminary in Finkenwalde.
From 1941 on they met fairly frequently in Berlin. Zimmermann
lived at that time in Werder an der Havel, not far from Berlin, and
later he several times described an incident that evidently made a
deep impression on him.[22] On his birthday on November 7, 1942,
according to Zimmermann, a discussion arose during the evening
in his apartment among a small group of friends about the difficult political situation; and this expectedly led to a dialogue lasting
several hours. For suddenly Werner von Haeften (Hans Bernd von
Haeften's younger brother) turned to Bonhoeffer and asked whether
shooting was permissible. He was in a position where he could gain
an armed entry to discussions in the Führer's headquarters, and he
was ready to risk his life in the attempt. In response to Bonhoeffer's
skeptical questions, the young officer explained how this would be
possible. After they had discussed the question about the oath of
loyalty, Bonhoeffer reverted to Haeften's initial question:

> He explained that the shooting in itself would have no
> significance. It would have to lead to a change in condi-
> tions. Just to get rid of Hitler would not help. Afterward
> something much worse could follow. The work of resis-
> tance was so difficult because the "afterward" would
> have to be exactly prepared. After the assassination a
> powerful group would have to be available which could
> at once take over power effectively. Haeften was still not
> satisfied. He found all that too theoretical. He saw a
> chance and was uncertain whether to take it. Bonhoef-
> fer enjoined prudence, and a clear weighing up of all

the possible complications. Haeften asked, "Should I? May I?" Bonhoeffer answered that he could not make the decision for him. If for him it would be guilt not to use the chance that offered, it would also be guilt to have dealt with the situation irresponsibly. No one gets out of such a situation guiltless. But Bonhoeffer's consolation was that guilt is always guilt borne by Christ.[23]

Irrespective of the question as to when exactly this meeting between Bonhoeffer and Werner von Haeften is supposed to have taken place,[24] we must see, in considering this winter dispute, that it looks exactly like an illustration of Bonhoeffer's approach to an ethic of responsibility and exemplifies his theoretical exposition in the *Ethics* on "the structure of responsible life" and "the acceptance of guilt." This provides a background to the dialogue between Haeften and Bonhoeffer, the officer and the theologian. The uncertainty of the one is matched by the hesitancy of the other. There is no ready-made answer. There is an answer, but no one can make it for anyone else. Everyone must take the responsibility for himself. A yes or no to a political murder can only be given in the face of a specific situation. The assassination of a dictator is not enough to change the evil reality. There must be sensible plans for a better reality afterward. And yet this is a yes to the assassination, but it is a yes that is aware that both the no and the yes involve guilt. Nevertheless—and this is said only "in hope"—guilt does not have the last word. Here the liberating element in Bonhoeffer's ethics and his relevance for the resistance take practical form. And this may be the enduring value of a reminiscence that in detail and in date may perhaps include one or the other inconsistency.

Apart from the varying recollections of his friends, we also have a whole number of Bonhoeffer's own statements that are worth thinking about. These reflect the erosions of the psyche through guilt and failure, but also his unshakable hope in God and the future. In the last weeks of 1942—the name Stalingrad symbolizes the catastrophe of the war, Auschwitz the catastrophe of the genocide—Bonhoeffer experienced inwardly the everyday catastrophe of dictatorship. He tried to render an account of what ten years of dictatorship had made of him, and chose the essay form for his characteristic account of his own experience. He wrote as "we," putting down these self-reflections for his immediate companions in the conspiracy. But he also writes—and why not in the first place?—for himself.

These reflections are a record from within of an existence in resistance, and they describe the psychological cost of an everyday life caught between resistance and concurrence, dissent and complicity. Bonhoeffer writes about the warping of the soul, about entanglement in guilt and lethargy, about loyalty, about unexpected experiences of trust, about helplessness, conformity, folly, courage, and optimism. He writes about processes of perception, about cordons of apathy, about the fatefulness of obedience, about confidence in the face of all appearances, about the "and yet," about life in the certainty of death—and about hope. There are fourteen closely typed pages, with several carbon copies. Its heading is "After Ten Years." The essay was finished at Christmas 1942, and he gave it to Hans Oster and Hans von Dohnanyi, to his friend Eberhard Bethge, and to his parents.[25]

The text consists of individual vignettes in which Bonhoeffer, under a particular heading or question, considers the point at issue. Not infrequently what he says is encoded and has to be deciphered. "After Ten Years" is a personal definition of his position and an assurance of his own conviction in a particular historical situation. And yet—and that is perhaps what gives the texts their fascination—some of his occasionally aphoristically expressed ideas have retained their topical reference over the years. Completely detached from their historical context, they are among the most frequently quoted of Bonhoeffer's dicta, as supposedly or in fact "timeless truths." His text is read with different eyes if what he says is seen strictly against the background of the situation in which he and his political friends were living at the end of 1942, tensed between paralysis in the face of the terror of war and dictatorship, and new hope in the face of plans for an overthrow that seemed at last to be assuming realistic form. Read with this sense for the contemporary situation, the text emerges in a new light. Here especially one can only echo the saying supposed to have been addressed to Augustine, "Take up and read!" Consequently, only a few points are touched on in our present framework.

In a "typology of failure"[26] Bonhoeffer describes the failure of individuals in all their many variations and the mechanisms of power that aim at subtle subjugation, showing how failure and power condition one another. He writes about conformity and disappointment, about rebellion and resignation, about self-deception and an overeager fulfilment of duty. About self-righteousness and the withdrawal into private life. About looking the other way and turning a deaf ear. Under the heading "Moral Courage" (a term not much used at that time), he writes that "in recent years we have seen a great deal of bravery and self-sacrifice but moral courage hardly anywhere, even among ourselves."[27] He describes how easily submissiveness, to the point of surrendering life, could be and is exploited.

What he has to say about folly reads like an essay within an essay. Here in his own way he describes the interaction between people and the circumstances in which they live and the latent mechanisms of power. People make fools of themselves and let others make fools of them too. Any evident display of power, whether it be religious or political, produces folly in a large part of the population: "The power of some needs the folly of the others."[28] He warns against contempt of other people, which is the main error of "our opponents," and against sticking fast in an atmosphere of betrayal and mutual self-isolation: "The air we breathe is so polluted by mistrust that it almost chokes us."[29] The passages under the heading of "the sense of quality" can only be understood against the background of the experiences of someone in and with Nazi Germany.[30] They are among the few utterances of Bonhoeffer's that are often quoted, and today they sound strange and disconcerting. But this was probably not so for people who were directly confronted with the pure arrogance of power, with frenetic masses, and with fanatical Nazi supporters—in short, with the simple terror encountered every day.

Toward the end of the essay he makes a plea for the optimism that is so much looked down upon by "the wise." Here as hardly anywhere else, as it seems to me, he writes with his main address-ees directly before his eyes. He seems to have in mind Hans Oster's apparently never-ebbing confidence, his repeated new attempts with continually vacillating generals; and Hans von Dohnanyi's appar-ently permanent struggle with himself, against resignation, against skepticism, against revulsion. Bonhoeffer paints a picture of opti-mism as a fundamental vital force and hope. "It enables a man to hold his head high when everything seems to be going wrong; it gives him strength to sustain reverses and yet to claim the future for himself instead of abandoning it to his opponent."[31] This is only in seeming contrast to the following passage about death, in which Bonhoeffer writes as "we," but in which he can ultimately only speak for himself.[32] It expresses his awareness of death and his love for life yet his composure in the face of death. It would seem that he had not only become used to the continual proximity of death but that he was reconciled to it, though without any heroic contempt for death and without any grandiose farewells.

seventeen

Death Zone

ON THE FIRST DAY of 1943, the final offensive of the Soviet army began and with it the final chapter in the battle of Stalingrad. The situation of the German soldiers was catastrophic, and such news as filtered through to the Reich about the real situation made many people grasp for the first time that the victorious progress of the war and the delusion of a victory for Hitler's Germany was inexorably beginning to disintegrate. A month later Field Marshal Paulus signed the capitulation of the Sixth Army, contrary to Hitler's will. For many people Stalingrad became the symbol of the senselessness of the war.

During these weeks, in the second half of January, a conference between the Western allies took place in the North African port of Casablanca. At this conference the president of the United States, Franklin D. Roosevelt, and the British prime minister, Winston Churchill, proclaimed the formula about Germany's unconditional surrender; only that could bring about an end to the war. This ruled out any (intermediate) solution on the basis of negotiations, a compromise, a partial withdrawal, or a separate peace. Before the forum of the world, an uncompromising message was sent in response to the fanatical German policy of conquest. This message was that there would only be one way to end the war. Churchill's earlier demand for "absolute silence" in response to any approaches from the German side now led in a logical step to the demand for unconditional surrender.[1]

Although Moltke and Trott, among others, still did not give up completely,[2] for opposition circles in Germany, this demand meant an end to all further attempts to convince London and Washington of their existence. It also ended the chances of sounding out the possibility of at least a temporary stop to military operations in the event of an overthrow. The reaction to Casablanca of the regime opponents was entirely negative. At that point the great majority rejected such an unconditional capitulation, which implied more than just military surrender. It was only Moltke who, in the course of 1943, seems to have abandoned his reservations toward the Allied formula.[3] If Bonhoeffer still stood by his Sigtuna "call for repentance"—and there is no reason to suppose anything else—he would not have resisted the Casablanca resolution. During the discussions in Sweden, more than six months previously, the bishop of Chichester noted down Bonhoeffer's words that "Christians do not wish to escape repentance, or chaos if God wills to bring it on us. We must accept this judgment as Christians."[4]

During these weeks the mood wavered between panic and resignation. There was "something like a feeling of catastrophe."[5] And for many people any future seemed illusory. But Maria von Wedemeyer broke through the depressed and depressing atmosphere that threatened to suffocate her home after the death at the front of her father and brother the previous year. She took the initiative that Bonhoeffer had hesitated to do, out of respect for her mother's grief. Now Maria confronted her mother directly with the fact that she wanted to marry Bonhoeffer and was going to do so. She broke through the bar to any contact to which they had agreed, and on January 13 wrote him a long letter. For them both, this letter counted as the date of their engagement. Its final sentence ran, "With all my happy heart, I can now say yes." Bonhoeffer replied by return of post. His answer reflects the happiness he had not dared to hope for, but also his tenuous sense of his own value and his anxieties: "It's only this 'yes' of yours that can give me the courage to stop saying 'no' to myself. Don't say anything about the 'false picture' I may have of you. I don't want a 'picture,' I want you; just as I beg you with all my heart to want me, not a picture of me—and you must surely know that those are two different things." He was willing to comply with her request that the next six months should be seen as a probationary period, as they had originally agreed, and to dispense with all contact, even though he could not understand why there had to be this "law of silence." On January 24, 1943, he wrote to her again: "The immediate future may hold events of such elemental importance, for our private lives as well, that it would be forced and unnatural for us to be unable to communicate, if only by letter."[6]

On February 8, after the two-day discussion with Constantin von Dietze of Freiburg about the memorandum project,[7] Bonhoeffer was once more in the train from Berlin to Munich, on his way to Switzerland "on business." The journey had already been postponed several times, and he had hardly arrived in Munich before he received a warning from Berlin, which again rested on the special contacts between the Oster group and Arthur Nebe, the SS lieutenant-general in the Reich Central Security Office. Against the background of Schmidhuber's interrogation—Schmidhuber being his "control" officer—Bonhoeffer was "urgently advised" not to travel, even though it now seemed a particularly appropriate time for him to demonstrate once again his role as indispensable spy into foreign affairs in the service of the Military Intelligence.[8] After an evening spent with his Intelligence colleague Josef Müller, Bonhoeffer returned to Berlin on February 12. During these weeks the atmosphere in the Oster group was nervous and anxious, the more so because Ludwig Beck had been diagnosed as suffering from a serious illness and had to undergo a complicated operation at the beginning of March.

Meanwhile there were evidently further travel plans for Bonhoeffer, as we know from a letter to Maria von Wedemeyer. It was again she who broke through the period of silence. On March 9 she phoned him in Berlin because she was suddenly unable to endure the uncertainty and her fear for him. In the letter Bonhoeffer wrote immediately after her phone call, he told her, "I'm now off to Rome for several weeks. When shall we go there together?"[9] But it would seem that this time he did not even get as far as Munich; at least we know nothing of it. What we do know, however, is that on March 13 he received an order from the Munich recruiting station to report for military service, upon which Hans Oster, with all the necessary haste, managed to arrange for a new "*uk*" position.[10]

In the historiography of the resistance movement (and especially in the biographies of Bonhoeffer and Dohnanyi), March 1943 is usually associated with two failed attempts on Hitler's life: the assassination attempt by Henning von Tresckow and Fabian von Schlabrendorff on March 13, and the attempt made by Rudolf-Christoph von Gersdorff on March 21. In their autobiographies, Schlabrendorff and Gersdorff have given detailed and vivid accounts of the events of these two March days, and the standard works on the resistance have followed them.[11] In the autumn of 1941, first contacts were made between Major General Oster and Colonel Henning von Tresckow, who was stationed on the eastern front. These contacts were intensified during 1942 and gave a new contour to plans for an overthrow, especially since a link was also established with General Friedrich Olbricht, a consistent and reliable Hitler opponent, who was chief of the general army office in Berlin and deputy commander of the reserve army. Tresckow's adjutant, Fabian von Schlabrendorff, acted as constant courier between the increasingly critical officer group around Tresckow in the Central Army Group (among them Gersdorff) and the Berlin "central office."[12]

Tresckow was one of the officers who, following his own complicity in the criminal occupation policy, and because of that, became an exponent of the military opposition.[13] Once the Führer had been eliminated, a coup d'etat was to smooth the way for a military dictatorship. Together with Olbricht, he began to consider various scenarios and increasingly tried to find realistic ways of killing Hitler, in order that his assassination should act as a detonator for the coup d'etat (*Initialzündung*, "detonator," was in fact the code name for the attempt). Hitler's projected visit to the headquarters of the Central Army Group in Smolensk on March 13 seemed to offer one of the few chances. A few days before, Dohnanyi supplied Tresckow and Schlabrendorff with explosives from supplies in the possession of the Military Intelligence. In his Bonhoeffer biography, Bethge recalls this brief journey of Dohnanyi's, a few days before March 13: "In his suitcase there was a special English explosive. . . . With no inkling of what was in the suitcase, I drove [him] in the car specially permitted to doctors that belonged to Bonhoeffer's father, to the night train that was to take him to East Prussia." From there Dohnanyi and Canaris flew to Smolensk on a routine visit to Intelligence officers there, taking this opportunity to settle details with Tresckow and Schlabrendorff.[14] In Marikje Smid's biography of Dohnanyi, she tells that in Christine von Dohnanyi's diary the entry for March 7, 1943, runs, "Hans to Smolensk," and this entry is specially marked. Smid adds that Bethge had driven Dohnanyi to Königsberg in his father-in-law's car. In Königsberg, Dohnanyi took a box with explosives on board Canaris's aircraft and flew with him to Smolensk. "During the stop in Smolensk on March 7, Dohnanyi was able to convey the box to Tresckow without being noticed."[15]

Tresckow, again, had a daring idea, and during Hitler's visit to Smolensk, he succeeded in depositing the explosive in the aircraft that was to take Hitler back again. The attempt failed because the detonator did not go off. It remained undetected because Tresckow was able to get rid of the traces in time. A second chance presented itself on March 21. Tresckow persuaded Gersdorff that a "suicide attack" was necessary and possible, since Gersdorff was able to be present at the opening of an exhibition in the Berlin arsenal that Hitler wanted to view. Gersdorff declared that he was prepared to blow up Hitler and, if necessary, himself too, during Hitler's visit. But Hitler unexpectedly left the exhibition so quickly that the explosive's time fuse had no chance to go off. But again Gersdorff was able to deactivate the bomb in time, so that this assassination attempt also went undiscovered.[16] The biographies of Bonhoeffer and Dohnanyi describe how, at the time, the Bonhoeffer family was practicing a birthday cantata in the Schleichers' house for Karl Bonhoeffer's impending seventy-fifth birthday. Ursula Schleicher remembered that her elder sister, Christine von Dohnanyi, was obviously nervous, and whispered to her, "It must go off any minute."[17]

It is impossible to decide now how much Bonhoeffer knew about the assassination attempts, or how in detail the fact of their failure was received in the Oster group. It is impossible to determine this because the timing of the intended assassinations must be viewed as problematical. "The exact dating is uncertain because the statements of the contemporary witnesses on which we are dependent in the matter are as a rule projections into the past of later events."[18] In addition, in recent times even the very fact of these attempts has in general been called in question.[19] In any case, what is untenable is the assertion that these assassination attempts by members of the military resistance were carried out "with the partly direct, partly indirect participation of Bonhoeffer."[20] This grossly exaggerates Bonhoeffer's role and importance in the resistance. What is certain is that in March 1943, among civilian and military representatives of the resistance, ideas about an assassination and a coup d'etat took form, and these then led to practical plans.[21] Apart from that, it is also certain that in the period in question members of the Oster circle, at least, were weighed down by very different thoughts about the future because of the imprisonment of Schmidhuber and Ickrath in the Reich Central Security Office's own prison.

The question: who was responsible for the suspicion about the Military Intelligence that emerged during the investigations, and for its consequences? This question was bandied about between the army's legal authorities and the Reich Central Security Office; and here the latter's covetous grasp at the autonomy of the army's own Intelligence doubtless played a considerable part. A scandal about the internal affairs of the "Canaris office" could be the beginning of that office's end. The background was the (ultimately speaking still obscure) competitive situation between the Reich Central Security

Office and the Military Intelligence Foreign Office, which, as we have seen, came under the army high command and had long been a thorn in the flesh of the Reich Security Office. The currency irregularities of a member of the staff of the Munich department of the Military Intelligence offered a welcome opportunity to intervene, to follow them up, and then to spread other suspicions.

Thus, what was basically a triviality in the systematic chaos of those war years was used as a pretext, initiated by leading quarters in the Gestapo as a way of, at long last, inflicting a wound on the long suspected institution at what was perhaps a vulnerable point. Canaris had long been an object of suspicion in the Reich Central Security Office; and if nothing could be laid personally at his door, perhaps at least his closest members of staff were open to attack. That in actual fact the attack reached the heart of one of the most important resistance cells was not realized at the time. When warnings increased to a threatening degree, suggesting that the network of investigations into alleged irregularities inside the Military Intelligence (especially in connection with Oster and Dohnanyi, Bonhoeffer and Josef Müller)[22] was about to be drawn tight, Dohnanyi and Oster decided to take certain precautionary measures. Among other things, Bonhoeffer's status as agent was to be "shored up." In the course of these tense weeks in February and March 1943, they therefore suggested to Bonhoeffer that backdated papers should be constructed as a way of lending more plausibility to the official Military Intelligence papers of the agent Bonhoeffer. The papers had ostensibly been issued by the Intelligence office in Munich, where Bonhoeffer was "controlled" by the at-present imprisoned Wilhelm Schmidhuber, while being actually employed by the central office in Berlin. True, Oster was hardly able to imagine that a sudden attack would be lodged by the Gestapo on the hitherto still inviolate Military Intelligence,[23] but it nevertheless seemed advisable to document in painstaking detail, and retrospectively, the perhaps not very convincing incorporation of Bonhoeffer as Military Intelligence agent. To produce fictitious material was normal practice in a secret service; deception and cover were part of the daily agenda. But here it was a matter of covering up internal conspiratorial activities. The cover had to be perfected for the protection of all those concerned. Bonhoeffer and Dohnanyi subsequently constructed his "letter of application," in which the internationally experienced churchman recommended himself to the Military Intelligence. In addition, official letters from Dohnanyi and Oster were now appended that acted as a backup for the Munich connection of the newly acquired agent; and the apparently conscientious agent drew up a travel diary.[24]

During the last week in March, Bonhoeffer again felt that he was living in suspense. "I shall probably, at long last, be leaving in the next few days," he wrote to Maria von Wedemeyer in his letter of March 24. She replied two days later, "I hope you have a wonderful trip. You'll tell me all about it later, won't you? I think about 'later' all day long and far too much if the truth be told!"[25] Bonhoeffer was supposed to travel to Rome with Josef Müller in order to intensify contacts with the Vatican. But the journey was again put off, evidently for reasons of security, and was finally planned for April 9. There was one incidental advantage: Bonhoeffer was able to help celebrate his father's seventy-fifth birthday on March 31; a photo shows that he was present.[26] The days that followed require a more exact chronology.[27]

On Saturday, April 3, 1943 Manfred Roeder was ordered to take up an appointment at the Reich War Court. Roeder was a doctor of law, was judge advocate at the air force court martial, and had been much praised for his recent intervention against the Rote Kapelle, which was outlawed and persecuted as a network of Communist agents. From August 1942, under that name, many members of variously oriented resistance circles had been indicted with Roeder's decisive participation, and for the most part executed. Now, at the Reich War Court, he was entrusted with further investigations of Schmidhuber's activities. Roeder was very much persona grata with the Reich Central Security Office, and he from his side also kept this department informed about the progress of the investigations. He combed through the Schmidhuber documents (with which he was already familiar for the most part) and came to the conclusion that he was on the track of currency offenses and a disregard of currency regulations, and that Schmidhuber was open to the suspicion of subversive treasonable activities.

On Sunday, April 4, one rumor followed hard on another. Canaris stepped in, so as to protect Oster and Dohnanyi. But information about the reasons for his intervention is contradictory. According to the account in Oster's biography, Canaris was warned about Roeder's activities by someone high up in army legal quarters, and this made him seek out Oster immediately, telling him to destroy all possibly incriminating documents, whereupon Oster tried to reassure him. According to the account in the Bonhoeffer biography, on the basis of the same information, Canaris told Dohnanyi and Bonhoeffer that nothing serious would happen during the next few days; if the matter had not already been successfully quashed, it had at least been taken out of the hands of the Gestapo. Dohnanyi's imminent arrest need not be expected, since the army prosecuting authorities had their hands full elsewhere; this was stated as an addendum to the "all clear" to Canaris in the report on Operation 7, which has already been mentioned several times.[28]

On Monday, April 5, at 7:00 P.M., Moltke wrote from Berlin to his wife, telling her, "Today it is a warm spring day. During the morning it was still overcast, but after about 11 o'clock a warm sun came out. Unfortunately it was a very busy day. . . . At 12.30 I was with Dohnanyi. . . . Consequently the day was fragmented into a lot of little pieces, so that nothing much came of it."[29] He evidently did not yet know anything about any serious events in his department. "Has something terrible happened? I'm afraid that it's something very terrible," wrote Maria von Wedemeyer in her diary for April 5. She did not yet know either what had happened that day in Berlin.[30]

Roeder had appeared in the building of the Military Intelligence Foreign Office in Berlin, accompanied by the Gestapo commissar Franz Xaver Sonderegger. The latter had subjected Schmidhuber and Ickrath to interrogations from the beginning of the year and now acted as assistant to the newly appointed head of the investigation into the *Depositenkasse*, this being the name given to the proceeding against members of the Military Intelligence for currency violations. For the whole complex, incidentally, the old code word "Schwarze Kapelle," earlier used in 1940, was once more pressed into service.[31] The details about Roeder's appearance in the rooms of the Military Intelligence Foreign Office on April 5 and the events that followed have often been recounted in detail and are described here only in brief.[32]

Roeder was careful to conform exactly to the official procedure. He first had himself announced to the head of the department, Canaris, in order to inform him that his staff member Dohnanyi was about to be arrested, and that his office was to be searched; he asked for an officer to be present during this search. Dohnanyi was suspected of diverse official and currency offenses, and in addition was under suspicion of treasonable activities. Canaris accompanied Roeder and Sonderegger to Dohnanyi, whose office was accessible only through Oster's. Oster immediately turned to Roeder, telling him to arrest him, Oster, himself, since Dohnanyi had done nothing without his knowledge. Roeder was unable to comply, but he more or less did so a little later with different means. Incidentally, we have Oster's official written assessment of this young hope of the army's judicial department and his Gestapo adjutant. It follows the normal style of such assessments.

> Young, arrogant, pathologically ambitious, compulsively uninhibited, criminologist of the most modern kind, full of fantasies, with the piercing eyes of a braggart, who sees his own opinion confirmed when he puts things together and sees them as *fact* in the interests of his own purposes and his hoped for success. Greatly overestimates his own ability and sees things as he wants to see them. In his choice of means and methods he is quite unscrupulous. He could be described as a sadist. He is flanked by a subaltern detective with a squint (Sonderegger)—probably belonging to the Security Office—who is unable to look one in the eye.[33]

During the search of Dohnanyi's office, Roeder managed to have Oster—Major General Oster!—sent out of the room. More: on the same Monday, giving as a reason "connivance," he managed by means of an official complaint to the army high command to have Oster put under house arrest, with immediate effect, and a week later to have him suspended from office. Roeder's pretext was that Oster wanted to get rid of suspicious material. What was meant was the "slips of paper affair," which was later described particularly often in detail.

This was an incident in connection with three notes or "slips of paper" in a folder—"Portfolio Z (grey)"[34]—that (without mentioning Bonhoeffer's name) had to do with his part in the Military Intelligence and also in the conspiracy, although at that time Roeder was unaware of this. These slips were, first, a handwritten note of Bonhoeffer's about the call-up of clergy for military service as hitherto practiced; second, the main heads of a discussion between Dohnanyi and Müller about possible influence on the Vatican, and the coordination of Protestant and Catholic aims; and third, the possibilities and conditions under which "a German Protestant pastor"[35] could be employed in the centers of the worldwide churches—Rome, Geneva, or Stockholm. To read them is to be reminded of a picture puzzle, and that was precisely what was intended. They had to do with secret interventions by Bonhoeffer on behalf of the anti-Hitler coalition, but they were so formulated that they could appear to be preliminary attempts at the necessary coded language used in "regular" agent activities.[36] Because of a misunderstanding between Oster and Dohnanyi, Oster tried to take possession of one of these slips of paper—which was reason enough for Roeder to suspect him both immediately and permanently, to arrange for his immediate suspension from his post, and to have him put under house arrest.[37]

Roeder had quickly brought about Dohnanyi's arrest, and by doing so—although he was not fully aware of the fact—he had eliminated one of the most resolute enemies of the Nazi system. Moreover, in the wake of this arrest he had also in equally rapid fashion put Oster out of harm's way; and Oster was the closest collaborator of

Canaris, the head of the Central Department of the Military Intelligence Foreign Office. In addition—which Roeder perhaps guessed but could not know—he was one of the earliest and most uncompromising protagonists of the conspiracy against Hitler. With this, one of the conspiracy's most important executive centers was put out of action. It has been stressed ever since that this surprise attack of April 5, 1943, was an event with the most serious implications for the German resistance.[38] And it certainly wrecked the work of many years of continuous and consistent opposition to the Nazi regime.

Dohnanyi was taken to the military remand prison in Berlin-Moabit. In Munich, after Roeder had arranged matters with the authorities there, Josef Müller, his wife, his secretary, and a former member of his staff were arrested on the same day. In Sakrow, near Berlin, also on April 5, Gestapo officials turned up about midday at Dohnanyi's house with a search warrant and a warrant for the arrest of his wife ("on the grounds of treasonable subversive activities").[39] Christine von Dohnanyi was taken to the women's prison in Berlin-Charlottenburg. About four o'clock Roeder and Sonderegger drew up in front of the Bonhoeffers' family house, in the Marienburger Allee 43.

Bonhoeffer was not taken unawares. During the morning he had worked on the *Ethics*, on the section headed "The Concrete Commandment and the Divine Mandates," and probably specifically on a passage about "the deficiency of the Protestant church."[40] There he deplores among other things "a liturgical poverty and uncertainty" in Protestant services, and finally the "frightening confusion or arrogance on the part of countless Protestant Christians with regard to Christians who refuse to take an oath" (that is, of loyalty to Hitler), conscientious objectors, etc.[41] A few sentences later, the text breaks off. At midday he tried to phone his sister in Sakrow, but the telephone was answered only by a voice unknown to him, and he immediately realized that the house was being searched. He told his sister Ursula and his brother-in-law Rüdiger Schleicher, who lived next door, as well as his friend Eberhard Bethge, who was with them at the time.[42]

Bonhoeffer once more cleared his writing desk in the attic room in his parents' house—he did not want to disturb his parents' afternoon rest—and then went over to the Schleichers again. There were questions and uncertainty and fear, and yet they could do nothing but wait. Finally, his father asked him to come over: two men were waiting for him in his room. What followed was for them routine: search, arrest, the removal of the person concerned. Roeder confiscated a copy of Bonhoeffer's outline for a new church order,[43] as well as parts of the *Ethics* manuscript, but these were soon returned to Bonhoeffer's parents; the Gestapo evidently found the reading of them too hard going; and Bonhoeffer's faked diary, which had also been lying on the desk, curiously enough roused no interest.[44]

In the late afternoon of April 5, 1943, Bonhoeffer was taken to the army remand prison in Berlin-Tegel. Two years and four days later, on April 9, 1945, Hans von Dohnanyi was executed—murdered—in Sachsenhausen concentration camp, and Wilhelm Canaris, Hans Oster, and Dietrich Bonhoeffer in the concentration camp in Flossenbürg.

eighteen

Postscript

THE DAY OF HIS arrest, April 5, 1943, marks the end of Bonhoeffer's pseudo-existence as agent of the Military Intelligence and at the same time the end of his active participation in resistance against the Nazi regime. The period of his imprisonment has, indeed, been interpreted as "a continuation of the resistance with other means and under completely different conditions,"[1] and with this interpretation the length of his activity in the resistance is considerably extended; but it must be asked whether this last phase of his life can really be described as a period of resistance. Certainly, for months Bonhoeffer was still able to draw attention away from his real field of activity and to keep up the appearance of having worked for the Military Intelligence precisely according to regulations. Certainly, too, while he was "inside" he knew about further plans for an overthrow that were still afoot "outside," and certainly he tried to do everything possible while he was "inside" to protect his associates both inside and out. In that sense his imprisonment can be seen as resistance after the resistance, as an indirect aiding and abetting of the resistance, but not as resistance itself; for the imprisonment made it completely impossible to resist the Nazi dictatorship in the more precise sense of the word. That is to say, it was impossible to participate actively in attempts to weaken the regime, to say nothing of bringing it down.

For that reason the individual phases of the imprisonment are here only briefly touched on, as a postscript. What followed directly on the committal to the military detention prison in Tegel were two weeks of total isolation, eighteen months of solitary confinement, interrogations, censured and smuggled correspondence, and theological reflections (what later came to be called his Tegel theology). There were also secret contacts with the others who were imprisoned, especially Hans von Dohnanyi, and with people who were still free, in order to cover for them. There were the (at first) successful attempts to hide the conspiratorial links that had existed. The initially vague but highly dangerous suspicion of treason or high treason was dropped, and the interrogations were increasingly concentrated on the *uk* positions he held—Operation 7 played only a minor part in the investigations against Bonhoeffer, as did his journeys abroad. In September 1943 he was indicted "only" for escaping the call-up or for "subverting military power," though it must be added that this was in principle subject to the death penalty.[2] However, no regular proceedings followed, and there remained a hope that the matter would drag on and then "fizzle out."

After the failed attempt on Hitler's life of July 20, 1944, the real connections threatened to come to light, and with the discovery of the "Zossen" files in the autumn of 1944, Bonhoeffer's situation—and Dohnanyi's too—finally became critical, as did those of Hans Oster and Wilhelm Canaris, both of whom had been arrested after July 20. These documents, discovered in a safe in an outpost of the Military Intelligence south of Berlin, were evidence of many years of resistance activities in the central department. There were Canaris's notes about ideas for an overthrow, dating from the end of the 1930s, Josef Müller's X report, Dohnanyi's dossiers and manifestos, a study by Oster on the resources and plans of the conspiracy, etc. At the beginning of October, Bonhoeffer was transferred to the

Gestapo cellar of the Reich Security Head Office. His last letter to his parents is dated January 17, 1945.

From the beginning of February until the beginning of April, Bonhoeffer was in an air-raid shelter cell in Buchenwald concentration camp, and then, after a week's odyssey, was taken to the concentration camp in Flossenbürg. There, on the same day, after a personal directive of Hitler's that followed the discovery of more documents, and at a summary court martial, the death sentence was passed by an SS judge on the thirty-nine-year-old Dietrich Bonhoeffer. He was executed at dawn on April 9, 1945, only a month before Germany's capitulation and the end of the war in Europe.[3]

In the written histories of the German resistance, Bonhoeffer was from the beginning acknowledged to be one of its most important figures, and right down to the present day he is still one of its most uncontroversial personalities.[4] That is true not only for Germany but also, for example, for Poland, Great Britain, and the United States. Moreover, "among opponents of Hitler, in the English-speaking world he undoubtedly takes first place."[5] In addition, Bonhoeffer enjoys a positively astonishing popularity far beyond the limits of the church and theology or any denominational boundaries. In the course of the second half of the twentieth century he became for many people an unquestioned model, even an idol.

We know him as the theologian who early on already chose the path that led him into the conspiracy against Hitler, consistently and in full awareness of the deadly risk. Bonhoeffer is the much-described hero of faith, highly praised resistance fighter, the militant saint on his pinnacle, and the antifascist pioneer. Bonhoeffer's resistance activity counts for us as the "permanent mark" of an almost uniquely lived consensus of thinking and living. His motives were clear: because of his faith he came out against the National Socialist persecution of the Jews, against the war, against the inhumanity of the dictatorship. His morality belongs to the martyrdom of modern life. I believe it was this bland interpretation of Bonhoeffer that helped to make him the icon both of Protestantism and of the resistance.

Through his interpretation, Bonhoeffer's biographer Eberhard Bethge may have helped to build up this picture in its many forms. At the same time, this finding contrasts strongly with the very modest statements Bethge makes about Bonhoeffer's role in the resistance, and which today, in my view, should be noted all the more carefully: "Bonhoeffer's position in the Resistance Movement was of no great importance politically. . . . Regarding the planning for a future Germany and its constitutional forms Bonhoeffer's share in the conspiracy was comparatively small."[6] Or, "He is not a 'hero'; he is an accomplice conscious of his guilt."[7] And what did Bonhoeffer himself write to Maria von Wedemeyer? He begged her to want *him*, not a picture of him, "and you must surely know that those are two different things."[8]

In the prefaces to my two first books about Bonhoeffer, I pointed out at the beginning that every book has its own history. And that is true of the present book as well. In the framework of my work on Bonhoeffer hitherto, my eye was increasingly drawn to what I called the political Bonhoeffer, and there I was particularly interested in the question of what was really meant by Bonhoeffer "in the resistance" in concrete terms and without the gloss of the iconization. How did he get involved? When exactly did his involvement begin? What did it mean for his everyday normal life? What did everyday life in the resistance look like? Why was he an agent for the Military Intelligence? What did that mean, and what were the assignments he had to carry out? What part did he play in the resistance? With whom did he work—and with whom did he not? What was he able to achieve?

There is copious biographical material and a whole series of individual studies in Bonhoeffer research about this subject as well as a wealth of literature on the resistance, in which Bonhoeffer has a firm and sometimes a preeminent place, but there has been no self-contained account. I wanted to trace the history behind the history in order to arrive at a better understanding of what it means to say that Bonhoeffer joined the resistance. I wanted to communicate the events of that time through a compact, comprehensible account. And I wanted to proceed cautiously. How quickly we invoke the great, irreproachable members of the resistance, operate with slogans, and intensify or distort traditional spruced-up pictures! How casually we glorify Bonhoeffer and stylize him into the saint of Protestantism! I had long asked myself how far one contributes oneself, passively or actively, to this process of idolization—and I now asked myself how it could be avoided, especially with regard to his part in the resistance.

What began as a question about Bonhoeffer the person and as a specific "search for things past" led to further questionings[9] and to unexpected learning processes. It became all of sudden a critical analysis of the dominating picture of Bonhoeffer, of the redundant leitmotifs in Bonhoeffer reception, of fixed points and patterns of thought in Bonhoeffer research. In the previous chapters, I have drawn attention to this at the relevant points. Looking back, I would concentrate on ten points as focuses of the question about Bonhoeffer and the resistance.

1. At the beginning of Bonhoeffer's participation in the political resistance was the question about his call-up for military service. Bonhoeffer was unwilling to perform military service for reasons of faith and conscience, but he of course knew that the penalty for refusal was death. Helped by Hans Oster, Bonhoeffer's brother-in-law Hans Dohnanyi developed a particular construction that made the necessary "*uk*" status possible. From then on Bonhoeffer counted officially as agent for the Military Intelligence, for which his first-class contacts abroad were supposed to be of use. And, in fact, he really was able to put these contacts to use on behalf of the resistance group around Oster and Dohnanyi. So from the beginning of 1941, Bonhoeffer began to act for this group. In the foreground, therefore, was not a unique (let alone a datable) fundamental decision by Bonhoeffer to join the resistance. It was because of his personal, difficult, and risky decision to refuse to perform military service that he entered into the political work of the resistance with what was for him (theo)logical consistency.

2. The share of Hans von Dohnanyi and Hans Oster in this resistance work is very much greater than Bonhoeffer's, not least

because of the posts they held. And the same is true of their significance for the civilian opposition against the Nazi system in general.
Recent thorough investigations have provided impressive evidence
for Dohnanyi's importance.[10] Similar, more modern and well-
founded studies of Oster are still much needed in the framework of
research into the resistance.

3. Bonhoeffer's involvement in Operation 7 must be seen with
the appropriate objectivity, solely in its real extent, and must not
be unrealistically exaggerated. It is a fact that the pseudo-agents of
Operation 7 were able to remain in Switzerland and were thus able
to survive. Fourteen people were saved from the ethnic murder of
European Jews, and for this Hans von Dohnanyi's efforts were decisive. Bonhoeffer contributed as far as he could and used his contacts as far as was possible. Moltke wrote in March 1943 to England
that the opposition saved the lives of individuals. "We cannot prevent wild commands from being given, but we can save individual
people."[11]

4. The importance of Bonhoeffer's journey to Sweden and his
meeting with Bishop Bell in Sigtuna in 1942 has been particularly
emphasized, both elsewhere and in the present book. It was undoubtedly the high point of his conspiratorial activities. And yet we have
to ask: were Bonhoeffer's role and message not from the beginning—
that is to say from the time of Bell's reports—set in contrast to the
role and message of Hans Schönfeld—understandably, perhaps, but
improperly? Was Bonhoeffer's share in the Sigtuna meeting and the
special character of what he said not thereby exaggerated? And how
ought we to judge the actual value of the information that Bonhoeffer gave Bell?

5. The next question, too, is a question not so much about Bonhoeffer himself as about the picture of him that has developed during
recent decades. As we know, Bonhoeffer laid great stress on intellectual honesty. It would be intellectually dishonest, for example, to
ignore the political categories in which he—or the people in whose
name he spoke—thought at that time. He had joined what was later
called the civilian opposition and—much more emphatically—the

"national conservative opposition," and this came to be a matter of considerable controversy.[12] In Bonhoeffer research, Bonhoeffer's closeness to decidedly conservative circles in the resistance has become a disputed subject.[13] What he said in Sigtuna in 1942, for example, testifies to the specific context to which he belonged, and certain texts in the *Ethics*, for example, show that at that time his political thinking was conservative in tendency. To deny this conservative leaning or to see it as a later discrimination of Bonhoeffer and therefore to reject it is in my view unjustified factually and the sign of what might be bluntly called insufficiently developed tolerance. A Bonhoeffer reception that denied this tendency would be wearing ideological blinkers. The "theopolitical" structure constituted by the alloy of Prussianism and Protestantism permanently influenced him as well. "Bonhoeffer is an especially reflective representative of this form of living and thinking, a form that he himself described as the 'Prussian-Protestant world.'"[14] The question is not whether Bonhoeffer was conservative. The question is how far. His political thinking can certainly not be pressed into a fixed mold, but it was nevertheless characterized by markedly conservative values.

6. It is all the more remarkable that, in contrast, what is noticeable about the enormous posthumous influence that emanated from him are its mainly progressive and liberating impulses for thought and action. And it was often especially people in situations of oppression —in Latin America, South Africa, East Germany, Poland— who were influenced and impressed by him, and who drew from him political conclusions that were anything but conservative, and certainly not national-conservative. On the extensive scale that runs from elitist to egalitarian thinking, politically speaking Bonhoeffer could rather be put on the elitist side, but theologically on the egalitarian one. In theological questions and in matters of church politics, he was already at that time in many respects more "progressive," in the best sense of the word, than he was politically. In other words, his theological existence was ahead of his political awareness.

7. Apart from Bonhoeffer's practical participation in Operation 7, the question about his attitude to the persecution of the Jews

has for years been a matter of controversy. But this has a surprising sequel. A special problem in research into the resistance is, as is well known, the historically established fact that, with respect to the persecution of the Jews, the national conservative resistance—and not that only—was blind and deaf. The historian Hans Mommsen, however, stresses in his most recent studies on the resistance that Bonhoeffer was "a clear exception" to the disregard by members of the resistance of Jewish persecution; there he played an "outsider's role."[15] He sums up by saying that in fact the Jewish persecution played only a marginal part in the resistance. Even the churches intervened, if at all, only on behalf of baptized Jews, "if we disregard Bonhoeffer's largely isolated position." Mommsen then says, "Initiatives to put a spoke in the wheel of the regime and to circumvent the persecutory measures were initiated primarily by the highly motivated and extremely active group in the Military Intelligence around Oster, Dohnanyi, and Bonhoeffer."[16] In contrast to this viewpoint, in North American theological circles, and in the wake of post-Holocaust theology, Bonhoeffer's attitude to the Jewish persecution has been for years violently criticized.[17]

8. For me, confronting historical research into the resistance from the angle of Dietrich Bonhoeffer's participation presented a number of problems. In order to avoid misunderstanding, let me first stress yet again my tremendous regard for Bethge's great Bonhoeffer biography. At the same time, I should like to pass on the following observation. The biography's eminently high position in Bonhoeffer research is well known. It opens the door to the whole subject of Bonhoeffer. In examining the literature on the resistance movement that was relevant for the present book, I discovered that for this, too, the biography holds the same key position. The resulting interdependences are astonishing. There are endless circularities in the literary references in the Bonhoeffer literature. These are sometimes amusing but are not particularly helpful: basic biography, Bonhoeffer research, resistance studies, basic biography, and so on.

9. Not only is the Bonhoeffer reception no proof against certain tendencies toward legend-building. The same is evidently true of

resistance studies. At the moment, for example, the burning question seems to be how far the recent massively formulated doubts about plans for an overthrow and an assassination in 1938 onward and in 1943 are justified.[18] In any event, what is still acute is the question that comes under the heading of "crimes committed by the German army." Ever since the 1990s this has led to heated disputes among both scholars and the general public. There is historical evidence that members of the army participated in crimes against humanity, and this finding necessarily also leads to corrections of the generally accepted picture of those members of the resistance who were connected with the army. What has to be said about men of the resistance involved in the assassination attempt of July 20, 1944, is certainly not true of them alone: "Factually speaking . . . it has to be admitted that a considerable number of those who played a part on July 20, 1944, and who in many cases sacrificed their lives in doing so, were earlier involved in the war of racial extermination, occasionally at least approved it, and in some cases actively pursued it."[19]

10. When we turn to Bonhoeffer in particular, it is noticeable that he is considered to be the pioneer thinker and theologian of the resistance par excellence. Yet his biographer was certainly right when he said that he could not be described or understood as a Christian theorist of the resistance,[20] and the assertion that as early as the beginning of 1932 he worked out a "theology of resistance"[21] is hardly tenable. Even later, he did not develop any finished and systematic theology of resistance. Bonhoeffer was not the theologian of the resistance. He was a theologian in resistance. Nor did he act, as it might be, out of any distinct political theory. During one of their last meetings in the spring of 1945, Hans von Dohnanyi said to his wife, "When all is said and done, Dietrich and I didn't do the thing as politicians. It was simply the way a decent person had to go."[22]

Is any summing up possible? What part did Bonhoeffer play in the resistance, and how should his importance for the resistance be judged? If he was neither the heroic resistance fighter nor the spiritual leader of the German resistance, what then? What if what he did was not crowned with success and led to nothing? Our answer can only be a tentative one. What it really was we do not know. Or what it was we do not really know. It is true that a closer analysis shows that Bonhoeffer's real part in conspiratorial resistance activities was much slighter than is usually assumed, and this slight share brought hardly any demonstrable results. But perhaps he was also active in the resistance in ways about which, even today, we still know nothing.

What is a matter of certain knowledge in this respect is merely a modest balance sheet of operational steps, specific missions, and factual results. Bonhoeffer's importance does not lie so much in any quantitatively measurable contribution to resistance against the Nazi regime. His importance lies in the ethical foundation for resistance that he offered. He was important for what he said, perhaps less for what he did. The "internal role" that he played in his resistance circle can most readily be described as intellectual pastoral care. Today it might be called "mental support"; and something like the "religious factor" in the German resistance should probably not be undervalued. Bonhoeffer was a "spiritual," to borrow a term from the Catholic religious orders. He was a pastor, a father confessor, a spiritual adviser. But he was a pastor in an unorthodox sense, a father confessor without ritual, a spiritual adviser in unspiritual situations. Bonhoeffer strengthened other people in what they did at points where the church was silent, and therefore, in spite of some differences, among those involved in the resistance he strengthened believers especially—and of these believers there were not a few in his immediate circle, for example, Oster, Beck, Hans Bernd von Haeften, Goerdeler, Schleicher, and Ewald von Kleist-Schmenzin. They received little support from their official Protestant church and acted without its legitimation. This gap could be closed by Bonhoeffer's theological and pastoral counseling, which had to take place quite unpretentiously, without any official position, without pulpit or consistory, without absolution and sacrament. What is perhaps Bonhoeffer's least theological text is the essay "After Ten Years," which was meant for Hans Oster and Hans von Dohnanyi; but this contains a theologically based reflection about everyday life in the dictatorship. The fact that he wrote this text for these two men indicates an inward closeness and openness that has much to do with friendship and has more still to do with belief. It has to do with shared questions about faith and the lack of faith, about ethics, and about failure.

It was perhaps Bonhoeffer's sometimes positively audacious hope that made him look to the future, in spite of what looked like hard facts. He refused to say that resignation was in the right, and his optimism was insistent—hope against hope, but with confidence in God's promise. It was in this hope that his strength lay.[23] It seems that he lived this hope for God's greater reality to the end, and that he was able, to the last, to communicate it to other people.

Bonhoeffer was a pioneer of hope. To live with hope—and to live with guilt: that was what could be learned from him. His understanding of the Christian faith could bring about an ethical liberation that made action possible. Apparently it was his special concern and task "to set their consciences at rest."[24] To live with the dilemma that not to act meant guilt, and that to act meant guilt—by acting to become knowingly guilty, and to be able to live with that knowledge before God: that was the special thing about Bonhoeffer's liberating "guilt declaration." He knew what he was talking about. With his knowledge about plans for an assassination and his complicity in the conspiracy, he had deliberately taken guilt on himself. We make ourselves guilty, but we have to do so—and we can live before God with this guilt. Perhaps it was particularly important in the specific situation of the time that this was said not just by "someone," "in good faith," but that it was said by a Lutheran theologian. This liberation to accept guilt is the special thing about Bonhoeffer, and it must be seen as his particular share in the ethical foundation of the resistance.

This summing up sounds very modest. It is not intended to diminish Bonhoeffer's importance, let alone is it meant to be a demolition. It is intended to demythologize a construct—for Bonhoeffer's own sake. The reconstruction of his activity in the resistance has led to a deconstruction—not to the destroying of the object but to the correction of what were pictures or images.

Bonhoeffer did not fit the image of the resistance fighter, working underground and waging a consistent and unrelenting struggle from the beginning of the Third Reich until its end. He was not the "pure martyr" who in selfless surrender allowed himself to be killed for his faith. He was a man of flesh and blood who did not seek death but wanted to live, marry, go on working—in short, who wanted to have a future. And this was so although he was aware of the risk of death, or just because of his awareness—although (as he wrote at the end of 1942) he had "almost come to terms" with the death that was perhaps so imminent, or for that very reason.[25] He was someone who did not try to escape even his own insufficiency. In the middle of his essay "After Ten Years," there is a section headed "A few articles of faith on the sovereignty of God in history." It interrupts the style and flow of his ideas—even the somewhat wooden heading is out of line with the rest of the text—but it includes a passage in which Bonhoeffer ceases to speak as "we," as he does elsewhere in the essay, but talks as "I" and formulates a personal creed:

> I believe that God can and will bring good out of evil, even out of the greatest evil. For that purpose he needs men who make the best use of everything. I believe that God will give us all the strength we need to help us to resist in all time of distress. But he never gives it in advance, lest we should rely on ourselves and not on him alone. A faith such as this should allay all our fears for the future. I believe that even our mistakes and shortcomings are turned to good account, and that it is no harder for God to deal with them than with our supposedly good deeds. I believe that God is no timeless fate, but that he waits for and answers sincere prayers and responsible actions.[26]

This understanding of existence was based on the certainty of God's presence—in spite of this world and in the face of this world; in spite of the frontier of death and in the face of that frontier. In this certainty Bonhoeffer experienced what he described in the last section of his *Ethics* manuscript: "The cross of reconciliation sets us free to live before God in the midst of the godless world."[27] His theology of the world and worldliness, and his matter-of-fact, undivided devotion were not mutually exclusive. They included each other. The this-worldliness of faith, based on the existence and presence of the Nazarene, which he so vehemently maintained, and his commitment to the conspiracy corresponded to each other. His resistance did not issue from a grudging acknowledgment that "he was bound to resist" the Nazi regime in spite of his Christian faith. It resulted from his theological self-understanding, the conviction that he had to seek a way of resistance in the world in which he lived just because of his faith. And here we come upon his question about the reality of God in the reality of the world, and upon Bonhoeffer's own answer: a worldly Christian existence in a godforsaken time.

In the interplay between research and reflection, I have tried to reconstruct the phase of Bonhoeffer's life that counts as the period of his resistance. I wanted to fetch him down from the heaven of blind admiration onto the ground of the life he lived—"to put him on his feet again."[28] Not in order to diminish him, let alone to defame him, not in the polemical sense of pontificating exposure literature, but in order to do him justice, with his "imperfect," his even contradictory and fragmented life, and in that very way to offer him the respect—more: the honor—that he deserves. And we should be careful not to elevate him to the dead-and-gone Olympus of heroes of the resistance and of faith. For his own sake, we should see to it that he remains fallible and questionable, understandable and conceivable. It is only in this way that the stagnation of remembrance can be counteracted: the remembrance of Bonhoeffer as one of the people in resistance.

In Memoriam

THE FOLLOWING MEN MENTIONED in this book lost their lives because of their participation in resistance against the Nazi regime.

Ludwig Beck on July 20, 1944
Dietrich Bonhoeffer on April 9, 1945
Klaus Bonhoeffer on April 23, 1945
Wilhelm Canaris on April 9, 1945
Justus Delbrück in October 1945
Alfred Delp on February 2, 1945
Hans von Dohnanyi on April 9, 1945
Georg Elser on April 9, 1945
Carl Friedrich Goerdeler on February 2, 1945
Karl Ludwig von Guttenberg on April 23, 1945
Hans-Bernd von Haeften on August 15, 1944
Werner von Haeften on July 20, 1944
Ernst von Harnack on March 5, 1945
Ulrich von Hassell on September 8, 1944
Erich Hoepner on August 8, 1944
Hans John on April 23, 1945
Ewald von Kleist-Schmenzin on April 9, 1945
Julius Leber on January 5, 1945
Wilhelm Leuschner on September 29, 1944

Helmuth James von Moltke on January 23, 1945
Friedrich Olbricht on July 20, 1944
Hans Oster on April 9, 1945
Friedrich Justus Perels on April 23, 1945
Rüdiger Schleicher on April 23, 1945
Claus Schenk von Stauffenberg on July 20, 1944
Hermann Stöhr on June 21, 1940
Henning von Tresckow on July 21, 1944
Adam von Trott zu Solz on August 26, 1944
Peter Yorck von Wartenburg on August 8, 1944
Erwin von Witzleben on August 8, 1944

Abbreviations

The following abbreviations are used in the notes:

Bethge, DB Biog. Eberhard Bethge, *Dietrich Bonhoeffer: Theologian—Christian—Contemporary* (1970). The standard English language edition is now *Dietrich Bonhoeffer, A Biography: Theologian, Christian, Man for His Times* (rev. and ed. Victoria J. Barnett; Minneapolis: Fortress Press, 2000).

DBW *Dietrich Bonhoeffer Werke* (17 volumes; ed. E. Bethge et al.; Munich, 1986–98).

DBWE *Dietrich Bonhoeffer Works*, a translation into English of DBW (gen. ed. Wayne Whitson Floyd Jr. et al.; Minneapolis: Fortress Press 1996–).

GS Dietrich Bonhoeffer, *Gesammelte Schriften* (ed. E. Bethge; Munich, 1957; 2nd ed. 1965).

Notes

1. Courier—In Whose Service?

1. DBWE 16:305f.
2. Ibid., 401.
3. DBW 14:126.
4. DBWE 16:329.
5. See Dorothee von Meding, *Mit dem Mut des Herzens: Die Frauen des 20. Juli* (Berlin, 1992), 39.
6. DBW 15:175f.
7. E. Bethge, DB Biog., 557–60; also DBW 15:227 and 225f.
8. Christoph Strohm, *Theologische Ethik im Kampf gegen den Nationalsozialismus: Der Weg Dietrich Bonhoeffers mit den Juristen Hans von Dohnanyi und Gerhard Leibholz in den Widerstand* (Munich, 1989), 3.
9. DBW 15:227 and 225f.
10. Ibid., 252, 647.
11. E. Bethge, DB Biog., 559; also DBW 15:644.
12. DBW 15:650f. Since the translation of this volume has not yet appeared, the above letter, originally written in English, is given here in paraphrase. The prime minister at the time was Neville Chamberlain, one of the signatories of the Munich agreement in the autumn of 1938.

2. A Change of Course

1. In considering processes and caesuras in anyone's life, different emphases are always possible. Cf., e.g., E. Bethge, DB Biog., 526, and idem, "Bonhoeffers Weg vom 'Pazifismus' zur Verschwörung," in *Frieden—das unumgängliche Wagnis: Die Gegenwartsbedeutung der Friedensethik D. Bonhoeffers* (ed. H. Pfeifer; Munich, 1982), 126f.; Christoph Strohm, *Theologische Ethik im Kampf gegen den Nationalsozialismus: Der Weg Dietrich Bonhoeffers mit den Juristen Hans von Dohnanyi und Gerhard Leibholz in den Widerstand* (Munich, 1989), 5; and Peter Steinbach, *Widerstand im Widerstreit: Der Widerstand gegen den Nationalsozialismus in der Erinnerung der Deutschen. Ausgewählte Studien* (2nd ed.; Paderborn, 2001), 450f.

2. Peter Hoffmann, *Widerstand, Staatsstreich, Attentat: Der Kampf der Opposition gegen Hitler* (3rd ed.; Munich, 1979), 66; Engl. trans. by R. Barry: *The History of the German Resistance 1933–1945* (Cambridge, 1977).

3. Winfried Meyer, "Staatsstreichplanung, Opposition und Nachrichtendienst: Widerstand aus dem Amt Ausland/Abwehr im Oberkommando der Wehrmacht," in *Widerstand gegen den Nationalsozialismus* (ed. P. Steinbach and J. Tüchel; Bonn, 1994), 320.

4. According to Klaus-Jürgen Müller, "Der nationalkonservative Widerstand," in *Widerstand gegen den Nationalsozialismus* (ed. P. Steinbach and J. Tuchel; Munich and Zurich, 1985), 55, and Joachim Fest, *Staatsstreich: Der lange Weg zum 20. Juli* (Berlin, 1994), 101, the terms "fundamental opposition" or "resistance" are already appropriate, and their plans count as having had the greatest chances of success at the time. H. Mommsen, on the other hand ("Die Stellung der Militäropposition," in *Alternative zu Hitler: Studien zur Geschichte des deutschen Widerstands* [Munich, 2000], 7; Engl. trans. by A. McGeoch: *Alternatives to Hitler: German Resistance under the Third Reich* [Princeton, 2003]), remarks merely that they "were still, as we know, episodes." They "remained vague and unstructured," in the view of Karl Heinz Roth's recently formulated sharp criticism (Roth and Angelika Ebbinghaus, eds., *Rote Kapellen—Kreisauer Kreise—Schwarze Kapellen: Neue Sichtweisen auf den Widerstand gegen die NS-Diktatur 1938–1945* [Hamburg, 2004], 42). He further states that these were by no means already plans for an assassination: "The memoirs of certain historians of the resistance have passed on the theory that at that time the Oster-Gisevius group already planned the assassination of Hitler; but this belongs to the realm of legend."

5. According to Christine von Dohnanyi, quoted in J. Fest, *Staatsstreich*, 87.

6. There was for a time an idea that Hitler should be arrested and that a panel of doctors headed by the professor for psychiatry, Karl Bonhoeffer (Dohnanyi's father-in-law and Dietrich Bonhoeffer's father), should declare

him insane and incapable of acting. See Bethge, DB Biog., 535, and, e.g.,
J. Fest, *Staatsstreich*, 93.

7. Hans von Dohnanyi to Bonhoeffer in April 1945, quoted in Marikje Smid,
   Hans von Dohnanyi—Christine Bonhoeffer: Eine Ehe im Widerstand gegen Hitler
   (Gütersloh, 2002), 361.

8. Eberhard Bethge, *In Zitz gab es keine Juden: Erinnerungen aus meinen ersten vierzig
   Jahren* (Munich, 1989), 104. In this connection attention must be drawn to
   the great importance of Christine von Dohnanyi's statements for what we
   know today.

9. E. Bethge, DB Biog., 534.

10. Discussions about the term are legion; see, e.g., the contributions by Ian
    Kershaw, "Widerstand ohne Volk? Dissens und Widerstand im Dritten
    Reich," in *Der Widerstand gegen den Nationalsozialismus* (ed. J. Schmädeke und
    P. Steinbach; Munich and Zurich, 1985), 781f.; Franciszek Ryszka, "Wid-
    erstand: Ein wertfreier oder ein wertbezogener Begriff?" in *Der Widerstand
    gegen den Nationalsozialismus* (ed. K. Schmädeke and P. Steinbach; Munich
    and Zurich, 1985), 1107ff.; or P. Steinbach, *Widerstand im Widerstreit*, 51ff.;
    as well as the discussions about the forms and wide spectrum of the resis-
    tance contained in the standard words, e.g., P. Hoffmann, *Widerstand* (34ff.),
    or K. von Klemperer, *German Resistance against Hitler: The Search for Allies
    Abroad, 1938–1945* (Oxford, 1992), 2–4. 10ff.

11. Peter Steinbach, "Der Widerstand gegen die Diktatur: Hauptgruppen und
    Grundzüge der Systemopposition," in *Deutschland 1933–1945* (ed. K. D.
    Bracher, M. Funke, and H.-A. Jacobsen; Düsseldorf, 1992), 453.

12. Hans Mommsen, "Der Widerstand gegen Hitler und die deutsche Gesell-
    schaft," in *Der Widerstand gegen den Nationalsozialismus* (ed. J. Schmädeke
    and P. Steinbach; Munich and Zurich, 1985), 11. His work, as he himself
    stresses (7), aims "to describe the resistance as a political process, in large
    part also as a political learning process that . . . broke through the totalitar-
    ian glass-house of non-communication with the outer world."

13. Cf., e.g., the much-noted successive stages of resistance recorded in Bethge's
    early (1963) work on Adam von Trott ("Adam von Trott und der deutsche
    Widerstand," *Vierteljahreshefte für Zeitgeschichte* 11 [1963], 221f.) (passive
    resistance, open ideological resistance, shared knowledge, active prepara-
    tion, responsible conspiratorial action). In connection with Bonhoeffer, and
    in his biography, he varies this and pins it down (526). For K. von Klem-
    perer (*German Resistance against Hitler*, 2) the range of resistance to National
    Socialism includes, e.g., conscientious objection, sabotage, betrayal of state
    secrets, secret memoranda about a new order and attempts at assassina-
    tion, individual actions and plotting. He writes "The road into resistance

is an unpaved one. . . . In most instances resistance is not even a matter of a clear decision. Resistance, the momentous step, is mainly a matter of gradual and intensified awareness translated into political action which, in turn, is propelled by chance as much as by conviction. In any case it becomes operative at the point when the burden becomes so unsupportable as to sweep away all considerations of conforming and coasting along and to call for the leap into extreme counter-action."

14. K. von Klemperer points this out on several occasions ("Sie gingen ihren Weg: Ein Beitrag zur Frage des Entschlusses und der Motivation zum Widerstand," in *Der Widerstand gegen den Nationalsozialismus* [ed. J. Schmädeke und P. Steinbach; Munich and Zurich, 1985], 1098; *German Resistance against Hitler*, 1) as does J. Fest similarly (*Staatsstreich*, 339). However, the term "resistance *movement*" does crop up, e.g., on the leaflet of the White Rose group "Aufruf an alle Deutschen," already printed in 1953 in Günther Weisenborn, ed., *Der lautlose Aufstand: Bericht über die Widerstandsbewegung des deutschen Volkes 1933–1945* (Hamburg, 1953), 314f., and on the leaflet of a Berlin group in 1945 (ibid., 318).

15. Quoted in Eberhard Bethge, "Zwischen Bekenntnis und Widerstand: Erfahrungen in der Altpreußischen Union," in *Der Widerstand gegen den Nationalsozialismus* (ed. J. Schmädeke and P. Steinbach (Munich and Zurich, 1985), 286.

16. Quoted in Dorothee von Meding, *Mit dem Mut des Herzens: Die Frauen des 20. Juli* (Berlin, 1992), 132, 202, 251.

17. F. Ryszka, "Widerstand," 1113. The passage goes on: "To overcome the fear in order to obey one's moral conviction and to translate it into action was not just the first commandment; it was also the prime characteristic of someone fighting in the resistance."

18. DBW 13, 128.

19. C. Strohm, *Theologische Ethik*, 6.

20. Karl Dietrich Bracher, "Rüdiger Schleicher," in *Zeugen des Widerstands* (ed. J. Mehlhausen; Tübingen, 1996), 231f.

21. E. Bethge, DB Biog., 530.

3. When Did the Commitment Begin?

1. E. Bethge, DB Biog., 601.

2. DBW 2f.; this preface is not included in the English translation, published in 2006. The document was discovered in the Archive for Military History in Prague in 1990–91 and was then analyzed for the first time.

3. See chap. 2.

4. All quotations are from DBWE 16:439.

5. See chaps. 7 and 17.

6. Bonhoeffer, DBWE 16, "Afterword," 665 and n. 97. In order to avoid any possible misunderstanding, it must be stressed here that volume 16 of DBWE in particular provides an indispensable basis for the present book and that the immense importance of the volume—and not for the historiographer alone—is in no way diminished.

7. DBWE 16:441.

8. Ibid., 418–19, n.23

9. This fact is then also already mentioned in the two investigations on Bonhoeffer and Dohnanyi respectively, which appeared *after* the discovery of the indictment. Cf. Martin Heimbucher, *Christusfriede—Weltfrieden: Dietrich Bonhoeffers kirchlicher und politischer Kampf gegen den Krieg Hitlers und seine theologische Begründung* (Gütersloh, 1997), 330, and Marikje Smid, *Hans von Dohnanyi—Christine Bonhoeffer: Eine Ehe im Widerstand gegen Hitler* (Gütersloh, 2002), 244. Smid even states as a fact, for example, that on the instructions of Oster or Canaris, Bonhoeffer undertook an (official) journey to Bethel in the early summer of 1940 (Smid, 250). Nevertheless, we are still dependent on presumptions with respect to journeys of this kind.

10. Elisabeth Chowaniec, *Der "Fall Dohnanyi" 1943–1945: Widerstand, Militärjustiz, SS-Willkür* (Munich, 1969), 82.

11. DBWE 16:357f. and 287 n.1.

12. Ibid., 356.

13. See also chap. 15.

14. DBWE 16:357f.

15. Paul Leverkuehn, *Der geheime Nachrichtendienst der deutschen Wehrmacht im Kriege* (Frankfurt am Main, 1957), 6. The author, who himself worked for the Military Intelligence, goes on: "At the branch offices we burnt with special satisfaction all the papers that had accumulated." The files of the Berlin Central Office for the Intelligence that were still in existence at the end of the war are deposited in Washington and have meanwhile been made available for research.

16. Eberhard Bethge, *Dietrich Bonhoeffer, mit Selbstzeugnissen und Bilddokumenten* (Reinbek, 1976, 1999), 83; Engl. trans. by R. Ockenden, *Dietrich Bonhoeffer: An Illustrated Biography in Documents and Photographs* (London, 1979).

17. See, e.g., Günther Weisenborn, ed., *Der lautlose Aufstand: Bericht über die Widerstandsbewegung des deutschen Volkes 1933–1945* (Hamburg, 1953), 17, or Gerhard Ritter, *Carl Goerdeler und die deutsche Widerstandsbewegung* (Stuttgart, 1954), 7.

18. Heinz Eduard Tödt, "Der Bonhoeffer-Dohnanyi-Kreis in der Opposition und im Widerstand gegen das Gewaltregime Hitlers," in *Die Präsenz des verdrängten Gottes: Glaube, Religionslosigkeit und Weltverantwortung nach Dietrich Bonhoeffer* (ed. C. Gremmels and Ilse Tödt; Munich, 1987), 208f. and 263; on Dohnanyi, see also M. Smid, H. v. *Dohnanyi—C. Bonhoeffer*, passim.

4. A Monkey Wrench in the Machinery of the Intelligence

1. Eberhard Zeller, *Geist der Freiheit: Der zwanzigste Juli* (Munich, 1952; 4th ed., 1963), 35.
2. Gert Buchheit, *Der deutsche Geheimdienst: Geschichte der militärischen Abwehr* (Munich, 1966), 13f., 107, 290f.
3. Romedio von Thun-Hohenstein, *Der Verschwörer: General Oster und die Militäropposition* (Munich, 1984), 17. Cf. also Hermann Graml, "Der Fall Oster," *Vierteljahreshefte für Zeitgeschichte* 14 (1966), 28, and Klemens von Klemperer, *German Resistance against Hitler: The Search for Allies Abroad, 1938–1945* (Oxford, 1992), 194.
4. Cited in R. von Thun-Hohenstein, *Der Verschwörer*, 21.
5. Quoted in Annedore Leber, *Das Gewissen steht auf* (Berlin and Frankfurt am Main, 1954), 155; Engl. trans. by T. S. McClymont, *The Conscience in Revolt: Portraits of the German Resistance 1933–1945* (Mainz, 1994).
6. Romedio von Thun-Hohenstein, "Widerstand und Landesverrat am Beispiel des Generalmajors Hans Oster," in *Der Widerstand gegen den Nationalsozialismus* (ed. J. Schmädeke and P. Steinbach; Munich and Zurich, 1985), 753f.
7. Oster in the later interrogation, 1944; cf. Hans-Adolf Jacobsen, ed., *"Spiegelbild einer Verschwörung": Die Opposition gegen Hitler und der Staatsstreich vom 20. Juli 1944 in der SD-Berichterstattung* (2 vols.; Stuttgart, 1984), 1:430.
8. Fabian von Schlabrendorff stated soon after the war that with Oster he arrived at "the center of the resistance movement"; he was "to some extent the director and clearing house of the resistance movement—a man after God's own heart" (*Offiziere gegen Hitler* [ed. G. von Schulze-Gaevernitz; Zurich, Vienna, and Konstanz, 1951], 42). H. B. Gisevius dedicated his (later highly controversial) book, *Bis zum bittern Ende*, to Oster's memory. For him Oster counted as being among "the most resolute and toughest fighters . . . who ever risked their lives in the army against terror and for justice and decency" (135). For the military historian Gert Buchheit (*Der deutsche*

Geheimdienst, 284), with Hans Oster the Military Intelligence became "the organizational center" of the plotting. In his research into the resistance, Klemens von Klemperer (*German Resistance against Hitler*, 194) sees him as "the driving force in all resistance activities" from 1938 onward.

9. On Oster in general, cf. H. Graml, "Der Fall Oster," 26–39, and R. von Thun-Hohenstein, *Der Verschwörer*.

10. Cf. the classic Canaris biographies by Karl Heinz Abshagen, *Canaris: Patriot und Weltbürger* (Stuttgart, 1956); André Brissaud, *Canaris 1887–1945* (1976); Engl. trans. by I. Colvin, *Canaris* (London, 1973); and Heinz Höhne, *Canaris: Patriot im Zwielicht* (Munich, 1976); Engl. trans. by J. M. Brownjohn, *Canaris: Hitler's Master Spy* (New York, 1999).

11. Paul Leverkuehn, *Der geheime Nachrichtendienst der deutschen Wehrmacht im Kriege* (Frankfurt am Main, 1957), 187, 10.

12. A few examples may suffice. Moltke talked about him as "the little sailor," though not disrespectfully—the context does not permit a contemptuous interpretation of the description (letter of May 5, 1943, in Helmuth James von Moltke, *Briefe an Freya 1939–1945* [2nd ed.; Munich, 1991], 480; Engl. trans. by B. Ruhm von Oppen, *Letters to Freya: 1939–1945* [New York, 1990]). For Allen W. Dulles (see n. 13 below) he was a pessimist, a fatalist, and a mystic (*Germany's Underground* [New York, 1947]). For one of his biographers he remained "surely the most puzzling figure among the prominent functionaries in the Third Reich" (H. Höhne, *Canaris*, 405). For K. von Klemperer (*German Resistance against Hitler*, 24) he was ultimately the "all too wily intelligence chief."

13. H. Höhne, "Canaris und die Abwehr zwischen Anpassung und Opposition," 407. From 1942 to 1945, Allen Welsh Dulles, brother of the American secretary of state John Foster Dulles, headed the Swiss branch of the American secret service, that is, as OSS representative in Bern. He estimated the number of "anti-Nazis" in the Military Intelligence as about 5 percent. They sporadically provided material for the plotters proper, that is, those who were grouped around Oster (cf. Dulles, *Germany's Underground*).

14. Jürgen Schmädeke, "Militärische Umsturzversuche und diplomatische Oppositionsbestrebungen zwischen der Münchener Konferenz und Stalingrad," in *Widerstand gegen den Nationalsozialismus* (ed. P. Steinbach and J. Tuchel; Bonn, 1994), 302.

15. Winfried Meyer, *Unternehmen Sieben: Eine Rettungsaktion für vom Holocaust Bedrohte aus dem Amt Ausland/Abwehr im Oberkommando der Wehrmacht* (Frankfurt am Main, 1993), 20.

16. H. Höhne, "Canaris und die Abwehr," 411.

17. W. Meyer, *Unternehmen Sieben*, 263, and Marikje Smid, *Hans von Dohnanyi—Christine Bonhoeffer: Eine Ehe im Widerstand gegen Hitler* (Gütersloh, 2002), 304.

18. M. Smid, ibid., 411.

19. Quoted in Heinz Eduard Tödt, "Der Bonhoeffer-Dohnanyi-Kreis in der Opposition und im Widerstand gegen das Gewaltregime Hitlers," in *Die Präsenz des verdrängten Gottes: Glaube, Religionslosigkeit und Weltverantwortung nach Dietrich Bonhoeffer* (ed. C. Gremmels and Ilse Tödt; Munich, 1987), 236f.

20. Quoted in M. Smid, *H. v. Dohnanyi—C. Bonhoeffer*, 211.

21. Cf. P. Steinbach in the foreword to M. Smid, *H. v. Dohnanyi—C. Bonhoeffer*, XVIII.

22. Notes made by Christine Dohnanyi in 1945–46, printed as an appendix in E. Bethge, DB Biog., German ed., 1047–1052, quotation from 1047. This appendix is omitted from the English translation. On Christine von Dohnanyi in general, cf. M. Smid's double biography of her and her husband, *Hans von Dohnanyi—Christine Bonhoeffer*. For Gürtner's official diary, Dohnanyi's "Chronicle," Oster's "Study" and collection of material, as well as Canaris's documentation, cf. Christoph Strohm, *Theologische Ethik im Kampf gegen den Nationalsozialismus: Der Weg Dietrich Bonhoeffers mit den Juristen Hans von Dohnanyi und Gerhard Leibholz in den Widerstand* (Munich, 1989), 243ff.; Winfried Meyer, "Staatsstreichplanung, Opposition und Nachrichtendienst: Widerstand aus dem Amt Ausland/Abwehr im Oberkommando der Wehrmacht," in *Widerstand gegen den Nationalsozialismus* (ed. P. Steinbach and J. Tüchel; Bonn, 1994), 321f.; and Gerd R. Ueberschär, ed., *Der deutsche Widerstand gegen Hitler: Wahrnehmung und Wertung in Europa und den USA* (Darmstadt, 2002), 14ff.

23. Cf. C. Strohm, *Theologische Ethik*, 247, and W. Meyer, "Staatsstreichplanung," 14ff.

24. Michael R. D. Foot, "Britische Geheimdienste und deutscher Widerstand 1939–1945," in *Großbritannien und der deutsche Widerstand* (ed. K.-J. Müller and D. N. Dilks; Munich, 1994), 16ff., and J. Schmädeke, "Militärische Umsturzversuche," 308 n.58.

25. One of the two British agents was Payne Best, who was later in prison with Dietrich Bonhoeffer.

26. On Josef Müller in general, see F. H. Hettler's biography and his own autobiography. According to Harold C. Deutsch, *Verschwörung gegen den Krieg: Der Widerstand in den Jahren 1939–40* (Munich, 1969), 113 (Engl. orig.: *The Conspiracy against Hitler in the Twilight War* [Minneapolis, 1968]), his and Dohnanyi's idea, which was supported by Beck, that the Vatican should be introduced as mediating authority, was "in the given circumstances undoubtedly the most reasonable attempt" to find a mediator between

Germany and England. Incidentally, he goes on: "The fact that Beck, Oster, and Dohnanyi were Protestants in no way deterred them."

27. On the compiling of the X Report, cf. Josef Müller, *Bis zur letzten Konsequenz: Ein Leben für Frieden und Freiheit* (Munich, 1975), 128f., and M. Smid, *H. v. Dohnanyi—C. Bonhoeffer*, 237ff. In connection with the X Report, Dohnanyi also prepared a memorandum for Generals Halder and von Brauchitsch. Bonhoeffer was evidently also involved in the preliminary ideas about its composition; cf. K. von Klemperer, *Die verlassene Verschwörer*, 164, referring to E. Bethge, DB Biog., 578f.

28. K. von Klemperer, *German Resistance against Hitler*, 25.

29. *Die Verschwörung gegen den Krieg* (Engl. orig.: *The Conspiracy against Hitler in the Twilight War*) was the title of H. C. Deutsch's investigation of the resistance in 1939 and 1940. Cf. here in general, e.g., Peter Hoffmann, *Widerstand, Staatsstreich, Attentat: Der Kampf der Opposition gegen Hitler* (3rd ed.; Munich, 1979), 130ff.; Engl. trans. by R. Barry, *The History of the German Resistance 1933–1945* (Cambridge, Mass., 1977); Joachim Fest, *Staatsstreich: Der lange Weg zum 20. Juli* (Berlin, 1994), 105ff., or K. von Klemperer, *Die verlassene Verschwörer*, 139ff.

5. Fit for Active Service

1. Hermann Graml, "Der Fall Oster," *Vierteljahreshefte für Zeitgeschichte* 14 (1966), 36ff.; Romedio von Thun-Hohenstein, *Der Verschwörer: General Oster und die Militäropposition* (Munich, 1984), 154f. and 187ff.; Klemens von Klemperer, *German Resistance against Hitler: The Search for Allies Abroad, 1938–1945* (Oxford, 1992), 195–198.

2. Quoted in H. Graml, "Der Fall Oster," 39.

3. K. von Klemperer, *German Resistance against Hitler*, 15–16.

4. Hans Mommsen, "Die Opposition gegen Hitler und die deutsche Gesellschaft 1933–1945," in *Der deutsche Widerstand 1933–1945* (ed. K.-J. Müller; 2nd ed.; Paderborn, 1900), 24.

5. German Criminal Code, §83 and §91, reprinted in Hans-Adolf Jacobsen, ed., *"Spiegelbild einer Verschwörung": Die Opposition gegen Hitler und der Staatsstreich vom 20. Juli 1944 in der SD-Berichterstattung* (2 vols.; Stuttgart, 1984), 2:963.

6. R. von Thun-Honenstein, *Der Verschwörer*, e.g., 147 and 223f. It seems, however, that Oster did not take Beck into his confidence in the matter at that point; cf. Harold C. Deutsch, *Verschwörung gegen den Krieg: Der Widerstand in den Jahren 1939–40* (Munich, 1969), 352 (Engl. orig.: *The Conspiracy against Hitler in the Twilight War* [Minneapolis, 1968]).

7. Quoted in H. C. Deutsch, *Verschwörungen*, 351; cf. also Winfried Meyer, "Staatsstreichplanung, Opposition und Nachrichtendienst: Widerstand aus dem Amt Ausland/Abwehr im Oberkommando der Wehrmacht," in *Widerstand gegen den Nationalsozialismus* (ed. P. Steinbach and J. Tüchel; Bonn, 1994).

8. DBWE 16:438.

9. E. Bethge, DB Biog., 579.

10. Marikje Smid, *Hans von Dohnanyi—Christine Bonhoeffer: Eine Ehe im Widerstand gegen Hitler* (Gütersloh, 2002), 246, with reference to the chronological table in DBWE 16:676; cf. also, ibid., 646.

11. See chap. 2 n.20.

12. See chap. 3.

13. Quoted in Annedore Leber, *Das Gewissen steht auf* (Berlin and Frankfurt am Main, 1954), 15 (Engl. trans. by T. S. McClymont, *The Conscience in Revolt: Portraits of the German Resistance 1933–1945* [Mainz, 1994]). See chap. 4 above.

14. E. Bethge, DB Biog., 579.

15. Ibid, 528, 530.

16. DBW 13:299.

17. Ibid., 300.

18. On Bonhoeffer's will for peace and struggle against war, cf. Martin Heimbucher, *Christusfriede—Weltfrieden: Dietrich Bonhoeffers kirchlicher und politischer Kampf gegen den Krieg Hitlers und seine theologische Begründung* (Gütersloh, 1997), passim; on Fanö, especially 113ff.; also Sabine Dramm, *Dietrich Bonhoeffer: Eine Einführung in sein Denken* (Gütersloh, 2001), 164ff.

19. E. Bethge, DB Biog., 352; idem, *In Zitz gab es keine Juden: Erinnerungen aus meinen ersten vierzig Jahren* (Munich, 1989), 94f.

20. Bonhoeffer knew Hermann Stöhr from Stettin. He was a radical Christian pacifist, whose aims and objectives Bonhoeffer did not share in detail, but the consequences of which nevertheless shocked him (E. Bethge, DB Biog., 353). Stöhr was a declared opponent of the war—as far as I know the first case on record of conscientious objection in the ranks of the Protestant church—and because of his fundamental pacifist convictions rejected for himself any compromise. He was arrested in March 1939 and, after negotiations that were at least long drawn out, was condemned to death a year later by court martial on the ground that he had undermined the country's defense. He was executed in June 1940; cf. Helmut Gollwitzer, Käthe Kuhn, and Reinhold Schneider, eds., *Du hast mich heimgesucht bei Nacht: Abschiedsbriefe und Aufzeichnungen des Widerstandes von 1933 bis 1945* (3rd ed.; Munich and Hamburg, 1969), 146ff.

21. Sabine Leibholz-Bonhoeffer, *The Bonhoeffers: Portrait of a Family* (London, 1971), 119.

22. DBW 15:625.

23. Ibid., 164.

24. See chap. 4.

25. E. Bethge, DB Biog., 575.

26. M. Smid, *H. v. Dohnanyi—C. Bonhoeffer*, 261.

27. DBWE 16:454.

28. In the later interrogations, the impression had to be avoided that these were church (and hence inner-political) reports, for according to the agreement between the different intelligences, such reports were the preserve of the SS's security service. It was only military and to some extent also foreign-political matters that belonged within the competence of the Military Intelligence Foreign Office.

29. Helmuth Groscurth, *Tagebücher eines Abwehroffiziers 1938–1940* (ed. H. Krausnick et al.; Stuttgart, 1970), 245. A few weeks later Groscurth was drafted to the front because of his unequivocal information policy in army circles about the brutal procedure of the SS in Poland. He died in a Russian prisoner of war camp in 1943.

30. E. Bethge, DB Biog., 594; H. Groscurth, *Tagebücher*, 245, n.679; Ulrich Kabitz, "Einige Tage nach Weihnachten 1939: Ein Fallbeispiel der Bonhoeffer-Forschung," in *Dietrich Bonhoeffer Jahrbuch* 2003 (ed. C. Gremmels, H. Pfeifer, et al.; Gütersloh, 2003), 121ff.

31. Heinz Eduard Tödt, "Der Bonhoeffer-Dohnanyi-Kreis in der Opposition und im Widerstand gegen das Gewaltregime Hitlers," in *Die Präsenz des verdrängten Gottes: Glaube, Religionslosigkeit und Weltverantwortung nach Dietrich Bonhoeffer* (ed. C. Gremmels and Ilse Tödt; Munich, 1987), 213.

32. Thus in the reports of the Security Service about the interrogations in the autumn of 1944; H. A. Jacobsen, ed., "Spiegelbild einer Verschwörung," 1:444.

33. DBWE 16:445.

6. Interim

1. E. Bethge, DB Biog., 585.

2. Ibid., 601. On these consequences, see below in the present chapter.

3. Chronological table in DBWE 16:678.

4. Quoted in Marikje Smid, *Hans von Dohnanyi—Christine Bonhoeffer: Eine Ehe im Widerstand gegen Hitler* (Gütersloh, 2002), 263. For more about Schönfeld, see chap. 14 below.

5. On Schönfeld's recruitment into the Military Intelligence Foreign Office and his later position, cf. Eugen Gerstenmaier, *Streit und Friede hat seine Zeit: Ein Lebensbericht* (Frankfurt, Berlin, and Vienna, 1981), 143f.; Elisabeth Chowaniec, *Der "Fall Dohnanyi" 1943–1945: Widerstand, Militärjustiz, SS-Willkür* (Munich, 1969), 84; Winfried Meyer, "Staatsstreichplanung, Opposition und Nachrichtendienst: Widerstand aus dem Amt Ausland/Abwehr im Oberkommando der Wehrmacht," in *Widerstand gegen den Nationalsozialismus* (ed. P. Steinbach and J. Tüchel; Bonn, 1994), 324; and M. Smid., *H. v. Dohnanyi—C. Bonhoeffer*, 362. It is still not quite clear when and for how long Schönfeld actually worked for the Military Intelligence Foreign Office.

6. E. Bethge, DB Biog., 601: chronological table in DBWE 16:678; also M. Smid, *H. v. Dohnanyi—C. Bonhoeffer*, 263.

7. H. Höhne, "Canaris und die Abwehr zwischen Anpassung und Opposition," 405f. The picture drawn of Gisevius is often not a flattering one. He is described as being "a man . . . of keen intellect and vivid imagination" who in Switzerland "had it both ways" (*er habe auf zwei Schultern getragen*) inasmuch as he acted as "chief informer for American espionage organizations" (Wolfgang Venohr, *Stauffenberg, Symbol der deutschen Einheit: Eine politische Biographie* [Frankfurt am Main and Berlin, 1986], 345). The expression "er habe auf zwei Schultern getragen" was used in the so-called Kaltenbrunner Reports too in connection with Gisevius; see, e.g., Hans-Adolf Jacobsen, ed., *"Spiegelbild einer Verschwörung": Die Opposition gegen Hitler und der Staatsstreich vom 20. Juli 1944 in der SD-Berichterstattung* (2 vols.; Stuttgart, 1984), 1:503. For K. von Klemperer he was "at first sight, of distinctly questionable make-up and background" who certainly from 1934 onward was "an inveterate conspirator against the regime" but who in resistance circles "was always a quite controversial figure" (Klemens von Klemperer, *German Resistance against Hitler: The Search for Allies Abroad, 1938–1945* [Oxford, 1992], 319–20). In the specific reports about Gisevius's activities, on the other hand, the picture that Klemperer paints of him is much more positive in tenor (cf. Klemperer, ibid., 66 n.31, as well as 399 n.38).

8. Jürgen Schmädeke, "Militärische Umsturzversuche und diplomatische Oppositionsbestrebungen zwischen der Münchener Konferenz und Stalingrad," in *Widerstand gegen den Nationalsozialismus* (ed. P. Steinbach and J. Tüchel; Bonn, 1994), 300.

9. In his book *Bis zum bittern Ende* (Zurich, 1946, 1954; Engl. trans. by R. and C. Winston, *To the Bitter End* [London, 1948]), which he had already begun to write a few years before the end of the war and only published for the first time in 1946, Hans Bernd Gisevius developed a view of Dohnanyi

that was biased against him in many respects. His view found its way into journalism and the history books until well into the postwar period, even, as can be shown, in the 1980s (cf. P. Steinbach in M. Smid, *H. v. Dohnanyi— C. Bonhoeffer*, XVII, and ibid., 6ff.). Only the investigations of Winfried Meyer, *Unternehmen Sieben: Eine Rettungsaktion für vom Holocaust Bedrohte aus dem Amt Ausland/Abwehr im Oberkommando der Wehrmacht* (Frankfurt am Main, 1993) and M. Smid (which were of pioneer importance where Dohnanyi was concerned) finally proved that Gisevius's allegations were groundless. His most important misrepresentations of Dohnanyi have to do with alleged inconsistencies in money matters and the circumstances that led to the finding of the Zossen papers in 1944. What is also interesting, incidentally, is the judgment of Dohnanyi and Bonhoeffer about the parts of Gisevius's book that they themselves were still able to read: "Dietrich said: 'yellow press.'" "Hans thinks the matter is too serious for him to want to read it," wrote Christine von Dohnanyi in a letter to her sister-in-law Sabine Leibholz in London (quoted in M. Smid, *H. v. Dohnanyi— C. Bonhoeffer*, 7).

10. Notes of Hans von Dohnanyi's from the autumn of 1943, which his wife was able to smuggle out of his prison, give an impression of how tense and problematical the relationship between him and Gisevius must have been, as well as that between Gisevius and Bonhoeffer. Cf. DBWE 16:446f.

11. E. Bethge, DB Biog., 601, and DBWE 16:71.

12. On this retreat see also above in the present chapter.

13. DBWE 16:62–68, quotations from pp. 65 and 68.

14. Ibid., 62.

15. Ibid., 68.

16. Ibid., 64.

17. Ibid., 71.

18. E. Bethge, DB Biog., 602.

19. For more about Perels, see chap. 11 below.

20. E. Bethge, DB Biog., 603.

21. Ernst Wolf, "Zum Verhältnis der politischen und moralischen Motive in der deutschen Widerstandbewegung," in *Der deutsche Widerstand gegen Hitler* (ed. W. Schmitthenner and H. Buchheim; Cologne and Berlin, 1966), 230.

22. E. Bethge, DB Biog., 358.

23. Cf. Jane Pesja, *Matriarch of Conspiracy: Ruth von Kleist 1867–1945* (Minneapolis, 1991).

24. In the foreword to Dorothee von Meding, *Mit dem Mut des Herzens: Die Frauen des 20. Juli* (Berlin, 1992), 12, von Klemperer describes her as "a

Prussian loyal to the government through and through, who nevertheless
through her family relationships . . . and through her friendship with Dietrich Bonhoeffer was drawn willy-nilly into the world of the conspirators,
participating in it, as it were, with stoic detachment."

25. E. Bethge, DB Biog., 454 and 527.

26. See on this also chap. 2. In Ekkehard Klausa's judgment, "In the years
before 1938, only a few lone wolves such as Ewald von Kleist-Schmenzin
pursued conservative opposition" ("Politischer Konservatismus und Widerstand," in *Der Widerstand gegen den Nationalsozialismus* [ed. P. Steinbach
and J. Tüchel; Munich and Zurich, 1994], 222). On Kleist-Schmenzin in
general, cf. Bodo Scheurig, *Ewald von Kleist-Schmenzin: Ein Konservativer gegen
Hitler* (Oldenburg and Hamburg, 1968). For details of his 1938 London
mission, cf. also Romedio von Thun-Hohenstein, *Der Verschwörer: General
Oster und die Militäropposition* (Munich, 1984), 92ff.

27. Bethge, DB Biog., 666f.

28. On his *Ethics* in general, cf., e.g., E. Bethge, DB Biog., 619ff., and the preface
and postscript to DBWE 6. Also Reinhold Mokrosch, Friedrich Johannsen,
and Christian Gremmels, *Dietrich Bonhoeffers Ethik: Ein Arbeitsbuch für Schule,
Gemeinde und Studium* (Gütersloh, 2003), passim, as well as Sabine Dramm,
Dietrich Bonhoeffer: Eine Einführung in sein Denken (Gütersloh, 2001), 113ff.

29. Now DBWE 1, 2, 4, and 5 respectively.

30. Editors' afterword to DBWE 6:419.

31. DBWE 16:77f.

7. Ecumenism Rewritten

1. The details of Bonhoeffer's incorporation into the Military Intelligence
and its bureaucratic implications can be seen or indirectly deduced from
the extracts from later, but meanwhile published, statements of Bonhoeffer,
Dohnanyi, Oster, and Canaris, or from the trial documents; cf., e.g., Elisabeth Chowaniec, *Der "Fall Dohnanyi" 1943–1945: Widerstand, Militärjustiz,
SS-Willkür* (Munich, 1969); Winfried Meyer, *Unternehmen Sieben: Eine Rettungsaktion für vom Holocaust Bedrohte aus dem Amt Ausland/Abwehr im Oberkommando der Wehrmacht* (Frankfurt am Main, 1993); Marikje Smid, *Hans von
Dohnanyi—Christine Bonhoeffer: Eine Ehe im Widerstand gegen Hitler* (Gütersloh,
2002); and DBWE 16.

2. E. Bethge, DB Biog., 629f., and Winfried Meyer, "Staatsstreichplanung,
Opposition und Nachrichtendienst: Widerstand aus dem Amt Ausland/

Abwehr im Oberkommando der Wehrmacht," in *Widerstand gegen den Nationalsozialismus* (ed. P. Steinbach and J. Tüchel; Bonn, 1994), 336 n.68.

3. See on this the minutes of the interrogations of Dohnanyi and Canaris, as well as the indictments of Dohnanyi and Oster of 1943 (DBWE 16:407f., 411f., and 433f.); also n.14 below.

4. For example, later on Christine von Dohnanyi (as witness in the postwar proceedings against the National Socialist representatives of the accused) stated via W. Schmidhuber, who was directly responsible for Bonhoeffer in the Munich office of the Military Intelligence (see below): "Schm, must, since B. was directly under him, have been informed in broad terms about the need for the journey to Sweden" (quoted in Friedrich Hermann Hettler, *Josef Müller ["Ochsensepp"]: Mann des Widerstandes und erster CSU-Vorsitzender* [Munich, 1991], 140).

5. Oster stated later—after the arrest of Dohnanyi and Bonhoeffer—that he thought he could remember "that the Gestapo who were responsible in Munich were informed through the Intelligence office in Munich and made no objection" (Oster's note on the file to Bonhoeffer's *uk* position of November 3, 1943, quoted in Romedio von Thun-Hohenstein, *Der Verschwörer: General Oster und die Militäropposition* (Munich, 1984), 253. In an interrogation in connection with the Bonhoeffer/Canaris case—also after their arrest—Canaris said about this complex (DBWE 16:412): "Dohnanyi gave me no indication that state police measures were in effect against Bonhoeffer at the time of his involvement with the Military Intelligence. I was informed neither of the ban on Bonhoeffer's speaking nor of the restrictions on his place of residence. If this had been the case, it would have been no immediate reason to prohibit engaging Bonhoeffer for the purposes of the Military Intelligence. I would, however, have arranged for contact to be made with the Gestapo in order to find a modus vivendi concerning him."

6. Quoted in E. Bethge, DB Biog., 604. This argument is indirectly in line with that of Canaris (see n. 5 above), and it was entirely along these lines that Bonhoeffer expressed himself in his later interrogations (DBWE 16): "To my occasional question whether difficulties might not arise for either Military Intelligence or for me because of my state police record, I was told these things did not mean anything for military duty and, in addition, Military Intelligence works with all sorts of people who are useful to it."

7. See chap. 4. On the negotiations with the Vatican in general, cf., e.g., Klemens von Klemperer, *German Resistance against Hitler: The Search for Allies Abroad, 1938–1945* (Oxford, 1992) 171–80.

8. M. Smid, *Dohnanyi—Christine Bonhoeffer*, 263f.

9. The relevant papers are printed in DBWE 16:108f.

10. Ibid., 437f. (Indictment of September 21, 1943); cf. also E. Bethge, DB Biog., 604, and the chronological table in DBWE 16:680, where the date is given as January 14, 1941.

11. Peter Steinbach, *Widerstand im Widerstreit: Der Widerstand gegen den Nationalsozialismus in der Erinnerung der Deutschen, Ausgewählte Studien* (2nd ed.; Paderborn, 2001), 42.

12. We must again return to the question of the date when Bonhoeffer officially "entered the service." It was not an official entry, for he was neither appointed to the Military Intelligence nor was he a civilian worker for this department, but simply a "V-man," and that too only for appearance' sake. In this connection there are occasionally problematical formulations. For example, in an essay by Klaus-Jürgen on Dohnanyi, Bonhoeffer, and Josef Müller, he is said to have been appointed to the *Abwehr* (Military Intelligence) "as officer or special leader" (Müller, "Struktur und Entwicklung der national-konservativen Opposition," in *Aufstand des Gewissens* (ed. T. Vogel; 5th ed.; Hamburg, Berlin, and Bonn, 2000), 117. Klemperer states that Bonhoeffer was appointed in the autumn of 1940 and with the help of Oster and Dohnanyi given a job in the *Abwehr* (K. von Klemperer, *German Resistance against Hitler*, 271.). In another passage (ibid., 159) Klemperer writes that at the same time that Josef Müller was won over for the *Abwehr* (that is, in autumn 1939) Oster saw to it "that Dietrich Bonhoeffer also joined the *Abwehr*"—which again brings us back to the question about the beginning of his "service" (see chap. 3 above).

13. E. Bethge, DB Biog., 605f., and W. Meyer, *Staatsstreichplanung*, 323.

14. That emerges, for example, from a formulation in the indictment against Oster and Dohnanyi of September 16, 1943 (DBWE 16:434; see also n. 3 above): ". . . because no V-men or agents were controlled by 'Z' and the appointment of a particular agent or V-man for reconnaissance lay entirely outside the assigned duties of 'Z.'" On the other hand, according to the minutes of the interrogation of April 16, 1943, Dohnanyi apparently used the terms V-Mann and agent as synonyms: ". . . that Z had no agents to command" (ibid., 408). (This being so, except for the above explanation, in the present translation the distinction between "agent" and "V-Mann" has been dropped, and the term "agent" has been used throughout, thus following Dohnanyi's practice as well as the usage in DBWE 16, and in view of the fact that "V-mann" has no precise correspondence in English [trans.].)

15. Thus the defense brief for Dohnanyi, DBWE 16:458.

16. DBWE 16:407, E. Bethge, DB Biog., 629; R. von Thun-Hohenstein, *Der Verschwörer*, 253; and M. Schmid, *H. v. Dohnanyi—C. Bonhoeffer*, 263f.

17. W. Meyer, *Unternehmen Sieben*, 354.

18. He was "an enterprising businessman," writes Thun-Hohenstein (*Der Verschwörer*, 148), "almost too enterprising, as was to emerge." In spite of his hostility to the Nazis, Oster is supposed from the beginning to have had an uncomfortable feeling about him, to put it mildly, but he was unfortunately sometimes indispensable "with his dubious business deals" (ibid., 236; cf. also Heinz Höhne, *Canaris: Patriot im Zwielicht* (Munich, 1976), 475; Engl. trans. by J. M. Brownjohn, *Canaris: Hitler's Master Spy* (New York, 1999). Schmidhuber was "the offspring of an old officers' family who, however, found the main purpose of his life in business deals of every kind" (Höhne, ibid., 366). He generously lavished presents on his friends, including the Dohnanyis, for example (cf. ibid., 475), and kept a meticulous account of them (thus the Munich Intelligence officer Josef Müller (quoted in ibid., 480).

19. K. von Klemperer, *German Resistance against Hitler*, 171–72.

20. See chaps. 3 and 17. For the date of this letter, cf. DBWE 16:395, notes 1 and 2. The original of the faked letter was destroyed in a bombing attack in November 1943, but it was probably dated November 11, 1940, and played an important role in the later interrogations of Dohnanyi and Bonhoeffer, it not being evident that it was faked. Bonhoeffer's typewritten draft (on which the quotation here is based) was dated November 4, 1940, at which time Bonhoeffer was already in Munich.

21. DBWE 16:400.

22. Ibid., 395f.

23. Ibid., 397f.

24. At Bonhoeffer's request, Bell had arranged for this invitation, which Bonhoeffer was then after all, to his regret, unable to accept. Cf. E. Bethge, DB Biog., 329ff., as well as DBW 13:213f.

25. DBWE 16:399.

26. Ibid., 396f.

27. The French term *fronde* was originally applied to a small upper-class group that was opposed to the ruler and his absolute rule.

28. E. Bethge, DB Biog., 146; cf. here also Sabine Dramm, *Dietrich Bonhoeffer: Eine Einführung in sein Denken* (Gütersloh, 2001), 179ff.

29. One of the main reasons was the continual, nerve-racking minor war as to whether members of the Confessing Church should be recognized as full German representatives, and who should claim sole representation in the various committees. Should it be members of the oppositional Confessing

Church, or should it be the (official) German Evangelical Church, which was in bondage to the government?

30. DBWE 6:98.

31. E. Bethge, DB Biog., 604f.

32. See above and chap. 4. For the term "Black Chapel" (*Schwarze Kapelle*) cf. W. Meyer, "Staatsstreichplanung," 331; Karl Heinz Roth and Angelika Ebbinghaus, eds. *Rote Kapellen—Kreisauer Kreise—Schwarze Kapellen: Neue Sichtweisen auf den Widerstand gegen die NS-Diktatur 1938–1945* (Hamburg, 2004), 49, as well as chap. 17 n.31 below.

33. Josef Müller, *Bis zur letzten Konsequenz: Ein Leben für Frieden und Freiheit* (Munich, 1975), 12ff.

34. Ibid., 257.

35. DBWE 16:81, 86, 88f., 96.

36. Ibid., 87.

37. Laurentius Koch, "Die Benediktinerabtai Ettal," In *Das Erzbistum München und Freising in der Zeit der nationalsozialistischen Herrschaft* (ed. Georg Schwaiger; vol. 2; Munich and Zurich, 1984), 382.

38. Neuhäusler remained imprisoned in the concentration camps in Sachsenhausen and Dachau until April 1945.

39. E. Bethge, *Bonhoeffer*, 629.

40. DBWE 16:155.

8. The Swiss Connection

1. Klemens von Klemperer, *German Resistance against Hitler: The Search for Allies Abroad, 1938–1945* (Oxford, 1992), 27.

2. For example, in the letter to Beckmann of February 4, 1941; DBWE 16:138.

3. See chaps 10 and 13. On the question about the date of Barth's initial mistrust with regard to Bonhoeffer's possible journey and his missions, cf. DBWE 16:278 n.3. For a different version, cf. E. Bethge, DB Biog., 631f., with a reference to Jørgen Glenthøj, "Bonhoeffer und die Ökumene," in *Die mündige Welt II* (ed. E. Bethge; Munich, 1956), 198; cf. also ibid., 185.

4. E. Bethge, DB Biog., 632 n.138.

5. Thus in one of Dohnanyi's notes for his wife, which were smuggled out of prison in the autumn of 1943 (DBWE 16:447). Cf. also E. Bethge, DB Biog., 631.

6. Quoted in Marikje Smid, *Hans von Dohnanyi—Christine Bonhoeffer: Eine Ehe im Widerstand gegen Hitler* (Gütersloh, 2002), 7.

7. DBWE 16:167.

8. K. von Klemperer, *German Resistance against Hitler*, 59.

9. Lothar Kettenacker, "Die britische Haltung zum deutschen Widerstand während des Zweiten Weltkriegs," en *Das "Andere Deutschland"* (ed. L. Kettenacker; Stuttgart, 1977), 59. For more informaion on Goerdeler, see chap. 9.

10. "Swiss roads" was the name given to the connections and means of communication between the European resistance movements, exile governments, etc., via neutral Switzerland. Cf. on this Willem A. Visser't Hooft, *Memoirs* (London and Philadelphia, 1973), and Jürgen Heideking, "Die 'Schweizer Straßen' des europäischen Widerstands," in *Geheimdienste und Widerstandsbewegungen im Zweiten Weltkrieg* (ed. Gerhard Schulz; Göttingen, 1982), 143ff.; also chap. 13 below.

11. L. Kettenacker, "Die britische Haltung," 59f. n.47, and Armin Boyens, *Kirchenkampf und Ökumene 1939–1945: Darstellung und Dokumentation unter besonderer Berücksichtigung der Quellen des Ökumenischen Rates der Kirchen* (Munich, 1973), 208.

12. L. Kettenacker, "Die britische Haltung," 58f.

13. Quoted in ibid., 59

14. E. Bethge, DB Biog., 630f., and K. von Klemperer, *German Resistance against Hitler*, 271.

15. See chap. 15.

16. W. A. Visser't Hooft, *Memoirs*, 108f.

17. Ibid., 109.

18. Ibid., 88.

19. DBWE 16:69f.

20. Ibid.

21. The French writer and later Nobel prize winner Albert Camus, who lived near Le-Chambon-sur-Lignon in 1942–43 and who was involved in the resistance from 1943, worked many impressions about people and events in Le-Cambon-sur-Lignon into his novel *La Peste* (Engl. trans.: *The Plague*). The names of protagonists in this plague chronicle are borrowed from them. Cf. on this Sabine Dramm, "Camus und die Christen: Kontroverse und Dialog 'jenseits von Lästerung und Gebet,'" 110.

22. DBWE 16:169f.

23. Visser't Hooft, *Memoirs*, 88. Cf. E. Bethge, DB Biog., 648. On the question of the date of this conversation, cf. Martin Heimbucher, *Christusfriede— Weltfrieden: Dietrich Bonhoeffers kirchlicher und politischer Kampf gegen den Krieg*

Hitlers und seine theologische Begründung (Gütersloh, 1997), 334; and DBWE
16:178 n.13.

24. Cf. DBWE 16:170.

25. Jacques Courvoisier in Wolf-Dieter Zimmermann, ed., *Begegnungen mit
Dietrich Bonhoeffer: Ein Almanach* (Munich, 1964), 138f.; Engl. trans. by
K. Gregor Smith, *I Knew Dietrich Bonhoeffer* (London and New York, 1966).
The date emerges only from the course of Courvoisier's account as a whole;
Ehrenströhm's daily notes suggest that the date was March 15, 1941.

26. W. A. Visser't Hooft, *Memoirs*, 153. He offers this recollection in the context
of Bonhoeffer's second journey to Switzerland, but it will have belonged to
March 15, 1941. Cf. here n. 25 above, and M. Heimbucher, *Christusfriede—
Weltfrieden*, 331.

27. E. Bethge, DB Biog., 633f.

28. A. Boyens, *Kirchenkampf und Ökumene*, 202f.

29. Printed in ibid., 353ff.

30. K. von Klemperer, *German Resistance against Hitler*, 271.

31. W. A. Visser't Hooft, *Memoirs*, 152.

32. Quoted in K. von Klemperer, *German Resistance against Hitler*, 272.

33. DBWE 16:172.

34. Visser't Hooft, *Memoirs*, 152.

35. In 1977 Kettenacker established that "most historians of the resistance
have remained ultimately as remote from the realities of foreign policy
as the resistance fighters themselves" (L. Kettenacker, "Die britische Haltung," 49), and in what follows he supports this thesis. And yet we find
the image of the vicious circle, for example, in Joachim Fest, *Staatsstreich:
Der lange Weg zum 20. Juli* (Berlin, 1994), 13, when in talking about the
year 1942 he talks about "the rigid old front" which every attempt ran up
against and then came to nothing: "It was a deadly circle." Heimbucher,
Christusfriede—Weltfrieden, 353, also talking about 1942, speaks of the vicious
circle "in which the hesitant generals of the German resistance and the
mistrustful British diplomacy were caught up."

36. DBWE 16:173.

37. Ibid., 173 n.4.

38. Ibid., 178.

39. Ibid., 178, n.15.

40. DBW 10:331f.

9. Networks

1. See the chronological table in DBWE 16:682.
2. Ibid., 182.
3. E. Bethge, DB Biog., 620f.
4. Bethge was at this time at the Berlin Gossner Mission. Niesel was a member of the Old Prussian Council of Brethren, one of the leading committees of the Confessing Church in Berlin-Brandenburg. Jannasch was manager of the Pastors' Emergency League (*Pfarrernotbund*) in Berlin, and Rott belonged to the provisional administration of the Confessing Church.
5. The final passage in a letter of Bonhoeffer's to Dohnanyi, cited in this connection in the indictment against Bonhoeffer. It is dated "presumably in March 1942" (DBWE 16:442f.).
6. Marikje Smid, *Hans von Dohnanyi—Christine Bonhoeffer: Eine Ehe im Widerstand gegen Hitler* (Gütersloh, 2002), 265.
7. In the later interrogations of Dohnanyi, Bonhoeffer, Oster, and Canaris, these *uk* positions played an important part.
8. Josef Müller, *Bis zur letzten Konsequenz: Ein Leben für Frieden und Freiheit* (Munich, 1975), 80.
9. See chaps. 4 and 7.
10. Cf. Günther Weisenborn, ed., *Der lautlose Aufstand: Bericht über die Widerstandsbewegung des deutschen Volkes 1933–1945* (Hamburg, 1953), 88.
11. Quoted in Gert Buchheit, *Ludwig Beck—ein preußischer General* (Munich, 1966), 353.
12. A religious element of whatever kind is evident not only in the case of Beck but, for example, in the case of Goerdeler too, and especially in some members of the Kreisau circle. As far as I know, the only discussion hitherto published about the religious attitude of those involved in the resistance is to be found in Klemens von Klemperer's article "Glaube, Religion, Kirche und der deutsche Widerstand gegen den Nationalsozialismus," *Vierteljahreshefte für Zeitgeschichte* 28 (1980), 293–309.
13. Quoted in Heinz Eduard Tödt, *Komplizen, Opfer und Gegner des Hitlerregimes: Zur "inneren Geschichte" von protestantischer Theologie und Kirche im "Dritten Reich"* (Gütersloh, 1997), 388.
14. Beck's central role as "the recognized leader of the conspiracy" (Annedore Leber, *Das Gewissen steht auf* [Berlin and Frankfurt am Main, 1954], 154; Engl. trans. by T. S. McCymont, *The Conscience in Revolt: Portraits of the German Resistance 1933–1945* [Mainz, 1994]) was ascribed to him not only in the historiography of the resistance. To give an example: Ulrich von Hassell noted on March 24,1942, after an evening discussion with

General Friedrich Olbricht in Beck's apartment in Lichterfeld: "At one
in our opinion that it is he who must gather all the threads together"(*Die
Hassell Tagebücher, 1938-1944: Aufzeichnungen vom Andern Deutschland* [Zurich,
1946], 306; Engl. trans.: *The von Hassell Diaries 1938–1944: The Story of the
Forces against Hitler inside Germany as Recorded by Ambassador Ulrich von Hassell*
[London, 1948]). And Fabian von Schlabrendorff stressed after the war
(*Offiziere gegen Hitler* [ed. G. von Schulze-Gaevernitz; Zurich, Vienna, and
Konstanz, 1951], 90): "Diverse though the backgrounds and the individual groups of the German resistance movement were, a doubt was never
expressed about [Beck] as the recognized head of the opposition." Historians of varying provenance and periods agree in their view of Beck's
central role. "Around him something like a thinking and responsible center
grew up in all attempts that up to July 20 were directed toward an overthrow": such is the summing up of Eberhard Zeller, *Geist der Freiheit: Der
zwanzigste Juli* (Munich, 1952; 4th ed., 1963), 33. According to Peter Hoffmann (*Widerstand, Staatsstreich, Attentat: Der Kampf der Opposition gegen Hitler*
[3rd ed.; Munich, 1979], 337; Engl. trans. by R. Barry, *The History of the
German Resistance 1933–1945* [Cambridge, Mass., 1977]), in 1942 Beck was
"explicitly 'constituted as centre.'" Klaus-Jürgen Müller, who according
to his own admission initially took a critical approach in his research into
"the anti-Hitler faction" (*General Ludwig Beck: Sudien und Dokument zur politisch-militärischen Vorstellungswelt und Tätigkeit des Generalstabschefs des deutschen
Heeres 1933–1938* [Boppard, 1980], 15), states distinctly at the beginning
of his study of Beck that he was undoubtedly "one of the central figures
of the national-conservative opposition movement" (ibid.). (For the dispute
about the term "national-conservative" resistance, see chaps. 15 and 18
below.) On the other hand, Beck's prewar role also attracts highly critical
comment. Cf., e.g., Karl Heinz Roth and Angelika Ebbinghaus, eds., *Rote
Kapellen—Kreisauer Kreise—Schwarze Kapellen: Neue Sichtweisen auf den Widerstand gegen die NS-Diktatur 1938–1945* (Hamburg, 2004), 31 and 35.

15. Quoted in F. von Schlabrendorff, *Offiziere gegen Hitler*, 44.

16. Quoted in Romedio von Thun-Hohenstein, *Der Verschwörer: General Oster und
die Militäropposition* (Munich, 1984), 70.

17. Quoted in E. Zeller, *Geist der Freiheit*, 13.

18. See chap. 4 above.

19. General Franz Halder was Beck's successor as general chief of staff. He was
dismissed in 1942 and arrested after July 20, 1944. General Erich Hoepner,
commander in chief of the 4th tank army, was dismissed from the army for
insubordination in 1942. General Friedrich Olbricht, chief of the general

army and commander in chief of the territorials, and Field Marshal Erwin von Witzleben (recalled from France as commander in 1942 and transferred to the reserve) were executed on or after July 20, 1944.

20. F. von Schlabrendorff describes the two in the framework of the resistance as a whole (*Offiziere gegen Hitler*, 90): "If one were to characterize Beck and Goerdeler, then Beck was the head and Goerdeler the heart of the German resistance movement." For his biographer Gerhard Ritter, Goerdeler stood "more than anyone else at the center of the conspiracy against the tyranny." He counted as "untiring driving force and 'recruiting officer' for the movement" and "at the same time as its most productive head" (Gerhard Ritter, *Carl Goerdeler und die deutsche Widerstandsbewegung* [Stuttgart, 1954], 13). Even forty years later Goerdler was held to be "one of the leading heads of the German resistance" (Jürgen Schmädeke, "Militärische Umsturzversuche und diplomatische Oppositionsbestrebungen zwischen der Münchener Konferenz und Stalingrad," in *Widerstand gegen den Nationalsozialismus* [ed. P. Steinbach and J. Tüchel; Bonn, 1994], 300). K. von Klemperer (*German Resistance against Hitler: The Search for Allies Abroad, 1938–1945*, 226) describes him as a conscientious man, full of ideas, with "deep religious convictions," someone who though at first a lone wolf, from 1940 onward belonged to the center of the resistance.

21. H. Mommsen has recently recorded that "Contemporaries who came into contact with Goerdeler were always impressed by his sincerity, his personal integrity and openness" (in Sabine Gillmann and Hans Mommsen, eds., *Politische Schriften und Briefe Carl Friedrich Goerdelers* [Munich, 2003], LXII). And even Roth's study (cf. K. H. Roth and A. Ebbinghaus, eds., *Rote Kapellen*), which is highly critical of the civilian resistance, stresses Goerdeler's courage and straightforwardness, as well as, for example, his early warning about the barbaric progress of the war.

22. Quoted in R. von Thun-Hohenstein, *Der Verschwörer*, 68.

23. Goerdeler's biographer still maintained in 1954 that there are not remotely as many sources for the activity, at almost every stage of his development, of any other politician in the German opposition as we have for Goerdeler (Ritter, *Goerdeler*, 13). But this has to be relativized since the publication and evaluation of the letters and diaries of, for example, Moltke or Hassell. At the same time, the source situation as regards finished texts is extremely copious in Goerdeler's case, and they have been recently edited afresh (cf. Gillmann and Mommsen, eds., *Politische Schriften und Briefe Goerdelers*).

24. H. E. Tödt, *Komplizen, Opfer und Gegner*, 234; and K. von Klemperer, *German Resistance against Hitler*.

25. Cf. Jacques Courvoisier, in W.-D. Zimmermann, ed., *Begegnungen mit D. Bon-hoeffer*, 139; P. Hoffmann, *Widerstand*, 245; Karl Dietrich Bracher, "Rüdiger Schleicher," in *Zeugen des Widerstands* (ed. J. Mehlhausen; Tübingen, 1996), 239; and M. Smid, *H. v. Dohnanyi—C. Bonhoeffer*, 233. Smid states in a later context that after Dohnanyi and Bonhoeffer had been arrested on April 5, 1943, Klaus Bonhoeffer very soon wrote a very warm letter to his brother-in-law (ibid., 362), whereas "he never got in touch with his brother Dietrich at all during the whole time of his imprisonment." On the other hand, it was certainly not by chance that it was a friend of Klaus Bonhoeffer's, Dr. Kurt Wergin, who was admitted as defending counsel for Bonhoeffer from the autumn of 1943 onward. We learn something about Klaus Bonhoeffer personally from the last letters written to his wife and children, and through a short sketch given by his wife Emmi, née Delbrück (in E. and B. Bethge, eds., *Letzte Briefe im Widerstand* [4th ed.; Gütersloh, 1997]), as well as from an instructive interview with Meding (ibid., 35ff.). Unfortunately, J. Molt-mann's essay on Klaus and Dietrich Bonhoeffer (ibid., 194ff.) is concerned mainly with Dietrich, much less with Klaus. Somewhat more informative (in spite of reservations) are the so-called Kaltenbrunn Reports about the interrogations after July 20, 1944, edited by H.-A. Jacobsen.

26. E. Bethge, *In Zitz gab es keine Juden: Erinnerungen aus meinen ersten vierzig Jahren* (Munich, 1989), 126.

27. Quoted in M. Smid, *H. v. Dohnanyi—C. Bonhoeffer*, 264.

28. E. Bethge, DB Biog., 605.

29. M. Smid, *H. v. Dohnanyi—C. Bonhoeffer*, 264.

30. On this whole complex there are also a few pointers in the letter drafts Bonhoeffer made in prison later, in connection with the interrogations (DBWE 16:415), as well as in the indictment of September 1943 (ibid., 441f.). At the same time, the passages concerned refer only to the question about subsidies for railway tickets and the payment for "business trips in the period until his recruitment into AST VII" (ibid.)—that is to say, in the period before his *uk* position, to which particular importance was attached in the interrogations and the indictment. Here the indictment reads (ibid., 441f.): "These official trips were never reimbursed by the office but . . . his brother-in-law occasionally contributed since he himself never had any sal-ary. He maintains that he did not know whether these subsidies were given from personal or official funds." But these subsidies were only occasional payments for a sleeping car and other supplements.

31. E. Bethge, DB Biog., 605.

32. Cf., e.g., Bonhoeffer DBWE 16:103, 119, or 123.

33. E. Bethge, DB Biog., 605. Cf. here also, for example, a clarification of the question whether and to what amount the Pastors' Emergency League was responsible for the payment of Bonhoeffer's salary (DBWE 16:195f. and 240).

34. Letter of July 20, 1942, from M. Burgwitz to Pastor Jannasch, in Jørgen Glenthøj, ed., *Die mündige Welt V: Dokumente zur Bonhoeffer-Forschung 1928–1945* (Munich, 1969), 219f.

35. See n. 27 above.

36. Wolf Dieter Zimmermann, *Wir nannten ihn Bruder Bonhoeffer: Einblicke in ein hoffnungsvolles Leben* (Berlin, 2004), 25.

37. Quoted in M. Smid, *H. v. Dohnanyi—C. Bonhoeffer*, 279.

38. See chap. 16; also the end of Bonhoeffer's reflections in 1942–43, in "After Ten Years," in *Letters and Papers from Prison* (ed. E. Bethge; trans. R. H. Fuller et al.; enlarged ed.; London, 1971; cf. chap. 16 n.25 below).

39. In earlier phases of his life, Bonhoeffer felt and impressively described his feeling of *acedia tristitia*. I have discussed this in more detail elsewhere; see Sabine Dramm, *Dietrich Bonhoeffer und Albert Camus: Analogien im Kontrast* (Gütersloh, 1998), 71ff.: "Seelenverstörung."

40. M. Smid, *H. v. Dohnanyi—C. Bonhoeffer*, 244f.; E. Bethge, DB Biog., 529f.

41. DBWE 6:67.

42. Moltke was an "administrative counselor for the war" conscripted into the Military Intelligence Foreign Office, while Dohnanyi, for formally necessary reasons, had been named "special leader" (see chap. 4 above). For the closer contacts between the two at that time, cf. Freya von Moltke, Michael Balfour, and Julian Frisby, *Helmuth James von Moltke 1907–1945: Anwalt der Zukunft* (Stuttgart, 1975), 160ff., and M. Smid, *H. v. Dohnanyi—C. Bonhoeffer*, 289ff.

43. P. Hoffmann, *Widerstand*, 333, and Hans Mommsen, "Die Widerstand gegen Hitler und die deutsche Gesellschaft," in *Der Widerstand gegen den Nationalsozialismus* (ed. J. Schmädeke and P. Steinbach; Munich and Zurich, 1985), 403f.

44. Hans Mommsen, "Die Stellung der Militäropposition," in *Alternative zu Hitler: Studien zur Geschichte des deutschen Widerstands* (Munich, 2000), 369; Engl. trans. by A. McGeoch: *Alternatives to Hitler: German Resistance under the Third Reich* (Princeton, 2003).

45. According to H. Mommsen ("Die Stellung," 372), "there was a large measure of agreement between the civilian and the military conspirators in their basic national-conservative attitude and their moral outrage over the crimes of the regime; but it was only a minority that saw these crimes as resulting from the system itself."

46. Cf. on this, e.g., Peter Steinbach, "Zum Verhältnis der Ziele der militärischen und zivilen Widerstandgruppen," in *Der Widerstand gegen den Nationalsozialismus* (ed. J. Schmädeke and P. Steinbach; Munich and Zurich, 1985), and H. Mommsen, "Die Stellung," passim.

47. Ekkehard Klausa, "Politischer Konservatismus und Widerstand," in *Der Widerstand gegen den Nationalsozialismus* (ed. P. Steinbach and J. Tüchel; Munich and Zurich, 1994), 468.

48. Matthias Schreiber, *Friedrich Justus Perels: Ein Weg vom Rechtskampf der Bekennenden Kirche in den politischen Widerstand* (Munich, 1989), 172 and 188. On Perels see chap. 11.

49. E. Klausa, "Politischer Konservatismus und Widerstand," 231.

50. P. Steinbach, "Zum Verhältnis der Ziele," 989.

51. E. Klausa, "Politischer Konservatismus und Widerstand," 231. Cf. here also H. E. Tödt, "Der Dohnanyi-Bonhoeffer-Kreis," 230 and 232.

52. Cf. here Dorothee von Meding, *Mit dem Mut des Herzens: Die Frauen des 20. Juli* (Berlin, 1992), and M. Schmid, *H. v. Dohnanyi—C. Bonhoeffer*, passim.

53. Peter Steinbach, *Widerstand im Widerstreit: Der Widerstand gegen den Nationalsozialismus in der Erinnerung der Deutschen* (2nd ed.; Paderborn, 2001), 468.

54. Ulrich Hehl, "Die Kirchen in der NS-Diktatur: Zwischen Anpassung, Selbstbehauptung und Widerstand," in *Deutschland 1933–1945* (ed. K. D. Bracher, M. Funke, and H.-A. Jacobsen (Düsseldorf, 1992), 179.

55. DBWE 16:517f.

10. Signals for the Future?

1. DBWE 16:215.

2. Ibid.

3. Thus the title of one of the earliest postwar accounts written by a survivor, Fabian von Schlabrendorff. It was also the title of a three-part German documentary film (2004) by Maurice Philip Remy.

4. This was the much-quoted title under which the diaries of Ulrich von Hassell were posthumously published. Von Hassell was ambassador in Rome until he was recalled in 1937 and was one of the most acute conservative critics of the Nazis. He maintained many conspiratorial contacts. The phrase "the other Germany" was especially current in 1941 in England and in the BBC's German service (cf. DBWE 16:382, n.7).

5. Thus Moltke's frequently quoted phrase in a letter to his English friend Lionel Curtis of July 1935; cited in Klemens von Klemperer, "Die 'Aussenpolitik' des deutschen Widerstandes," in *Großbritannien und der deutsche Widerstand* (ed. K.-J. Müller and D. N. Dilks; Paderborn, 1994), 84.

6. Willem Visser't Hooft, *Memoirs* (London and Philadelphia, 1973), 152f.

7. DBWE 16:173.

8. Adolf Freudenberg, in W.-D. Zimmermann, ed., *Begegnungen mit Bonhoeffer* (Munich, 1964), 134. On Freudenberg see chap. 8 above.

9. Otto Salomon, in W.-D. Zimmermann, ed., *Begegnungen mit Bonhoeffer*, 136.

10. Jørgen Glenthøj, "Bonhoeffer und die Ökumene," in *Die mündige Welt II* (ed. E. Bethge; Munich, 1956), 185; and "Dietrich Bonhoeffer vor Kalten-brunner: Zur Begegnung mit Lordbischof Bell in Schweden 1942," *Evangelische Theologie* 26 (1966), 490; also DBWE 16:278 n.3.

11. J. Glenthøj, "Bonhoeffer vor Kaltenbrunner," 491; also DBWE 16:280 n.7.

12. On Bonhoeffer's service passport, see chap. 3 above.

13. J. Glenthøj, "Bonhoeffer vor Kaltenbrunner," 490, and DBWE 16:280 n.7. E. Bethge, on the other hand (DB Biog., 646f.), maintains that in his conversation with Barth at this time Bonhoeffer was not perhaps so much expressing his own personal view as those of some of Beck's confidants. Cf. on this also Martin Heimbucher, *Christusfriede—Weltfrieden: Dietrich Bonhoeffers kirchlicher und politischer Kampf gegen den Krieg Hitlers und seine theologische Begründung* (Gütersloh, 1997), 342 n.272.

14. Willem Visser't Hooft, *Memoirs* (London and Philadelphia, 1973), 117.

15. DBWE 16:530.

16. Ibid., 531.

17. Ibid., 531–33.

18. Points in common and differences between the two writings have been discussed in detail elsewhere, e.g., in E. Bethge, DB Biog., 644f.; M. Heimbucher, *Christusfriede—Weltfriede*, 337ff.; and K. von Klemperer, *German Resistance against Hitler: The Search for Allies Abroad, 1938–1945* (Oxford, 1992), 272–74. For the historian Klemperer—very much an admirer of Bonhoeffer—the draft about Paton's book is "a tortured document which attests little to the clarity and serenity which usually mark Bonhoeffer's thought and writing," 273.

19. DBWE 16:533–35.

20. Ibid., 535 and 538.

21. Ibid., 536, 539.

22. W. Visser't Hooft, *Memoirs*, 154.

23. E. Bethge, DB Biog., 645f.

24. Printed in Armin Boyens, *Kirchenkampf und Ökumene 1939–1945: Darstellung und Dokumentation unter besonderer Berücksichtigung der Quellen des Ökumenischen Rates der Kirchen* (Munich, 1973), 176. John Foster Dulles was secretary of state in the United States during the 1950s.

25. W. Visser't Hooft, *Memoirs*, 154.

26. See chap. 8. In September 1941 Churchill once more emphasized to Eden the policy of absolute silence; cf. Lothar Kettenacker, "Der deutsche Widerstand aus britischer Sicht," in *NS-Verbrechen* (ed. G. R. Ueberschär; Darmstadt, 2002), 27.

27. W. Visser't Hooft, *Memoirs*, 155.

28. E. Bethge, DB Biog., 646.

29. DBWE 16:224.

30. U. von Hassell, *Die Hassell-Tagebücher, 1938–1944: Aufzeichnungen vom Andern Deutschland* (Zurich, 1946); Engl. trans.: *The von Hassell Diaries 1938–1944: The Story of the Forces against Hitler inside Germany as Recorded by Ambassador Ulrich von Hassell* (London, 1948), 278. See also chap. 9 above.

31. Cf. here Peter Hoffmann, *Widerstand, Staatsstreich, Attentat: Der Kampf der Opposition gegen Hitler* (3rd ed.; Munich, 1979), 327ff.; and Hans Mommsen, "Die Stellung der Militäropposition," in *Alternative zu Hitler: Studien zur Geschichte des deutschen Widerstands* (Munich, 2000), 369ff.; Engl. trans.: *Alternatives to Hitler: German Resistance under the Third Reich* (trans. A. McGeoch; Princeton, N.J., 2003).

11. "The Desperation is Unprecedented . . ."

1. Matthias Schreiber, *Friedrich Justus Perels: Ein Weg vom Rechtskampf der Bekennenden Kirche in den politischen Widerstand* (Munich, 1989), 168f., and Winfried Meyer, *Unternehmen Sieben: Eine Rettungsaktion für vom Holocaust Bedrohte aus dem Amt Ausland/Abwehr im Oberkommando der Wehrmacht* (Frankfurt am Main, 1993), 462 n.7.

2. DBWE 16:228f.

3. Ibid., 225ff.

4. M. Schreiber, *Perels*, 99.

5. E. Bethge, DB Biog., 471. Cf. M. Schreiber, *Perels*, 110.

6. M. Schreiber, *Perels*, 154f., and 175; also chap. 6 above.

7. See chaps. 4 and 18.

8. E. Bethge, DB Biog., 650, and W. Meyer, *Unternehmen Sieben*, 8.

9. Cf. DBWE 16:227f. n.6

10. W. Meyer, *Unternehmen Sieben*, 76. On what follows, see pp. 76ff.

11. DBWE 16:230f.

12. More than fifty years after the events of autumn 1941, in the autumn of 1998 a short handwritten letter was discovered in the Karl Barth archive in Basel. It was headed "Zurich, 29 October 1941" and began, "Dear

Baroness," ending with an illegible signature, "Dr. Sch. . ." (DBW 17:139). The background of this small yet interesting discovery is as follows (cf. Bethge, DB Biog., 653f., and Meyer, *Unternehmen Sieben*, 79 and 479): In his Bonhoeffer biography, Bethge started from the assumption that in the second half of October Schmidhuber had received in Munich from Rott, in addition to his long letter to Koechlin, another personal letter of Bonhoeffer's to Barth. However, there is no evidence for this in the papers of either Barth or Bonhoeffer. Through the discovery of 1998 it emerges that Barth, or his assistant Charlotte von Kirschbaum—whose code name at that time was "baroness"—did indeed receive the same letter as that to Koechlin, together with the letter that has now been found. This accompanying letter runs (DBW 17:139): "On behalf of Mr D. Bonhoeffer and Mr. D. Rott I enclose a copy of a letter addressed to President D. Köchlin. The gentlemen ask you on your side too to support this request as far as possible. . . . Both gentlemen ask you to destroy this and the enclosed letter after you have read them. I would ask you to do the same with the present letter." The last request, at least, was not complied with, and it is only because this letter was not destroyed that we have any evidence for the existence of the letter to Barth, which itself, however, has still not been found. The question still remains: who was the author of this accompanying letter? The illegible signature has prevented this from being cleared up. I believe that the answer to the riddle can be found by piecing together the following mosaic stones: the note now appended to this letter suggests that the signature is Schmidhuber's, because of the three letters that are legible; but the writing otherwise does not permit this conclusion. Moreover Schmidhuber traveled directly from Munich to Koechlin in Bern. But there is another hint in this connection (DBW 17:139 n.1): "The writer was evidently a source living in Zurich of the Munich Intelligence office." And in a quite different connection (Meyer, *Unternehmen Sieben*, 303 and 615), we learn that one of the code names for Hans Bernd Gisevius, then the representative in Munich of the Military Intelligence, was Dr. Schicht. According to this, it may in my view be assumed that no one other than Gisevius was the writer or messenger of this letter to Barth, especially since he found contacts to Barth very important (see chaps. 8 and 13). So much for this small discovery of 1998. "Occasionally," writes Ulrich Kabitz ("Einige Tage nach Weihnachten 1939: Ein Fallbeispiel der Bonhoeffer-Forschung," in *Dietrich Bonhoeffer Jahrbuch* 2003 [ed. C. Gremmels, H. Pfeifer, et al.; Gütersloh, 2003], 125), ". . .even tiny particles are illuminating."

13. Cited in W. Meyer, *Unternehmen Sieben*, 81.

14. Ibid., 82.

15. Cf. ibid., passim.

16. Ibid., 395.

17. Ibid., 69.

18. Ibid., 303.

19. DBWE 16:352f.

20. We may assume with some degree of certainty that on August 30, 1942, Hans Bernd Gisevius, the German Military Intelligence representative in Switzerland, visited Koechlin, and it is conceivable that Bonhoeffer's letter reached Koechlin by this means. Cf. here DBWE 16:353 n.2, W. Meyer, *Unternehmen Sieben*, 303, and Marikje Smid, *Hans von Dohnanyi—Christine Bonhoeffer: Eine Ehe im Widerstand gegen Hitler* (Gütersloh, 2002), 391f.

21. From Charlotte Friedenthal's diary of September 5, 194, cited in W. Meyer, *Unternehmen Sieben*, 394. This impressive diary, a copy of which was kindly put at my disposal by Winfried Meyer, contains the entries from September 4, 1942, to December 31, 1944. As it goes on there are also mentions of Albertz, Rott, Bell, and Schönfeld, but not (as we should perhaps expect) of Dohnanyi or Bonhoeffer. The reason could be that for reasons of security she did not wish to mention them. Meyer (*Unternehmen Sieben*, 336 and 545) points to another factor: Charlotte Friedenthal (as a precaution in her own interests) was not fully informed about the special preconditions of her emigration in the context of Operation 7.

22. W. Meyer, *Unternehmen Sieben*, 479 n.347. Cf. in contrast Bethge's description in DB Biog., 651ff. Here it should, however, be noted that Bethge especially greatly valued Meyer's justified corrections, and his study in general.

23. W. Meyer, *Unternehmen Sieben*, 70, and M. Smid, *H. v. Dohnanyi—C. Bonhoeffer*, 300.

24. Thus the beginning of the heading to the relevant chapter in Meyer, *Unternehmen Sieben*.

25. A few examples of such idealizations may be mentioned: Many years ago Wilhelm Rott himself described his recollections of Operation 7, but the dates and description of the action today seem problematical (Rott in W.-D. Zimmermann, ed., *Begegnungen mit Bonhoeffer: Ein Almanach* [Munich, 1964], 108; Engl. trans. by K. Gregor Smith, *I Knew D. Bonhoeffer* [London and New York, 1966]): "The 'equivocal' Bonhoeffer was untiringly concerned with the rescue of the victims. At the end of 1941 he and his friends in the Military Intelligence succeeded in bringing a number of wearers of the yellow star into Switzerland." A biography published in 1998, talking about autumn 1941, the reports of the deportations, and "Operation 7," maintains (Christian Feldmann, *Wir hätten schreien müssen: Das Leben des*

Dietrich Bonhoeffer [Freiburg, 1998], 108): "Bonhoeffer . . . sent the documents to oppositional military personnel in order to encourage them to a putsch. He helped Canaris . . . to get another group of persecuted people into neutral Switzerland." In 2004 a Protestant monthly published a report about Bonhoeffer's stay in America in 1939, supplemented by an "infobox" headed "Dietrich Bonhoeffer," which stated not only that he acted as a "double agent" but added specifically, "In the framework of this activity he brings fourteen Jews threatened by deportation to Switzerland" (*Chrismon* 2004/3, 32).

26. On the general subject of Bonhoeffer and the Jews, cf. among contributions in German, e.g., Pinchas E. Lapide's essay of 1979, "Bonhoeffer und das Judentum," in *Verspieltes Erbe?* (ed. E. Feil; Munich, 1979); Bethge's essay of 1980, "Dietrich Bonhoeffer und die Juden," in *Konsequenzen: Dietrich Bonhoeffers Kirchenverständnis heute* (ed. E. Feil and I. Tödt; Munich, 1980; the collection edited in 1982 by Wolfgang Huber and I. Tödt, *Ethik im Ernstfall: Dietrich Bonhoeffers Stellung zu den Juden und ihre Aktualität* (Munich, 1982); Wolfgang Gerlach's study, *Als die Zeugen schwiegen: Bekennende Kirche und die Juden* (2nd ed.; Berlin, 1993) (Engl. trans. by V. J. Barnett, *And the Witnesses Were Silent: The Confessing Church and the Jews* [Lincoln, Neb., 2000]); and that of Christine-Ruth Müller, *Dietrich Bonhoeffers Kampf gegen die nationalsozialistische Verfolgung und Vernichtung der Juden: Bonhoeffers Haltung zur Judenfrage im Vergleich mit Stellungnahmen aus der evangelischen Kirche und Kreisen des deutschen Widerstandes* (Munich, 1990). See also the chapter "Und die Juden?" in Sabine Dramm, *Bonhoeffer: Eine Einführung in sein Denken* (Gütersloh, 2001), 191ff.

27. On the question about the German resistance and the Jews, cf. especially Christof Dipper's "Der Widerstand und die Juden," in *Der Widerstand gegen den Nationalsozialismus* (ed. J. Schmädeke and P. Steinbach; Munich and Zurich), 1985; Peter Hoffman's reply, "Motive," in *Der Widerstand gegen den Nationalsozialismus* (ed. J. Schmädeke and P. Steinbach; Munich and Zurich, 1985); as well as Dipper's "Der 'Aufstand des Gewissens' und die 'Judenfrage': ein Rückblick," in *NS-Verbrechen* (ed. G. R. Ueberschär; Darmstadt, 2000); and especially Hans Mommsen's essay "Die Widerstand gegen Hitler und die deutsche Gesellschaft," in *Der Widerstand gegen den Nationalsozialismus* (ed. J. Schmädeke and P. Steinbach; Munich and Zurich, 1985). Here Mommsen discusses Bonhoeffer (393 and 399) and, taking up his well-known formulation (DBW 13:353), establishes (399), "Initiatives to put a spoke in the wheel of the system and to circumvent the persecuting measures took their starting point in the first place from the highly motivated and extremely active group in the Military Intelligence around Oster,

Dohnanyi, and Bonhoeffer, and culminated in the well-known 'Operation 7' action."

28. DBWE 6:128.

29. Ibid.

30. P. Lapide, "Bonhoeffer und das Judentum," 118.

12. Is There Such a Thing as Spring?

1. See chap. 9.

2. Thus the formulation that provided the title for the reports of the interrogations of the security service that followed the attack of July 20, 1944, the so-called Kaltenbrunn Reports; see Hans-Adolf Jacobsen, ed., *"Spiegelbild einer Verschwörung": Die Opposition gegen Hitler und der Staatsstreich vom 20. Juli 1944 in der SD-Berichterstattung* (2 vols.; Stuttgart, 1984).

3. Hans Mommsen, "Die Opposition gegen Hitler und die deutsche Gesellschaft 1933–1945," in *Der deutsche Widerstand 1933–1945* (ed. K.-J. Müller; 2nd ed.; Paderborn, 1900), 38.

4. DBWE 16:146.

5. The expression "divided trust" is used in the Kaltenbrunn Reports (cf. n.2 above) in the context of the Gördeler's interrogation (cf. H.-A. Jacobsen, ed., *"Spiegelbild einer Verschwörung,"* 1:522). Even Beck only mentioned names to him with the greatest reluctance: "Secrecy even toward the people to whom one was closest had become second nature to this old general staff officer."

6. E. Bethge, DB Biog., 619.

7. Harold C. Deutsch, *Verschwörung gegen den Krieg: Der Widerstand in den Jahren 1939–40* (Munich, 1969), 8; Engl. orig.: *The Conspiracy against Hitler in the Twilight War* (Minneapolis, 1968).

8. Joachim Fest, *Staatsstreich: Der lange Weg zum 20. Juli* (Berlin, 1994), 339, with reference to Schlabrendorff.

9. Dorothee von Meding, *Mit dem Mut des Herzens: Die Frauen des 20. Juli* (Berlin, 1992), 54.

10. Ibid., 52.

11. Ibid., 53.

12. See chap. 12.

13. Matthias Schreiber, *Friedrich Justus Perels: Ein Weg vom Rechtskampf der Bekennenden Kirche in den politischen Widerstand* (Munich, 1989), 188.

14. Marikje Smid, *Hans von Dohnanyi—Christine Bonhoeffer: Eine Ehe im Widerstand gegen Hitler* (Gütersloh, 2002), 306.

15. E. Bethge, *DB Biog.*, 654; also the chronological table in DBWE 16:686.

16. Ulrich von Hassell, *Die Hassell-Tagebücher, 1938–1944: Aufzeichnungen vom Andern Deutschland* (Zurich, 1946), 300; Engl. trans.: *The von Hassell Diaries 1938–1944: The Story of the Forces against Hitler inside Germany as Recorded by Ambassador Ulrich von Hassell* (London, 1948).

17. DBWE 16:235.

18. Ibid., 246.

19. Ibid., 255.

20. Ger van Roon, "Graf Moltke als Völkerrechtler im OKW," *Vierteljahreshefte für Zeitgeschichte* 18 (1970), 21.

21. Bonhoeffer used this now well-known phrase "to put a spoke in the wheel" in 1933 in connection with "the Jewish question" (DBW 12:353). It occurs similarly in a letter of Moltke's to his wife. Talking about "liquidations" in the east in the middle of November 1941, he talks allusively about his daily work in Berlin at the time (quoted in Freya von Moltke, Michael Balfour, and Julian Frisby, *Helmuth James von Moltke 1907–1945: Anwalt der Zukunft* [Stuttgart, 1975], 174) and says that he "really had succeeded in putting a spoke in the wheel of the Jewish persecution, or could at least hamper it a little." A day later he was able to tell his wife: "In the Jewish matter, I have managed to get a veto for the moment from the army high command" (cf. G. van Roon, "Moltke als Völkerrechtler," 39f.). The matter in question was a written protest to army headquarters directed against the murder of Jewish-Russian prisoners of war. The "liquidation" was at least staved off. On Moltke's warnings to Denmark and Sweden, see, e.g., Hans Mommsen, "Die Widerstand gegen Hitler und die deutsche Gesellschaft," in *Der Widerstand gegen den Nationalsozialismus* (ed. J. Schmädeke and P. Steinbach; Munich and Zurich, 1985), 395f. According to Mommsen (ibid., 395), because of the information available to him in the Military Intelligence, Moltke was "positively the seismograph of the opposition with regard to the intensified action against the Jews."

22. This is the subtitle of the Moltke biography published by Michael Balfour and Julian Frisby, with the cooperation of Freya von Moltke (cf. n. 21 above).

23. Thus the documents of the security service of September 12, 1944, covering the interrogations following July 20 with regard to Steltzer (cf. H.-A. Jacobsen, ed., *"Spiegelbild einer Verschwörung,"* 1:381). The death sentence passed on Steltzer was set aside by Himmler personally because of interventions by Norwegian friends, and he was released on April 25, 1945 (cf. Klemens von Klemperer, *German Resistance against Hitler: The Search for Allies*

Abroad, 1938–1945 [Oxford, 1992], 414 n.277). A marginal note brings out the many fortuitous interactions of those years: Eberhard Bethge (*In Zitz gab es keine Juden: Erinnerungen aus meinem ersten vierzig Jahren* [Munich, 1989], 208) remembered that after he himself had been released from prison at the end of April, he met Steltzer's wife during the bombardment of Berlin. At that time she was living in the house of her parents-in-law, Ursula and Rüdiger Schleicher, at Marienburger Allee 42.

24. Armin Boyens writes (*Kirchenkampf und Ökumene 1939–1945: Darstellung und Dokumentation unter besonderer Berücksichtigung der Quellen des Ökumenischen Rates der Kirchen* [Munich, 1973], 163) that "Berggrav got Steltzer to tell him about the experiences of the Confessing Church in Germany, whereas Steltzer asked about the mood of the Norwegian population."

25. Theodor Steltzer, *Sechzig Jahre Zeitgenosse* (Munich, 1966), 142.

26. F. von Moltke, M. Balfour, and J. Frisby, *Moltke*, 182.

27. DBWE 16:266.

28. Printed in full in Helmuth James von Moltke, *Briefe an Freya 1939–1945* (2nd ed.; Munich, 1991), 360ff.; Engl. trans. by B. Ruhm von Oppen, *Letters to Freya: 1939–1945* (New York, 1990); extracts in DBWE 16:267ff.

29. H. J. v. Moltke, *Briefe an Freya*, 360.

30. Ibid., 361.

31. Ibid., 362f., 363, and 364.

32. Ibid., 365.

33. Ibid.

34. F. v. Moltke, M. Balfour, and J. Frisby, *Moltke*, 183.

35. H. J. v. Moltke, *Briefe an Freya*, 364.

36. Cf. ibid., 366 n.4; also DBWE 16:267f. There are earlier, disparate statements on this in G. van Roon, "Moltke als Völkerrechtler," 327; E. Bethge, DB Biog., 659; and Jørgen Glenthøj, ed., *Die mündige Welt V: Dokumente zur Bonhoeffer-Forschung 1928–1945* (Munich, 1969), 262f. n.13. Van Roon states (327) that Berggrav, "who had been smuggled out of prison for the discussion," was present; but this can no longer be maintained.

37. Cf. F. v. Moltke, M. Balfour, and J. Frisby, *Moltke*, 183, and E. Bethge, DB Biog., 659.

38. H. J. v. Moltke, *Briefe an Freya*, 365.

39. The discrepancies in the dating have meanwhile been resolved. The last part of Moltke's detailed account in his letter to his wife about the Oslo mission which began on April 15, 1942, bears the date April 17, 1942. But the editor of the letters (*Briefe an Freya*, 364 and 366 n.3), in accordance with a statement of Moltke himself (ibid., 365) and with Bonhoeffer's diary

entries (DBWE 16:266), assigns the account to Thursday April 16, 1942: "Today, Thursday morning, we left at 7 o'clock for Stockholm."

40. H. J. v. Moltke, *Briefe an Freya*, 365f. and 367.

41. DBWE 16:266.

42. Quoted in J. Glenthøj, *Die mündige Welt V*, 263 n.13.

43. E. Bethge, DB Biog., 658, and the corresponding quotation in the afterword to DBWE 16:658. It need hardly be said that no reflection is intended here on these outstanding volumes.

44. E. Bethge, ibid., and J. Glenthøj, *Die mündige Welt V*, 263 n.13.

45. Cf. J. Glenthøj, *Die mündige Welt V*, 264 n.13, and T. Steltzer, *Sechzig Jahre Zeitgenosse*, 142; also DBWE 16:275 n.2.

46. T. Steltzer, *Sechzig Jahre Zeitgenosse*, 142.

47. From the Bonhoeffer literature it is only necessary to cite here a few examples that unintentionally suggest that the mission and visit of Bonhoeffer and Moltke were directly connected with the at least relative and provisional "success" in the Berggrav matter. Bethge (DB Biog., 657f.) points out on the one hand that "Berlin had intervened," and the formulation on the following pages does not expressly construe a causal connection between their stay and the bishop's release from prison; but the suggestion is nevertheless given: "On the day that Berggrav was exiled to the forest chalet near Asker . . . Moltke and Bonhoeffer left on their return journey." Jørgen Glenthøj in his "Dietrich Bonhoeffer vor Kaltenbrunner: Zur Begegnung mit Lordbischof Bell in Schweden 1942," *Evangelische Theologie* 26 (1966), 474, proceeded from the assumption that in April 1942 Berggrav "barely escaped with his life, with the help of Dietrich Bonhoeffer and J. von Moltke." But three years later, in *Die Mündige Welt* V (263f n.13), he put it in a very much more differentiated way: "To what extent Moltke and Bonhoeffer contributed to the saving of Berggrav's life cannot be clearly established." Yet a few sentences further on he sums up: "At all events Berggrav was saved from the gallows through intervention from the German side. . . . Moltke and Bonhoeffer at least contributed essentially to this turn of events." The 1986 edition of *Bonhoeffer: Bilder aus seinem Leben* (ed. E. and R. Bethge and C. Gremmels; Munich) (Engl. trans. by John Bowden: *Dietrich Bonhoeffer: A Life in Pictures* [Philadelphia: 1986]) states: "The Abwehr and their emissaries used the security of the German occupying forces as an argument: if the Bishop was eliminated the whole Norwegian population would be in an uproar. So Berggrav was released from prison" (Engl. ed., p. 190). This statement no longer appears in this form in the 2005 German edition.

48. By historians too the Norwegian mission of Moltke and Bonhoeffer has
    been assigned great importance—sometimes unduly great. Ger van
    Roon, for example, writes (*Widerstand im Dritten Reich: Ein Überblick* [6th ed.;
    Munich, 1994], 36f.) that Moltke saved Berggrav's life "by hastening to
    Oslo at the height of the conflict between the occupying power and the
    church and, by way of reports to Canaris, managing to have Berggrav
    interned." However, in another place (*Moltke als Völkerrechtler*, 51) Ger van
    Roon had characterized the report to Canaris in more differentiated terms:
    the account of the situation had caused Canaris "to point out that the
    interests of the army were endangered, this being a way of avoiding even
    worse things." Peter Hoffmann, for example (*Widerstand, Staatsstreich, Atten-
    tat: Der Kampf der Opposition gegen Hitler* [3rd ed.; Munich, 1979], 303; Engl.
    trans. by R. Barry: *The History of the German Resistance 1933–1945* [Cam-
    bridge, Mass., 1977]), has a brief mention of the journey with a mistaken
    account of the events themselves, and—with reference to Roon—points to
    the attempt to make contact with the Allies: Steltzer, Moltke, Bonhoeffer,
    and Canaris "freed the Norwegian bishop Berggrav from life-threatening
    imprisonment in April 1942 but also did not miss the chance to use the
    connection achieved to appeal to the Allies for intervention, so that they
    might make contact with the German resistance movement. Admittedly
    the Norwegian discussion partners believed that the time for this 'was not
    yet ripe.' " In research into the resistance, the Norwegian journey of Mol-
    tke and Bonhoeffer is occasionally held to be an important example of the
    relations between German and non-German resistance groups, through
    which, again, other links with the Allied governments were to be forged.
    Also referring to Roon, Klemperer writes: "The first feelers to the Nor-
    wegian Resistance were actually put out on the occasion of Moltke's and
    Bonhoeffer's visit to Norway in April 1942. Together with Bonhoeffer and
    Steltzer, Moltke then explored whether the Norwegian Resistance could
    induce the King or Crown Prince to intercede with the Allies to establish
    ties with the German Resistance; but the idea was dropped as being pre-
    mature" (K. von Klemperer, *German Resistance against Hitler*, 413 n.269.).

49. F. v. Moltke, M. Balfour, and J. Frisby, *Moltke*, 184. Moltke and Berggrav
    met later on (see n. 61 below), but Klemperer confirms that Bonhoeffer
    never met Berggrav. (*German Resistance against Hitler*, 308 n.143.).

50. Quoted in F. v. Moltke, M. Balfour and J. Frisby, *Moltke*, 185. Moltke's letter
    has here been translated back from German. Here too there are discrep-
    ancies in the dates, for the letter to Curtis is headed "Stockholm, 18 April
    1942." But according to Bonhoeffer's diary, the two already traveled to

Malmö on the evening of the 17th, in order to fly from there to Berlin via Copenhagen the next day.

51. E. Bethge, *DB Biog.*, 656.

52. Ibid., 659.

53. Quoted in F. von. Moltke, M. Balfour, and J. Frisby, *Moltke*, 73, and in K. von Klemperer, *German Resistance against Hitler*.

54. Klemens von Klemperer, "Glaube, Religion, Kirche und der deutsche Widerstand gegen den Nationalsozialismus," *Vierteljahreshefte für Zeitgeschichte* 28 (1980), 296.

55. During the imprisonment that preceded their murder, both Moltke and Bonhoeffer experienced an intensity and power of faith that in its depth is beyond anything that might be called "normal" standards.

56. K. von Klemperer, *German Resistance against Hitler*, 48.; cf. his earlier essay "Glaube, Religion, Kirche," 295.

57. Thus Freya von Moltke in the middle of the 1970s according to K. von Klemperer, *German Resistance against Hitler*, 48.

58. F. von Moltke, M. Balfour and J. Frisby, *Moltke*, 187.

59. E. Bethge, *DB Biog.*, 659; also Ger van Roon, *Neuordnung im Widerstand: Der Kreisauer Kreis* (Munich, 1967), 327 n.15; Engl. trans. by P. Ludlow: *German Resistance to Hitler: Count von Moltke and the Kreisau Circle* (London, 1971). See also chap. 16 below.

60. F. von Moltke, M. Balfour and G. Frisby, *Moltke*, 207.

61. Incidentally, it was Berggrav, in his function as Lutheran bishop, to whom Moltke, when he was again in Oslo in February 1943, put the question about the justification for an assassination (ibid., 211).

62. E. Bethge, *DB Biog.*, 656.

63. DBWE 6:275.

64. Quoted in F. von Moltke, M. Balfour and J. Frisby, *Moltke*, 176. The letter has been translated back from German; cf. also n. 50 above.

13. Under Suspicion

1. DBWE 16:286f.

2. Ibid. 287 (see also chaps. 8 and 11 above).

3. Ibid., 274f.

4. Ibid., 276.

5. Ibid., 277f., translation slightly altered.

6. See chap. 10.

7. All quotations ibid., 278ff.

8. On Wilhelm Schmidhuber, see chap. 7 above. For details about the background of this currency affair, cf. Heinz Höhne, *Canaris: Patriot im Zwielicht* (Munich, 1976), 475ff.; Engl. trans. by J. M. Brownjohn, *Canaris: Hitler's Master Spy* (New York, 1999), and Winfried Meyer, *Unternehmen Sieben: Eine Rettungsaktion für vom Holocaust Bedrohte aus dem Amt Ausland/Abwehr im Oberkommando der Wehrmacht* (Frankfurt am Main, 1993), 351ff.

9. On the earlier "Ten Commandments," see chap. 7 n.2.

10. See chap. 10. Hans Schönfeld, Eugen Gerstenmaier, and Hans Bernd von Haeften among others were involved in the composition of this Trott memorandum. It is published in Hans Rothfels, ed., "Zwei aussenpolitische Memoranden der deutschen Opposition (Frühjahr 1942)," *Vierteljahreshefte für Zeitgeschichte* 5 (1957): 392ff.; cf. Klemens von Klemperer, *German Resistance against Hitler: The Search for Allies Abroad, 1938–1945* (Oxford, 1992), 16 n.41.

11. Quoted in K. von Klemperer, *German Resistance against Hitler*, 305 n.111.

12. E. Bethge, DB Biog., 574, and Clarita von Trott zu Solz, *Adam von Trott zu Solz: Eine Lebensbeschreibung* (Berlin, 1994), 155. In retrospect, incidentally, many parallels deserving of research emerge between their biographies. On Adam von Trott cf., e.g., Eberhard Bethge, "Adam von Trott und der deutsche Widerstand," *Vierteljahreshefte für Zeitgeschichte* 11 (1963), 213–23, Clarita von Trott, *Adam von Trott*, passim, and Joachim Fest, *Staatsstreich: Der lange Weg zum 20. Juli* (Berlin, 1994), 1–18.

13. Cf. W. Visser't Hooft's *Memoirs* (London and Philadelphia, 1973), 136ff. For the term "Swiss road," see chap. 8, n. 10 above. Visser't Hooft's endeavors have been repeatedly recognized. He acted "in awareness of the total European dimension of the resistance against National Socialism" (Jürgen Heideking, "Die 'Schweizer Straßen' des europäischen Widerstands," in *Geheimdienste und Widerstandsbewegungen im Zweiten Weltkrieg* [ed. Gerhard Schulz; Göttingen, 1982], 160), and it was probably due to him especially that the German resistance was accepted and understood abroad (K. von Klemperer, *German Resistance against Hitler*, 438), especially in the WCC and among other resistance groups, in Holland and Scandinavia particularly.

14. J. Heideking, "Die 'Schweizer Strassen,'" 159.

15. Karl Dietrich Bracher, "Rüdiger Schleicher," in *Zeugen des Widerstands* (ed. J. Mehlhausen; Tübingen, 1996), 229f.; and J. Fest, *Staatsstreich*, 12.

16. E. Bethge, DB Biog., 661.

17. DBWE 16:286 n.2.

18. Ibid., 280 n.7; also chap. 10 above.

19. Thus E. Bethge, DB Biog., 661. In Meyer's reconstruction of the prepa-
    rations for Operation 7 (W. Meyer, *Unternehmen Sieben*; see also chap. 11
    above), there is admittedly no evidence for this.

20. For the most probable date of Bonhoeffer's return journey, cf. DBWE
    16:287 n.1 and 288 n.1, together with Otto Salomon's recollection (in
    Wolf-Dieter Zimmermann, ed., *Begegnungen mit Dietrich Bonhoeffer: Ein Alma-
    nach* [Munich, 1964], 136; Engl. trans. by K. Gregor Smith: *I Knew Dietrich
    Bonhoeffer* [London and New York, 1966]), which, however, leaves a precise
    date open: "One afternoon, after he had collected his poste restante (gen-
    eral delivery) letters, we found him depressed. He said, 'Things are serious
    for me,' and departed the same day." Bethge (DB Biog., 661) was sure that
    the initiative to break off his Swiss visit and to prepare for the next journey,
    which was immediately impending, came from Bonhoeffer himself.

14. Sigtuna

1. There is a wealth of material on this episode, which took place on Swedish
   soil at the end of May/beginning of June 1942: commentaries, interpretations, evaluations, and polemics about which it is impossible to enter into
   detail here. With regard to the sources, it may suffice to say the following:
   Hans Schönfeld is the author of the *Statement by a German Pastor at Stockholm
   31st May 1942* (see DBWE 16:306ff.). Bell offers most of the eyewitness
   accounts; see his diary notes of May 13 to June 6, 1942 (ibid., 289ff.). Bell's
   Memorandum of Conversations is dated 19.6.1942. This report, together with
   Schönfeld's *Statement* was intended for Anthony Eden (the British Foreign
   Secretary) or for the Foreign Office in London (ibid., 319ff.). Also available
   are letters, minutes, etc. from the Foreign Office, as well as the correspondence of that time between Eden and Bell (ibid., 318f. and 331ff.).

   After the war, in October 1945, Bell published in an English periodical his recollections of the events in Sweden under the title "The Background of the Hitler Plot." This report also appears in his book *The Church
   and Humanity* (1946). In May 1957 Bell gave a lecture at the universities
   of Göttingen and Bonn with the title "The Church and the Resistance
   Movement," which was a further report about the events in Sweden. This
   was published in German translation in Bonhoeffer's *Gesammelte Schriften*
   1:399ff. and in the periodicals *Vierteljahreshefte für Zeitgeschichte* 5, 1957, and
   Evangelische Theologie, 1957.

   The following account is based mainly on Bell's diary notes because
   of their close contemporary reference; but when the facts require it, later

descriptions have also been drawn upon. It would undoubtedly be interesting to make a detailed "synoptic comparison" of the various reminiscence strata, which emerge, for example, from Bell's accounts of 1942, 1945, and 1957.

On Stockholm, Sigtuna, and the consequences as a whole, cf. earlier literature, especially Hans Rothfels, *Die deutsche Opposition gegen Hitler: Eine Würdigung* (Zurich, 1949; 2nd ed. 1994), 280ff.; further, since 1967, the biographies by R. C. D. Jasper, *George Bell, Bishop of Chichester* (London, New York, and Toronto, 1967), 266ff., and E. Bethge, DB Biog., 661ff.; also Jørgen Glenthøj, ed., *Die mündige Welt V: Dokumente zur Bonhoeffer-Forschung 1928–1945* (Munich, 1969), 268ff.; and Peter Hoffmann, *Widerstand, Staatsstreich, Attentat: Der Kampf der Opposition gegen Hitler* (3rd ed.; Munich, 1979), 268ff. (Engl. trans. by R. Barry: *The History of the German Resistance 1933–1945* [Cambridge, Mass., 1977]); and finally Klemens von Klemperer, *German Resistance against Hitler: The Search for Allies Abroad, 1938–1945* [Oxford, 1992], 285–86, *Welt V*, 304f. and Martin Heimbucher, *Christusfriede—Weltfrieden: Dietrich Bonhoeffers kirchlicher und politischer Kampf gegen den Krieg Hitlers und seine theologische Begründung* (Gütersloh, 1997), 353ff.

2. Published in J. Glenthøj, ed., *Die mündige Welt V*, 304f. As official representative of the WCC, Schönfeld needed in each case only a visa from the country to be visited; see n.18 below; also K. von Klemperer, *German Resistance against Hitler*, 414 n.287

3. E. Bethge, DB Biog., 663. Schönfeld's political friends in 1942 still included Eugen Gerstenmaier, as well as Hans Bernd von Haeften and Adam von Trott.; cf., e.g., K. von Klemperer, *German Resistance against Hitler*, 304 n.92.

4. K. von Klemperer, *German Resistance against Hitler*, 307 n.130.

5. Marikje Smid, *Hans von Dohnanyi—Christine Bonhoeffer: Eine Ehe im Widerstand gegen Hitler* (Gütersloh, 2002), 313. See also chap. 13, n.20, above.

6. See chap. 3 above.

7. Theodor Steltzer, *Sechzig Jahre Zeitgenosse* (Munich, 1966), 140.

8. Thus Bonhoeffer to Kaltenbrunner, cited in DBWE 16:463. In the later interrogations Bonhoeffer tried to present the character of this alleged Military Intelligence assignment and the meeting with Bell convincingly. The conspiratorial mission and purpose of his journey were not in fact discovered at that time. Cf. here the whole report of January 4, 1945 given by Kaltenbrunner to Ribbentrop (DBWE 16:462ff.; also Jørgen Glenthøj, "Dietrich Bonhoeffer vor Kaltenbrunner: Zur Begegnung mit Lordbischof Bell in Schweden 1942," *Evangelische Theologie* 26 [1966]: 462ff.).

9. Quoted in M. Smid, *H. v. Dohnanyi—C. Bonhoeffer*, 314.

10. Ger van Roon, *Neuordnung im Widerstand, Der Kreisauer Kreis* (Munich, 1967), 154, 313; Engl. trans. by P. Ludlow: *German Resistance to Hitler: Count von Moltke and the Kreisau Circle* (London, 1971); also K. v. Klemperer, *German Resistance against Hitler*, 308 n.149. On Hans Bernd von Haeften, cf. Gerhard Ringshausen, "Evangelische Kirche und Widerstand," in *Deutscher Widerstand—Demokratie heute: Kirche, Kreisauer Kreis, Ethik, Militär und Gewerkschaften* (ed. H. Engel; Bonn and Berlin, 1992), 86ff., and K. v. Klemperer, *German Resistance against Hitler*, 30–32. According to Clarita von Trott's recollection, Haeften's sense of justice was so sensitive and vulnerable "that his horror and suffering over the crimes round about him threatened to destroy him physically" (Clarita von Trott zu Solz, *Adam von Trott zu Solz: Eine Lebensbeschreibung* [Berlin, 1994], 164).

11. E. Bethge, DB Biog., 662. Cf. K. v. Klemperer, *German Resistance against Hitler*, 282–83., for a clarification of this riddle, as Bethge calls it. On the question as to whether Bonhoeffer and Schönfeld knew about each other, cf. J. Glenthøj, *Die mündige Welt V*, 271, and K. v. Klemperer, *German Resistance against Hitler*, 285.

12. Schönfeld's friend, the theologian Eugen Gerstenmaier, assumed forty years later, in the account of his life, that Schönfeld and Bonhoeffer flew to Stockholm together (Eugen Gerstenmaier, *Streit und Friede hat seine Zeit: Ein Lebensbericht* [Frankfurt, Berlin, and Vienna, 1981], 141): "I accompanied Schönfeld to Tempelhof airport. We could never be sure of getting through the passport and customs controls unscathed. In front of the narrow passage leading to the passport control we met Dietrich Bonhoeffer. He was holding a green service passport in his hand and was obviously astonished at meeting us. There was no longer any time for much conversation. We did not mention Chichester by so much as a word. Both Schönfeld and Bonhoeffer passed through the passport control without any difficulty." But when Bonhoeffer flew to Sweden, Schönfeld was undoubtedly already there. This reminiscence demonstrates the problems involved in reconstructing reality *and* recollection, and reality *in* recollection.

13. DBWE 16:401, and chap. 1 above.

14. Armin Boyens, *Kirchenkampf und Ökumene 1939–1945: Darstellung und Dokumentation unter besonderer Berücksichtigung der Quellen des Ökumenischen Rates der Kirchen* (Munich, 1973), 165.

15. Thus Johansson's 1954 report, quoted in Jørgen Glenthøj, "Dietrich Bonhoeffer vor Kaltenbrunner: Zur Begegnung mit Lordbischof Bell in Schweden 1942," *Evangelische Theologie* 26 (1966), 479, as well as in idem, *Die mündige Welt V*, 270f. They are hence in agreement with K. v. Klemperer, *German Resistance against Hitler*, 309 n.153.

16. Bell's diary entries of 1942 and his 1945 and 1957 accounts differ in detail on this point. The diary, for example, says only that Schönfeld joined Bell and Bonhoeffer after their private talk, which does not necessarily mean that Schönfeld arrived later. On May 31, 1942 (DBWE 16:297f.), Bell tells about Sigtuna, mentioning Johansson and Björkquist and—suddenly— Bonhoeffer: "After tea Bonhoeffer spoke [*sic*] messages for sister." Then he only notes (298): "S. [that is, Schönfeld] joined us later." The confidential discussion had finished, and the other visitors to Sigtuna, notably Schönfeld, joined them (ibid.). In Bell's later accounts of 1945 and 1957 (cf. GS 1:507f., 518), he stresses that Bonhoeffer and Schönfeld arrived in Sigtuna separately, and Schönfeld at all events later than Bonhoeffer.

17. In accounts of church history during these years, Schönfeld is still a shadowy figure, as can be seen from the fact, among other things, that as far as I know up to now no biographical study of him has been published, merely a few—highly emotional—pages of *"hommage"* from Eugen Gerstenmaier ("Zum Gedenken an Hans Schönfeld," in *Reden und Aufsätze* II [Stuttgart, 1962], 421ff.). Gerstenmaier has numerous other effusive and not very helpful comments about his friend Schönfeld in his autobiographical book *Streit und Friede*. But this contrasts with a largely negative picture in Bonhoeffer reception. This was influenced by the undoubtedly extremely cool relationship between Bonhoeffer and Schönfeld that was passed on and loaned permanence by Bethge's Bonhoeffer biography, although Bethge himself pointed to the later rapprochement between the two (cf. E. Bethge, DB Biog., 698). Where Schönfeld is concerned, U. Kabitz rightly regrets "the lack of a thorough biographical assessment" (Ulrich Kabitz, "Einige Tage nach Weihnachten 1939: Ein Fallbeispiel der Bonhoeffer-Forschung," in *Dietrich Bonhoeffer Jahrbuch* 2003 [ed. C. Gremmels, H. Pfeifer, et al.; Gütersloh, 2003], 120).

18. K. v. Klemperer, also n. 2 above, *German Resistance against Hitler*, 414 n.287.

19. The most useful contribution to an assessment of Schönfeld seems to me Klemperer's approach. He weighs up objectively his weaknesses—indeed blindness—where the church's policies were concerned but sets over against this his efforts for the ecumenical movement and finally for the resistance too—a commitment made at the risk of his life (cf. ibid., 52ff., 314 ff., 484).

20. W. Visser't Hooft, *Memoirs* (London and Philadelphia, 1973), 94, 99.

21. Quoted in E. Bethge, DB Biog., 310. For Bonhoeffer's Fanö lecture, see chap. 5 above.

22. Quoted in J. Glenthøj, ed., *Die mündige Welt V*, 248.

23. See chap. 6 above.

24. Freya von Moltke, Michael Balfour, and Julian Frisby, *Helmuth James von Moltke 1907–1945: Anwalt der Zukunft* (Stuttgart, 1975), 190; Clarita von Trott, *Trott*, 178 and 181f.; also Allen Welsh Dulles, *Germany's Underground* (New York, 2000).

25. K. v. Klemperer, *German Resistance against Hitler*, 357.

26. A. Boyens, *Kirchenkampf und Ökumene*, 165, and K. v. Klemperer, *German Resistance against Hitler*, 16 n.44.

27. R. C. D. Jasper, *George Bell*, 267.

28. DBWE 16:290.

29. GS 1:594.

30. Ibid., 505.

31. DBWE 16:295f.

32. Ibid., 297, and GS 1:517.

33. R. C. D. Jasper, *George Bell*, 267.

34. Bell stressed in 1945, for example, Schönfeld's sympathy for the Confessing Church (GS 1:504), and in 1957 pointed out that through his travels he continually put his life in danger (GS 1:514 and 526). Nevertheless, in spite of this high regard for Schönfeld, the bishop in his 1945 account made it explicitly clear that he encountered him with a certain ambivalence. Schönfeld's ties with Heckel's External Affairs Office in the official Protestant church, which was well-disposed toward the regime, was too suspect for Bell to ignore it, in spite of his sympathy for Schönfeld's bold courier activity and in spite of his respect for his work in Geneva.

35. Quoted in E. Bethge, DB Biog., 283.

36. GS 1:514.

37. E. Bethge, DB Biog., 288f.

38. Ibid., 570.

39. Ibid., 289.

40. Winfried Meyer, *Unternehmen Sieben: Eine Rettungsaktion für vom Holocaust Bedrohte aus dem Amt Ausland/Abwehr im Oberkommando der Wehrmacht* (Frankfurt am Main, 1993), 74.

41. The literature on Bonhoeffer and the resistance ascribes great importance to Bell. He was "the postman for German opposition circles" (J. Glenthøj, "Bonhoeffer vor Kaltenbrunner," 477), and he was "a unique advocate and ally" for the German resistance movement (E. Bethge, DB Biog., 676). As such, he was for a long time an isolated figure, according to the view of one historian and expert on English affairs (Lothar Kettenacker, "Der deutsche Widerstand aus britischer Sicht," in *NS-Verbrechen* [ed. G. R. Ueberschär;

Darmstadt, 2002], 28). The assessment of a British author in the framework of his study of the British secret service and the German resistance is less positive (Michael R. D. Foot, "Britische Geheimdienste und deutscher Widerstand 1939–1945," in *Großbritannien und der deutsche Widerstand* [ed. K.-J. Müller and D. N. Dilks; Munich, 1994]). Foot writes that Bell was a wonderful man and a true Christian but otherwise a quite impossible ambassador for delicate political assignments and handicapped by his prominent position. In discussing the attempts at contacts made by representatives of the German resistance in Sweden at the end of May 1942, Foot's judgment is that Bell was the most unsuitable person conceivable for this mission (164). K. von Klemperer's view is quite different. According to him, Bell was one of the most committed advocates of the German resistance (*German Resistance against Hitler*, 11), whose particular mark was that he acted as "a churchman without much political weight," and he built up a varied network of contacts (16 n.44). Klemperer dedicated *German Resistance against Hitler* to the memory of Bell and Visser't Hooft.

42. GS 1:507.
43. DBWE 16:304.
44. See chap. 5.
45. DBWE 304; see on this chap. 3 above.
46. DBWE 16:305.
47. GS 1:508 and 518.
48. DBWE 16:297f.
49. Ibid. 298–300.
50. Ibid (translation slightly altered).
51. After the death in action of the eldest son of Crown Prince William of Prussia, in conservative circles his second son, Prince Louis Ferdinand, was given the preference as potential monarch. According to K. v. Klemperer (*German Resistance against Hitler: The Search for Allies Abroad, 1938–1945* [Oxford, 1992], Louis Ferdinand had always kept his distance from National Socialism. Klaus Bonhoeffer knew him through his service in the German air force, and Dietrich Bonhoeffer met him through his brother.
52. DBWE 16:301.
53. GS 1:520.
54. DBWE 16:302.
55. E. and R. Bethge and C. Gremmels, *Dietrich Bonhoeffer: A Life in Pictures* (trans. John Bowden; Philadelphia, 1986), 193.
56. J. Glenthøj, ed., *Die mündige Welt V*, 272.
57. GS 1:522.
58. DBWE 16:311.

59. Sabine Leibholz-Bonhoeffer, *The Bonhoeffers: Portrait of a Family* (London, 1971), 167.

60. GS 1:522.

61. DBWE 16:310–12.

62. G. van Roon, *Neuordnung im Widerstand*, 314, and M. Smid, *H. von Dohananyi—C. Bonhoeffer*, 313. Bonhoeffer drew up a report of his conversations with Bell in Sigtuna. Through Josef Müller, who received such a report from Bethge, who gave it to him in the Berlin zoo, a copy arrived in the Vatican, according to J. Glenthøj, *Bonhoeffer vor Kaltenbrunner*, 465. However, up to now it has not been possible, as far as I know, to confirm the presumptions about the existence and character of this report.

63. Quoted in L. Kettenacker, "Die britische Haltung," 57; also K. von Klemperer, *German Resistance against Hitler: The Search for Allies Abroad, 1938–1945* (Oxford, 1992). On Churchill's silence directive, cf. chaps. 8 and 10 above.

64. DBWE 16:318.

65. Ibid., 331.

66. All documents are published in DBWE 16:306ff.

67. Quotations from Hans Schönfeld's *Statement by a German Pastor*, in DBWE 16:306–10.

68. Quotations from George Bell's *Memorandum of Conversations*, in DBWE 16:319–24.

69. GS 1:525.

70. Quotations from Foreign Office: Minutes of Proceedings, June 18–23, 1942. Germany: Peace Moves; published in DBWE 16:325f.

71. DBWE 16:346.

72. GS 1:411.

73. Quoted in J. Fest, *Staatsstreich*, 211, and L. Kettenacker, "Die britische Haltung," 70. (This marginal note was not a private impertinence of Eden's, however; he was quoting King Henry II's legendary ill-fated reference to Thomas à Becket [trans.]).

74. K. von Klemperer's book *German Resistance against Hitler* is written with great sympathy and admiration for the resistance and is at the same time objective and thorough. He devotes the book exclusively to the present subject. Cf. also his essay "Die 'Außenpolitik' des deutschen Widerstandes," in *Großbritannien und der deutsche Widerstand* (ed. K.-J. Müller and D. N. Dilks; Paderborn, 1994), 639ff., and, in contrast, Bernd Martin, "Deutsche Opposition und Widerstandskreise und die Frage eines separaten Friedensschlusses im Zweiten Weltkrieg," in *Der deutsche Widerstand 1933–1945* (ed. K. J. Müller; 2nd ed.; Paderborn, 1990), 79ff. On the subject in general, cf.

Klaus-Jürgen Müller and David N. Dilks, eds., *Großbritannien und der deutsche Widerstand 1933–1944* (Paderborn, 1994); and Jürgen Schmädeke, "Militärische Umsturzversuche und diplomatische Oppositionsbestrebungen zwischen der Münchener Konferenz und Stalingrad," in *Widerstand gegen den Nationalsozialismus* (ed. P. Steinbach and J. Tüchel; Bonn, 1994), 294ff. On Sigtuna, Hedva Ben-Israel, "Im Widerstreit der Ziele: Die britische Reaktion auf den deutschen Widerstand," in *Der Widerstand gegen den Nationalsozialismus* (ed. J. Schmädeke and P. Steinbach; Munich and Zurich, 1985), 741f., and in general on the interpretation of the British attitude, L. Kettenacker, ed., "Die britische Haltung," 49ff., and "Der deutsche Widerstand aus britischer Sicht," 25f. Three examples of the way London's silence was retrospectively judged may suffice. In his *Memoir* of 1973, Visser't Hooft summed up by saying that, right to the end, the conversation between the German resistance and the Allies remained a conversation between the deaf. The church historian A. Boyens sharply condemns the British rejection: "The Germans in opposition were condemned to death by the Nazis because of their efforts on behalf of a free Germany in a free Europe, and were condemned to oblivion by the nationalists in the Foreign Office." The historian J. Fest's judgment (or condemnation) is similar: looking back at the appeals by Bonhoeffer, Moltke, and Trott, he writes: "There was . . . no help and not even a sign of encouragement. Instead only obtuse, unmovable, armor-plated silence" (*Staatsstreich*, 212).

75. GS 1:504.

76. GS 1:526. Bell writes that Schönfeld's health deteriorated sharply after the war and he was struck down by a prolonged neurological disease. He died in Frankfurt/Main on September 1, 1954, aged fifty-four. Cf. here also E. Gerstenmaier, "Gedenken an H. Schönfeld," 426f. and K. von Klemperer, *German Resistance against Hitler*, 44, referring to Visser't Hooft. Schönfeld, Visser't Hooft says, was a highly introverted and mysterious personality who was weighed down by the conflicts of his double life and in the end broke down under them. The allusive and ambivalent character of what is said about Schönfeld's personality and his death are still further evidence that a biography of him is much needed (see n.17 above).

77. E. Bethge, DB Biog., 662f.: "It seems fairly certain . . ." "Presumably . . ." "It seems fairly certain . . ." and "I think I can remember . . ."

78. E. Bethge, DB Biog., 667. Even a historian as much impressed by Bonhoeffer as Klemperer notes that here Bethge was perhaps overstating the contrast (K. von Klemperer, *German Resistance against Hitler*, 309 n.157.).

79. H. Rothfels comments on Bonhoeffer's assertion in Sigtuna that the attitude of the opponents must be understood as an act of repentance: "Although it

was without any political intention, it was for that very reason highly political" (*Die deutsche Opposition*, 284).

80. Moltke expressed similar ideas in his letters during the autumn of 1941. Writing to Freya von Moltke on August 26, for example, he talked about "a blood guilt that will not be expiated in our lifetime and can never be forgotten" (Helmuth James von Moltke, *Briefe an Freya 1939–1945* [2nd ed.; Munich, 1991], 278; Engl. trans. by B. Ruhm von Oppen: *Letters to Freya: 1939–1945* [New York, 1990]). On September 16, 1941, he wrote: "Everything will come crashing down on us, and rightly" (ibid., 288). Later, during the period of imprisonment especially, but not only then, categories such as repentance and expiation also play a not unimportant role for Carl Goerdeler and Peter Yorck von Wartenburg, for example. Wartenburg was arrested after the assassination attempt on Hitler of July 20, 1944. In his last letter to his wife, he wrote: "My death will I hope be accepted as expiation for all my sins and as atonement for that which we all share. It will perhaps lessen to a tiny degree the remoteness from God of our time." Carl Goerdeler, also arrested after July 20, 1944, wrote in his farewell letter to his wife (quoted in H. Rothfels, *Die deutsche Opposition*, 319): "But I would beg the world to accept our martyr fate as expiation for the German people."

81. Cf., e.g., the chapter "Umsturz als Akt der Buße" (Overthrow as an Act of Expiation) in M. Heimbucher, *Christusfriede—Weltfriede*, 353ff., or K. von Klemperer, *German Resistance against Hitler*, 286, who writes that by making the question of repentance a theme in Sigtuna, Bonhoeffer reached the heart of all the attempts at dialogue between the German resistance and the outside world.

82. See n. 1 above.

83. J. Glenthøj, *Die mündige Welt V*, 289f., already drew attention to difficulties of this kind. It should also be noted that in his first discussion with Bell, Schönfeld also talked about repentance, and that Bell recorded what he said in this connection in 1942, 1945, and 1957: "Many Germans convinced they must sacrifice much of personal income to atone for damage in occupied territories": thus Bell's notes of 1942 (DBWE 16:292f.); similarly in 1945 (GS 1:506) and 1957 (GS 1:516.).

84. See on this chaps. 15 and 18 below. What Schönfeld put into writing is incidentally more ambivalent. It shows an affinity with the less conservative thinking of the Kreisau circle, but also unmistakeably contains a "reactionary" element. In what Schönfeld said in Stockholm and Sigtuna in 1942, we find the categories of international law and elements of federalist and socialist thinking, such as were characteristic of Trott and Moltke,

for example. But in addition there were remarks in which he talked about fighting 'to the bitter end' if the Allies were resolved on a 'fight to the finish' (cf. Bonhoeffer, DBWE 16:308).

85. See chaps. 9 and 15.

86. See above and DBWE 16:297, 298. Of these names Kurt von Hammerstein-Equord is probably the least well-known today, because of his early death in 1943. Hammerstein, who was "an opponent from the beginning" (P. Hoffmann, *Widerstand*, 147), was from the outset extremely hostile toward the Nazi party and its followers. He resigned from his commanding position in the army after a few months of Nazi government, out of protest against its policies. When he was recalled at the beginning of the war, he quickly and practically conceived a plan, entirely by himself, to kill Hitler. But this unfortunately could not be implemented. As early as the end of September 1939 he was retired. He remained in contact with resistance circles until his death from cancer in 1943. Wilhelm Leuschner, a Social Democrat and trade unionist belonging to the Confessing Church, spent two years in a concentration camp but in spite of that decided to go on with conspiratorial activity. Together with Jakob Kaiser he played a decisive part in establishing contacts between trade union oriented and civilian and military resistance circles (K. von Klemperer, *German Resistance against Hitler*, 52.). Kaiser was also a trade unionist, though as a practicing Catholic it was the Catholic trade union movement he belonged to. He also stood out from early on and consistently against the Nazi regime. Both men fought against the Nazi regime until July 20, 1944. Afterward Kaiser was able to disappear underground, but Leuschner was not one of those who survived the plot. For Leuschner and Kaiser, see also chaps. 9 and 15.

87. See above and DBWE 16:297, 305. K. von Klemperer (*German Resistance against Hitler*, 220) calls Schacht "Germany's financial wizard." In the 1930s, as president of the German national bank and minister for commerce, he served the interests of the National Socialist economic policy and was, among other things, generally responsible for the economic conduct of the war. In 1939, because of several conflicts with the government arising from Göring's escapades and Hitler's ignorance, he did, at least, resign, but until 1943 he remained minister without portfolio. He certainly had contacts with the conspirators, but according to Klemperer (ibid.), he was not fully trusted in the inner circles of the resistance.

88. See above, as well as DBWE 16:298. Field Marshal Hans Günther von Kluge—nicknamed "the clever [*kluge*] Hans"—was in overall charge of the campaigns in Poland, France, and Russia. He was an eternal ditherer, famous for his continual vacillating between "yes," "perhaps," and "no"

in response to any plans for a coup d'etat. Tresckow would have been the most likely person to convince the "continually wavering Kluge" (P. Hoffmann, *Widerstand*, 338), but right to the end he was unable to win through to a definite stance, and committed suicide after July 20, 1944. Fedor von Bock, also from 1940 onward a field marshal, was also initially in overall command of the attacks on Poland and the neighboring countries in the west. Until the beginning of 1942 he was head of the Central Army Group, and until July 1942 head of the Southern Army Group. In response to the approach of his nephew and his, for a while, close colleague Henning von Tresckow, he refused to take any active part in plans for a putsch (P. Hoffmann, *Widerstand*, 337f.). Georg von Küchler was from the beginning of 1942 head of the Northern Army Group and was appointed field marshal at the end of June 1942. He was relieved of his command for a time shortly after the outbreak of war because of his opposition to the inhumane German occupation policy. However, there is as far as I know no evidence that he had close contacts with the resistance, apart from a conversation with Goerdeler in August 1942.

89. Yet it was Witzleben about whom Bonhoeffer had reservations, saying, according to Bell's diary notes, that he was "not so likely to come up in the front" (DBWE 16:298). In his memorandum Bell mentions "possibly Witzleben" (ibid., 322). These reservations probably did not apply to his probity, but to the fact that Field Marshal von Witzleben was ill, and for reasons of health had resigned only shortly before (in the middle of March 1942). It was Witzleben above all who from 1938 onward continuously and actively supported the diverse plans for an overthrow (cf. K. von Klemperer, *German Resistance against Hitler*, 106, 163), and even after March 1942 he remained closely in touch with the conspiracy. It was intended that after the assassination and the coup d'etat—on Day X in July 1944—Witzleben should become the future supreme commander of the army. He was condemned to death and executed on August 8, 1944.

90. DBWE 16:659.

15. Home Affairs

1. DBWE 16:329f.
2. See chap. 6 above.
3. Dietrich Bonhoeffer and Maria von Wedemeyer, *Love Letters from Cell 92* (ed. R.-A. von Bismarck and U. Kabitz; trans. J. Brownjohn; London, 1994), 283f.

4. There are differences in detail here between E. Bethge, DB Biog., 676f.; Elisabeth Chowaniec, *Der "Fall Dohnanyi" 1943–1945: Widerstand, Militärjustiz, SS-Willkür* (Munich, 1969), 31f.; DBWE 16:402 n.9 and the chronological table, 689; and Marikje Smid, *Hans von Dohnanyi—Christine Bonhoeffer: Eine Ehe im Widerstand gegen Hitler* (Gütersloh, 2002). Josef Müller even remembered, in 1960 and 1975, respectively, several Rome stays with Bonhoeffer and Dohnanyi (in Harold C. Deutsch, *Verschwörung gegen den Krieg: Der Widerstand in den Jahren 1939–40* [Munich, 1969], 131; Engl. orig.: *The Conspiracy against Hitler in the Twilight War* [Minneapolis, 1968], and Josef Müller, *Bis zur letzten Konsequenz: Ein Leben für Frieden und Freiheit* [Munich, 1975], 241).

5. There were surely a number of meetings that recalled times in Ettal (see chap. 7). But we know nothing about the content of the conversations held with prominent Catholic clergy in Rome in 1942 (cf. E. Bethge, DB Biog., 676f.). The subject may have been ecumenical topics in the widest sense, and the sounding out, via the Vatican, of possible other contacts between the Berlin opposition and London government circles.

6. DBWE 16:34.

7. Ibid., 402f.

8. See chap. 9. For 1942 see the chronological table in DBWE 16:686ff.

9. See chap. 11.

10. DBWE 16:354.

11. Ibid., 356f.

12. See chaps 3. and 10.

13. DBWE 16:357.

14. Ibid., 355 n.1. Arthur Nebe held a leading position in the SS-dominated state, and yet from time to time and from case to case he cultivated oppositional contacts, for example by deliberately passing on internal information. From 1937 he had been criminal director of the Reich Central Security Office, and during the war he played a decisive part in numerous mass killings. Hans Mommsen points out emphatically that Nebe "must count as one of the most prominent representatives of the annihilation policy" ("Die Stellung der Militäropposition," in *Alternative zu Hitler: Studien zur Geschichte des deutschen Widerstands* [Munich, 2000], 377; Engl. trans.: *Alternatives to Hitler: German Resistance under the Third Reich* [trans. A. McGeoch; Princeton, 2003]).

15. E. Bethge, DB Biog., 686; DBWE 16:357 n.2, where it is suggested, again cautiously, that the purpose might have been to give help to the suffering Greek population.

16. It is presumed that this idea was put forward by Bishop Bell in Switzerland (cf. Jørgen Glenthøj, ed., *Die mündige Welt V: Dokumente zur Bonhoeffer-Forschung 1928–1945* [Munich, 1969], 282ff., and the afterword in DBWE 16:662).

17. Gerhard Ritter in 1945, in the foreword to the memorandum; Philipp von Bismarck and Helmut Thielicke, eds., *In der Stunde Null: Die Denkschrift des Freiburger "Bonhoeffer-Kreises: Politische Gemeinschaftsordnung, Ein Versuch zur Selbstbesinnung des christlichen Gewissens in den politischen Nöten unserer Zeit* (Tübingen, 1979), 27f.

18. On the Freiburg circle (or circles in general), cf. Dagmar Rübsam and Hans Schadek, eds., *Der "Freiburger Kreis": Widerstand und Nachkriegsplanung 1933–1945, Katalog einer Ausstellung* (Freiburg, 1990), also on the question about the various names given to it (ibid., 17). Some of those who belonged to the "working party" on the Memorandum were later arrested. However, Klemens von Klemperer's judgment seems to me exaggerated (*German Resistance against Hitler: The Search for Allies Abroad, 1938–1945* [Oxford, 1992]): "Within the spectrum of the German Resistance the Freiburg group occupied a central place and possessed a considerable potential as a mediating force. Through the participation of Goerdeler a tie was established with the activist branch of the Resistance."

19. Published in D. Rübsam and H. Schadek, *Der "Freiburger Kreis,"* 78.

20. DBWE 16:361ff.

21. Cf. Dietze's secret message to his wife of October 28, 1944 (DBWE 16:459) and the indictment against him of April 9, 1945 (ibid., 466f.). On Perels see chap. 11 above.

22. Gerhard Ringshausen, "Die Überwindung der Perversion des Rechts im Widerstand," In *Widerstand und Verteidigung des Rechts* (ed. G. Ringshausen and R. von Voss; Bonn, 1997), 222, n.63, and DBWE 16:382 n.1; also the chronological table, 692.

23. Editors' afterword, DBWE 16:672.

24. This thesis was propounded by G. Ringshausen ("Überwindung," 222ff.) and convincingly substantiated. This applies especially to the theological reasons for the rift between Bonhoeffer and Ritter. A central point with regard to this complex can be found in Dietze's notes about the discussion on February 6–7, 1943 (DBWE 16:390f.). A further indication, though in the *Ethics* (DBWE 6:352ff.), can be seen in the existence of Bonhoeffer's unfinished text as it was discussed in Freiburg on October 9, 1942. Its title is "On the Possibility of the Church's Message to the World." Cf. here also G. Ringshausen, "Überwindung," 212f., n.9.

25. G. Ringshausen, "Überwindung," 224. This also makes superfluous the question whether Bonhoeffer knew the final text of the memorandum, including appendix 5, or had agreed to it (Matthias Schreiber, *Friedrich Justus Perels: Ein Weg vom Rechtskampf der Bekennenden Kirche in den politischen Widerstand* [Munich, 1989], 178; Christine-Ruth Müller, *Dietrich Bonhoeffers Kampf gegen die nationalsozialistische Verfolgung und Vernichtung der Juden: Bonhoeffers Haltung zur Judenfrage im Vergleich mit Stellungnahmen aus der evangelischen Kirche und Kreisen des deutschen Widerstandes* [Munich, 1990], 274ff.; Wolfgang Gerlach, *Als die Zeugen schwiegen: Bekennende Kirche und die Juden* [2nd ed.; Berlin, 1993] [Eng. trans. by V. J. Barnett, *And the Witnesses Were Silent: The Confessing Church and the Jews* (Lincoln, Nebraska, 2000)]; Hans Mommsen, *Alternative zu Hitler: Studien zur Geschichte des deutschen Widerstands* [Munich, 2000] [Engl. trans. by A. McGeoch, *Alternatives to Hitler: German Resistance under the Third Reich* (Princeton, 2003)]). This appendix 5 was written by Dietze, was entitled "Suggestions for a Solution of the Jewish Question," and after the war was the most controversial part of the memorandum.

26. Ernst Schulin, in Dagmar Rübsam and Hans Schadek, eds., *Der "Freiburger Kreis": Widerstand und Nachkriegsplanung 1933–1945, Katalog einer Ausstellung* (Freiburg, 1990), 16 n.28. This description, proposed by Christine Blumenberg-Lampe in 1973, became part of the published title of the memorandum in 1979 (Philipp von Bismarck and Helmut Thielicke, eds., *In der Stunde Null: Die Denkschrift des Freiburger "Bonhoeffer-Kreises": Politische Gemeinschaftsordnung. Ein Versuch zur Selbstbesinnung des christlichen Gewissens in den politischen Nöten unserer Zeit* [Tübingen, 1979]).

27. G. Ringshausen, "Überwindung," 225f.

28. Cf. n. 24 above and the afterword of the German editors of DBW 16:707, in which it is conceded, with reasons, that "the direction of the *political* ideas coincide with those of Bonhoeffer" (emphasis added).

29. Thus the memorandum, ed. P. von Bismarck, *In der Stude Null*, 74.

30. Ibid.

31. In "After Ten Years," in *Letters and Papers from Prison* (ed. E. Bethge; trans. R. H. Fuller et al.; enlarged ed.; London, 1971), 12f.

32. DBWE 16:502ff. About the origin of this text we know very little. Cf. ibid., 506 n.1.

33. Ibid., 527f.

34. Ibid., 517f.

35. Thus the German editors of DBW 16:5.

36. DBWE 16:572f.

37. Ibid., 574 n.1.

38. Ibid., 577.

39. See above and ibid. 527f.

40. D. Bonhoeffer and M. von Wedemeyer, *Love Letters from Cell 92*, 285 (translation slightly altered).

41. Ibid., 287f.

42. Thus, e.g., Karl Heinz Roth and Angelika Ebbinghaus, eds., *Rote Kapellen—Kreisauer Kreise—Schwarze Kapellen: Neue Sichtweisen auf den Widerstand gegen die NS-Diktatur 1938–1945* (Hamburg, 2004), 91.

43. Ibid., 130ff. On important, more long-term contacts between Tresckow and Olbricht, cf. also H. Mommsen, "Die Stellung der Militäropposition," 371.

44. K. von Klemperer, *German Resistance against Hitler*, 233. and Peter Hoffmann, *Widerstand, Staatsstreich, Attentat: Der Kampf der Opposition gegen Hitler* (3rd ed.; Munich, 1979), 245f.; Engl. trans. by R. Barry: *The History of the German Resistance 1933–1945* (Cambridge, Mass., 1977).

45. For a different view, see E. Bethge, DB Biog., 678: "The Bonhoeffer brothers assented to those considerations, mainly on pragmatic grounds, and without royalist motives. What Bonhoeffer wanted to see brought about by a revolt was not a 'restoration'; but if a monarchical beginning could offer advantages when the revolt was launched, it had to be considered as a possibility."

46. Hans Mommsen takes a different view ("Die Widerstand gegen Hitler und die deutsche Gesellschaft," in *Der Widerstand gegen den Nationalsozialismus* [ed. J. Schmädeke and P. Steinbach; Munich and Zurich, 1985], 393). He maintains that Bonhoeffer belonged within "the German-national tradition." But we know, for example, that in the last, only partially "free," Reichstag election on March 5, 1933, Bonhoeffer voted for the Catholic Center party, and not, as he might have done, for the German-National People's Party. Cf. on this E. Bethge, DB Biog., 200, and Christoph Strohm, *Theologische Ethik im Kampf gegen den Nationalsozialismus: Der Weg Dietrich Bonhoeffers mit den Juristen Hans von Dohnanyi und Gerhard Leibholz in den Widerstand* (Munich, 1989), 87.

47. See above and DBWE 16:527.

48. On the political worldview of the conservative resistance, cf. still Hans Mommsen's early "Gesellschaftsbild und Vefassungsplänen des deutschen Widerstands," in *Der deutsche Widerstand gegen Hitler* (ed. W. Schmitthenner and H. Buchheim; Cologne and Berlin, 1966), 73–167 as a whole, and idem, "Verfassungs- und Verwaltungsreformpläne der Widerstandsgruppen des 20. Juli 1944," in *Der Widerstand gegen den Nationalsozialismus* (ed. J. Schmädeke and P. Steinbach; Munich and Zurich, 1985), 570ff.

49. See above and DBWE 16:526f.

50. DBW 17:138.

16. The Dilemma of Guilt

1. Cf. here also the specific examples in Peter Hoffmann, *Widerstand, Staats-streich, Attentat: Der Kampf der Opposition gegen Hitler* (3rd ed.; Munich, 1979), 347; Engl. trans. by R. Barry: *The History of the German Resistance 1933–1945* (Cambridge, Mass., 1977), as well as the general question in Karl Heinz Roth and Angelika Ebbinghaus, eds., *Rote Kapellen—Kreisauer Kreise—Schwarze Kapellen: Neue Sichtweisen auf den Widerstand gegen die NS-Diktatur 1938–1945* (Hamburg, 2004), 8.

2. *Letters and Papers from Prison* (ed. E. Bethge; trans. R. H. Fuller et al.; enlarged ed.; London, 1971), "After Ten Years," 5, 6 (translation altered). Also DBW 8:22 and 24. For more on this text, see below.

3. Jürgen Schmädeke, "Militärische Umsturzversuche und diplomatische Oppositionsbestrebungen zwischen der Münchener Konferenz und Stalingrad," in *Widerstand gegen den Nationalsozialismus* (ed. P. Steinbach and J. Tüchel; Bonn, 1994), 314. Similarly, Klaus-Jürgen Müller, "Über den 'militärischen Widerstand,'" in *Widerstand gegen den Nationalsozialismus* (ed. P. Steinbach and J. Tüchel; Bonn, 1994), 277, who speaks of "the result of an inner reconstruction process" and "a letting-go of the traditions and standards of behavior of a traditional elite, which younger members of the opposition, such as Tresckow, Oster, Olbricht, Bonhoeffer, and Stauffenberg, found necessary in face of the challenges of the totalitarian dictatorship." Admittedly, Oster and Olbricht did not belong to the younger generation of the opposition.

4. E. Bethge, DB Biog., 655f., 659; also chap. 12 above.

5. Klemens von Klemperer, "Glaube, Religion, Kirche und der deutsche Widerstand gegen den Nationalsozialismus," *Vierteljahreshefte für Zeitgeschichte* 28 (1980).

6. Peter Hoffmann, *Widerstand*, 455ff.

7. On "State and Church" see also chap. 15 above. All quotations here are from DBWE 16:516f.

8. Christian Gremmels, in C. Gremmels and Heinrich W. Grosse, *Dietrich Bonhoeffer: Der Weg in den Widerstand* (2nd ed.; Gütersloh, 2004), 71.

9. DBWE 16:376.

10. "The veiled language that characterizes the *Ethics* manuscript accords with the conspiratorial requirement for silence." Thus Gremmels, in Reinhold Mokrosch, Friedrich Johannsen, and Christian Gremmels, *Dietrich Bonhoeffers Ethik: Ein Arbeitsbuch für Schule, Gemeinde und Studium* (Gütersloh, 2003), 37.

11. Cf. on this Sabine Dramm, *Bonhoeffer: Eine Einführung in sein Denken* (Gütersloh, 2001), 121ff.

12. DBWE 6:274f.
13. A. Camus, *Oeuvres complète* (Paris, 1955), 241 (from the diary of 1947).
14. Heinz Eduard Tödt, "Der Bonhoeffer-Dohnanyi-Kreis in der Opposition und im Widerstand gegen das Gewaltregime Hitlers," in *Die Präsenz des verdrängten Gottes: Glaube, Religionslosigkeit und Weltverantwortung nach Dietrich Bonhoeffer* (ed. C. Gremmels and Ilse Tödt; Munich, 1987), 242.
15. See chap. 14, n.1, above.
16. E. Bethge, DB Biog., 626f.
17. Ibid., 627.
18. Ibid.
19. It was taken over into R. C. D. Jasper's biography of Bell from Bell's own book, *The Church and Humanity* (London and New York, 1946); see there p. 281.
20. Cf., e.g., Hans Rothfels, *Die deutsche Opposition gegen Hitler: Eine Würdigung* (Zurich, 1949, 1994), 281; Harold C. Deutsch, *Verschwörung gegen den Krieg: Der Widerstand in den Jahren 1939–40* (Munich, 1969), 383 (Engl. orig.: *The Conspiracy against Hitler in the Twilight War* [Minneapolis, 1968]); Uta von Aretin, "Preußische Tradition als Motiv für den Widerstand gegen das NS Regime," in *Aufstand des Gewissens* (ed. T. Vogel; Hamburg, Berlin, and Bonn, 2000), 284; According to Otto John, who knew Bonhoeffer through his brother Klaus, Bonhoeffer countered *him*, during a discussion in the winter of 1941–42, by saying, "If we have grasped that Hitler is the personification of all evil, and that he is the Antichrist, we must combat him with all the means at our disposal, and destroy him, whether the German people initially understand it or not!" (Otto John, *"Falsch und zu spat": Der 20. Juli 1944. Epilog* [Berlin, 1984], 211). Joachim Fest, *Staatsstreich: Der lange Weg zum 20. Juli* (Berlin, 1994), 211, even writes: "In his intellectual radicalism, Bonhoeffer repeatedly demanded that Hitler must be 'eliminated' regardless of the conceivable political consequences."
21. Cf., e.g., Andreas Pangritz, "Dietrich Bonhoeffers theologische Begründung der Beteiligung am Widerstand," *Evangelische Theologie* 55, NF 50 (1995): 501ff.; Heinz Eduard Tödt, *Komplizen, Opfer und Gegner des Hitlerregimes: Zur "inneren Geschichte" von protestantischer Theologie und Kirche im "Dritten Reich"* (Gütersloh, 1997), 342ff.; R. Mokrosch, F. Johannsen and C. Gremmels, *Bonhoeffers Ethik*, passim.; also G. Ringshausen's forthcoming book on Bonhoeffer and the resistance; see chap. 9 n.12 above.
22. Cf. Wolf-Dieter Zimmermann, ed., *Begegnungen mit Dietrich Bonhoeffer: Ein Almanach* (Munich, 1964), 155; Engl. trans. by K. Gregor Smith, *I Knew Dietrich Bonhoeffer* (London and New York, 1966), the version of Zimmermann's account underlying Gerhard Ringshausen, "Evangelische Kirche

und Widerstand," in *Deutscher Widerstand—Demokratie heute: Kirche, Kreisauer Kreis, Ethik, Militär und Gewerkschaften* (ed. H. Engel; Bonn and Berlin, 1992), 104f. Also W.-D. Zimmermann's own book *Wir nannten ihn Bruder Bonhoeffer* (Berlin, 2004), 100f.

23. W.-D. Zimmermann, *Wir nannten ihn Bruder Bonhoeffer*, 101.

24. Cf. on this G. Ringshausen, "Evangelische Kirche und Widerstand," 104f., n.144, and 116f. For his recent discussion about the date of this conversation between Bonhoeffer and Stauffenberg's later adjutant, cf. chap. 9, n.12.

25. See "After Ten Years," in *Letters and Papers from Prison*, 1ff. This was added by E. Bethge to the *Letters and Papers* after the first edition of the book, and given the subtitle: "A Reckoning Made at New Year 1943." The final passage, "The View from Below," is evidently an unfinished text, probably written at the end of 1942. It appeared on a separate page and was not added by Bonhoeffer himself to the text of "After Ten Years." About the origin of the text, Bethge says that "it was written during one of the most promising phases of the resistance, in order to strengthen his friends in their course of action" (E. Bethge, DB Biog., 702). He gave it as a Christmas present in 1942 to his parents and to Dohnanyi and Oster and also left Bethge a copy (ibid., 693). There are detailed commentaries on the text in H. E. Tödt, "Der Bonhoeffer-Dohnanyi-Kreis," 239ff., Peter Steinbach, *Widerstand im Widerstreit: Der Widerstand gegen den Nationalsozialismus in der Erinnerung der Deutschen. Ausgewählte Studien* (2nd ed.; Paderborn, 2001), and Marikje Smid, *Hans von Dohnanyi—Christine Bonhoeffer: Eine Ehe im Widerstand gegen Hitler* (Gütersloh, 2002), 320ff.

26. H. E. Tödt, "Der Bonhoeffer-Dohnanyi-Kreis," 241.

27. *Letters and Papers*, 5 (translation altered).

28. Ibid., 8.

29. Ibid., 11.

30. See chap. 15.

31. *Letters and Papers*, 15.

32. Impressive though this essay of Bonhoeffer's is, I find Peter Steinbach's judgment exaggerated ("Zum Verhältnis der Ziele der militärischen und zivilen Widerstandgruppen," in *Der Widerstand gegen den Nationalsozialismus* [ed. J. Schmädeke and P. Steinbach; Munich and Zurich, 1985], 996), when in reference to the passages about the contempt for other people, optimism, and death he maintains for the resistance in general: the National Socialists "understood Bonhoeffer's claim that the resistance movement must not practice the contempt for others practiced by their opponents as a threat." The resistance movement's own claim to the future

and their surmounting of the fear of death had, he believes, restricted the claim to rule of the Nazi leadership. "In this sense Dietrich Bonhoeffer invoked the future when he invoked *optimism as the fundamental driving power of the resistance.*" This optimism was the mark of the whole of the resistance against the Nazis and ultimately united the different groups where the assassination attempt was concerned.

17. Death Zone

1. Cf. on this, e.g., Lothar Kettenacker, "Die britische Haltung zum deutschen Widerstand während des Zweiten Weltkriegs," in *Das "Andere Deutschland"* (ed. Kettenacker; Stuttgart, 1977), 61, and Klemens von Klemperer, *German Resistance against Hitler: The Search for Allies Abroad, 1938–1945* (Oxford, 1992), 237.
2. Peter Hoffmann, *Widerstand, Staatsstreich, Attentat: Der Kampf der Opposition gegen Hitler* (3rd ed.; Munich, 1979), 275ff.; Engl. trans. by R. Barry, *The History of the German Resistance 1933–1945* (Cambridge, Mass., 1977).
3. Klemens von Klemperer, "Nationale oder internationale Außenpolitik des Widerstands," in *Der Widerstand gegen den Nationalsozialismus* (ed. J. Schmädeke und P. Steinbach; Munich and Zurich, 1985), 643f.
4. DBWE 16:300; also chap. 14 above.
5. P. Hoffmann, *Widerstand, Staatsstreich, Attentat*, 346.
6. Dietrich Bonhoeffer and Maria von Wedemeyer, *Love Letters from Cell 92* (ed. R.-A. von Bismarck and U. Kabitz; trans. J. Brownjohn; London, 1994), 290ff.
7. See chap. 15 above.
8. DBWE 16:391f.; also E. Bethge, DB Biog., 690.
9. *Love Letters from Cell 92*, 295 (translation slightly altered).
10. E. Bethge, DB Biog., 690.
11. Fabian von Schlabrendorff, *Offiziere gegen Hitler* (ed. G. von Schulze-Gaevernitz; Zurich, Vienna, and Konstanz, 1951), 116ff., and Rudolf-Christoph von Gersdorff, *Soldat im Untergang* (Frankfurt, Berlin, and Vienna, 1977), 126ff.; also P. Hoffmann, *Widerstand, Staatsstreich, Attentat*, 350ff., and Joachim Fest, *Staatsstreich: Der lange Weg zum 20. Juli* (Berlin, 1994), 195ff.
12. Hans Mommsen, "Die Stellung der Militäropposition," in *Alternative zu Hitler: Studien zur Geschichte des deutschen Widerstands* (Munich, 2000), 370ff.; Engl. trans. by A. McGeoch: *Alternatives to Hitler: German Resistance under the Third Reich* (Princeton); also chaps 10, 15, and 16 above.

13. Ibid., 376: "In all essentials it can be stated that in the Central Army Group particularly, in the wake of the fight against the partisans, not only were a great number of uninvolved civilians killed but the indigenous Jewish population was liquidated." There is evidence for Tresckow's active involvement in the inhumane occupation policy, and for his later renewed employment at the eastern front—that is, for the period from the autumn of 1943 until the summer of 1944 (cf. Karl Heinz Roth and Angelika Ebbinghaus, eds., *Rote Kapellen—Kreisauer Kreise—Schwarze Kapellen: Neue Sichtweisen auf den Widerstand gegen die NS-Diktatur 1938–1945* [Hamburg, 2004], 122).

14. E. Bethge, DB Biog., 685.

15. Marikje Smid, *Hans von Dohnanyi—Christine Bonhoeffer: Eine Ehe im Widerstand gegen Hitler* (Gütersloh, 2002), 327.

16. For accounts of these assassination attempts, see n.11 above.

17. Cf. E. Bethge, DB Biog., 685, and M. Smid, *H. v. Dohnanyi—C. Bonhoeffer*, 327.

18. H. Mommsen, "Die Stellung der Militäropposition," 371.

19. K. H. Roth writes (Roth and Ebbinghaus, eds., *Rote Kapellen*,136) that how far these attempts were actually made "has still to be verified, for as source material the memoir literature on the subject is problematical." He notes that it could well be "that the assassination attempts described were the wishful fantasies of 1943 which gradually in the process of recollection acquired the character of fact." To verify the events "is an urgent requirement for research" (ibid., 136, n.142).

20. Reinhold Mokrosch, Friedrich Johannsen, and Christian Gremmels, *Dietrich Bonhoeffers Ethik: Ein Arbeitsbuch für Schule, Gemeinde und Studium* (Gütersloh, 2003), 175.

21. Jürgen Schmädeke, "Militärische Umsturzversuche und diplomatische Oppositionsbestrebungen zwischen der Münchener Konferenz und Stalingrad," in *Widerstand gegen den Nationalsozialismus* (ed. P. Steinbach and J. Tüchel; Bonn, 1994), 317f.

22. Winfried Meyer, *Unternehmen Sieben: Eine Rettungsaktion für vom Holocaust Bedrohte aus dem Amt Ausland/Abwehr im Oberkommando der Wehrmacht* (Frankfurt am Main, 1993), 375.

23. Thus H. Höhne, *Canaris: Patriot im Zwielicht* (Munich, 1976), 491; Engl. trans. by J. M. Brownjohn, *Canaris: Hitler's Master Spy* (New York, 1999).

24. DBWE 16:395ff.; also chaps. 1, 3, 7, 14, and 15 above.

25. *Love Letters from Cell 92*, 295f.

26. For the events leading up to these days, see above.

27. On what follows, cf. the biographies of Bonhoeffer, Oster, and Dohnanyi, as well as the study of Operation 7: E. Bethge, DB Biog., 691ff.; Romedio von Thun-Hohenstein, *Der Verschwörer: General Oster und die Militäropposition* (Munich, 1984), 240ff.; M. Smid, *H. v. Dohnanyi—C. Bonhoeffer*, 341ff.; and W. Meyer, *Unternehmen Sieben*, 383ff.

28. R. von Thun-Hohenstein, *Der Verschwörer*, 244; E. Bethge, DB Biog., 690; and W. Meyer, *Unternehmen Sieben*, 383.

29. Helmuth James von Moltke, *Briefe an Freya 1939–1945* (2nd ed.; Munich, 1991), 465; Engl. trans. by B. Ruhm von Oppen: *Letters to Freya: 1939–1945* (New York, 1990). At first sight this looks like something of a discrepancy as regards the timing. For it is generally assumed that Dohnanyi was already arrested during the morning, Bonhoeffer during the afternoon. In both cases the arrests were ordered by Roeder in the presence of Sonderegger. Since Bethge was present at Bonhoeffer's arrest, we can assume that here we are on safe ground. According to him, Bonhoeffer was arrested toward 4 o'clock in his parents' house in the Marienburger Allee. Nevertheless, what Moltke says can accord with the facts: even if he was only with Dohnanyi "about 12:30," and for at most half an hour (Moltke gives as his next appointment: "About 1:15 Gablentz ate with me"), his arrest in the office on the Tirpitzufer could quite well have taken place afterward, so that Roeder could have arrived in the Marienburger Allee in the afternoon in order to arrest Bonhoeffer. H. Höhne (*Canaris*, 492) incidentally pinpoints Roeder's appearance in the Tirpitzufer office quite precisely. He presents his research on the matter in his own way as follows: "On 5 April 1943 towards 10 o'clock the opponent broke into the central office of the Military Intelligence. . . . He came quietly and as it were officially."

30. *Love Letters from Cell 92*, 297 (translation altered).

31. Under this code name the Gestapo had at that time tried in vain to elucidate the betrayal of the Western offensive. In Gestapo jargon the code name "Schwarze Kapelle" was intended to cover generally attempts at betrayal or espionage that drew on help from the churches. Cf. W. Meyer, *Unternehemen Sieben*, 369, and idem, "Staatsstreichplanung, Opposition und Nachrichtendienst: Widerstand aus dem Amt Ausland/Abwehr im Oberkommando der Wehrmacht," in *Widerstand gegen den Nationalsozialismus* (ed. P. Steinbach and J. Tüchel; Bonn, 1994), 331; K. H. Roth and A. Ebbinghaus, eds., *Rote Kapellen—Kreisauer Kreis—Schwarze Kapellen*, 49; and also chap. 7 n.32 above.

32. See n.27 above; also H. Höhne, *Canaris*, 492ff.

33. Quoted in R. von Thun-Hohenstein, *Der Verschwörer*, 492ff.

34. DBWE 16:404, n.1. On the sudden appearance of these three "notes," or slips of paper, as well as their wording and importance, cf. ibid. The fact that one of these notes was marked "signed O" only played a part later, not yet on April 5, 1943. The person meant was not Oster but Beck, whose code name was "Nadelöhr" (eye of a needle). Beck had been involved in the deliberations, as was ambiguously formulated in the third of the slips.

35. Ibid., 406.

36. These notes purport (fictitiously) to be evidence of previous and future activities by agents of the Military Intelligence, and were supposed to document especially Bonhoeffer's employment in espionage matters. They were—officially—supposed to be "rough drafts of the coded words to be used by an agent who was to be sent to the Vatican," according to Christine von Dohnanyi later (quoted in W. Meyer, *Unternehmen Sieben*, 385)—specifically for an ostensible mission to the Vatican by the ostensible agent Bonhoeffer—more specifically still, for the journey to Rome that really was planned for Bonhoeffer and Müller on April 9, 1943. All three notes could also be read differently, which called in question their character as notes meant internally for the Military Intelligence, and which behind their official interpretation would have revealed hidden questions about previous and conceivable future contacts—between the central office of the Military Intelligence on the one hand, and Geneva, the Vatican, and the Allies on the other. It was, however, possible in the later interrogations to divert attention from this reading (see E. Bethge, DB Biog., 691f.).

37. R. von Thun-Hohenstein, *Der Verschwörer*, 245f. Following Oster's isolation, he was dismissed from the army at the end of 1943, after all contact with members of the Military Intelligence had been forbidden. The end of the Military Intelligence Foreign Office followed only a little later. After Canaris had been relieved of his post at the beginning of 1944, and had subsequently been put under house arrest, measures were taken for the Military Intelligence to be taken over by the Reich Central Security Office. Oster was arrested on July 21, 1944; Canaris on July 23.

38. In much-read works on the resistance—from G. Ritter and G. Buchheit to P. Hoffmann and J. Fest—there is unanimity about the supreme importance of this day. According to Gert Buchheit, *Ludwig Beck—ein preußischer General* (Munich, 1966), 284, with Oster's elimination, the conspiracy lost what had hitherto been the center of its organization. Gerhard Ritter writes similarly (*Carl Goerdeler und die deutsche Widerstandsbewegung* [Stuttgart, 1954], 346). The blow for the opposition was so dangerous or annihilating that, in Hoffmann's view (*Widerstand*, 365), "for the time being further actions were inconceivable." Fest maintains (*Staatsstreich*, 216) that through

the action of April 5, 1943, the resistance "did not only lose its 'manager' but its whole center, and with that almost everything it possessed of inner coherence."

39. Quoted in ibid., 343.

40. DBWE 6:388ff.

41. Ibid., 407.

42. Hence the detailed account in E. Bethge, DB Biog., 690ff. Since the end of 1942, Bethge had been engaged to Renate Schleicher, one of the Schleichers' daughters, and therefore meanwhile belonged to the family officially too.

43. DBWE 16:574, n.1; also chap. 15 above.

44. Eberhard Bethge, "Bonhoeffers Weg vom 'Pazifismus' zur Verschwörung," in *Frieden—das unumgängliche Wagnis: Die Gegenwartsbedeutung der Friedensethik D. Bonhoeffers* (ed. H. Pfeifer; Munich, 1982), 132; and DBWE 16:400 n.1.

18. Postscript

1. Heinz Euard Tödt, "Der Bonhoeffer–Dohnanyi Kreis in der Opposition und im Widerstand gegen das Gewaltregime Hitlers," in *Die Präsenz des verdrängten Gottes: Glaube, Religionslosigkeit und Weltverantwortung nach Dietrich Bonhoeffer* (ed. C. Gremmels and Ilse Tödt; Munich, 1987), 252; similarly Marikje Smid, *Hans von Dohnanyi—Christine Bonhoeffer: Eine Ehe im Widerstand gegen Hitler* (Gütersloh, 2002), 339f., and earlier E. Bethge, DB Biog., 526.

2. Indictment files, DBWE 16:435ff.

3. The Zossen files discovered at the beginning of April 1945 were notes, further to his diaries, written by Canaris (Winfried Meyer, *Unternehmen Sieben: Eine Rettungsaktion für vom Holocaust Bedrohte aus dem Amt Ausland/Abwehr im Oberkommando der Wehrmacht* [Frankfurt am Main, 1993], 456). On the SS court in Flossenbürg, cf. Christoph U. Schminck-Gustavus, *Der "Prozeß" gegen Dietrich Bonhoeffer und die Freilassung seiner Mörder* (Bonn, 1995), 35ff.

4. Beginning with what are meanwhile viewed as classic accounts of the early history (Hans Rothfels, *Der deutsche Opposition gegen Hitler: Eine Würdigung* [Zurich, 1949], Eberhard Zeller, *Geist der Freiheit: Der zwanzigste Juli* [Munich, 1952; 4th ed., 1963], and Günther Weisenborn, ed., *Der lautlose Aufstand: Bericht über die Widerstandsbewegung des deutschen Volkes 1933–1945* [Hamburg, 1953]), this line can be traced via Peter Hoffmann, *Widerstand, Staatsstreich, Attentat: Der Kampf der Opposition gegen Hitler* (3rd ed.; Munich, 1979) (Engl. trans. by R. Barry, *The History of the German Resistance 1933–1945* [Cambridge, Mass., 1977]), above all to the investigations of the 1980s and 1990s

by P. Steinbach and K. von Klemperer, who both, each in his own way, especially stresses the importance of Bonhoeffer for the German resistance. Even in the studies of H. Mommsen, who is known for his sober analysis, a markedly high value is attached to Bonhoeffer's role in the resistance.

5. Lothar Kettenacker, "Die britische Haltung zum deutschen Widerstand während des Zweiten Weltkriegs," in *Das "Andere Deutschland"* (ed. L. Kettenacker; Stuttgart, 1977), 28.

6. E. Bethge, DB Biog., 700f.

7. E. Bethge, "Bonhoeffers Weg vom 'Pazifismus' zur Verschwörung," in *Frieden—das unumgängliche Wagnis: Die Gegenwartsbedeutung der Friedensethik D. Bonhoeffers* (ed. H. Pfeifer; Munich, 1982), 34.

8. Dietrich Bonhoeffer and Maria von Wedemeyer, *Love Letters from Cell 92* (ed. R.-A. von Bismarck and U. Kabitz; trans. J. Brownjohn; London, 1994), 292.

9. For example, it would be worth investigating more exactly the picture of Bonhoeffer that emerges in resistance research, and especially in studies about the German resistance and the Jews; or to develop a sociogram of the civilian resistance, and to work out the closer parallels and differences between, for example, Moltke and Bonhoeffer or between Trott and Bonhoeffer.

10. Cf. W. Meyer, *Unternehmen Sieben*, and M. Smid, *H. v. Dohnanyi—C. Bonhoeffer*.

11. Moltke's letter of March 25, 1943, to Lionel Curtis in London, quoted in Freya von Moltke, Michael Balfour, and Julian Frisby, *Helmuth James von Moltke 1907–1945: Anwalt der Zukunft* (Stuttgart, 1975), 217.

12. As a suggestion, it would be worthwhile investigating in detail the history and nuances of this label, which has existed since the 1960s and has been in widespread use since the 1980s, and to discuss it with reference to Bonhoeffer. Not least following Klemens von Klemperer, *German Resistance against Hitler: The Search for Allies Abroad, 1938–1945* (Oxford, 1992), and Ekkehard Klausa, "Politischer Konservatismus und Widerstand," in *Der Widerstand gegen den Nationalsozialismus* (ed. P. Steinbach and J. Tüchel; Munich and Zurich, 1994), 227, I would prefer the description "conservative resistance."

13. Such attributions were decisively rejected, and it was suggested that the group around Dohnanyi should be described as a "republican conservative group" (H. E. Tödt, "Der Bonhoeffer–Dohnanyi Kreis," 262). Christoph Strohm, *Theologische Ethik im Kampf gegen den Nationalsozialismus: Der Weg Dietrich Bonhoeffers mit den Juristen Hans von Dohnanyi und Gerhard Leibholz in den Widerstand* (Munich, 1989), 346, takes a similar view: the group can

best be described as "republican" or "liberal conservative." It is true that Bonhoeffer's thinking cannot be described as "*national*-conservative" (see chap. 15 above), but he did in fact belong to circles in the resistance that can be called, in the widest sense, "bourgeois conservative."

14. Yorick Spiegel, "Dietrich Bonhoeffer und die 'protestantisch-preußische Welt,'" in *Verspieltes Erbe?* (ed. E. Feil; Munich, 1979), 68.

15. Hans Mommsen, *Alternative zu Hitler: Studien zur Geschichte des deutschen Widerstands* (Munich, 2000), 393; Engl. trans. by A McGeoch, *Alternatives to Hitler: German Resistance under the Third Reich* (Princeton, 2003).

16. Ibid.

17. See on this already E. Bethge, "Bonhoeffers Weg vom Pazifismus," 32ff.

18. Karl Heinz Roth and Angelika Ebbinghaus, eds., *Rote Kapellen—Kreisauer Kreise—Schwarze Kapellen: Neue Sichtweisen auf den Widerstand gegen die NS-Diktatur 1938–1945* (Hamburg, 2004), 42 and 136. See chap. 2, n.4 above; also chap. 17 n.19.

19. H. Mommsen, *Alternative zu Hitler*, 377f.

20. E. Bethge, DB Biog., 702.

21. Thus K. von Klemperer, *German Resistance against Hitler*, 45.

22. Quoted in W. Meyer, *Unternehmen Sieben*, 458.

23. E. Bethge, DB Biog., 638: "Because of that basic attitude, not a few of the conspirators were glad of the pastor's support."

24. Ibid., 533, and similarly H. E. Tödt, "Der Bonhoeffer–Dohnanyi Kreis," 247.

25. Dietrich Bonhoeffer, *Letters and Papers from Prison* (ed. E. Bethge; trans. R. H. Fuller et al.; enlarged ed.; London, 1971), 16.

26. Ibid., 11.

27. DBWE 6:400.

28. Cf. Engels's 1888 dictum about Marx's handling of Hegel's dialectic, that he "wanted to stand it on its feet again instead of on its head."

Bibliography

Primary Sources

Bethge, Eberhard. *Dietrich Bonhoeffer: A Biography: Theologian, Christian, Man for His Times*. Revised and edited by Victoria J. Barnett. Minneapolis: Fortress Press, 2000. This is now the standard English language edition.

——. *Dietrich Bonhoeffer: Theologian—Christian—Contemporary*. Edited by E. Robertson. Translated by E. Mosbacher et al. London and New York, 1970. Citations in this book are from this edition.

Bonhoeffer, Dietrich. *Gesammelte Schriften*. Edited by E. Bethge. Munich, 1957. 2nd ed., 1965.

——. *Letters and Papers from Prison*. Edited by E. Bethge. Translated by R. H. Fuller et al. Enlarged edition. London, 1971.

Bonhoeffer, Dietrich, and Maria von Wedemeyer. *Love Letters from Cell 92*. Edited by R.-A. von Bismarck and U. Kabitz. Translated by J. Brownjohn. London, 1994.

Dietrich Bonhoeffer Werke. 17 volumes. Edited by E. Bethge et al. Munich, 1986–98.

Dietrich Bonhoeffer Works. General editor Wayne Whitson Floyd Jr. Minneapolis 1996–. A translation of DBW. Not all seventeen volumes have as yet appeared.

Further Literature

Abshagen, Karl Heinz. *Canaris: Patriot und Weltbürger*. Stuttgart,1956.

Aretin, Uta von. "Preußische Tradition als Motiv für den Widerstand gegen das NS Regime." In *Aufstand des Gewissens*, edited by T. Vogel. Hamburg, Berlin, and Bonn, 2000.

Bedürftig, Friedemann. *Drittes Reich und Zweiter Weltkrieg: Das Lexikon*. Munich, 2002.

Ben-Israel, Hedva. "Im Widerstreit der Ziele: Die britische Reaktion auf den deutschen Widerstand." In *Der Widerstand gegen den Nationalsozialismus*, edited by J. Schmädeke and P. Steinbach. Munich and Zurich, 1985.

Benz, Wolfgang, and Walter H. Pehle, eds. *Lexikon der deutschen Widerstandes*. Frankfurt am Main, 2001.

Bethge, Eberhard. "Adam von Trott und der deutsche Widerstand." *Vierteljahreshefte für Zeitgeschichte* 11 (1963).

———. *Dietrich Bonhoeffer, mit Selbstzeugnissen und Bilddokumenten*. Reinbek, 1976, 1999. Engl. trans.: *Dietrich Bonhoeffer: An Illustrated Biography in Documents and Photographs*. Translated by R. Ockenden. London, 1979.

———. "Dietrich Bonhoeffer und die Juden." In *Konsequenzen: Dietrich Bonhoeffers Kirchenverständnis heute*, edited by E. Feil and I. Tödt. Munich, 1980.

———. "Dietrich Bonhoeffers Weg vom 'Pazifismus' zur Verschwörung." In *Frieden—das unumgängliche Wagnis: Die Gegenwartsbedeutung der Friedensethik D. Bonhoeffers*, edited by H. Pfeifer. Munich, 1982.

———. *In Zitz gab es keine Juden: Erinnerungen aus meinen ersten vierzig Jahren*. Munich, 1989.

———. "Nichts scheint mehr in Ordnung." In *Ethik im Ernstfall*, edited by W. Huber and I. Tödt. Munich, 1982.

———. "Zwischen Bekenntnis und Widerstand: Erfahrungen in der Altpreußischen Union." In *Der Widerstand gegen den Nationalsozialismus*, edited by J. Schmädeke and P. Steinbach. Munich and Zurich, 1985.

Bethge, Eberhard, and Renate Bethge, eds. *Letzte Briefe im Widerstand.* 4th edition. Gütersloh, 1997. Engl. trans.: *Last Letters of Resistance: Farewells from the Bonhoeffer Family.* Translated by D. Slabaugh. Philadelphia, 1986.

Bethge, Eberhard, Renate Bethge, and Christian Gremmels. *Dietrich Bonhoeffer: A Life in Pictures.* Translated by John Bowden. Philadelphia, 1986, from *Dietrich Bonhoeffer: Bilder aus seinem Leben.* Munich 1986.

———. *Dietrich Bonhoeffer, mit Selbstzeugnissen und Bilddokumenten.* Reinbek, 1976, 1999.

Bismarck, Philipp von, and Helmut Thielicke, eds. *In der Stunde Null: Die Denkschrift des Freiburger "Bonhoeffer-Kreises: Politische Gemeinschaftsordnung. Ein Versuch zur Selbstbesinnung des christlichen Gewissens in den politischen Nöten unserer Zeit.* Tübingen, 1979.

Boyens, Armin. *Kirchenkampf und Ökumene 1939–1945: Darstellung und Dokumentation unter besonderer Berücksichtigung der Quellen des Ökumenischen Rates der Kirchen.* Munich, 1973.

Bracher, Karl Dietrich. "Rüdiger Schleicher." In *Zeugen des Widerstands.* Edited by J. Mehlhausen. Tübingen, 1996.

Bracher, Karl Dietrich, Manfred Funke, and Hans-Adolf Jacobsen, eds. *Deutschland 1933–1945: Neue Studien zur nationalsozialistischen Herrschaft.* Düsseldorf, 1992.

Brissaud, André. *Canaris 1887–1945.* Translated from French by I. Colvin. London, 1973.

Buchheit, Gert. *Der deutsche Geheimdienst: Geschichte der militärischen Abwehr.* Munich, 1966.

———. *Ludwig Beck—ein preußischer General.* Munich, 1966.

Camus, Albert. *Oeuvres complètes.* Paris, 1955.

Chowaniec, Elisabeth. *Der "Fall Dohnanyi" 1943–1945: Widerstand, Militärjustiz, SS-Willkür.* Munich, 1969.

Deutsch, Harold C. *The Conspiracy against Hitler in the Twilight War.* Minneapolis, 1968. German trans.: *Verschwörung gegen den Krieg: Der Widerstand in den Jahren 1939–40.* Munich, 1969.

Dipper, Christof. "Der 'Aufstand des Gewissens' und die 'Juden-frage': ein Rückblick." In *NS-Verbrechen*, edited by G. R. Ueber-schär. Darmstadt, 2000.

————. "Der Widerstand und die Juden." In *Der Widerstand gegen den Nationalsozialismus*, edited by J. Schmädeke and P. Steinbach. Munich and Zurich, 1985.

Dramm, Sabine. "Camus und die Christen: Kontroverse und Dia-log 'jenseits von Lästerung und Gebet.'" In *Albert Camus und die Christen. Eine Provokation.*, edited by S. Dramm and H. Düringer. Frankfurt am Main, 2002.

————. *Dietrich Bonhoeffer: Eine Einführung in sein Denken*. Gütersloh, 2001.

————. *Dietrich Bonhoeffer und Albert Camus: Analogien im Kontrast*. Gütersloh, 1998.

Dulles, Allen Welsh. *Germany's Underground*. New York, 2000.

Feil, Ernst, ed. *Verspieltes Erbe? Dietrich Bonhoeffer und der deutsche Nach-kriegsprotestantismus*. Munich, 1979.

Feldmann, Christian. *Wir hätten schreien müssen: Das Leben des Dietrich Bonhoeffer*. Freiburg, 1998.

Fest, Joachim. "Spiel mit hohem Einsatz: Über Adam von Trott." *Vier-teljahreshefte für Zeitgeschichte* 46 (1998).

————. *Staatsstreich: Der lange Weg zum 20. Juli*. Berlin, 1994.

Foot, Michael R. D. "Britische Geheimdienste und deutscher Wider-stand 1939–1945." In *Großbritannien und der deutsche Widerstand*, edited by K.-J. Müller and D. N. Dilks. Munich, 1994.

Gerlach, Wolfgang. *Als die Zeugen schwiegen: Bekennende Kirche und die Juden*. 2nd edition. Berlin, 1993. Engl. trans.: *And the Witnesses Were Silent: The Confessing Church and the Jews*. Translated by V. J. Barnett. Lincoln, Nebraska, 2000.

Gersdorff, Rudolf-Christoph von. *Soldat im Untergang*. Frankfurt, Ber-lin, and Vienna, 1977.

Gerstenmaier, Eugen. *Streit und Friede hat seine Zeit: Ein Lebensbericht*. Frankfurt, Berlin, and Vienna, 1981.

————. "Zum Gedenken an Hans Schönfeld." In *Reden und Aufsätze II*. Stuttgart, 1962.

Gillmann, Sabine, and Hans Mommsen, eds. *Politische Schriften und Briefe Carl Friedrich Goerdelers*. Munich, 2003.

Gisevius, Hans Bernd. *Bis zum bittern Ende*. Zurich, 1946, 1954. Engl. trans.: *To the Bitter End*. Translated by R. and C. Winston. London, 1948.

Glenthøj, Jørgen. "Bonhoeffer und die Ökumene." In *Die mündige Welt II*, edited by E. Bethge. Munich, 1956.

————. "Dietrich Bonhoeffer vor Kaltenbrunner: Zur Begegnung mit Lordbischof Bell in Schweden 1942." *Evangelische Theologie* 26 (1966).

————, ed. *Die mündige Welt V: Dokumente zur Bonhoeffer-Forschung 1928–1945*. Munich, 1969.

Gollwitzer, Helmut, Käthe Kuhn, and Reinhold Schneider, eds. *Du hast mich heimgesucht bei Nacht: Abschiedsbriefe und Aufzeichnungen des Widerstandes von 1933 bis 1945*. 3rd edition. Munich and Hamburg, 1969.

Graml, Hermann. "Der Fall Oster." *Vierteljahreshefte für Zeitgeschichte* 14 (1966).

Gremmels, Christian, and Heinrich W. Grosse. *Dietrich Bonhoeffer: Der Weg in den Widerstand*. 2nd edition. Gütersloh, 2004.

Groscurth, Helmuth. *Tagebücher eines Abwehroffiziers 1938–1940*, with further documents on the military opposition against Hitler. Edited by H. Krausnick and H. C. Deutsche, with Hildegard von Kotze. Stuttgart, 1970.

Hassell, Ulrich von. *Die Hassell-Tagebücher, 1938–1944: Aufzeichnungen vom Andern Deutschland*. Zurich, 1946. Engl. trans.: *The von Hassell Diaries 1938–1944: The Story of the Forces against Hitler inside Germany as Recorded by Ambassador Ulrich von Hassell*. London, 1948.

Hehl, Ulrich von. "Die Kirchen in der NS-Diktatur: Zwischen Anpassung, Selbstbehauptung und Widerstand." In *Deutschland 1933–1945*. Edited by K. D. Bracher, M. Funke, and H.-A. Jacobsen. Düsseldorf, 1992.

Heideking, Jürgen. "Die 'Schweizer Straßen' des europäischen Widerstands." In *Geheimdienste und Widerstandsbewegungen im Zweiten Weltkrieg*. Edited by Gerhard Schulz. Göttingen, 1982.

Heimbucher, Martin. *Christusfriede—Weltfrieden: Dietrich Bonhoeffers kirchlicher und politischer Kampf gegen den Krieg Hitlers und seine theologische Begründung*. Gütersloh, 1997.

Hettler, Friedrich Hermann. *Josef Müller ("Ochsensepp"): Mann des Widerstandes und erster CSU-Vorsitzender*. Munich, 1991.

Höhne, Heinz. *Canaris: Patriot im Zwielicht*. Munich, 1976. Engl. trans.: *Canaris: Hitler's Master Spy*. Translated by J. M. Brownjohn. New York, 1999.

———. "Canaris und die Abwehr zwischen Anpassung und Opposition." In *Der Widerstand gegen den Nationalsozialismus: Die deutsche Gesellschaft und der Widerstand gegen Hitler*, edited by J. Schmädeke and P. Steinbach. Munich and Zurich, 1985.

Hoffmann, Peter. *Widerstand, Staatsstreich, Attentat: Der Kampf der Opposition gegen Hitler*. 3rd edition. Munich, 1979. Engl. trans.: *The History of the German Resistance 1933–1945*. Translated by R. Barry. Cambridge, Mass., 1977.

———. "Motive." In *Der Widerstand gegen den Nationalsozialismus*. Edited by J. Schmädeke und P. Steinbach. Munich and Zurich, 1985.

Huber, Wolfgang, and Ilse Tödt, eds. *Ethik im Ernstfall: Dietrich Bonhoeffers Stellung zu den Juden und ihre Aktualität*. Munich, 1982.

Jacobsen, Hans-Adolf, ed. *"Spiegelbild einer Verschwörung": Die Opposition gegen Hitler und der Staatsstreich vom 20. Juli 1944 in der SD-Berichterstattung. Geheime Dokumente aus dem ehemaligen Reichssicherheitshauptamt*. 2 volumes. Stuttgart, 1984.

Jasper, R. C. D. *George Bell, Bishop of Chichester*. London, New York, and Toronto, 1967.

John, Otto. *"Falsch und zu spat": Der 20. Juli 1944 Epilog*. Berlin, 1984.

Kabitz, Ulrich. "Einige Tage nach Weihnachten 1939: Ein Fallbeispiel der Bonhoeffer-Forschung." In *Dietrich Bonhoeffer Jahrbuch*

2003. Edited by C. Gremmels, H. Pfeifer, et al. Gütersloh, 2003.

Kershaw, Ian. "Widerstand ohne Volk? Dissens und Widerstand im Dritten Reich." In *Der Widerstand gegen den Nationalsozialismus.* Edited by J. Schmädeke und P. Steinbach. Munich and Zurich, 1985.

Kettenacker, Lothar. "Die britische Haltung zum deutschen Widerstand während des Zweiten Weltkriegs." In *Das "Andere Deutschland."* Edited by L. Kettenacker. Stuttgart, 1977.

———. "Der deutsche Widerstand aus britischer Sicht." In *NS-Verbrechen.* Edited by G. R. Ueberschär. Darmstadt, 2002.

———, ed. *Das "Andere Deutschland" im Zweiten Weltkrieg: Emigration und Widerstand in internationaler Perspektive.* Stuttgart, 1977.

Klausa, Ekkehard. "Politischer Konservatismus und Widerstand." In *Der Widerstand gegen den Nationalsozialismus.* Edited by P. Steinbach and J. Tüchel. Munich and Zurich, 1994.

Klemperer, Klemens von. "Die 'Außenpolitik' des deutschen Widerstandes." In *Großbritannien und der deutsche Widerstand.* Edited by K.-J. Müller and D. N. Dilks. Paderborn, 1994.

———. *German Resistance against Hitler: The Search for Allies Abroad, 1938–1945,* Oxford, 1992.

———. "Glaube, Religion, Kirche und der deutsche Widerstand gegen den Nationalsozialismus." *Vierteljahreshefte für Zeitgeschichte* 28 (1980).

———. "National oder internationale Außenpolitik des Widerstands." In *Der Widerstand gegen den Nationalsozialismus.* Edited by J. Schmädeke und P. Steinbach. Munich and Zurich, 1985.

———. "Sie gingen ihren Weg: Ein Beitrag zur Frage des Entschlusses und der Motivation zum Widerstand." In *Der Widerstand gegen den Nationalsozialismus.* Edited by J. Schmädeke and P. Steinbach. Munich and Zurich, 1985.

Koch, Laurentius. "Die Benediktinerabtai Ettal." In *Das Erzbistum München und Freising in der Zeit der nationalsozialistischen Herrschaft.* Edited by Georg Schwaiger. Volume 2. Munich and Zurich, 1984.

Lapide, Pinchas E. "Bonhoeffer und das Judentum." In *Verspieltes Erbe?* Edited by E. Feil. Munich, 1979.

Leber, Annedore, with Willy Brandt and Karl Dietrich Bracher. *Das Gewissen steht auf.* Berlin and Frankfurt am Main, 1954. Engl. trans.: *The Conscience in Revolt: Portraits of the German Resistance 1933–1945.* Translated by T. S. McClymont. Mainz, 1994.

Leibholz-Bonhoeffer, Sabine. *The Bonhoeffers: Portrait of a Family.* London, 1971.

Leverkuehn, Paul. *Der geheime Nachrichtendienst der deutschen Wehrmacht im Kriege.* Frankfurt am Main, 1957.

Martin, Bernd. "Deutsche Oppositions- und Widerstandskreise und die Frage eines separaten Friedensschlusses im Zweiten Weltkrieg." In *Der deutsche Widerstand 1933–1945.* Edited by K. J. Müller. 2nd edition. Paderborn, 1990.

Meding, Dorothee von. *Mit dem Mut des Herzens: Die Frauen des 20. Juli.* Berlin, 1992.

Mehlhausen, Joachim, ed. *Zeugen des Widerstands.* Tübingen, 1996.

Meyer, Winfried. "Staatsstreichplanung, Opposition und Nachrichtendienst: Widerstand aus dem amt Ausland/Abwehr im Oberkommando der Wehrmacht." In *Widerstand gegen den Nationalsozialismus.* Edited by P. Steinbach and J. Tüchel. Bonn, 1994.

———. *Unternehmen Sieben: Eine Rettungsaktion für vom Holocaust Bedrohte aus dem Amt Ausland/Abwehr im Oberkommando der Wehrmacht.* Frankfurt am Main, 1993.

Mokrosch, Reinhold, Friedrich Johannsen, and Christian Gremmels. *Dietrich Bonhoeffers Ethik: Ein Arbeitsbuch für Schule, Gemeinde und Studium.* Gütersloh, 2003.

Moltke, Freya von, Michael Balfour, and Julian Frisby. *Helmuth James von Moltke 1907–1945: Anwalt der Zukunft.* Stuttgart, 1975.

Moltke, Helmuth James von. *Briefe an Freya 1939–1945.* 2nd edition. Munich, 1991. Engl. trans.: *Letters to Freya: 1939–1945.* Translated by B. Ruhm von Oppen. New York, 1990.

Moltmann, Jürgen. "Klaus und Dietrich Bonhoeffer." In *Zeugen des Widerstands.* Edited by J. Mehlhausen. Tübingen, 1996.

Mommsen, Hans. *Alternative zu Hitler: Studien zur Geschichte des deutschen Widerstands.* Munich, 2000. Engl. trans.: *Alternatives to Hitler: German Resistance under the Third Reich.* Translated by A. McGeoch. Princeton, N.J., 2003.

———. "Gesellschaftsbild und Verfassungspläner des deutschen Widerstandes." In *Der deutsche Widerstand gegen Hitler.* Edited by W. Schmitthenner and H. Buchheim. Cologne and Berlin, 1966.

———. "Die Opposition gegen Hitler und die deutsche Gesellschaft 1933–1945." In *Der deutsche Widerstand 1933–1945.* Edited by K.-J. Müller. 2nd edition. Paderborn, 1990.

———. "Die Stellung der Militäropposition im Rahmen der deutschen Widerstandsbewegung gegen Hitler." In H. Mommsen, *Alternative zu Hitler.* Munich 2000. Engl. trans.: *Alternatives to Hitler*, Princeton, N.J., 2003.

———. "Verfassungs- und Verwaltungsreformpläne der Widerstandsgruppen des 20. Juli 1944." In *Der Widerstand gegen den Nationalsozialismus.* Edited by J. Schmädeke and P. Steinbach. Munich and Zurich, 1985.

———. "Der Widerstand gegen Hitler und die deutsche Gesellschaft." In *Der Widerstand gegen den Nationalsozialismus.* Edited by J. Schmädeke and P. Steinbach. Munich and Zurich, 1985.

———. "Der Widerstand gegen Hitler und die Nationalsozialistische Judenverfolgung." In H. Mommsen, *Alternative zu Hitler*, 2003. Eng. trans.: *Alternatives to Hitler.* Princeton, N.J., 2003.

Müller, Christine-Ruth. *Dietrich Bonhoeffers Kampf gegen die nationalsozilistische Verfolgung und Vernichtung der Juden: Bonhoeffers Haltung zur Judenfrage im Vergleich mit Stellungnahmen aus der evangelischen Kirche und Kreisen des deutschen Widerstandes.* Munich, 1990.

Müller, Josef. *Bis zur letzten Konsequenz: Ein Leben für Frieden und Freiheit.* Munich, 1975.

Müller, Klaus-Jürgen. *General Ludwig Beck: Studien und Dokumente zur politisch-militärischen Vorstellungswelt und Tättogkeit des Generalstabschefs des deutschen Heeres 1933–1938.* Boppard, 1980.

————. "Der nationalkonservativen Widerstand 1933–1940." In *Der deutsche Widerstand 1933–1940.* Edited by K.-J. Müller. 2nd edition. Paderborn, 1990.

————. "Struktur und Entwicklung der national-konservativen Opposition." In *Aufstand des Gewissens.* Edited by T. Vogel. 5th edition. Hamburg, Berlin, and Bonn, 2000.

————. "Über den militärischen Widerstand." In *Widerstand gegen den Nationalsozialismus.* Edited by P. Steinbach and J. Tüchel. Bonn, 1994.

————, ed. *Der deutsche Widerstand 1933–1945.* 2nd edition. Paderborn, 1990.

Müller, Klaus-Jürgen, and David N. Dilks, eds. *Großbritannien und der deutsche Widerstand 1933–1944.* Paderborn, 1994.

Pangritz, Andreas. "Dietrich Bonhoeffers theologische Begründung der Beteiligung am Widerstand." *Evangelische Theologie* 55, NF 50 (1995).

Pesja, Jane. *Matriarch of Conspiracy: Ruth von Kleist 1867–1945.* Minneapolis, 1991.

Ringshausen, Gerhard. "Evangelische Kirche und Widerstand." In *Deutscher Widerstand—Demokratie heute: Kirche, Kreisauer Kreis, Ethik, Militär und Gewerkschaften.* Edited by H. Engel. Bonn and Berlin, 1992.

————. "Die Überwindung der Perversion des Rechts im Widerstand." In *Widerstand und Verteidigung des Rechts.* Edited by G. Ringshausen and R. von Voss. Bonn, 1997.

Ritter, Gerhard. *Carl Goerdeler und die deutsche Widerstandsbewegung.* Stuttgart, 1954.

Roon, Ger van. "Graf Moltke als Völkerrechtler im OKW." *Vierteljahreshefte für Zeitgeschichte* 18 (1970).

————. *Neuordnung im Widerstand: Der Kreisauer Kreis.* Munich, 1967. Engl. trans.: *German Resistance to Hitler: Count von Moltke and the Kreisau Circle.* Translated by P. Ludlow. London, 1971.

————. *Widerstand im Dritten Reich: Ein Überblick.* 6th edition. Munich, 1994.

Roth, Karl Heinz, and Angelika Ebbinghaus, eds. *Rote Kapellen—Kreisauer Kreise—Schwarze Kapellen: Neue Sichtweisen auf den Widerstand gegen die NS-Diktatur 1938–1945.* Hamburg, 2004.

Rothfels, Hans. *Die deutsche Opposition gegen Hitler: Eine Würdigung.* Zurich, 1949, 1994.

———, ed. "Zwei außenpolitische Memoranden der deutschen Opposition (Frühjahr 1942)." *Vierteljahreshefte für Zeitgeschichte* 5 (1957).

Rübsam, Dagmar, and Hans Schadek, eds. *Der "Freiburger Kreis": Widerstand und Nachkriegsplanung 1933–1945, Katalog einer Ausstellung.* Freiburg, 1990.

Ryska, Franciszek. "Widerstand: Ein wertfreier oder ein wertbezogener Begriff?" In *Der Widerstand gegen den Nationalsozialismus.* Edited by K. Schmädeke and P. Steinbach. Munich and Zurich, 1985.

Scheurig, Bodo. *Ewald von Kleist-Schmenzin: Ein Konservativer gegen Hitler.* Oldenburg and Hamburg, 1968.

Schlabrendorff, Fabian von. *Offiziere gegen Hitler.* Edited by G. von Schulze-Gaevernitz. Zurich, Vienna, and Konstanz, 1951.

Schmädeke, Jürgen. "Militärische Umsturzversuche und diplomatische Oppositionsbestrebungen zwischen der Münchener Konferenz und Stalingrad." In *Widerstand gegen den Nationalsozialismus.* Edited by P. Steinbach and J. Tüchel. Bonn, 1994.

Schmädeke, Jürgen, and Peter Steinbach, eds. *Der Widerstand gegen den Nationalsozialismus: Die deutsche Gesellschaft und der Widerstand gegen Hitler.* Munich and Zurich, 1985.

Schminck-Gustavus, Christoph U. *Der "Prozeß" gegen Dietrich Bonhoeffer und die Freilassung seiner Mörder.* Bonn, 1995.

Schmitthenner, Walter, and Hans Buchheim, eds. *Der deutsche Widerstand gegen Hitler.* Cologne and Berlin, 1966. Engl. trans.: *The German Resistance to Hitler.* Translated by P. and B. Ross. London, 1970.

Schreiber, Matthias. *Friedrich Justus Perels: Ein Weg vom Rechtskampf der Bekennenden Kirche in den politischen Widerstand.* Munich, 1989.

Smid, Marikje. *Hans von Dohnanyi—Christine Bonhoeffer: Eine Ehe im Widerstand gegen Hitler.* Gütersloh, 2002.

Spiegel, Yorick. "Dietrich Bonhoeffer und die 'protestantisch-preußische Welt.'" In *Verspieltes Erbe?* Edited by E. Feil. Munich, 1979.

Steinbach, Peter. "Der Widerstand gegen die Diktatur: Hauptgruppen und Grundzüge der Systemopposition." In *Deutschland 1933–1945.* Edited by K. D. Bracher, M. Funke, and H.-A. Jacobsen. Düsseldorf, 1992.

―――. "Zum Verhältnis der Ziele der militärischen und zivilen Widerstandgruppen." In *Der Widerstand gegen den Nationalsozialismus.* Edited by J. Schmädeke and P. Steinbach. Munich and Zurich, 1985.

―――. *Widerstand im Widerstreit: Der Widerstand gegen den Nationalsozialismus in der Erinnerung der Deutschen, Ausgewählte Studien.* 2nd edition. Paderborn, 2001.

Steinbach, P., and J. Tüchel, eds. *Lexikon des Widerstandes 1933–1945.* Munich, 1966.

―――. eds. *Widerstand gegen den Nationalsozialismus.* Bonn, 1994.

Steltzer, Theodor. *Sechzig Jahre Zeitgenosse.* Munich, 1966.

Strohm, Christoph. *Theologische Ethik im Kampf gegen den Nationalsozialismus: Der Weg Dietrich Bonhoeffers mit den Juristen Hans von Dohnanyi und Gerhard Leibholz in den Widerstand.* Munich, 1989.

Thun-Hohenstein, Romedio von. *Der Verschwörer: General Oster und die Militäropposition.* Munich, 1984.

―――. "Widerstand und Landesverrat am Beispiel des Generalmajors Hans Oster." In *Der Widerstand gegen den Nationalsozialismus.* Edited by J. Schmädeke and P. Steinbach. Munich and Zurich, 1985.

Tödt, Heinz Eduard. "Der Bonhoeffer-Dohnanyi-Kreis in der Opposition und im Widerstand gegen das Gewaltregime Hitlers." In *Die Präsenz des verdrängten Gottes: Glaube, Religionslosigkeit und Weltverantwortung nach Dietrich Bonhoeffer.* Edited by C. Gremmels and Ilse Tödt. Munich, 1987.

―――. *Komplizen, Opfer und Gegner des Hitlerregimes: Zur "inneren Geschichte" von protestantischer Theologie und Kirche im "Dritten Reich."* Gütersloh, 1997.

Trott zu Solz, Clarita von. *Adam von Trott zu Solz: Eine Lebensbeschreibung.* Berlin, 1994.

Ueberschär, Gerd R. *NS-Verbrechen und der militärische Widerstand gegen Hitler.* Darmstadt, 2000.

————, ed. *Der Deutsche Widerstand gegen Hitler: Wahrnehmung und Wertung in Europa und den USA.* Darmstadt, 2002.

Venohr, Wolfgang. *Stauffenberg, Symbol der deutschen Einheit: Eine politische Biographie.* Frankfurt am Main and Berlin, 1986.

Visser't Hooft, Willem A. *Memoirs.* London and Philadelphia, 1973.

Vogel, Thomas, ed. *Aufstand des Gewissens: Militärischer Widerstand gegen Hitler und das NS-Regime 1933 bis 1945.* Begleitband zur Wanderausstellung des Militärgeschichtlichen Forschungsamtes. 5th edition. Hamburg, Berlin, and Bonn, 2000.

Weisenborn, Günther, ed. *Der lautlose Aufstand: Bericht über die Widerstandsbewegung des deutschen Volkes 1933–1945.* Hamburg, 1953.

Wolf, Ernst. "Zum Verhältnis der politischen und moralischen Motive in der deutschen Widerstandbewegung." In *Der deutsche Widerstand gegen Hitler.* Edited by W. Schmitthenner and H. Buchheim. Cologne and Berlin, 1966.

Zeller, Eberhard. *Geist der Freiheit: Der zwanzigste Juli.* Munich, 1952; 4th edition, 1963.

Zimmermann, Wolf-Dieter, ed. *Begegnungen mit Dietrich Bonhoeffer: Ein Almanach.* Munich, 1964. Engl. trans.: *I Knew Dietrich Bonhoeffer.* Translated by K. Gregor Smith. London and New York, 1966.

————. *Wir nannten ihn Bruder Bonhoeffer: Einblicke in ein hoffnungsvolles Leben.* Berlin, 2004.

Index

Japan, 133
Jews, 34, 82–83, 118–19, 123–31,
133–34, 203, 233, 237–38,
276–77n25, 304n13
Johansson, Harry, 170, 171, 178,
180, 181
John, Hans, 97, 244
John, Otto, 97

Kaiser, Jakob, 96, 97, 178, 186,
190, 203, 294n86
Kalckreuth, Christine von, 66, 73
Keitel, Wilhelm, 13, 200
Kieckow (Kleist-Retzow estate),
59, 137
Kirschbaum, Charlotte von, 155,
156, 160
Klein-Krössin, 58, 60, 108, 193,
195
Kleist-Retzow, Ruth von, 58, 59,
106, 137, 193, 259–60n24
Kleist-Retzow estate, 58, 59, 137
Kleist-Schmenzin, Ewald von, 59,
60, 97, 107, 240, 244
Kluge, Hans Günther von, 178,
185, 190, 294–95n88
Koechlin, Alphons, 110, 124, 125,
128–29, 160, 195
Königsberg, 54, 55, 222
Kreisau circle/group, 105, 107–8,
140–41, 166, 168–69, 188, 203,
208, 267n12
Kreisau estate, 139, 140, 167
Küchler, Georg von, 178, 185,
295n88
Kupfer, Angelus, 76

Lampe, Adolf, 197
Le-Chambon-sur-Lignon, 82–83
Leber, Julius, 107, 244
Lehmann, Paul, 10–11
Leiber, Father Robert, 38, 76
Leibholz, Gerhard, 105, 181

Leibholz, Sabine-Bonhoeffer, 8,
9, 45, 46, 80, 105, 150, 168,
181
Leibholz family, 9, 49, 98
Leipzig, 96
Leuschner, Wilhelm, 96, 178, 186,
190, 203, 244, 294n86
Life Together (Dietrich Bonhoeffer),
60, 64
London, 8, 9, 19, 45, 80–81, 177,
186
Luther, Martin, 57
Luxembourg, 39–40

martyrdom, Bonhoeffer and, 233
*Memorandum of Conversations and
Statement by a German Pastor* (Hans
Schönfeld), 184
Mendelssohn, Felix, 96
Military Intelligence *(Abwehr)*, 1–3,
9, 22–27, 29–33, 38, 47, 52–54,
63–69, 77–79, 94, 98, 102–4,
108, 110, 126, 129–31, 134,
137, 139, 142, 144, 149, 157–8,
160, 167, 169, 171, 177, 194–95,
203, 220, 223–24, 226–29, 231,
261nn5–6
Ministry of Justice, 34
Molotov, Vyacheslav, 158
Moltke, Freya von, 18, 107, 134,
140, 151
Moltke, Helmuth Graf von, 139
Moltke, Helmuth James Graf von,
28, 102, 103, 105, 107–8, 130,
134, 136, 139–53, 169, 173, 181,
208, 219, 226, 236, 245, 271n42,
279n21, 282n48
Mommsen, Hans, 238
monarchism, 31, 204–205
monasticism, 74, 75, 76
money. *See* salary, Bonhoeffer's
Moscow, 133
Müller, Josef, 38, 68, 73, 76, 93,